RECEIVING SCRIPTURE IN THE PENTECOSTAL TRADITION

A RECEPTION HISTORY

RECEIVING SCRIPTURE IN THE PENTECOSTAL TRADITION

A RECEPTION HISTORY

EDITED BY

DANIEL D. ISGRIGG

MARTIN W. MITTELSTADT

RICK WADHOLM, JR

CPT

CPT Press
Cleveland, Tennessee

Receiving Scripture in the Pentecostal Tradition
A Reception History

Published by CPT Press
900 Walker ST NE
Cleveland, TN 37311
USA
email: cptpress@pentecostaltheology.org
website: www.cptpress.com

ISBN-13: 978-1-953358-06-6

TABLE OF CONTENTS

ABBREVIATIONS

Pentecostal Periodicals

AE	*Australian Evangel*
AEGTM	*Australian Evangel and Glad Tidings Messenger*
AF	*Apostolic Faith* (Los Angeles, CA)
BC	*Bridal Call*
BCF	*Bridal Call Foursquare*
BCCF	*Bridal Call Crusader Foursquare*
CE	*Christian Evangel*
CGE	*Church of God Evangel*
FC	*Foursquare Crusader*
FM	*The Foursquare Magazine*
LRE	*Latter Rain Evangel*
PE	*The Pentecostal Evangel*
PHA	*The Pentecostal Holiness Advocate*
TBM	*The Bridegroom's Messenger*
TCO	*The Christian Outlook*
TP	*The Pentecost*
WE	*The Weekly Evangel*
WW	*Word and Witness*
WWM	*White Wing Messenger*

Other

JBL	*Journal of Biblical Literature*
JPT	*Journal of Pentecostal Theology*
JPTSup	*Journal of Pentecostal Theology,* Supplement Series
JSNT	*Journal for the Study of the New Testament*
THNTC	Two Horizons New Testament Commentary

1

INTRODUCTION: THE DISCIPLINES OF HUNTING AND GATHERING, AND THE REWARDS OF DISCOVERY

MARTIN W. MITTELSTADT[*]

In the spring of 2017, I was elected for a four-year term to the Executive Committee of the Society for Pentecostal Studies (SPS). I immediately began to process possibilities for my second year as Vice President and Program Chair. Though I found the privilege and responsibility of selecting the conference theme somewhat daunting, I settled quickly on the topic of reception history. As I shared my vision with friends, I received an array of responses. Some simply quipped, 'What's reception history?' Others recognized its methodological validity for interest groups such as Biblical Studies and Philosophy, but they wondered 'what has reception history to do with ethics, practical theology, or missions?' Even my Biblical Studies colleagues offered a mixed response. While many responded with enthusiasm, others envisioned only a short hiatus with a faddish method. If hindsight is indeed 20/20 – at least through my own eyes – I was thrilled with the success of the theme and the outstanding work that emerged from the conference. Since the contributions to this volume – save one – are the product of this conference, it seems

* Martin W. Mittelstadt (PhD, Marquette University) is professor of New Testament at Evangel University, Springfield, MO, USA.

fitting for me to celebrate and, if necessary, defend the work before us with my original call for papers distributed to the SPS membership.

Receiving Scripture in the Pentecostal and Charismatic Traditions

The recent evolution and success of reception history fits well with the current allure of postmodernity and the rise of interdisciplinarity. If proponents of historical criticism strive to recreate the world behind a text, and literary critics seek to encounter the Bible as story, reception historians take another step forward – or backward. Whereas the historical critic employs a formulaic 'two-step' hermeneutic from 'what the text meant' to 'what it means', reception historians choose a slow, scenic, and meandering path to rediscover 'what the text has meant'. Reception historians return to stories of the Scriptures read, interpreted, viewed, and performed through the centuries. In a move postmodernists should celebrate, these scholars give voice to the 'other' and the many. Reception histories offer a museum-like tour of the reading of Scriptures between original authors and current readers. In this conference we invite scholars to contribute further to – even rescue – current readers prone to believe they should view this intervening period as an obstacle to avoid.

Though some might seek to reduce reception history to an adventure primarily for biblical scholars, the method demands interdisciplinary analysis. Hans-Georg Gadamer introduces the term *Wirkungsgeschichte* (literally, 'history-effected consciousness'); H.R. Jauss and W. Iser describe a chain of readings on the same material as *Rezeptionsgeschichte* (literally, 'reception history'); New Testament scholar Ulrich Luz explores the 'history of influences', specifically the 'history, reception, and actualizing of text in media other than a commentary; e.g. in sermons, canonical law, hymnody, art, and in the actions of sufferings of the church'; and Anthony C. Thiselton cleverly likens the discipline to the Bible's *Nachleben* (literally, its 'afterlife' or post-history).

As Pentecostals and Charismatics cast their theological and praxeological vision into the twenty-first century, we must take more than an occasional glance in our rearview mirror. Though we represent a comparatively young movement in the drama of Christian history, some would opine that only Catholics produced more Christian literature in the twentieth century than print-happy Pentecostals. One cannot overstate the opportunities to explore our history of exegesis on roads previously travelled. Pentecostals and Charismatics march forward not in a vacuum, but as communities made up of theologians and practitioners, both formal and informal, amateur and professional, past and present. Reception historians, akin to hunters and gathers, provide us (and others) the opportunity simply to hear what the Bible has been saying.[1]

The Volume Before Us

Following the 2019 conference, I received an invitation from Daniel Isgrigg and Rick Wadholm to contribute to a collection of essays on the conference theme of reception history. My response may have surprised them. Because I was already working on some publications in this field, I said 'no', but I gladly offered to serve with them as fellow editors for this work.[2] They graciously accepted my bullish request, and I have enjoyed the opportunity to grow with them in our discipline and to develop our friendship.

The title of this volume has been altered only slightly from the theme of the 2019 Annual Conference. Whereas the conference call included a request for contributors to address both the Pentecostal

---

[1] Adapted from my call for papers in the 2019 Program for the Annual Meeting of the Society for Pentecostal Studies: *Reception History: Receiving Scripture in the Pentecostal and Charismatic Traditions*, pp. 13-14, https://s3.amazonaws.com/media.cloversites.com/1e/1e4f8ff8-e013-43f7-b6706fe754785d4e/documents/SPS_Program_2019_2_8_19_2.pdf, (Accessed Feb 20, 2020).

[2] I have been active with recent publications, some published and others forthcoming. See my 'Receiving Luke–Acts in the Pentecostal Tradition: The Rise of Reception History and a Call to Pentecostal Scholars', in *Pneuma* 40 (2018), pp. 367-88; 'Nothing to Sneeze At: Receiving Acts 19.11-12 in the Canadian Pentecostal Tradition', in R. Tuppurainen, *Reading St. Luke's Text and Theology: A Pentecostal Voice. Essays in Honour of Roger Stronstad on His 75th Birthday* (Eugene, OR: Pickwick Publications, 2019), pp. 73-84. Two further essays have been delayed due to the 2020 Coronavirus pandemic: 'A Century in the Making: Receiving the Samaritan Pentecost (Acts 8:4-25) in the Pentecostal and Charismatic Tradition' was to be my 2020 Presidential Address for the Society for Pentecostal Studies at Vanguard University in Costa Mesa, CA. Similarly, 'On Prodigals, Elder Brothers, and Fathers? The Reception of Luke 15 in the Pentecostal and Charismatic Traditions' was scheduled for the 27th Annual Youngsan International Theological Lectureship at Hansei University in Seoul, Korea (May 22, 2020). Both presentations have been postponed until 2021 and will be published in *Pneuma* and the *Youngsan International Theological Symposium*, respectively.

and Charismatic traditions, as fate would have it, the pieces submitted to this volume only addressed the classical Pentecostal tradition.[3] Since our search for possible contributions on the conference theme yielded only classical Pentecostal contributors, I would suggest that possibilities for reception history in the broader Charismatic traditions are readily available for interested students and scholars.[4]

The order of an edited volume often proves tricky. Though the essays stand alone, we sought to create a suitable sequence for the chapters. The first three essays are introductory and methodological; the contributors provide an excellent foundation for the novice student and a summary for the seasoned scholar. We arranged the subsequent essays according to canonical order. Sadly, and to the chagrin of my unnamed fellow editor, we discovered only one essay from the Old Testament (OT), and this paper is no less from his hand! Similarly, in our turn to the New Testament (NT), only two contributions focus on biblical passages outside the Gospels.[5]

The Essays Before Us

Robert Berg delivered the opening plenary address for the 2019 conference. Bob, if I may, is my dear colleague at Evangel University. Upon selection of the conference theme, I knew of no one better to launch the conference with an introduction to the interdisciplinary complexities of reception history. His breadth concerning biblical, philosophical, theological, and historical disciplines, as well as his astute cultural and artistic awareness, are vividly on display in his test case: 'All Men are Created Equal'. Berg demonstrates masterfully that this iconic American motto has undergone a complex history of interpretations. In as much as this seminal statement requires ongoing articulation of the 'obvious' beliefs and values for the young republic,

---

[3] We include both Trinitarian and Oneness perspectives in this tradition.

[4] See chapter 4 by John Christopher Thomas. In his survey of reception histories, Thomas demonstrates that Classical Pentecostals have been the most responsive to the opportunities afforded through this method. I would add that this response has been greater among my friends in the Church of God (Cleveland, TN) than my colleagues in the Assemblies of God.

[5] We are both saddened and pleased to say that other presenters and would-be contributors to this volume had secured contracts to extend their paper into a larger project or submitted a proposal to other journals. Their success speaks further to the rise of this method among Pentecostal scholars.

Berg infers that reception historians reveal no less evolution and diverse interpretations of biblical texts and motifs. Ironically, I heard only one criticism of his address. Presenters at the conference, many of whom ventured into reception history for the first time, wished that they had seen his essay ahead of the conference. With his opening chapter, the context for this volume has been set.

Alicia Jackson takes readers from Berg's introduction of reception history to the hermeneutical challenges and opportunities before twenty-first century Pentecostal exegetes. Jackson traces specifically the complex hermeneutical history of Pentecostal scholarship. Since many Pentecostal scholars 'have been schooled' in historical criticism, particularly grammatical and syntactical analysis, these scholars remain committed to a quest for authorial intent and original audiences. With the advent of literary criticism and the rise of various reader-based approaches (feminist, post-colonial, African-American, LGBTQ, and Global South, to name a few), many of our own scholars embraced the opportunity to produce Pentecostal readings. Jackson seeks to build a bridge between reception historians, who trace 'what the text has meant' to Pentecostal communities, and historical-critical scholars, who committed to the pursuit of 'what the text meant'.

John Christopher Thomas became my second obvious choice as a plenary speaker for the 2019 conference. I knew of no Pentecostal scholar with more investment and experience in reception history. He is not only a prolific author of monographs and essays on the topic, but he has also guided countless Pentecostal students both formally, through thesis and dissertation supervision, and informally, as a mentor to rising students and scholars in SPS. Indeed, Rick, Daniel, and I have been enriched through his scholarship and through the Bangor University PhD program that has advanced this methodology. For his plenary session, I invited 'Chris' to produce a documentary history of Pentecostal scholarship on reception history. I was utterly amazed at the wealth of published works on Pentecostal scholarship already available. His survey – not unlike an annotated bibliography – will remain an invaluable resource of Pentecostal contributions to date thus far.

Though we have only one contribution from the OT, Rick Wadholm's essay focusing on Deborah aligns well with the work of Lisa Stephenson's essay on Mary. As Wadholm mines the Pentecostal periodicals, he discovers in Deborah a paradigmatic Pentecostal woman of the Spirit. Pentecostals, unlike many of their evangelical counterparts, generally read the story of Deborah as a clarion call for women to join in full proclamation and service of the gospel. With Stephenson's essay on the mother of Jesus, she tells first of the pro-vocative inspiration for her essay. Stephenson challenges the hasty con-clusions of the late Jerry Sandidge, a premier Pentecostal ecumenist who suggested that Pentecostals, unlike their Catholic brothers and sis-ters, have 'no theology' of Mary. In response, Stephenson reveals a remarkable mosaic of a Pentecostal Mary, namely as a model of faith and discipleship, humility and obedience, and disciplined spirituality. Mary's character and behavior produce for Pentecostals not '*The* [Cath-olic] Mother of God', but *A* consummate Pentecostal sister and/or Pentecostal mother (italics mine).

In the next cluster of essays, contributors turn to the Gospels. In so doing, they hunt through Pentecostal literature to locate the mean-ings and trajectories applied to various Scriptures, doctrines, and mo-tifs critical to Pentecostal theology and praxis. Clayton Coombs takes readers on a fascinating journey through Pentecostal readings of Mk 16.17-18. Though most biblical scholars defend the shorter ending of Mark (16.8), many Pentecostal preachers and practitioners rely heavily on the longer ending (16.9-20), particularly Jesus' extensive commissioning emphases (compare Mt. 28.19-20). Ironically, reliance on this longer ending requires Pentecostal nuancing of the five man-ifestations to be employed in evangelism. Coombs compares Pente-costal and patristic interpretations concerning the three 'less contro-versial' manifestations of signs and wonders, tongues, and healing versus the 'more problematic' apprehensions over the handling of snakes and drinking poison.

Pamela Engelbert and Daniel Isgrigg take readers to the ending of the Third Gospel. Engelbert turns to the Emmaus story and pro-vides both a reception and contemporary application of Jesus' 'pres-ence in absence'. Engelbert examines Pentecostal responses to dis-traught disciples unable to recognize the 'presence' of the resurrected Jesus. She applies Pentecostal interpretations of the present but not yet recognizable Jesus to opportunities for pastoral care, particularly among the grieving. Isgrigg examines a spiritual discipline dear to the heart of Pentecostals: tarrying. The word 'tarry', found only in the KJV translation of Lk. 24.49 and Acts 1.4, functions for Pentecostals as a worshipful ritual of 'waiting' before God for Spirit reception. To mine the early understandings of this term, Isgrigg digs through the thirteen surviving issues of the *Apostolic Faith*, the official organ of the Azusa Street Revival. Though the leaders of the revival did not produce a manual for tarrying, Isgrigg unveils tarrying tendencies through his data, namely the correlation of testimonies. Tarrying tendencies generally included both a plain reading of Jesus' commandment to 'Tarry ye … until' you receive the Spirit, and a call to persevere, patiently and fervently if necessary, for the Bible evidence of tongues. Isgrigg collaborates these accounts and discovers a captivating spectrum of answers for questions such as 'how long must I/we tarry?', 'where should I tarry?', and 'who should do so?'.

Matthew Paugh delivers an invaluable contribution on the underexamined Pentecostal captivation with John's 'Living Water' motif. Paugh offers the only essay not presented at the 2019 SPS conference. He and I had talked many times of his interest in this motif, and I finally convinced him that the time was right. Paugh examines Pentecostal use of Jesus' exchange with the Samaritan woman in John 4 and then Jesus' pronouncement that those who thirst will experience 'rivers of living water' according to Jn 7.37-39. As Paugh wades through both Wesleyan-Holiness and Finished Work camps, he argues convincingly that Pentecostals find in the living water motif a vocabulary that provides an array of Spirit/ual encounters. Living water might speak to an effect on the believer, namely, tongues speech, praise and worship, intensified longing and prayer, love and joy, or unity. However, Pentecostal pragmatism also meant implications of living water for its effect through the believer, namely, proclamation, mighty deeds, and endurance during hardship.

Andrew Williams contributes the first of our NT essays beyond the Gospels. Not surprisingly, Williams' examination of Acts 2.38 elicits immediate resonance with Oneness Pentecostal scholarship. He surveys early African-American Oneness Pentecostals and reveals not only their traditional interpretations of Acts 2.38 concerning baptism in Jesus' name (only), but also the necessity of baptismal immersion and threefold salvation. I am most struck by Williams' discovery that Oneness Pentecostals testify to water baptism rather sacramentally (undoubtedly unaware of any such tendencies). In so doing, Williams draws a parallel to Chris Green's discovery of sacramental application of the Lord's Supper by Trinitarian Pentecostals.

Williams' work should elicit further research for sacramentalists and ecumenists.

Finally, Denise Austin and Steven Mawston close this volume with a turn to Paul's letter to the Romans. They trace the reception of Rom. 8.37 upon Australian Pentecostal thought and practice. According to Austin and Mawston, Pentecostals employ Paul's use of *hypernikomen*, typically rendered 'conquerors' or 'victors', as a term for community identity formation. Austin and Mawston discover an evolving interpretation based upon the ever-changing contexts of Australian Pentecostalism. Whether used for personal or corporate identity, inspiration to stand against external or internal challenges, a call for endurance, or a summons to a victorious life, these Pentecostals demonstrate that new circumstances give rise to new – or at least nuanced – meanings to Paul's exhortation that 'we are more than conquerors'.

The Rewards of Discovery!

My co-editors and I believe this work will be valuable for several reading audiences. First, the volume continues the conversation on the value of reception theory. Though a relatively new methodology, reception history continues to gain traction in biblical, theological, and philosophical studies. I believe this volume demonstrates that vast opportunities are available. Scholars are increasingly willing to supervise theses and dissertations through this method, and not least by Pentecostals and/or on the Pentecostal and Charismatic traditions. Further, I also expect to see methodological maturation. On one end, the most basic form of reception history functions primarily as documentary history, namely, the gathering and compiling of material related to a specific text or topic. On the other hand, a robust reception history should produce analytical results. Beyond compilation, questions should include: What factors contribute to changing interpretations? (e.g. sociological, cultural, demographic, political, ethnic, gendered, etc.). Does a trajectory reveal the need for retrieval and/or progress? How do Pentecostals read Scripture across the world? How do Pentecostal readings and interpretations compare across the various charismatic streams and to other Christian traditions? And how might reception histories contribute to current worldview formation and praxis?

The contributions in this volume add first-time analysis of several passages and practices loaded with meaning in our Pentecostal history. In so doing, reception histories serve as a reminder that Pentecostal doctrines and practices are not discovered *ex nihilo* or in an ivory tower, but they evolve through those who live among us. These accounts encourage us to appreciate our one hundred-year-old Pentecostal family, and to build humbly and faithfully on their efforts. At the risk of presumption, I offer the final words from my 2019 call for papers:

> In this conference, we take a U-turn and revisit the Scriptures interpreted and experienced by both the giants of our Pentecostal/Charismatic story and less-celebrated, often forgotten interpreters. Join us as we read and receive afresh the biblical story shaped and performed by our Pentecostal foremothers and forefathers. We will retell our story, not only in the manner of church historians, but also built upon our collective reading, application, and performance of the biblical text across the Pentecostal stage. Join us not simply to reproduce the Bible's post-history among Pentecostals, but offer critical analysis of our received readings. We will celebrate the rich contributions of Pentecostals, take an honest look at our 'warts', share them with one another, and build a better future. Together our examination of interpreters both new and old will help locate our role in the grand symphony of interpretations, a never-ending succession of Pentecostal performances on the biblical story. [6]

Readers will experience through this volume a 'Pentecostal' sample of complicated biblical characters, theologies, and practices. Let's keep looking and digging! Rich rewards remain to be discovered.

Holy Week 2020.[7]

---

[6] 2019 Program: *Reception History*, p. 14.

[7] I and my fellow-editors wish to acknowledge the editorial contributions of Keilah Rodgers and Anna Mitchell, my undergraduate TAs at Evangel University.

2

'ALL MEN ARE CREATED EQUAL': AN INTRODUCTION TO RECEPTION HISTORY

ROBERT BERG[*]

I'm going to address the phrase 'All men are created equal' to intro-
duce reception history, the theme of our conference.[1] My goal is to
pique your interest in the field and set the table for the diversity of
offerings over the next two days. 'All men are created equal'. Now,
wouldn't it be fascinating to interact with those next to you about
what this phrase *means*? What did it mean to the delegates of the
Constitutional Congress in 1776? And what did it mean to Thomas
Jefferson when he penned it in his draft of the Declaration of Independence of the American colonies from the British crown? I cannot
resist in this introduction referring to the events of the week. On
Wednesday, the Supreme Court heard arguments on the constitution-
ality of a forty-foot-tall cross standing on public land near a busy
intersection four miles from where we sit today. It was erected in 1925
to honor veterans of World War I from Prince George's County. Two
quotes are noteworthy. Justice Kagan observed that the monument
was a product of a 'historic moment in time', and Justice Breyer implied that although such a monument would not be acceptable if

---

[*] Robert Berg (PhD, Drew University) is Professor of New Testament at Evangel University, Springfield, MO, USA.
[1] This chapter is derived from a plenary address delivered on March 1, 2019 for
the 49th Annual Meeting of the Society for Pentecostal Studies held in College Park,
MD. The author graciously allowed us to include this address in its presented for-
mat and thus with minimal references.

proposed today, one erected in a different, earlier context, might well be. 'History counts.' And all the historians said … (Amen!). Indeed it does count. History counts with texts in particular. It counts in the writing of texts. It counts in the reception of texts.

Reception Studies

Like it or not, we must briefly talk theory, and in particular, about two Germans named Hans who contributed to what has become Reception Studies. The first Hans is Hans-Georg Gadamer, a student of Martin Heidegger. His major work, *Truth and Method*, originally published in 1960, is one of the most influential philosophical works of the twentieth century.[2] For Gadamer, 'understanding is a historically effected event'. A written text, like a play or a piece of music, must be performed to be understood. That is, understanding begins when something – a drama, a poem, a symphony – *addresses us*, in the viewing, in the hearing, in the reading. As in Heidegger, being, expressed in language, is the underlying human principle. Reading texts, viewing plays, and hearing great music enables us to understand human being – including our own. This is what links, for example, a reader today to a text from the past. Any text, of course, is created in a particular time and place, with what Gadamer calls a 'horizon of understanding' (a horizon meaning everything that can be viewed from a certain perspective). A reader today comes to such a text with her own 'horizon of understanding'. So, what must occur is a 'fusion' of these different horizons. Being – in language – is what *addresses* the reader – one might say *responds* to the initiation of the reader. By means of the words of an author in a text, being makes possible a *conversation* with the reader. The reader is after the meaning of a text – what being has to say – which far exceeds what the author intends and what the text itself says. For those of us with biblical backgrounds, it may sound analogous to how NT writers handle certain texts from the Hebrew Bible: there is more there – divinely intended – than even the biblical writer perceived.

For Gadamer, tradition is not something to be overcome, but is the essential context for all human understanding. We are all products

---

2 Hans-Georg Gadamer, *Wahrheit und Methode: Grudzuge einer philosophischen Hermeneutik* (Tubingen: J.C.B. Mohr, 1960); Additional citations from Hans-Georg Gadamer, *Truth and Method* (New York: Continuum, 1975).

of our historical and cultural contexts – our tradition or situatedness. As he famously wrote, 'history does not belong to us; we belong to it'.[3] Our history 'determines in advance both what seems to us worth inquiring about and what will appear as an object of investigation'.[4] Distance from the writing is not an obstacle at all. Rather, it allows later readers a better perspective of the meaning of a text, since we can see how it has been understood over various contexts.

The second person who shaped reception history is Hans Robert Jauss, often identified as the father of reception theory.[5] Jauss utilizes much of the work of Gadamer, while focusing a bit more specifically on how Gadamer's philosophical insights might work out in practice. One revision that he made relates to the role of the author. Gadamer's approach minimizes such a role, because it is being that speaks through language, above and beyond the intention of the author. Jauss advocated an approach to interpretation that integrated three elements: the work, the author, and the reader.

We owe at least the name of the topic for our conference to Jauss and what he called *Rezeptionaesthetik* (reception theory), from which one gets *Rezeptiongeschichte* (reception history). We should note the difference between this word and a term coined by Gadamer, *Wirkungsgeschichte* (effective history). Gadamer's term stresses the *effect* of a work, in that the focus is on the text and the influence it has in history. Jauss' term stresses the *reception* of a work, in that the focus is on the way a particular audience interprets a work.

Jauss adapts Gadamer's analogy of a horizon and speaks of a 'horizon of expectations'. The original horizon of expectations is that of the original readers in their historical cultural context. Readers of a later time and context will, of course, bring different perspectives to the reading of this same text, with different horizons of expectations. Horizons necessarily change with time and further life and reading experiences. Texts will be read and have different effects as the circumstances of audiences change. A text's meaning, as a result, evolves without any end to the process. One comes to understand a text from the past by reconstructing the horizon of

---

[3] Gadamer, *Truth and Method,* pp. 288-89.
[4] Gadamer, *Truth and Method,* p. 311.
[5] Hans Robert Jauss, *Toward an Aesthetic of Reception* (trans. Timothy Bahti; Minneapolis: University of Minnesota Press, 1982).

expectations of the author and the original audience. The history of the effects of an event or work enables us to understand the plurality of meanings that was not yet perceivable to its contemporaries. Our present horizon always includes the original horizon of the past as it has passed through the tradition. If this were not true, understanding a text from the past would be impossible. It is the task of historical understanding to take both horizons into account through conscious effort. Affirming Gadamer, Jauss reminds us that such an approach is not 'objective' – as supposedly managed in the natural sciences – but involves the reader's choices, perspectives, and evaluations.

Summing up, the crucial principles for Gadamer and Jauss for what comes to be known as reception history are as follows:

- All human existence, language, and artistic work are historically situated, and hence subject to change.
- Objectivity, that is, standing outside this historical situatedness, is impossible.
- Readers play a crucial role in the discovery of meaning in a text.
- Meaning in a text transcends that of the intention of the author.
- The horizon of a reader has some elements that are common with the horizon of a text and some elements that are alien to it.

All Men Created Equal

With this background, let's consider the words of the Declaration of Independence:

> We hold these truths to be self-evident, that all men are created equal, that they are endowed by their Creator with certain unalienable Rights, that among these are Life, Liberty and the pursuit of Happiness.[6]

Though drafted by Thomas Jefferson, the Declaration was the product of considerable discussion and revision both by the 'Committee of Five' and then the whole of the Continental Congress

---

[6] Declaration of Independence, July 4, 1776, https://www.archives.gov/founding-docs/declaration-transcript (accessed May 7, 2020).

meeting in Philadelphia in 1776. The stated purpose of the document was to justify the extreme action of separating from the British crown, stating the 'long train of abuses' that require a declaration of independence.

Our interest is in the opening words that appeal to the 'self evident' truth that 'men' are endowed by the Creator with natural rights that cannot be taken away. It is well known that such concepts were in the air at the time, a part of the original horizon. We know, for example, that when Jefferson was called upon to write a draft, he had in hand a draft of Virginia's Declaration of Rights, written by George Mason, that read: 'That all men are born equally free and independent, and have certain inherent natural rights ...'

Because the drafters adapted the language of prior documents, the Declaration itself is a reception. Historians for many years have been doing a sort of reception history in their examination of how the words of John Locke or Thomas Paine or the English Declaration of Rights of 1689 were used and interpreted by Jefferson and the other drafters. It is interesting that during the 1800 election campaign against John Adams, Jefferson was accused of plagiarizing John Locke and others. There are nearly one hundred resolutions of independence created by towns, counties, and colonies in the two months prior to the Continental Congress. These, in addition to the writings of the members of the Congress, newspaper articles, personal letters, and the like, would provide the basis for an understanding of how contemporaries of the Declaration would have understood it.

Reception

Reception theory claims that the text cannot 'mean' anything unless and until it is received (read, heard, or seen). As noted above, the reader initiates a conversation with the text; the result is meaning. The 'reader', then, must give careful thought to his or her horizon. What has been called a 'reader-response' approach, with its emphasis on the individual reader, actually reflects modernism's emphasis on the individual. Postmodernism, though not dismissing the importance of the individual, focuses on the group of which an individual is a part. We reflect the values and perspectives of our cultural groups.

Reception history reflects postmodernism in bringing to hermeneutics a new attention to the corporately-molded horizon of the reader and the reception tradition behind this horizon. Popular support for independence was crucial, and Jefferson and his colleagues had their colonial audience in mind when composing the Declaration. This is seen in how Jefferson made marks in at least one section of his draft to indicate when the reader should pause. The original audience would often hear, rather than read this document, and so the Declaration was written to be performed.

Historians have found that the Declaration fell into relative obscurity for the fifty years after its creation, its purpose having been served. Political events, however, led to a sharp rise in the country's interest in its history. According to Pauline Maier, this interest reached a high point in 1826 with the fiftieth anniversary of independence. 'In that critical period, members of the revolutionary generation were heroicized and the Declaration began to assume a certain holy quality.'[7] This was only heightened by one of the most remarkable coincidences of American history: the death of both Thomas Jefferson and John Adams on July 4, 1826, the country's 50th birthday.

Beginning in the 1820s, all sorts of groups began to cite the equality language of the Declaration to protest against the 'tyranny' of factory owners, railroad bosses, and corporation heads. The title of one scholarly survey says it all: *We, The Other People. Alternative Declarations of Independence by Labor Groups, Farmers, Woman's Right Advocates, Socialists, and Blacks, 1829–1975.*[8] So, in 1844, for example, The 'Declaration of Independence of the Producing from the Non-Producing Class' stated: 'We hold these truths to be self-evident: That as the natural wants and powers of production of all men are nearly equal, all should be producers as well as consumers'. Four years later, in 1848, at Seneca Falls, NY, the Women's Rights Convention created a 'Declaration of Sentiments and Resolutions' that asserted: 'We hold these truths to be self-evident: that all men and women are created equal'.

Here is a demonstration that this particular reading of the Declaration remains in the cultural air today. This excerpt is from the

---

[7] Pauline Maier, *American Scripture: Making the Declaration of Independence* (New York: Vintage, 1998), p. 175.

[8] Philip Sheldon Foner, *We The Other People: Alternative Declarations of Independence by Labor Groups, Farmers, Woman's Right Advocates, Socialists, and Blacks, 1829–1975* (Urbana, IL: University of Illinois Press, 1976).

Broadway smash, *Hamilton*, where the Schuyler Sisters go out in Manhattan, filled with optimism about what is possible in the new America.

> I've been reading *Common Sense* by Thomas Paine
> So men say that I'm intense or I'm insane
> You want a revolution? I want a revelation
> So listen to my declaration:
> 'We hold these truths to be self-evident
> That all men are created equal'
> And when I meet Thomas Jefferson
> I'm 'a compel him to include women in the sequel![9]

In the summer and fall of 1858, a lawyer from Springfield, IL, engaged US Sen. Stephen Douglas in a series of seven debates generally agreed to be one the most important electoral campaigns in American history. The previous year, in the Dred Scott case, the US Supreme Court decided that a slave is not a citizen of the United States and so could not sue in a federal court.

> In the opinion of the court, the legislation, and the history of the times, and the language of the Declaration of Independence, show, that neither the class of persons who had been imported as slaves, nor their descendants ... were then acknowledged as a part of the people, nor intended to be included in the general words used in that memorable instrument.[10]

In this case, the reception of the Declaration influenced the law of the land. That lawyer, Abraham Lincoln, appealed to the principle underlying the Declaration: all men are created equal. In this case, 'all' includes negroes. Douglas responded:

> I believe that the Declaration of Independence, in the words 'all men are created equal', was intended to allude only to the people of the United States, to men of European birth or descent, being white men, that they were created equal, and hence that Great Britain had no right to deprive them of their political and religious privileges; but the signers of that paper did not intend to include

---

[9] Lin-Manuel Miranda, 'The Schuyler Sisters', *Hamilton (Original Broadway Cast)*, Produced by Bill Sherman *et al.* Atlantic Records, 2015.

[10] Henry Steele Commager (ed.), *Documents of American History*, I (New York: Appleton-Century-Crofts, 8th edn, 1968), p. 341.

the Indian or the negro in that declaration, for if they had would they not have been bound to abolish slavery in every state and colony from that day?[11]

He added that the American government in its actions towards Native Americans proves it did not view Native peoples as the equal of white men.

Lincoln knew that most of the voters in Illinois in 1858 thought that black men were inferior to white men. He had to choose his words carefully. In the debates, he denies any desire to give negroes the right to be voters or jurors, or to allow them to intermarry with whites. But to be 'equal' meant at least equal in their right to 'life, liberty, and the pursuit of happiness'.[12] What is perhaps most intriguing for us is that Lincoln challenged Douglas on the intention of the creators and signers of the Declaration. The framers of the Constitution did the best they could, he said, given their historical and cultural limitations. Though they practically could not abolish slavery in 1781, they deplored its evil and anticipated the abolition of the slave trade explicitly by 1808.

It is in the Gettysburg Address, however, that Lincoln most memorably establishes the language of the Declaration as a national principle. At the dedication of the cemetery for those killed at the Battle of Gettysburg in 1863, he began his four minute speech, 'Fourscore and seven years ago our fathers brought forth on this continent a new nation, conceived in liberty and dedicated to the proposition that all men are created equal'. Though Lincoln doesn't quote from the Bible, he draws on its tradition, even in his use of 'fourscore and seven years ago' rather than 'eighty-seven years ago', or even, 'in 1776'. His language is evocative. The fathers didn't 'found' a nation, they 'brought it forth'. And most pertinent, those crafters and signers of the Declaration conceived of this new nation *dedicated to a proposition*. As some have claimed, the first nation ever formed based on a *concept*. And it is the task of those left alive to complete the unfinished business of more fully realizing this concept.

This ideology is illustrated in Dr Martin Luther King Jr's 'I Have a Dream' speech in the 1963 March on Washington:

---

[11] Paul M. Angle (ed.), *Created Equal? The Complete Lincoln–Douglas Debates of 1858* (Chicago: University of Chicago Press, 1958), pp. 62-63.
[12] Angle (ed.), *Created Equal?*, p. 82.

When the architects of our republic wrote the magnificent words of the Constitution and the Declaration of Independence, they were signing a promissory note to which every American was to fall heir. This note was a promise that all men, yes, black men as well as white men, would be guaranteed the unalienable rights of life, liberty, and the pursuit of happiness.

It is obvious today that America has defaulted on this promissory note insofar as her citizens of color are concerned. Instead of honoring this sacred obligation, America has given the Negro people a bad check, a check which has come back marked insufficient funds …

I say to you today, my friends, so even though we face the difficulties of today and tomorrow, I still have a dream. It is a dream deeply rooted in the American dream. I have a dream that one day this nation will rise up and live out the true meaning of its creed. 'We hold these truths to be self-evident, that all men are created equal'.[13]

Those words, of course, are not Lincoln's; they are Jefferson's. But it is Lincoln who makes those words sacred words. For Jefferson, they were the basis for breaking away from England and forming a new government. It is the Lincoln *reception* of those words that makes the Lincoln Memorial the appropriate location for the 'I Have a Dream' speech.

Reception in Media

This is a good time to emphasize how reception historians are particularly interested in receptions in media other than those traditionally studied, and among those who have not traditionally been heard. Reception studies are being pursued across the cultural spectrum: music, sculpture, drawing, film, theater, and architecture. And reception historians often are drawn to groups who have not written books or scholarly articles.

Let's look at a few examples from the time of the 1963 rally in Washington, each from a somewhat different horizon. First, consider

---

[13] Martin Luther King Jr, 'I Have a Dream', March on Washington, Washington DC, August 28, 1963.

Harper Lee's *To Kill a Mockingbird* and Atticus Finch's closing argument at the trial of Tom Robinson:

> And so, a quiet, humble, respectable negro, who has had the unmitigated TEMERITY to feel sorry for a white woman, has had to put his word against two white people. The defendant is not guilty. But somebody in this courtroom is.

> Now, gentlemen, in this country our courts are the great levelers. In our courts, all men are created equal. I'm no idealist to believe firmly in the integrity of our courts and of our jury system. That's no ideal to me.[14]

Finch receives the Declaration's words to defend the legal rights of Robinson. Both the novel in 1960 and the film in 1962 were immediate successes.

A second example is Jacob Lawrence, one of the first African American artists to gain recognition in the mainstream art world. In 1941, at age 24, he became the first artist of African descent to be represented by a major commercial art gallery. Inspired by the experience of young blacks being threatened as they entered newly integrated schools, in 1963, the same year of King's 'I Have a Dream' speech, Lawrence painted a work he titled *The Ordeal of Alice*. The young girl, pierced by arrows in the manner of St. Sebastian, symbolizes the struggle for equal rights a century after Emancipation.[15]

A third example could be the 1962 Bob Dylan song 'Blowing in the Wind' that became popular in the Civil Rights Movement, which was performed by Peter, Paul, and Mary in the same rally as the 'I Have a Dream' speech. Though Dylan was always evasive about what he meant when he wrote the words, the references to being accepted as a man and being allowed to be free were certainly taken to align perfectly with King's evocation of Lincoln:

> How many years can a mountain exist
> Before it's washed to the sea?
> How many years must some people exist
> Before they're allowed to be free

---

[14] Harper Lee, *To Kill a Mocking Bird* (1963) https://americanrhetoric.com/MovieSpeeches/moviespeechtokillamockingbird.html (accessed Nov 17, 2019).
[15] https://web.stanford.edu/dept/suma/news_room/Jacob-Lawrence.html (accessed January 27, 2020).

And how many times can a man turn his head
And pretend that he just doesn't see – the answer
The answer, my friend, is blowin' in the wind
The answer is blowin' in the wind.[16]

It is not Dylan's intention, but the *public reception* that grabs the attention of the reception historian. The popularity of the song, after the Peter, Paul, and Mary release, was immediate and worldwide. A different reception historian might trace the reception of the same song in protests against the Vietnam War just a few years later.

Reception and Modern Media

I now turn to more recent receptions of 'all men are created equal'. You may know the bioethicist and animal rights activist Peter Singer. His contribution to a work in 1989 was a chapter not surprisingly titled 'All Animals Are Equal', arguing against speciesism whereby humans distinguish themselves from other animals.[17]

With an article entitled 'All Animals Are Equal', we recognize the reception of reception, as we cannot confront such a title without thinking of George Orwell's *Animal Farm,* written in 1945. In what Orwell called a 'fairy story', he pictures the takeover of communism in Russia with an animal seizure of a farm from human control. One of the Seven Commandments of the revolution was 'All animals are equal'. The pigs manipulate matters so that the Commandments are simplified to the single phrase: 'All animals are equal, but some animals are more equal than others'. A biographer of Orwell has suggested that he drew from two texts in fashioning this phrase. One was Jefferson's phrase 'all men are created equal'. Orwell's use of the Declaration seems fairly certain, given that, in the Appendix to *1984* discussing the principles of Newspeak, he cites Jefferson's 'we hold these truths to be self-evident'.[18]

---

[16] Bob Dylan, 'Blowing in the Wind', *The Freewheeling,* 1962 by Warner Bros. Inc.; renewed 1990 by Special Rider Music, http://www.bobdylan.com/songs/blowin-wind/
[17] Tom Regan and Peter Singer, *Animal Rights and Human Obligations* (Englewood Cliffs, NJ: Prentice Hall, 1976).
[18] George Orwell, *Animal Farm* and *1984* (Orlando: Harcourt Books, 2002), p. xiii.

One last example: In February 2017, the European Union Parliament voted in favor of a report destined to create a legal framework around artificial intelligence. One of the report's most controversial proposals is the suggestion that electronic personality be granted to robots, thereby making them legal agents. Some commentators have stated that this amounts to giving robots the ability to possess human rights. Amanda Wurah argued in a paper that year the EU's decision is not only sound, but warranted. Can you guess the title of her paper? Yes, indeed: 'We Hold These Truths to Be Self-Evident, That All Robots Are Created Equal'.[19]

What might a reception historian find noteworthy from this brief survey of the afterlife of the text, 'all men are created equal' from the Declaration of Independence? A careful reconstruction of the probable meaning or meanings of the text for the writers and their contemporary audience is an essential part of the process of interpretation.

The tradition has revealed the fullness of the meaning of the text to far exceed the intentions of the writer(s). To understand the significance of the language of the Declaration, one must become familiar with the tradition, although for most Americans, this would already be a part of their understanding of the original text. Reception of the text has been influenced significantly by the horizon of the receivers. Various groups over time have found that the words and principles these groups inferred addressed their own situations. These receptions developed with larger cultural changes and were not uncontested.

Reception Since Gadamer and Jauss

This much we could have proposed based on our study of Gadamer and Jauss. But Reception Studies have moved beyond their word. Versions of Reception have blossomed in Communication Studies, for example, that examine the reception of television programming or advertising by different audiences. In marketing studies in particular, identifying the intention of the originator (the 'encoder') is much more important than was identifying the author in Gadamer's

---

[19] Amanda Wurah, 'We Hold These Truths to Be Self-Evident, That All Robots Are Created Equal', *Journal of Future Studies* 22.2 (2017), pp. 61-74.

framework. Some examples might include 'Women Watching Oprah in an African American Hair Salon',[20] the reception of the 'Telenovela' among rural viewers in Brazil,[21] and mapping the identity of Christian emerging adults through a reception study of the Colbert Report.[22]

One could point out that the humanities, as represented by Gadamer and Jauss, have lost considerable influence in the past fifty years. Financial resources, and therefore studies housed in particular academic fields, now flow toward technology, the media, and sociopolitical trends. And the internet has complicated the whole question of 'interpretive communities' because individuals now are members of diverse communities, some with overlapping interests, and some with competing interests.

The diversity within Reception Studies reflects the postmodern dismissal of a controlling center, of claims that one can characterize a cultural or historical period with generalities. Emphasis now is on the diversity of perspectives in any one period or group. Look at the following ads and note that they all appeal not to equality but to inequality. Some past ads for things that are **not** created equal include the following:

- A Michelob ad says, 'Dedicated to the proposition that all beers are not created equal'.
- A Metamucil ad that notes, 'All fiber is not created equal'.
- A Nike ad states, 'All feet are not created equal'.
- A Kobalt Tools ad that proclaims, 'Not all sockets are created equal'.

Reception and the De-Centering of Postmodernism

Back in the day, there was one Coke, and everybody watched Johnny Carson on the Tonight Show. Now there are dozens of versions of

---

[20] https://www.baltimoresun.com/features/baltimore-insider/bs-fe-oprah-exhibit-national-museum-african-american-history-culture-20180606-story.html (accessed Nov 17, 2019).

[21] Antonio C. La Pastina, 'Telenovela Reception in Rural Brazil: Gendered Readings and Sexual Mores', *Critical Studies in Media Communication* 21.2 (2004), pp. 162-81.

[22] Jill Elizabeth Dierberg, *Searching for Truth(iness): Mapping the Religio-Political Landscape and Identity of Christian Emerging Adults through a Reception Study of The Colbert Report* (PhD dissertation, University of Denver, August 2012).

Coke and of late-night comedy shows. We are not all the same in what we think tastes good or is funny. The framework of the reception historian, then, is this 'de-centering' associated with postmodernism. There is a special interest in those who have not been heard, those on the cultural fringes, and minorities. The anti-elitist character of Reception Studies is seen also in its interdisciplinary breadth. Film, pop music, and memes on social media – all are to be studied both as receiver and received. There is no interest in doing what has already been done, that is, a 'history of interpretation' by the experts. The development of Reception Studies thus aligns with the rise of multi-culturalism.

In this contemporary context – contrary to the claim of the Declaration of Independence – there are no truths that are self-evident. Truth, like everything else, has been de-centered. Truth is what one's interpretive community agrees upon. Reception history conferences should feature no academic papers with a title or subtitle with the word 'towards', if the 'towards' refers to any universal truth or principle. There are no 'grand narratives' that override all group horizons. There is no modern illusion of 'development' or 'progress' toward some ideal end. All cultural products are receptions of previous cultural products. Lincoln used Jefferson, who used Locke, who used Grotius, and so on.

According to Gadamer (though not Jauss, since Jauss gave more attention to the author), receptions are not 'better' or 'worse', only 'different'. From such a perspective, then, both Abraham Lincoln and Stephen Douglas had valid receptions of the Declaration because each had an interpretive community that affirmed his respective reception. Conversely, although postmodern de-centering has precluded any universal pretenses, it has fostered claims openly based on the prejudices (the word used here without the negative connotation of common usage) of particular interpretive communities. Note how this aligns with the postmodern emphasis on the voice of communities that have not been heard. The African American community, for example, would believe that Lincoln's reception of these words were 'better' given the community's openly-stated prejudices.

A truly interesting example of reception of the language of the Declaration of Independence comes from an IKEA ad featuring a same-sex couple relaxing in their home and a flag saying, 'All Homes are Created Equal'. The ad clearly affirms the company's support for gay rights, and, no doubt, its interest in sales among those who share that support. The explicit use of the original words of the Declaration is striking. It blatantly appeals to the American creed – the 'proposition' – that everyone is equal in the pursuit of life, liberty, and happiness. I am under no illusion that the executives of IKEA are religious people who believe that God created us and gave us inalienable rights. Equality is the point, and this ad powerfully demonstrates how the tradition continues to resound in the American ear. The question for the reception historian is not: did Jefferson and his colleagues have gay rights in mind? It's not even whether Lincoln's transformative reception – and hence the American tradition – has had gay rights in mind. The question is whether the IKEA 'marketing reception' rings true to the audience of the ad. This is no 'self-evident' truth that IKEA would appeal to in *Reader's Digest* as well as in *Gay Times*. Reception history, then, faces the same question that postmodernism does more generally: can anything be said that applies outside one's interpretive community?

Reception and Pentecostalism

Finally, how might this discussion speak to an interest common to all of us here gathered, twentieth-century Pentecostalism? How, for example, have Pentecostals used and interpreted the phrase 'all men are created equal'? The first example I found in Pentecostal periodicals was in 1911 in the text of a sermon preached by William Piper honoring the 300th anniversary of the King James Version of the Bible.[23] He cited the phrase, in this case via the Gettysburg Address, but his sermon was not so much about equality as it was how Lincoln was a man of the Bible. Jefferson was certainly not a man of the Bible, so by this time, the words of the Declaration were being read as those of Lincoln rather than those of Jefferson.

Articles in the *Christian Evangel* in 1919 and the *Foursquare Crusader* in 1928 cite the opening words of the Declaration and Scripture as jointly proclaiming the truth that all men are created equal with the right to worship God freely. As they did for Piper, the words of the

---

[23] William Hamner Piper, 'The Story of the Bible', *LRE* 3.8 (May 1911), pp. 2-8.

Declaration mean what they mean through the Lincoln reception.[24]

During the Second World War, references to the wording of the Declaration of Independence multiply. This is in a sense not surprising. The liberty of both nation and church was being threatened, and expressions of loyalty and devotion seemed only natural. Interestingly, writers speak of the inspiration and value of faith and nation on nearly equal levels of fervor. One arresting example came in the June 28, 1941 edition of the *Church of God Evangel* in an article that cites the Declaration language at length. The cover declares, 'My Bible, My Church, My Flag', and a poem within refers to those three as 'earth's greatest trinity'.[25]

This increased support for the nation and its war effort coincides with the erosion of the pacifism of many Pentecostals earlier in the century. To use Gadamer's language, Pentecostal horizons had changed.

Some historians of Pentecostalism may recognize the name Marie Burgess Brown. From Eau Claire, WI, she joined Alexander Dowie's community in Zion, IL and received her Pentecostal baptism in the Spirit in 1906. That same year, Charles Parham asked her to go to New York to start a Pentecostal mission, and though initially she resisted because she felt a call to mission work in China, she went when she sensed it was God's direction. She founded what became Glad Tidings Tabernacle, one of the leading churches in the Assemblies of God (AG) for years. She married Robert A. Brown, a former Irish policeman, who became her husband and a general presbyter of the AG in its early years. They were my great aunt and uncle, and I was named after him. I was aware that Uncle Robert had referred to 'our boys' from Glad Tidings fighting in Europe during WWII, so I was rather taken aback when I first read his statement against participation in WWI. In the March 1917 edition of the Glad Tidings periodical *The Midnight Cry,* he writes:

> How do you account for so many Christians fighting in this war, we have been asked time and again. The answer is plain and positive: there are none so doing (according to scriptural standard) and

---

[24] A.P. Collins, 'The Competency of the Soul Under God or Soul Liberty', *CE* 305/306 (September 6, 1919), p. 3; Dorothy H. Martin, 'The Great Task of Which Lincoln Speaks', *FC* 2.11 (February 8, 1928), p. 2.

[25] Laura Adrene Sanders, 'My Bible, My Church, My Flag', *CGE* 32.8 (June 28, 1941), p. 1, 3.

if they ever were God's children they have backslidden and are engaged in the work of the devil.[26]

His belief was that war is murder. 'And no murderer shall inherit the kingdom of God'. Apparently, Uncle Robert's reception of that text changed. And he was not alone. Many Pentecostal horizons changed between 1917 and 1945.

How might a reception historian approach a study of changing Pentecostal receptions of biblical texts?

- Pursue the voices of those who have not been heard. Find diaries, letters, or testimonies of Pentecostals to discern whether the statements in periodicals and other published works reflect the diversity among Pentecostals.

- Ask the question: How important, relatively speaking, was identity as a Pentecostal in forming views of violence and war? Were other factors such as previous religious affiliation or tradition, gender, social class, race, and geographic region more important? (e.g. Arthur Booth-Clibborn and his background in The Salvation Army.)

- Ask the question: What is my own horizon and how does it influence my reception of the original text and of the earlier reception I am studying?

- Remember that there can be no universal claims. There are no 'self-evident' truths. The most the historian can do is stake a position based on the conversation she has had with the text and its reception, representing her interpretive group. A pacifist may not claim that twentieth-century Pentecostalism should be understood as a 'fall' from a pure work of the Spirit into militarism and nationalism. A just war advocate may not claim that early Pentecostals should be dismissed as naïve sectarians. Each is free to evaluate the data from their group's perspective, as long as each is open and honest about the prejudices they bring to their study.

Reception history, like reader response criticism, is a postmodern phenomenon in that it emphasizes the role of the reader in determining meaning. I hope that we can acknowledge that we are all now

---

[26] 'Editoral', *The Midnight Cry* (March 1917), p. 4.

working in a postmodern context. For those of us who lament the de-centering to which I have referred, allow me one final observation. If we cannot enthusiastically embrace all the characteristics that are commonly associated with postmodernism, let's embrace at least the intellectual humility that it warrants. The AG, in its Statement of Fundamental Truths in 1916, set down what its adherents confidently believed was the teaching of the Bible, confirmed by the work of the Holy Spirit among them. Yet even these single-minded Pentecostals in the preface affirmed: 'This statement is not inspired or contended for' and 'No claim is made that it contains all biblical truth'. The formulation served only as a 'basis of fellowship'. Most postmodernists don't deny that there is such a thing as truth. The key point, they would insist, is that we *don't know* and we *can't know* truth apart from an inevitably prejudiced viewpoint. I think we all would do well to acknowledge this reality. Regardless of whether you can or not, you can't understand or practice reception history without taking that principle as a starting point. We can gain much from studies in reception history. I daresay Christians in 2019 would benefit mightily from a greater knowledge of the church tradition lying behind our reading of the Bible. We are not aware how much our interpretation has been affected by readings over the past 2,000 years, most for the better, some for the worse. I look forward to hearing the presentations over the next couple of days and having my own horizon clarified and challenged.

Bibliography

Angle, Paul M. (ed.), *Created Equal? The Complete Lincoln–Douglas Debates of 1858* (Chicago: University of Chicago Press, 1958).

Commager, Henry Steele (ed.), *Documents of American History,* I (New York: Appleton-Century-Crofts, 8th edn, 1968).

Declaration of Independence, July 4, 1776, https://www.archives.gov/founding-docs/declaration-transcript (accessed May 7, 2020).

Dierberg, Jill Elizabeth, 'Searching for Truth(iness): Mapping the Religio-Political Landscape and Identity of Christian Emerging Adults through a Reception Study of The Colbert Report' (PhD dissertation, University of Denver, August 2012).

Foner, Philip Sheldon, *We The Other People: Alternative Declarations of Independence by Labor Groups, Farmers, Woman's Right Advocates, Socialists, and Blacks, 1829–1975* (Urbana, IL: University of Illinois Press, 1976).

Gadamer, Hans-Georg, *Truth and Method* (New York: Continuum, 1975).
—*Wahrheit und Methode: Grundzuge einer philosophischen Hermeneutik* (Tübingen: J.C.B. Mohr, 1960).
Jauss, Hans Robert, *Toward an Aesthetic of Reception* (trans. Timothy Bahti; Minneapolis: University of Minnesota Press, 1982).
La Pastina, Antonio C., 'Telenovela Reception in Rural Brazil: Gendered Readings and Sexual Mores', *Critical Studies in Media Communication* 21.2 (2004), pp. 162-81.
Maier, Pauline, *American Scripture: Making the Declaration of Independence* (New York: Vintage Books, 1999).
Miranda, Lin-Manuel, 'The Schuyler Sisters', *Hamilton (Original Broadway Cast),* Produced by Bill Sherman *et al.* Atlantic Records, 2015.
Regan, Tom and Peter Singer, *Animal Rights and Human Obligations* (Englewood Cliffs, NJ: Prentice-Hall, 1976).
Wurah, Amanda, 'We Hold These Truths to Be Self-Evident, That All Robots Are Created Equal', *Journal of Future Studies* 22.2 (2017), pp. 61-74.

Websites
https://web.stanford.edu/dept/suma/news_room/Jacob-Lawrence.html (accessed Jan 27, 2020).
Dylan, Bob, 'Blowing in the Wind', *The Freewheeling,* 1962 by Warner Bros. Inc.; renewed 1990 by Special Rider Music, http://www.bobdylan.com /songs/blowin-wind/.
Lee, Harper, *To Kill a Mocking Bird* (1963) https://americanrhetoric.com/ MovieSpeeches/moviespeechtokillamockingbird.html (Accessed Nov 17, 2019).

3

RECEPTION HISTORY AS LITERARY-HISTORICAL METHODOLOGY: IMPLICATIONS FOR PENTECOSTAL HERMENEUTICS

ALICIA R. JACKSON[*]

For Pentecostal scholars working in the field of biblical studies, conversations continue regarding the prioritization of Enlightenment-based historical methodologies exploring the 'world behind the text', or literary methodologies emphasizing the 'world of the text'. In this chapter, I will argue that reception history is inherently a literary-historical approach to biblical interpretation, taking 'the best of both worlds'. While reception history cannot be reduced to either a historical or literary analysis of the text's interpretation, it may possess potential to bridge the divide between two methodological camps, potentially creating fresh perspective and space for discussion in the field of Pentecostal hermeneutics. I will begin with a brief overview of reception history, followed by a summary of contemporary conversations regarding literary and historical methodological approaches as they relate to Pentecostal hermeneutics. After offering what I hope is a nuanced view, I will conclude by exploring ways in which reception history may provide common ground for literary and historical approaches to biblical interpretation, considering some

* Alicia R. Jackson (PhD, University of Birmingham, UK) is Assistant Professor of Old Testament at Vanguard University, Costa Mesa, CA, USA.

of the benefits and limitations of reception history for Pentecostal interpreters.

In his introduction to the *Oxford Handbook of the Reception History of the Bible*, Jonathan Roberts aptly defines reception history as 'the practice of making worldly records of those manifest and mysterious individual and corporate experiences of the biblical text'.[1] Based in the hermeneutics of Hans-Georg Gadamer, reception history of the Bible involves selecting and organizing 'reception material' of the biblical text into a 'narrative frame'.[2] Gadamer's work on reception history emphasized the 'situated nature of all historical acts',[3] and thus he writes, 'History does not belong to us; we belong to it'.[4] According to Gadamer, by locating ourselves historically, we as interpreters discover our own pre-dispositions and biases toward the text, thereby fusing the horizons of text and interpreter in the frameworks of both tradition and history.[5] Pentecostal theologian Amos Yong

---

[1] Jonathan Roberts, 'Introduction', in Michael Lieb, Emma Mason, and Jonathan Roberts (eds.), *The Oxford Handbook of the Reception History of the Bible* (Oxford: Oxford University Press, 2011), pp. 1-10 (8). This reception material of the biblical text is not limited to literature only, but it can also include various cultural expressions such as art, music, and politics. For the purposes of the constraints of this paper, I am narrowing my focus on reception history as it pertains to literary records of the experiences of biblical texts.

[2] See Roberts, 'Introduction', pp. 1-10 (1); and Timothy Beal, 'Reception History and Beyond: Toward the Cultural History of Scriptures', *Biblical Interpretation* 19 (2011), pp. 357-72 (359). Riches provides a multivalent understanding of the significance of reception history for biblical interpretation: 'These are texts to be lived out of – this too is part of what it is for them to be seen as canonical – and their meaning will be grasped only in such a process of social embodiment, lived or observed. This is what Jauss means when he says that the historical life of a literary work is inconceivable without the active participation of its addressee. Reception history of the Bible is not just a repository of readings, more or less interesting, more or less able to inform our understanding of the text (though it is certainly that); it is the record of a lived history, of the life of communities for whom these texts have provided direction and a sense of meaning, and who have discovered new meanings in them as they have lived with them and sought to make sense of their lives. And it is precisely within this historical process of engagement between text and community (and not in some supratemporal encounter) that these texts come alive, that new dimensions are discovered that were perhaps uncoverable before.' See John Riches, 'Reception History as a Challenge to Biblical Theology', *Journal of Theological Interpretation* 7.2 (2013), pp. 171-85 (185).

[3] Roberts, 'Introduction', p. 1.

[4] Hans-Georg Gadamer, *Truth and Method* (trans. Joel Weinsheimer and Donald G. Marshall; London: Continuum, 2nd edn, 2004), pp. 276-77; Roberts, 'Introduction', p. 2.

[5] Gadamer, *Truth and Method*, p. 305; Roberts, 'Introduction', pp. 2-3.

affirms the significance of Gadamer's work for the theological interpretation of Scripture when he claims that 'in a post-Gadamerian
frame there is no interpretation that is not a fusion of horizons between that of the text and that of the reader'.[6] Ulrich Luz, the well-
known German theologian who famously applied reception history
to the gospel of Matthew, yielded a reading which Donald Hagner
characterized as possessing 'revolutionary implications for traditional, historical-critical exegesis in its quest of a single, objective
meaning – the intention of the author'.[7] While Hagner celebrated the
way Luz unveiled the text's vast richness, he expressed concern that
the 'new meanings' of the text are placed on the same level of importance as the text's 'original sense', effectively rendering the idea
of a text's original meaning as either elusive or perhaps even irrele-
vant.[8]

The interpreter's answer to the question of whether the biblical
text even possesses an 'original sense' – in terms of either authorial
intent or meaning as received by the text's original audiences – may
reveal the interpreter's methodological preferences and priorities. Is
reception history yet another methodological approach that must be
prioritized over and against others, or does it potentially create space
in which to harmonize various approaches? Mark Knight rejects what
he sees as the polarization between the 'new interest' in reception and
the older emphasis on historical-critical methodologies, arguing, 'To
polarize our interpretative options is to ignore the ways in which

---

[6] Amos Yong, *The Hermeneutical Spirit: Theological Interpretation and Scriptural Imagination for the 21ˢᵗ Century* (Eugene, OR: Cascade Books, 2017), p. 260.

[7] Donald A. Hagner, review of *Matthew 8–20* (trans. James E. Crouch; Hermeneia, Minneapolis: Fortress, 2001) by Ulrich Luz, in *JBL* 121 (2002), pp. 766-69
(768); Roberts, 'Introduction', p. 4.

[8] Hagner, review of *Matthew 8–20*, p. 768. Roberts, 'Introduction', pp. 4-5,
writes, 'Luz's work demonstrates how the concept of "tradition" can be a way of
putting parameters on the multivalence of the biblical text by setting out what is
and is not acceptable to the interpreter'. Regarding how one defines the boundaries
of a particular tradition, in terms of how those within that tradition establish parameters of a text's meaning or prioritization of which voices are most significant
within a text's reception history, Roberts explains, 'It is impossible to judge these
matters from the outside, because the experiential truth of a particular tradition
may only be evident to those within it … Given the billions of individual lives
shaped for better or worse by the Bible over the millennia, it is a contentious task
to compile a work that says, "*these* are the voices that matter".' emphasis original.

different positions constantly collide, intersect and fuse'.[9] Similarly, Timothy Beal views reception history as nothing less than 'revolutionary for the field of biblical studies' in its 'welcome potential to overcome the tired, decades-old opposition between so-called historical-critical approaches (source-critical, form-critical, redaction-critical, and textual-critical) and literary-critical approaches (new-critical, reader-response, structuralist, poststructuralist, etc.) within the field of biblical studies'.[10] I concur with Knight and Beal, and I propose that reception history is literary-historical methodology. It is literary in the sense that the interpreter is collecting and analyzing literature written on the reception of the biblical text, and it is historical in the sense that the literary analysis of the selected texts focuses upon a particular time or setting in history, or even more broadly, the trajectory of reception within a certain tradition throughout history. Regardless of the parameters set for a reception history study of the biblical text, it necessarily involves both literary and historical analysis, thereby fusing methodological approaches, which have been (in my view) at times unnecessarily polarized.

Reception History as Literary-Historical Methodology and Pentecostal Hermeneutics

What implications may reception history as literary-historical methodology have for Pentecostal hermeneutics? As I have argued, I believe it demonstrates the ways in which literary and historical approaches to the text both hold tremendous value for interpreters. While some Pentecostal scholars discourage prioritization of historical-critical and historical-grammatical approaches to reading the Bible, others emphasize their foundational nature. Although these historical approaches arose from opposite spheres (one from fundamentalist/evangelical movements, and the other from mainline denominations and academia), both are rooted in scientific approach born in the rationalism of the Enlightenment. Those scholars who emphasize historical-grammatical methodologies seek to uncover the 'world behind the text' by examining the language, culture, and historical background of the text in order to interpret more accurately

---

[9] Mark Knight, 'Wirkungsgeschichte, Reception History, Reception Theory', *JSNT* 33 (2010), pp. 137-46 (144).
[10] Beal, 'Reception History and Beyond', p. 364.

the text's meaning as it would have been received and understood by its original audiences. Pentecostal NT scholar Craig Keener's voluminous and meticulously researched socio-cultural, linguistic, and historical background work illustrates this emphasis most extensively.[11] In Keener's recent contribution to the field of Pentecostal hermeneutics, he cautions interpreters against relying solely on experiential or communal interpretations. Keener argues that in addition to studying Scripture in community, interpreters must also consider the text's linguistic, cultural, and historical contexts.[12] Robert Menzies expresses similar concerns when he asks, 'If we loose the meaning of a text from its historical moorings, how shall we evaluate various and even contradictory interpretations? How shall we keep our own ideologies and prejudices from obliterating the text?'[13] John Poirer and B. Scott Lewis urge fellow Pentecostals to resist what they refer to as 'uncritical Enlightenment bashing', and instead to acknowledge that methodologies rooted in rational approaches are more helpful for accurate Scripture interpretation than postmodern methods.[14] Arden

---

[11] For a sample of Keener's historical background work on the biblical text, see Craig S. Keener, *The IVP Bible Background Commentary: New Testament* (Downers Grove, IL: InterVarsity Press, 1994); *Matthew* (IVP New Testament Commentary Series, Downers Grove, IL: InterVarsity Press, 1997); *A Commentary on the Gospel of Matthew* (Grand Rapids: Eerdmans, 1999); *Revelation* (The NIV Application Commentary, Grand Rapids: Zondervan, 2000); *The Gospel of John: A Commentary.* (2 vols; Peabody, MA: Hendrickson, 2003); *1–2 Corinthians* (New Cambridge Bible Commentary, Cambridge: Cambridge University Press, 2006); *Romans* (New Covenant Commentary Series, Eugene, OR: Cascade Books, 2009); *Acts: An Exegetical Commentary* (4 vols; Grand Rapids: Baker Academic, 2012–2015); *Galatians* (New Cambridge Bible Commentary, Cambridge: Cambridge University Press, 2018); and *Galatians: A Commentary* (Grand Rapids: Baker Academic, 2018).

[12] Craig S. Keener, *Spirit Hermeneutics: Reading Scripture in the Light of Pentecost* (Grand Rapids: Eerdmans, 2016), pp. 276-77.

[13] Robert P. Menzies, 'Jumping Off the Postmodern Bandwagon', *Pneuma* 16 (1994), pp. 115-20 (116-17).

[14] They write, 'Pentecostals should reject the uncritical Enlightenment-bashing of today's biblical-critical and theological guilds in favor of a more sensitive and informed treatment of how the Bible's commitments intersect with those of today's world'. See John C. Poirier and B. Scott Lewis, 'Pentecostal and Postmodern Hermeneutics: A Critique of Three Conceits', *JPT* 15 (2006), pp. 3-21 (21). In addition, Cargal lamented the state of most Pentecostal scholars, who according to Cargal 'have tended to align themselves with evangelicals in their move toward adopting the methods of higher criticism while maintaining a commitment to the reality of biblical narrative'. See Timothy B. Cargal, 'Beyond the Fundamentalist-Modernist Controversy: Pentecostals and Hermeneutics in a Postmodern Age', *Pneuma* 15 (Fall 1993), pp. 163-87; and see French L. Arrington, 'The Use of the Bible by Pentecostals', *Pneuma* 16 (1994), pp. 101-107 (101).

Autry argues that while the historical-critical methodology may be inadequate by itself, it is not 'inappropriate or unnecessary'.[15]

However, other Pentecostal scholars claim that a significant problem with prioritizing historical approaches to the text is that the focus on discovering the 'world behind the text' eclipses an emphasis on the 'world of the text'. In support of the literary approach of Pentecostal NT scholar John Christopher Thomas, Kenneth Archer explains, 'Thomas' concern for literary analysis would take precedent over the historical critical approaches. Hence, the world of the text and not the world behind the text would be the central concern.'[16] For Pentecostal theologian Chris Green, as well as for Thomas and Archer, emphasis on the significance of community for Pentecostal interpreters remains key, in which multiple readings may emerge.[17] French Arrington and Andrew Davies both note how early Pentecostals, who often found multiple meanings and applications in one text, more closely align with postmodern biblical hermeneutical approaches than with historical-critical methodologies.[18] Archer

---

[15] See Arden C. Autry, 'Dimensions of Hermeneutics in Pentecostal Focus', *JPT* 3 (1993), pp. 29-50 (33). Similarly, Harrington and Patten write, 'As long as we are working with a text that has been given to us through human activity in human language, sometimes through objectifiable channels, it is incumbent on us to study it for understanding in all ways possible. While the objective approach is admittedly partially subjective, a subjective approach alone would not be assessable at all.' Hannah K. Harrington and Rebecca Patten, 'Pentecostal Hermeneutics and Post-Modern Literary Theory', *Pneuma* 16 (Spring 1994), pp. 109-14 (113).

[16] See Kenneth J. Archer, *A Pentecostal Hermeneutic: Spirit, Scripture, and Community* (Cleveland, TN: CPT Press, 2009), p. 198; John Christopher Thomas, 'Reading the Bible from Within Our Traditions: A Pentecostal Hermeneutic as Test Case', in Joel Green and Max Turner (eds.), *Between Two Horizons: Spanning New Testament Studies and Systematic Theology* (Grand Rapids: Eerdmans, 2000), pp. 108-22; and John Christopher Thomas, 'Women, Pentecostals, and the Bible', *JPT* 5 (1994), pp. 41-56.

[17] See John Christopher Thomas, '"What the Spirit is Saying to the Church" – The Testimony of a Pentecostal in New Testament Studies', in Kevin L. Spawn and Archie T. Wright (eds.), *Spirit and Scripture: Exploring a Pneumatic Hermeneutic* (London: Bloomsbury T&T Clark, 2011), pp. 115-29, and 'Women, Pentecostals, and the Bible'; Archer, *A Pentecostal Hermeneutic*, pp. 212-60, and 'Pentecostal Hermeneutics: Retrospect and Prospect', *JPT* 4 (1996), pp. 63-81; and Chris E.W. Green, *Sanctifying Interpretation: Vocation, Holiness, and Scripture* (Cleveland, TN: CPT Press, 2015), pp. 150-53.

[18] Davies writes, 'We [Pentecostals] have rather more in common methodologically with the liberal progressive wing of biblical scholarship than the traditional evangelicals'. Andrew Davies, 'What Does It Mean to Read the Bible as a Pentecostal?' *JPT* 18 (2009), pp. 216-29 (222); and Arrington, 'The Use of the Bible by Pentecostals', pp. 101-102.

concurs, expressing great concern for what he views as an overuse of historical-critical methodologies among Pentecostals. Similarly, Hannah Harrington and Rebecca Patten explain how postmodern literary approaches may be helpful for Pentecostals:

> Indeed, limiting the meaning of the text to only what the ancient authors intended to convey to their audiences may cause the reader to miss the creative work of the Spirit in making the text relevant to life. Thus, it appears that there is a niche in postmodern literary criticism for Pentecostal hermeneutics, a scholarly apparatus for explaining the Pentecostal process of reading Scripture.[19]

Along these lines, Timothy Cargal expresses concern that Pentecostal interpreters, in aligning themselves with evangelicals, are in danger of losing their Pentecostal distinctives.[20] Cargal's concern can be illustrated by examining Bradley Truman Noel's assessment of Gordon Fee's work. Fee advocates the use of historical-grammatical interpretation, with an emphasis on discovering original authorial intent, primarily because he believes it 'serves as a corrective, limiting the possible meanings a text might be given'.[21] However, Noel argues that when Fee employs the interpretive criteria of authorial intent rigidly to the book of Acts, he abandons belief in both subsequence and initial evidence, resulting in a theology of Spirit baptism that

---

[19] Harrington and Patten, 'Pentecostal Hermeneutics and Post-Modern Literary Theory', p. 109.

[20] See Cargal, 'Beyond the Fundamentalist-Modernist Controversy', pp. 163-87.

[21] See Gordon D. Fee, *Gospel and Spirit: Issues in New Testament Hermeneutics* (Grand Rapids: Baker Publishing Group, 1991), pp. 43, 91; and Bradley Truman Noel, 'Gordon Fee and the Challenge to Pentecostal Hermeneutics: Thirty Years Later', *Pneuma* 26 (2004), pp. 60-80 (62). Fee explains, 'Clearly descriptive history in Acts must not be translated into normative experiences for the ongoing church'. Noel summarizes Fee's position succinctly,

> Fee outlines three specific principles regarding hermeneutics and historical narrative: (1) Authorial intent is the chief factor in determining normative values from narratives. (2) That which is incidental to the primary intent of a narrative cannot have the same didactic value as the intended teaching, although it may provide insight into the author's theology. (3) For historical precedent to have normative value, it must be demonstrated that such was the specific intent of the author. If the author intended to establish precedent, then such should be regarded as normative.

more closely resembles that of Evangelicals than Pentecostals.[22] For example, Fee argues that because the author of the book of Acts did not intend to establish a repeatable pattern demonstrating Spirit-baptism as a subsequent experience to salvation, any discernable narrative pattern should not be considered normative due to the lack of authorial intent.[23]

Building upon the hermeneutical models of Gadamer and Ricoeur, Richard Israel, Daniel Albrecht, and Randal McNally locate the focus of hermeneutics not in authorial intent, but rather in the structural relations and meaning found in the text's language. They write:

> The focus of the hermeneutical task is not to delve into the subjectivity of the author, but to explain the structural relations and sets of meanings contained in the language of a text and understand the claims which the text is making about the world.[24]

Davies, Archer, and Green are also among those who find little value in pursuing knowledge of authorial intent. Davies articulates why such a concern remains tangential at best for most Pentecostals:

> Pentecostals read the Bible as dialogue partners with it and with the inspiring Spirit; we bring our own questions, circumstances and needs to the text, and through it to the Lord, and allow him to bring his own agenda about as he speaks to us. There is therefore little interest for us as spiritualizing readers in the surface meaning of the text, and scant attention paid to the original intention of the author. Rather we seek to push behind the plain sense

---

[22] Noel sees contradictions in Fee's assertions. 'For, although Fee claims to be Pentecostal in every regard, he nonetheless takes considerable exception to the stated form of two of their key (some would argue distinctive) doctrines: the baptism of the Holy Spirit as a subsequent act following conversion, and the declaration that the evidence of such baptism is speaking in tongues.' See Noel, 'Gordon Fee and the Challenge to Pentecostal Hermeneutics', p. 63. For a more thorough account of Fee's hermeneutics and Pentecostal responses to Fee's approach, see Bradley Truman Noel, *Pentecostal and Postmodern Hermeneutics: Comparisons and Contemporary Impact* (Eugene, OR: Wipf & Stock, 2010), pp. 73-95.

[23] Gordon D. Fee and Douglas Stuart, *How to Read the Bible for all Its Worth* (Grand Rapids: Zondervan, 4th edn, 2014), pp. 112-31.

[24] See Richard D. Israel, Daniel E. Albrecht, and Randal G. McNally, 'Pentecostals and Hermeneutics: Texts, Rituals, and Community', *Pneuma* 15 (1993), pp. 137-61 (138).

of the text to experience what Aquinas would have labeled its anagogic power, its capacity to edify and inspire.[25]

Archer pushes back not only against the need to discover authorial intent, but also against the idea of determinate meaning:

> A Pentecostal hermeneutical strategy is needed which rejects the quest for a past determinate meaning of the author and embraces the reality that interpretation involves both the discovery of meaning and the creation of meaning. Thus, texts are by their very nature, indeterminate.[26]

Similarly, Green shifts the emphasis away from past meaning and authorial intent to the Spirit's witness to Christ:

> When we come to the Scriptures, then, we are not trying to rediscover 'original intent', or trying to uncover what the words 'meant' in the ancient world so we can work out how they might be made to 'mean' something for us today. We are trying to hear the Spirit's witness to Christ. Nothing more or less than that.[27]

While I deeply appreciate the emphasis of Davies, Archer, and Green upon the pneumatic immediacy and experiential nature of the text for Pentecostal readers, and while I also acknowledge the somewhat subjective nature of seeking to identify authorial intent, I believe it is unnecessary to swing the pendulum too far in the other direction and thereby diminish the importance of historical approaches to the text. It is one thing to claim to know the internal motivations and intentions of an individual author, and quite another to read the text in light of helpful linguistic, historical, and cultural background information. As stated previously, Hagner's concern with Luz's reception history work on Matthew was that in uncovering new meanings in the text, Luz would essentially deconstruct 'a single, objective meaning – the intention of the author'.[28] Hagner's comment seems to imply that the existence of an original determinate meaning of a text must be based primarily upon authorial intent, but I disagree. I propose that interpreters may enhance their exegesis with

---

[25] See Davies, 'What Does It Mean to Read the Bible as a Pentecostal', pp. 221-22.

[26] See Archer, *A Pentecostal Hermeneutic*, p. 199

[27] See Green, *Sanctifying Interpretation*, pp. 153-54.

[28] Hagner, review of *Matthew 8–20*, p. 768.

knowledge of the text's linguistic, historical, and cultural background, in an effort to understand how the text would have been received and understood by its original audiences, without getting sucked into the vortex of basing interpretations solely upon authorial intent. Such an investigation into the 'world behind the text' does not detract from a deeper look into the 'world of the text'. In fact, I argue that research into the 'world behind the text' can greatly enhance the interpreters understanding of the 'world of the text'. This is not to say that each text only possesses a singular, narrow meaning in a fundamentalist sense, or that interpreters should reduce or flatten a text to one 'correct' meaning, but certainly investigating the 'world behind the text' in order to understand how the text was received serves as a foundation upon which to evaluate subsequent readings in the text's reception history.

Historical-Grammatical and/or Historical Critical Methodologies

Analogous to the neglect of historical-grammatical methodology by some scholars, due in part to either a disinterest in authorial intent or a recognition of its elusive nature, is the tendency to collapse historical-critical and historical-grammatical methodologies into one camp, or even to use the terminology interchangeably, when the goals of historical-critical and historical-grammatical methodologies can differ significantly. It may be helpful at this point to draw a distinction between what I see as diachronic and synchronic methodologies. Diachronic methodologies, including some of the historical-critical methods (such as source, form, tradition history, and redaction criticism), primarily seek to uncover the various layers of the text's construction.[29] By contrast, synchronic methodologies, including

---

[29] However, it should be noted that form and redaction criticism can also be employed synchronically. For example, Israel, Albrecht, and McNally affirm the limited value of a synchronic use of structuralism when they write, 'Structuralism can clarify how a text operates, how it functions, but provides no help in understanding or grappling with what the text is all about'. See Israel, Albrecht, and McNally, 'Pentecostals and Hermeneutics', p. 141. I think this is somewhat analogous to Muilenburg's appropriation of a sort of synchronic form criticism in his development of 'rhetorical criticism', springing from his growing dissatisfaction with the classical diachronic emphasis of the historical-critical methods.

approaches such as the historical-grammatical method, socio-cultural analysis, narrative criticism, canonical criticism, and rhetorical analysis, primarily seek to determine the meaning of the text as a whole in its canonical form.[30] Personally, I find the synchronic historical-grammatical method (emphasizing the location of a text's meaning in its reception by its original audiences), immensely helpful for biblical interpretation, and yet, regarding some of the diachronic historical-critical methods, I resonate with Alan Cooper's lament: 'At the very least, I find them uninteresting'.[31] Much of the emphasis of diachronic source criticism, form criticism, tradition history, and redaction criticism seems to me an unsatisfying attempt at uncovering hidden layers of the text's construction. While such pursuits may allow the interpreter to spin interesting hypotheses, theories resulting from such approaches remain tenuous at best – most often yielding conclusions based upon conjecture and circular reasoning.

However, concerning the interpretation of the text in its canonical form, I propose that, ironically, postmodern-based literary methodologies share more in common with the synchronic historical-

---

Muilenburg saw rhetorical criticism as a part of the field of form criticism, although today scholars would categorize it separately as a postmodern literary methodology. Muilenburg emphasized what he called 'stylistics', including analysis of literary structural devices such as chiasms, inclusios, repetition, and rhetorical questions. Muilenburg's work in biblical studies was analogous to the 'new criticism' introduced by twentieth-century literary critics in the sense that both rejected historical-critical approaches to the text. See James Muilenburg, 'Form Criticism and Beyond', *JBL* 88 (1969), pp. 1-18; Rolf Knierim, 'Criticism of Literary Features, Form, Tradition, and Redaction', in Douglas A. Knight and Gene M. Tucker (eds.), *The Hebrew Bible and Its Modern Interpreters* (Philadelphia: Fortress Press, 1985), pp. 123-66 (134-46); and Patricia K. Tull, 'Rhetorical Criticism and Intertextuality', in Steven L. McKenzie and Stephen R. Haynes (eds.), *To Each Its Own Meaning: An Introduction to Biblical Criticism and Their Application* (Louisville, KY: Westminster/John Knox Press, 1999), pp. 156-80 (158-60).

[30] For an explanation of the contrast between diachronic and synchronic approaches, see Michael J. Gorman, *Elements of Biblical Exegesis: A Basic Guide for Students and Ministers* (Grand Rapids: Baker Academic, 2009), pp. 13-17. Gorman employs the term 'historical criticism' in a similar way that I am using it here to denote a concern with 'historical events related to the genesis, development, production, and background of the text under investigation' (p. 16). I agree with Gorman, who acknowledges that while there are similarities between 'social-scientific' or socio-cultural concerns of a synchronic approach and the historical critical considerations of a diachronic approach, the two 'differ in emphasis'.

[31] See Alan Cooper, 'On Reading the Bible Critically and Otherwise', in Richard Elliott Friedman and H.G.M. Williamson (eds.), *The Future of Biblical Studies: Hebrew Scriptures* (Atlanta: Scholars Press, 1987), pp. 61-79 (61).

grammatical method than do many of the diachronic historical-critical methodologies. For example, rhetorical analysis, a specific type of literary analysis popularized first by James Muilenburg and developed further by Phyllis Trible and others, considers the text's historical context as well as literary artistry and persuasion. When literary artistry is the focus of rhetorical analysis, as it was for Muilenburg, discovering the author's intent becomes the primary end. However, when literary persuasion is emphasized, the focus shifts to the reception of the audience and the response of the reader, resembling in this aspect both the historical-grammatical method and reception history.[32] Therefore, in my view, it is unnecessary to view Enlightenment-based historical approaches as polarized from postmodern-based literary ones, when in fact the historical-grammatical method and a literary-critical analysis can be effectively employed together cohesively. Adrian Hinkle demonstrates this type of creative approach in *Pedagogical Theory of Wisdom Literature*, in which she 'uses a somewhat eclectic hermeneutical approach that combines grammatical-historical and literary criticism to draw attention to nuances within the texts'. She argues, 'Vital aspects of the biblical texts are not fully regarded when only viewing these texts through a single lens'.[33] Wonsuk Ma similarly affirms, 'A properly guided historico-

---

[32] The emphasis on rhetoric as a form of persuasion goes all the way back to Aristotle and reflects the emphasis of the classical period's definition of rhetoric. Contemporary biblical scholars who maintain this emphasis include George Kennedy, Yehoshua Gitay, and Meir Sternberg. Kennedy examines the rhetorical situation, or the contexts in which the texts arose, as well as the content and literary devices of the text, in order to address the text's rhetorical problem and purpose. Gitay emphasizes what he calls 'pragmatic persuasion', the idea that the text seeks to persuade the reader with a specific pragmatic goal. He investigates both structural and stylistic elements of the text to define this pragmatic persuasive goal. Sternberg views the biblical text as governed by three principles: ideology, historiography, and aesthetics, which complement rather than contrast one another in their rhetorical goal – to reveal a 'divine system of norms'. Sternberg argues that the reader lays aside his or her own interpretive opinions and becomes drawn into the biblical narrator's intent. See Tull, 'Rhetorical Criticism and Intertextuality', pp. 160-64; George Kennedy, *New Testament Interpretation through Rhetorical Criticism* (Chapel Hill: University of North Carolina Press, 1984), p. 4; Yehoshua Gitay, *Prophecy and Persuasion: A Study of Isaiah 40–48* (Bonn: Liguistica Biblica, 1981); and Meir Sternberg, *The Poetics of Biblical Narrative: Ideological Literature and the Drama of Reading* (Bloomington: Indiana University Press, 1985).

[33] Adrian E. Hinkle, *Pedagogical Theory of Wisdom Literature: An Application of Educational Theory to Biblical Texts* (Eugene, OR: Wipf & Stock, 2017), p. x.

literary reading will not only serve as guidance but will also set parameters for "affective" reading'.[34]

Viewing Pentecostalism as 'counter-modern', Jacqueline Grey
constructs a creative hermeneutical model in which text as symbol
encompasses historical-cultural context and present significance for
the reader, avoiding both the reduction of the text to a singular historical meaning and the openness of the text to any meaning; and
containing, rather, a 'constrained plurality of meanings'.[35] Referring
to Gadamer, Grey argues that disregard of the text's cultural and historical context causes a 'premature fusion of horizons' as 'the textual
horizon will have collapsed into that of the reader's own narrative
biography'.[36] Grey explains:

> This recognition of historical distance would affirm the reality
> that the biblical text emerges from a specific historical and cultural

---

[34] Wonsuk Ma, 'Biblical Studies in the Pentecostal Tradition: Yesterday, Today,
and Tomorrow', in Murray W. Dempster (ed. *et al.*), *The Globalization of Pentecostalism:
A Religion Made to Travel* (Carlisle: Paternoster Press, 1999), pp. 52-69 (62). Spawn
and Wright similarly argue that Pentecostal biblical scholarship may express itself
through historical-grammatical, historical-critical, and postmodern methodologies,
as a gift from God to the church. They argue, 'There is a *via media* that offers a
constructive role for the *charism* of scholarship which promotes a pneumatic hermeneutic'. Following O'Brien, Spawn and Wright view biblical scholarship as a *charism*, a gift from God to employ 'the tools of biblical scholarship in the renewal
tradition'. Spawn and Wright describe the views of those who seek to forge a middle road of recognizing the value of historical critical methods but also their limitations: 'these charismatic biblical realists do not balk at the historical critical
method per se, "but precisely an uncritical use of this method, whereby one im-
poses on the text a presupposition, such as an anti-supernatural bias, that is basi-
cally alien to the biblical world"'. See Kevin L. Spawn and Archie T. Wright (eds.),
Spirit and Scripture: Exploring a Pneumatic Hermeneutic (London: Bloomsbury T&T
Clark, 2011), pp. 20-21. Scott Ellington also finds both advantages and disad-
vantages in historical-critical and postmodern methodologies. While he describes
the historical-critical approach as 'an indispensable foundation for biblical interpretation', he acknowledges its limited value due to its foundations in rationalistic
thought. Although he identifies postmodern hermeneutics as helpful by providing
new insights, he cautions Pentecostal interpreters to employ these methodologies
carefully, recognizing that they spring from a worldview which deems the concept
of truth as relative and casts suspicion on authors of the biblical text. Ellington
suggests that in the convergence of testimony and complaint, Pentecostals may
find ways to articulate 'truth-as-testimony' in their biblical interpretations, viewing
God as an active agent in the biblical text as well as in the modern world. See Scott
Ellington, 'History, Story, and Testimony: Locating Truth in a Pentecostal Hermeneutic', *Pneuma* 23 (2001), pp. 245-63 (261-62).

[35] Grey, *Three's a Crowd*, pp. 126, 128.

[36] Grey, *Three's a Crowd*, p. 120.

context. Rather than dampen the dynamic quality of Pentecostal readings, this recognition can affirm the Pentecostal value of the immediacy of the text as it affirms the immanence of the divine voice in speaking to the people of God in a way that is culturally, linguistically, and historically relevant. It would lengthen and deepen the 'great narrative' in which Pentecostal readers find themselves as they conduct their identities as 'people of God'.[37]

Building upon Grey's compelling argument, I propose that taking into account the historical, cultural, and linguistic background of the text, for the purpose of understanding the meaning and reception of the text by its original audience (hearing what the Spirit *said*), will both ground and prepare the Pentecostal interpreter to then evaluate subsequent readings (hearing what the Spirit *has said*), and finally to interpret the text communally and personally (hearing what the Spirit *is saying*). It is my conviction that Pentecostal interpreters may employ multiple methodological approaches, allowing for various layers of meaning or *sensus plenior* in a given text, while still maintaining Pentecostal hermeneutical and theological distinctives and holding firmly to the belief that the text contains the authoritative, reliable, and infallible revelation of God, mediated both dynamically and personally by the Holy Spirit.

Returning then to my argument that reception history demonstrates ways in which both literary and historical approaches to the text remain invaluable, I also suggest that the aims of the historical-grammatical method are analogous to (but not equal with nor collapsed into) the aims of reception history – to understand how a particular audience received and assigned meaning to a text. Is not reception history a closer look at the 'world behind the reception of the text', in a way that is strikingly similar to the historical-grammatical inquiry into the 'world behind the text'? Are not the goals of those working on reception history, using a form of literary analysis to examine the reception of the text by a particular audience at a specific time in history (what the text *has meant*), surprisingly similar to those employing a historical-grammatical methodology to understand how the text may have been received and understood by a different audience at an earlier time in history (what the text *meant*)? In our too often polarized methodological camps of prioritizing the

---

[37] Grey, *Three's a Crowd*, p. 132.

'world behind the text' via Enlightenment-based historical methods or emphasizing the 'world of the text' via postmodern-based literary methods, reception history in a sense fuses both approaches, reminding interpreters on 'both sides of the aisle' that they may share more in common than they realize.

The Role of Reception History for Pentecostal Interpreters

Finally, I would like to explore briefly a couple of questions regarding the role of reception history for Pentecostal interpreters. First, to what extent should they rely upon reception history to define a text's meaning or meanings? Or more specifically, how should Pentecostal interpreters prioritize an early Pentecostal reading when it seems to contradict the way in which the text's original audience may have received or understood it? For example, in my reception history analysis of Pentecostal readings of 'Gog and Magog' texts, several readings in the first ten years of Pentecostal history identified 'Gog' as 'Russia', a notion that obviously would have been quite foreign not only to the original audience, but to any audience prior to the ninth century AD.[38] Second, should earlier Pentecostal readings always be prioritized over later ones, or can there be cases in which 'hindsight is 20/20'? For example, when Frank Cummings described 'Gog' in 1939 as 'a representative group of the colored and Mohammedan races, together with Russia and Germany', explaining that after Armageddon, 'the battle for the supremacy of the races is over, Germany, Russia, Asia, and colored races and Mohammedan nations are crushed', dare modern Pentecostal interpreters name such blatant

---

[38] Bartleman identified Gog as Russia, but he also wrote, 'The destruction of our fellow man must not enter into the principle of Christianity'. See Frank Bartelman, 'The War – Separation', *TBM* 9.178 (January 1916), p. 3. See also Arne Ilmoni, 'Letter From Kangasala, Finland', *TBM* 5.120 (November 1912), p. 1. Ilmoni writes, 'I believe that Gog and Magog, in Ez. 38 and 39, are Russia. The emperor of Russia was earlier called "Gog". A village in Siberia is called "Tubal".' In addition, Marquess refers to *Smith's Bible Dictionary* as his source for the identification of Rosh as Russia, Meshech as Moscow, and Tubal as Tobolosk. He writes, 'This scene is the finish of Russia and her allied armies, the European Powers, as graphically and minutely foretold 2500 years ago in the 38th and 39th chapters of Ezekiel … For 2500 years it has been prophecy. It will shortly be history.' See Ernest Marquess, 'The Latest War News', *LRE* (January 1915), pp. 21–24 (23). For a more thorough look at this topic in Pentecostal reception history, see Alicia R. Jackson, 'Wesleyan Holiness and Finished Work Pentecostal Interpretations of Gog and Magog Biblical Texts', *JPT* 25 (2016), pp. 168-83.

prejudice as unbiblical and racist, or are they to prioritize this reading since it was closer to the movement's founding?[39] I would argue that such a reading violates not only the text's meaning in its original historical context, but also the ethical values of the OT prophets and moral injunctions found throughout the Torah and the Sermon on the Mount, as well as numerous other biblical texts. Therefore, I suggest that when a Pentecostal reading, even an early one, clearly contradicts the meaning of the text as it would have been received and understood by its original audiences, or the consistent witness of Scripture, that reading should be re-examined.

In conclusion, reception history helps contemporary Pentecostals to understand their biblical and theological roots, and to locate their own readings in the historical and theological trajectory of Pentecostalism. However, these few brief examples of the Pentecostal reception history from 'Gog and Magog' texts may serve to remind us that no reading or individual is beyond critique. Additionally, reception history, viewed as literary-historical methodology, may also help to demonstrate the value of both historical and literary approaches, potentially opening creative methodological space in biblical exegesis. As Pentecostal interpreters applying various methodologies to the text – considering what the text *meant*, what the text *has meant*, and what the text *means* – may we continually evaluate all readings biblically, pneumatically, and communally, remembering that Bible reading for Pentecostals is not primarily, as Davies so eloquently expresses, for us 'to grasp it; but so that God might grasp us through it'.[40]

---

[39] In a subsequent article he writes, 'When Battle of Gog and Magog is over and the White Race has retained its supremacy, another World Peace Conference will be in session'. See Frank A. Cummings, 'What Next in World Events: Greatest Turning Point in Universal History Is Near at Hand', *FC* 12.31 (January 1939), pp. 1-2, 8 (2), and 'Nations to Abolish War: Era of World Peace Predicted Even as Nations Face New War Scares', *FC* 12.42 (April 1939), pp. 1-2, 6, 8. See also Jackson, 'Wesleyan Holiness and Finished Work Pentecostal Interpretations of Gog and Magog Biblical Texts', pp. 177-79.

[40] See Davies, 'What Does It Mean to Read the Bible as a Pentecostal?', p. 216, 223. Ellington expresses a similar sentiment when he writes, 'We do not simply know about God, but we "get to know" God experientially in direct encounter'. Scott A. Ellington, 'Pentecostalism and the Authority of Scripture', *JPT* 9 (1996), pp. 16-38 (26-27). Bridges-Johns also emphasizes the personal nature of Bible reading for Pentecostals, writing, 'Because there is a co-joining of God's presence with God's Word, to encounter the Scriptures is to encounter God'. See Cheryl Bridges-

Bibliography

Archer, Kenneth J., *A Pentecostal Hermeneutic: Spirit, Scripture, and Community* (Cleveland, TN: CPT Press, 2009).

—'Pentecostal Hermeneutics: Retrospect and Prospect', *JPT* 4 (1996), pp. 63-81.

Arrington, French L., 'The Use of the Bible by Pentecostals', *Pneuma* 16 (1994), pp. 101-107.

Autry, Arden C., 'Dimensions of Hermeneutics in Pentecostal Focus', *JPT* 3 (1993), pp. 29-50.

Beal, Timothy, 'Reception History and Beyond: Toward the Cultural History of Scriptures', *Biblical Interpretation* 19 (2011), pp. 357-72.

Bridges-Johns, Cheryl, 'A Pentecostal Perspective', in Jürgen Moltmann and Karl-Josef Kuschel (eds.), *Pentecostal Movements as an Ecumenical Challenge* (London: SPCK, 1996), pp. 45-51.

Cargal, Timothy B., 'Beyond the Fundamentalist–Modernist Controversy: Pentecostals and Hermeneutics in a Postmodern Age', *Pneuma* 15 (Fall 1993), pp. 163-87.

Cartledge, Mark, 'Text–Community–Spirit: The Challenges Posed by Pentecostal Theological Method to Evangelical Theology', in Kevin L. Spawn and Archie T. Wright (eds.), *Spirit and Scripture: Exploring a Pneumatic Hermeneutic* (London: Bloomsbury T&T Clark, 2011), pp. 130-42.

Cooper, Alan, 'On Reading the Bible Critically and Otherwise', in Richard Elliott Friedman and H.G.M. Williamson (eds.), *The Future of Biblical Studies: Hebrew Scriptures* (Atlanta: Scholars Press, 1987), pp. 61-79.

Davies, Andrew, 'What Does It Mean to Read the Bible as a Pentecostal?' *JPT* 18 (2009), pp. 216-29.

Ellington, Scott, 'History, Story, and Testimony: Locating Truth in a Pentecostal Hermeneutic', *Pneuma* 23 (2001), pp. 245-63.

—'Pentecostalism and the Authority of Scripture', *JPT* 9 (1996), pp. 16-38.

Johns, 'A Pentecostal Perspective', in Jürgen Moltmann and Karl-Josef Kuschel (eds.), *Pentecostal Movements as an Ecumenical Challenge* (London: SPCK, 1996), pp. 45-51 (47). Along these lines, Chris Green writes,

> Here is the wonder: those depths of possibility hidden in the Scriptures are nothing less than the depths of God's own self-understanding. To search those depths is to share in the Spirit's searching the deep things of God (1 Cor. 2.10) where Christ, our sanctification, is found. Therefore, as we are searching, we are participating in the divine life, knowing God as God knows God, and just so we are being drawn into fullness of joy, into our eternally-purposed share in Christ's life with God for the world.

See Green, *Sanctifying Interpretation*, p. 163.

Fee, Gordon D., *Gospel and Spirit: Issues in New Testament Hermeneutics* (Grand Rapids: Baker Publishing Group, 1991).

Fee, Gordon D. and Douglas Stuart, *How to Read the Bible for all Its Worth* (Grand Rapids: Zondervan, 4th edn, 2014).

Gadamer, Hans-Georg, *Truth and Method* (trans. Joel Weinsheimer and Donald G. Marshall; London: Continuum, 2nd edn, 2004).

Gitay, Yehoshua, *Prophecy and Persuasion: A Study of Isaiah 40–48* (Bonn: Liguistica Biblica, 1981).

Green, Chris E.W., *Sanctifying Interpretation: Vocation, Holiness, and Scripture* (Cleveland, TN: CPT Press, 2015).

Grey, Jacqueline, *Three's a Crowd: Pentecostalism, Hermeneutics and the Old Testament* (Eugene, OR: Pickwick Publications, 2011).

Hagner, Donald A., 'Review of Matthew 8–20 (trans. James E. Crouch, Hermeneia; Minneapolis: Fortress, 2001) by Ulrich Luz', *JBL* 121.4 (2002), pp. 766-69.

Harrington, Hannah K. and Rebecca Patten, 'Pentecostal Hermeneutics and Post-Modern Literary Theory', *Pneuma* 16 (Spring 1994), pp. 109-14.

Hinkle, Adrian E., *Pedagogical Theory of Wisdom Literature: An Application of Educational Theory to Biblical Texts* (Eugene, OR: Wipf & Stock, 2017).

Israel, Richard D., Daniel E. Albrecht, and Randal G. McNally, 'Pentecostals and Hermeneutics: Texts, Rituals, and Community', *Pneuma* 15 (1993), pp. 137-61.

Jackson, Alicia R., 'Wesleyan Holiness and Finished Work Pentecostal Interpretations of Gog and Magog Biblical Texts', *JPT* 25, (2016), pp. 168-83.

Keener, Craig S., *A Commentary on the Gospel of Matthew* (Grand Rapids: Eerdmans, 1999).

—*Acts: An Exegetical Commentary* (4 vols; Grand Rapids: Baker Academic, 2012–2015).

—*1–2 Corinthians* (New Cambridge Bible Commentary; Cambridge: Cambridge University Press, 2006).

—*Galatians* (New Cambridge Bible Commentary; Cambridge: Cambridge University Press, 2018).

—*Galatians: A Commentary* (Grand Rapids: Baker Academic, 2018).

—*Matthew* (IVP New Testament Commentary Series; Downers Grove, IL: InterVarsity Press, 1997).

—*Revelation* (The NIV Application Commentary; Grand Rapids: Zondervan, 2000).

—*Romans* (New Covenant Commentary Series; Eugene, OR: Cascade Books, 2009).

—*Spirit Hermeneutics: Reading Scripture in the Light of Pentecost* (Grand Rapids: Eerdmans, 2016).

—*The Gospel of John: A Commentary* (2 vols; Peabody, MA: Hendrickson, 2003).

—*The IVP Bible Background Commentary: New Testament* (Downers Grove, IL: InterVarsity Press, 1994).

Kennedy, George, *New Testament Interpretation through Rhetorical Criticism* (Chapel Hill: University of North Carolina Press, 1984).

Knierim, Rolf, 'Criticism of Literary Features, Form, Tradition and Redaction', in Douglas A. Knight and Gene M. Tucker (eds.), *The Hebrew Bible and Its Modern Interpreters* (Philadelphia: Fortress Press, 1985), pp. 123-66.

Knight, Mark, 'Wirkungsgeschichte, Reception History, Reception Theory', *JSNT* 33 (2010), pp. 137-46.

Ma, Wonsuk, 'Biblical Studies in the Pentecostal Tradition: Yesterday, Today, and Tomorrow', in Murray W. Dempster (ed. et al.), *The Globalization of Pentecostalism: A Religion Made to Travel* (Carlisle: Paternoster Press, 1999), pp. 52-69.

Menzies, Robert P., 'Jumping Off the Postmodern Bandwagon', *Pneuma* 16 (1994), pp. 115-20.

Muilenburg, James, 'Form Criticism and Beyond', *JBL* 88 (1969), pp. 1-18.

Noel, Bradley Truman, 'Gordon Fee and the Challenge to Pentecostal Hermeneutics: Thirty Years Later', *Pneuma* 26 (2004), pp. 60-80.

—*Pentecostal and Postmodern Hermeneutics: Comparisons and Contemporary Impact* (Eugene, OR: Wipf & Stock, 2010).

Poirier, John C. and B. Scott Lewis, 'Pentecostal and Postmodern Hermeneutics: A Critique of Three Conceits', *JPT* 15 (2006), pp. 3-21.

Riches, John, 'Reception History as a Challenge to Biblical Theology', *Journal of Theological Interpretation* 7.2 (2013), pp. 171-85.

Roberts, Jonathan, 'Introduction', in Michael Lieb, Emma Mason, and Jonathan Roberts (eds.), *The Oxford Handbook of the Reception History of the Bible* (Oxford: Oxford University Press, 2011), pp. 1-10.

Spawn Kevin L., and Archie T. Wright (eds.), *Spirit and Scripture: Exploring a Pneumatic Hermeneutic* (London: Bloomsbury T&T Clark, 2011).

Sternberg, Meir, *The Poetics of Biblical Narrative: Ideological Literature and the Drama of Reading* (Bloomington: Indiana University Press, 1985).

Thomas, John Christopher, 'Reading the Bible from Within Our Traditions: A Pentecostal Hermeneutic as Test Case', in Joel Green and Max Turner (eds.), *Between Two Horizons: Spanning New Testament Studies and Systematic Theology* (Grand Rapids: Eerdmans, 2000), pp. 108-22.

—'"What the Spirit is Saying to the Church" – The Testimony of a Pentecostal in New Testament Studies', in Kevin L. Spawn and Archie T. Wright (eds.), *Spirit and Scripture: Exploring a Pneumatic Hermeneutic* (London: Bloomsbury T&T Clark, 2011), pp. 115-29.

—'Women, Pentecostals, and the Bible', *JPT* 5 (1994), pp. 41-56.

Tull, Patricia K., 'Rhetorical Criticism and Intertextuality', in Steven L. McKenzie and Stephen R. Haynes (eds.), *To Each Its Own Meaning: An Introduction to Biblical Criticism and Their Application* (Louisville, KY: Westminster / John Knox Press, 1999), pp. 156-80.

Yong, Amos, *The Hermeneutical Spirit: Theological Interpretation and Scriptural Imagination for the 21ˢᵗ Century* (Eugene, OR: Cascade Books, 2017).

4

THE SPIRIT, THE TEXT, AND EARLY PENTECOSTAL RECEPTION: THE EMERGENCE OF A DISCIPLINE

JOHN CHRISTOPHER THOMAS*

It is an honor for me to be invited to contribute to the first volume dedicated exclusively to the issue of Pentecostal reception history. I would like to express my appreciation to Martin Mittelstadt for his kind invitation.[1]

Prolegomena

Before launching into the topic in earnest a few words of prole-gomena should, perhaps, be offered to make as clear as possible what I am and am not concerned with in this chapter. So, I begin with the following observations.

First, *Wirkungsgeschichte* is a methodology or approach of recent origins and as such does not exist in one agreed upon form, as the various English translations of the German word reveal. At first it seems the term was often translated as 'effective history' or 'the

* John Christopher Thomas (PhD, University of Sheffield) is Clarence J. Abbott Professor of Biblical Studies at Pentecostal Theological Seminary in Cleveland, TN USA and Director of the Centre for Pentecostal and Charismatic Studies at Bangor University in Bangor, Wales, UK.
[1] This chapter is derived from a plenary session delivered on March 2, 2019 for the 49th Annual Meeting of the Society of Pentecostal Studies in College Park, MD. The chapter includes only minor revisions by the author.

history of effects'. Other translations included 'impact history' focusing on the impact the text has had upon its readers and hearers. More recently, the translation 'reception history' has come into vogue and appears to be making much headway as the preferred nomenclature, but it is important to remember that none of these translations are a perfect fit.

Second, there is a remarkable amount of diversity amongst those who make use of the approach. For example, despite the fact that the method developed, in part, as a reaction to the limitations of historical critical approaches to the text of Scripture,[2] it has been amusing to me to see how many scholars doing work on reception have simply made it into yet another historical critical enquiry, replacing the historical critical examination of the biblical text with an historical critical examination of the readers or interpreters of the text. On this view, it is the same method with simply a change of subject matter. This move is not unlike the way in which some biblical interpreters have taken a postmodern approach like intertextuality and made it into a more subtle form of source criticism, which seems to miss the whole point. From my vantage point, moves like these tend to hijack such newer approaches and, in the process, rob the interpreters of the richness viewing the text from new angles has to offer. Thus, the task of understanding reception is complicated by the fact that there is no agreed upon definition for the approach.

Third, whilst being similar in some respects to history of interpretation approaches, there are significant differences. In many ways, history of interpretation efforts may be characterized as building upon the conviction that Enlightenment ways of thinking and writing are to be privileged over other approaches, sometimes to the exclusion of other approaches. This privileging might be illustrated by the way in which so-called 'pre-critical' works on the biblical text often found little place in such approaches, save to demonstrate the fanciful nature of such thought. Another characteristic of such approaches is their desire to determine correct and incorrect interpretations. On this view, texts have one meaning and interpreters are to be evaluated by how closely they come to that mark. The clear conclusion is that the further one is removed from the Enlightenment,

---

[2] Cf. for example the scathing critique of historical criticism offered by Ulrich Luz in his groundbreaking work on *Wirkungsgeschichte* in his *Matthew in History: Interpretation, Influence, and Effects* (Minneapolis: Fortress Press, 1994), pp. 5-22.

the less likely an interpretation is to be correct. Finally, for the most part, these approaches focus exclusively on texts, suggesting that 'interpretation' is confined to the world of textuality. As will be seen, reception approaches differ at most every turn. They do not necessarily privilege Enlightenment interpretations over 'pre-critical' ones; they are not nearly as concerned with distinguishing between correct and incorrect interpretations and judging the reception of texts by means of the one meaning of the text; and these approaches do not restrict reception to the world of textuality, but are interested in how biblical texts have been received across a variety of media, both inside and outside the church.

The Call to Pentecostal Reception

As far as I have been able to determine, the first call for Pentecostals to be intentional about the use of *Wirkungsgeschichte* came in my 1998 SPS Presidential Address.[3] This being the case, perhaps a few autobiographical reflections are in order. My own hermeneutical journey continued to develop after the completion of my PhD thesis, an exercise that had resulted in a methodological reprioritizing of the way I approached texts. For a variety of reasons, I had become convinced that one must privilege the text and its world as the starting point in the hermeneutical journey. In the thesis I had found that results reached at the narrative/literary level could then be placed into conversations with historical reconstruction with much profit, rather than the other way around. By this time, I had also become more interested in the theological implications of the canonical location of the various NT documents, despite the somewhat artificial arrangement of the NT canon. This interest caused me to appreciate the contributions reflection about a book's canonical location could make to an understanding of different aspects of the NT. I was beginning to view the NT as one might view a diamond. Every turn revealed surprising new facets as different points of examination revealed some never before observed dimensions. This was enabling me to view the text of the NT from a literary or narrative perspective without thinking about historical issues, or from a canonical

---

[3] J.C. Thomas, 'Pentecostal Theology in the Twenty-First Century', *Pneuma* 20 (1998), pp. 3-19 (16).

perspective without thinking about the historical and vice versa. In other words, I was becoming more fascinated by the hidden beauty the biblical text had to reveal when approached from a variety of perspectives.

It was during this time of methodological exploration and methodological openness that I encountered *Wirkungsgeschichte* through the work of Ulrich Luz, a Swiss NT scholar who had spent years working on the method and whom I met at meetings of the *Studiorum Novi Testamenti Societas* in Bonn and Durham. What I found in his work, *Matthew in History*, fascinated me very much indeed. According to Luz:

> biblical texts *have* a history of effects, which is the history between them and us ... [the history of effects] cannot be separated from the texts, because it is an expression of the texts' own power. It belongs to the texts in the same way that a river flowing away from its source belongs to the source. What is the hermeneutical significance of this history of effects for us? I think it can function as a bridge between the biblical texts and us. The history of effects makes it clear that the Bible and we are not separated from one another. I intend this to point beyond the objective truth that all historical results are interrelated. I am thinking of the more fundamental fact that we too are part of that great river that is nourished by the biblical texts. We, the present readers, are not independent from the history of effects of the Bible ... History of effects brings together the texts and us, their interpreters; or better: the history of effects shows us that we are already together and that it is an illusion to treat the texts in a position of distance and in a merely 'objective' way.[4]

As I reflected on Luz's proposal and thinking, I became convinced that the use of *Wirkungsgeschichte* would be immensely helpful in the construction of a Pentecostal approach to teaching an introductory course on the NT, which I incorporated into a course I would come to retitle 'Pentecostal Explorations of the NT' and in turn included this suggestion as part of my SPS Presidential address. There I proposed two ways in which *Wirkungsgeschichte* might prove helpful. First, I suggested that a section of the course acquaint the student with

---

[4] Luz, *Matthew in History*, pp. 24-25.

something of a particular book's impact upon the church as well as the broader culture. Specific examples offered included the impact of the Epistle to the Romans on Augustine, Martin Luther, John Wesley, and Karl Barth; the Sermon on the Mount upon John Wesley, L. Tolstoy, Dietrich Bonhoeffer, and Martin Luther King Jr; James 5 on Dr Cullis and Elizabeth Mix; as well as examples of a more mixed nature, like those related to Philemon, where both slave and slaveholder have appealed to the support of the text; the way in which Matthew 23 was utilized in Nazi Germany's anti-Semitic propaganda; or Charles Manson's interpretation of the four angels of Revelation 9 who would kill a third of humankind, as having reference to the Beatles, resulting in the Tate-LaBianca murders. Second, I proposed the use of *Wirkungsgeschichte* in a section of the course that would seek to locate a particular NT book within a Pentecostal context. This section would combine both testimonies of the book's effect in early Pentecostalism with implications this book may have for the contemporary movement. For example, the importance of Jude in early Pentecostalism is testified to by the fact that Jude 3 appears on the masthead of no less an important publication than *The Apostolic Faith* by William Seymour in the heyday of the Azusa Street revival. At the same time, Jude's harsh words about false teachers and their characteristics would appear to find application within a movement that has had to contend with false teachers from the beginning.

But before moving forward, a quick look backward.

Pentecostal Scholars who Anticipated the Use of Reception

Despite the fact that the first call for intentional use of reception by Pentecostal scholars came in 1998, there were at least three scholars whose work in some ways anticipated the use of reception as part of the interpretive arsenal at their disposal.

In 1991, Robert W. Herron published a revised version of his Rice University PhD dissertation entitled *Mark's Account of Peter's Denial of Jesus: A History of Its Interpretation.*[5] Though incorporating 'A History of Its Interpretation' in the title, Herron's work pushes very much in the direction of what would become known as *Wirkungsgeschichte*, a term Ernst Best, one of his reviewers, actually used to describe

---

[5] Robert W. Herron, *Mark's Account of Peter's Denial of Jesus: A History of Its Interpretation* (Lanham, MD: University Press of America, 1991).

Herron's method.[6] Specifically, Herron seeks to gain leverage on the interpretation of Mark's account of Peter's denial of Jesus, described in Mk 14.54, 66-72, by examining interpreters and interpretations of the passage in both the pre-modern period (including the apostolic and patristic eras, the middle ages, as well as the reformation and post-reformation era) and the modern period (including the nineteenth and twentieth centuries, as well as the post World War II period). Comparing the methodologies and interpretations from these diverse periods, Herron offers an assessment of the similarities and differences of their results while proposing a way forward in how Mk 14.54, 66-72 might best be understood. Herron's careful unearthing of numerous pre-modern treatments of this text – along with supplying these texts in original and translated forms – goes some way toward suggesting something of the fruit a reception history approach can bear. In this regard Herron might well be identified as the first Pentecostal to anticipate this methodological approach.

The very next year saw the appearance of a two-volume, 660 page Strasbourg ThD thesis from Hubert Jurgensen on 1 Thess. 4.13–5.11.[7] Unlike Herron, Jurgensen's work did not include representations from the pre-modern era, but rather focused on 'modern' interpreters and interpretations. Yet, Jurgensen's focus moved beyond history of interpretation in that his extensive historical work was brought to bear on his own produced interpretation. Thus, whilst not anticipating *Wirkungsgeschichte* in quite the same way as Herron, Jurgensen deserves a mention in this section.

Whilst Herron and Jurgensen made certain moves toward *Wirkungsgeschichte* by examining interpretations of specific texts throughout interpretive history, Larry R. McQueen appears to be the first to make use of early Pentecostal literature in a way that traces the influence of major themes of a given biblical book. In his slightly revised Columbia Theological Seminary ThM thesis, written under the direction of Walter Brueggemann, McQueen first offers a literary and theological analysis of the book of Joel focusing on the Spirit and

---

[6] Ernst Best, 'Review', *Journal of Theological Studies* 44.1 (1993), pp. 249-51.

[7] Hubert Jurgensen, 'Saint Paul et la parousia: I Thessaloniciens 4,13 - 5,11 dans l'exegesis modern et contemporaine' (ThD thesis, Universite dex Science Humaines de Strasbourg, 1992). Cf. also Hubert Jurgensen, 'Awaiting the Return of Christ: A Re-examination of 1 Thessalonians 4.13–5.11 from a Pentecostal Perspective', *JPT* 4 (1994), pp. 81-113.

lament, salvation, and judgment.[8] McQueen next traces these themes in the NT, before tracking the ways in which these themes from Joel are found in early Pentecostal literature, including the periodical literature, songs, poetry, and even some art. Though McQueen's work does not appropriate *Wirkungsgeschichte* language, as his work appeared at almost the same time as Luz's groundbreaking volume, McQueen rather clearly anticipates the move to use reception history as a hermeneutical tool and appears to be the first scholar actually to mine early Pentecostal literature in this attempt.

Early Reception Developments amongst Pentecostals

Within a year of the publication of my Presidential address, the *Journal of Pentecostal Theology* hosted a dialogue on *Wirkungsgeschichte* between Pentecostal NT scholar Emerson Powery and the aforementioned Ulrich Luz.[9] Powery's engagement with Luz sought to acquaint the readers of *JPT* with the contents and rationale of Luz's *Matthew in History* whilst at the same time pressing Luz to reflect on the potential his method might have for Pentecostal hermeneutics. Aside from a generally productive time of engagement, a few observations might be worthy of note. First, when Powery pressed Luz on what seemed to be an inconsistency with regard to his dependency on historical critical approaches, after having earlier rather ruthlessly critiqued them as having severe limits, Luz doubled down, indicating that he was not quite as methodologically adventurous as he had appeared to be in his book. Second, it also became clear that, despite Powery's encouragement to be more inclusive in the selection of his *Wirkungsgeschichte* examples, Luz was quite comfortable choosing cases with which his Western European mainline church would be familiar, rather than venturing out to include Pentecostals and examples from other parts of the Christian tradition. He seemed to imply that one is not really under any compulsion to include examples outside of one's orbit. Third, when Powery pressed Luz on expanding his 'criterion of love' as an interpretive grid to include the Spirit, Luz appeared to be unable to think of such Spirit illumination that was not problematic.

---

[8] Larry R. McQueen, *Joel and the Spirit: The Cry of a Prophetic Hermeneutic* (JPTSup 8; Sheffield: Sheffield Academic Press, 1995).

[9] Cf. Emerson B. Powery, 'Ulrich Luz's *Matthew in History*: A Contribution to Pentecostal Hermeneutics?', *JPT* 14 (1999), pp. 3-17 and Ulrich Luz, 'A Response to Emerson Powery', *JPT* 14 (1999), pp. 19-26.

It would not be until October 2002 that the first self-consciously intentional *Wirkungsgeschichte* treatment by a Pentecostal would appear. This article-length study by Heather Landrus would be devoted to a passage of some degree of significance within the Pentecostal and Charismatic movements: 3 John 2.[10] Specifically, Landrus traces the interpretation of 3 John 2 from early Christian writers to modern figures within our tradition. Specifically, Landrus examines the life and writings of Tertullian, Augustine, the Venerable Bede, Le Maistre de Sacy, Ambrosius, Catharinus, John Bird Sumner, Albert Barnes, Carrie Judd Montgomery, Oral Roberts, Kenneth Hagin, Raymond Brown, Frederick Price, and Paul Yonggi Cho. Landrus concludes:

> The interpretation of this passage has been undeniably altered in the hands of Christian theologians, apologists and church leaders throughout history. In utilizing the history of effects, I have been able to examine the life of the interpreter to determine how his or her experiences might have influenced the hermeneutical process. From this vantage point, Augustine's ascetic interpretation of 3 Jn 2 is better understood in view of his nine-year stint as a Manichean and his interest in Neo-Platonic philosophy. The Venerable Bede's notion of communal prosperity speaks loudly of his commitment to monastic life. And finally, Oral Roberts' interpretative dedication to the well-being of the body reflects much about the indigence of his childhood. These summations, though easily made now, only come as a by-product of research … One such reward is found in the way the researcher is able to ascertain the origin of new interpretations and follow those interpretations through subsequent adherents. Thus, Oral Roberts' understanding of 3 Jn 2 seems to be the first in a series of interpretations pointing to material success as a sign of God's goodness. His understanding of 3 Jn 2 very clearly armed the ministry of Paul Yonggi Cho with a 'deliverance message' suited for the poverty of post-war Korea. Price later finds solace in a similar 'deliverance message' in the work of Kenneth Hagin. Thus, one could confidently conclude that the message discovered by Price can be traced back to Oral Roberts.[11]

---

[10] Heather L. Landrus, 'Hearing 3 John 2 in the Voices of History', *JPT* 11.1 (2002), pp. 70-88.
[11] Landrus, 'Hearing 3 John 2 in the Voices of History', pp. 87-88.

According to Landrus this approach is 'the outgrowth of a herme-neutical method that values life as a seedbed for theology … the his-tory of effects allows us to listen to the sound of God's words in life, rather than trying to pull them apart from the very things for which they were first created'.[12]

The very next issue of the *Journal of Pentecostal Theology* would carry another work of *Wirkungsgeschichte*, this one jointly written by my col-league, Kimberly Alexander, and myself, on Mk 16.9-20.[13] This article included two major sections devoted to the *Wirkungsgeschichte* of Mk 16.9-20 in early Pentecostalism. The first section focused on the role and significance this longer ending played within the early days of the movement, whilst the second focused on early Pentecostalism's knowledge of and response to the text critical problems surrounding the ending of Mark's Gospel. Among other things, Mk 16.9-20 was found to have been the most popular by far of the NT commission-ing texts amongst Pentecostals. Specifically, a survey of the *Church of God Evangel* Scripture Index from 1910–19 reveals twenty-six refer-ences to Mt. 28.18-20, sixteen references to Acts 1.8, and seventy-five references to Mk 16.9-20. A similar comparison from the Scrip-ture Index of *The Apostolic Faith* from September 1906-May 1908 re-veals three references to the Matthew text, five to the Acts text, and twenty references to the Mark text, suggesting that for early Pente-costals Mk 16.9-20 was a litmus test of sorts. Interestingly enough, early Pentecostals were aware of and responded to the text critical problems surrounding the ending of Mark, including Tischendorf's discovery of Codex Sinaiticus, A.J. Tomlinson's embryonic canonical critique, an examination of Codex Washingtonianus, and quotations from early Christian writers including Papias, Justin Martyr, Irenaeus, Ambrose, Chrysostom, Jerome, and Augustine.[14]

---

[12] Landrus, 'Hearing 3 John 2 in the Voices of History', p. 88. In the same issue of *JPT* Mark E. Roberts offers a response to Landrus' study that advocates for a 'hermeneutic of charity' when engaging and critiquing views which one cannot necessarily endorse. Mark E. Roberts, 'A Hermeneutic of Charity: Response to Heather Landrus', *JPT* 11.1 (2002), pp. 89-97.

[13] John Christopher Thomas and Kimberly Ervin Alexander, '"And the Signs Are Following": Mark 16.9-20 – A Journey into Pentecostal Hermeneutics', *JPT* 11.2 (2003), pp. 147-70.

[14] Wesleyan NT scholar Robert W. Wall offered a response to the Mark 16 piece in which he strengthened the arguments laid out and concluded that 'a "Pentecos-tal" interpretation of Scripture extends meaning beyond Pentecostal readers to

The Canonical Lay of the Land

In the second major section of this essay, I depart from a chronological survey and will offer a canonical overview of relevant Pentecostal reception studies as a way to give some sense of the canonical lay of the land, so to speak. It should almost go without saying that not all the books in the canon have received attention to this point, with some books receiving an unexpected amount of consideration.

The Torah

This canonical survey begins with the Torah and the recently published PhD thesis by Steffen Schumacher, a lecturer in OT at the European Bible Seminary in Freudenstadt-Kniebis, Germany.[15] In chapter three of this work devoted to the role of the Spirit in the Torah, Schumacher surveys the reception by early Pentecostals of the pneumatological texts found within the Torah. Following the groundbreaking work of Kimberly Alexander, he traces this reception in the early Pentecostal periodical literature within the Wesleyan Pentecostal and Finished Work Pentecostal streams.

He concludes his exhaustive analysis by comparing and juxtaposing select periodicals within the Wesleyan Pentecostal stream with select periodicals in the Finished Work stream, finding both similarities and differences between the streams.

First, Schumacher finds that 'these early Pentecostals clearly underline the Spirit's presence and impact from Genesis 1 to Deuteronomy ... stress the Spirit's relevance throughout Scripture in general and read the Spirit in the Torah in particular in light of NT contexts paired with their personal spiritual experiences'.[16]

Second, by their efforts, these Pentecostals express a serious desire for the Spirit to be a

> means for living Spirit-generated, holy, and Spirit-filled lives. In fact, their portrayals of the Spirit are embedded in the contexts of regeneration, sanctification, and Spirit baptism. These Pentecostals affirm the Spirit's existence and activities in the OT, including

---

challenge and enrich the beliefs and practices of the church catholic'. Cf. Robert W. Wall, 'A Response to Thomas/Alexander, "And the Signs Are Following" (Mark 16.9-20)', *JPT* 11.2 (2003), pp. 171-83.

[15] Steffen Schumacher, *The Spirit of God in the Torah: A Pentecostal Exploration* (Cleveland, TN: CPT Press, 2020).

[16] Schumacher, *The Spirit of God in the Torah: A Pentecostal Exploration*, p. 220.

the confession of the existence and the bestowal of spiritual gifts.[17]

Third, all of these Pentecostals portray the Spirit in terms of character traits and activities. They use symbols, metaphors/images, and typification to express the Spirit's nature and works in a way that makes sense in light of their leaning toward the NT.

Within the Wesleyan-Pentecostal stream, a comparison of the *Church of God Evangel* and *The Pentecostal Holiness Advocate* reveals that, whilst both discuss the Spirit in the context of salvation, sanctification, and Spirit Baptism, the former sees a strong connection between the Spirit and identity and ecclesiastical structure, the latter focuses more on walking with and drawing nearer to God. The *Church of God Evangel* seems reticent to typify the Spirit (only in Genesis 24), whilst *The Pentecostal Holiness Advocate* makes more extensive use of typology and the Spirit (Gen. 24; Exod. 8.23; 14; 16.33-34).

Schumacher's comparison of these select Wesleyan Pentecostal journals with those of the Finished Work tradition reveals some significant differences. First, the Finished Work journals contain significantly more individual texts from the Torah that leave a reception footprint. Second, their reading approach is more vigorous, more creative, and bolder. This involves a greater willingness to make use of symbols, illustrations, metaphors, typology, and allegory. These periodicals reflect a greater freedom 'in dealing with pneumatological texts in the Torah and provide a diverse and rich description of the Spirit'.[18]

With regard to the use of *Wirkungsgeschichte* as a methodological tool, Schumacher identifies what he considers to be noteworthy.

(1) Experience. Early Pentecostals exhibit a high level of experiential spirituality. This experience is centered on the baptism of the Spirit, which – as an outcome – impacts the way Scripture is read.

(2) Community. Early Pentecostal literature demonstrates that early Pentecostals read the Bible together. Pentecostal theology and spirituality are a communal affair, shaped and informed by the community.

---

[17] Schumacher, *The Spirit of God in the Torah: A Pentecostal Exploration*, p. 220
[18] Schumacher, *The Spirit of God in the Torah: A Pentecostal Exploration*, p. 221.

(3) Integration. Early Pentecostals integrate heart and head, which includes orthodoxy (right faith), orthopraxy (right acting), and orthopathy (right passion). The outcome of these elements is transformation, which impacts the way Scripture is read, too.

(4) Text. Early Pentecostals show a strong affinity to narratives. In this sense, their focus is on the text as it lies before them.

(5) Time. Early Pentecostal literature reveals that Pentecostals reflect on the Spirit in the OT with the Spirit of the NT in mind. Considering the worldview and the desire of early Pentecostals to restore and re-experience the apostolic faith of the NT, it makes sense that early Pentecostals not only find the Spirit in the Torah, but provide a description of the Spirit's influence that is in some way or other different from the Spirit in the NT. It appears that, for them, both Testaments are linked by the Spirit leading up to the day of Pentecost and beyond. In this sense, early Pentecostals 'shaped and reshaped' Scripture.

(6) Relevance. The aspect of time is linked to the aspect of relevance. As the exploration of early Pentecostal literature reveals, early Pentecostals show a desire to have the biblical text make sense for them. They want God's word to be significant for life, and they explore the text with the intention and expectation 'to retrieve meaning and solace'.[19]

Schumacher concludes, along with Ulrich Luz, that Scripture interpretation is always contextual interpretation.

Accordingly, the text of Scripture is closely linked to the various contexts in which the reader/interpreter is integrated. Therefore, the interpretation of Scripture is influenced by aspects such as a personal divine encounter, the reader's own tradition, the desire to live out the text, contemporary history, and God's word producing new meanings. This observation is repeatedly demonstrated throughout this chapter.[20]

Another reception study on the Torah comes in the form of David Hymes's SBL/SPS presentation entitled, 'Pentecostal-

---

[19] Schumacher, *The Spirit of God in the Torah: A Pentecostal Exploration*, pp. 222-23.

[20] Schumacher, *The Spirit of God in the Torah: A Pentecostal Exploration*, p. 223.

Charismatic Reception History of the Book of Numbers'.[21] In this piece Hymes, Professor of Old Testament Studies at Northwest University, offers an initial assessment of the way in which Numbers has been received by a variety of Pentecostal readers. The essay is distinctive in several ways. First, for the most part it explores almost exclusively periodical literature in the Finished Work stream of the Pentecostal tradition, which is likely a result of the provisional nature of his research at that point. Second, it traces the reception of Numbers in this literature beyond the first generation all the way up to the 1960s. Third, it is one of the first, if not *the* first, attempt to trace the Pentecostal reception of a specific book as a whole, rather than the reception of specific texts within a book.

Hymes utilizes the literary shape of Numbers as a way of structuring his study. Thus, his examination focuses on the following sections:

- Numbers 1–4 and Organization
- Num. 6.1-21 – The Nazirite Vow as a pattern for Consecration
- Numbers 11–14, 16–17 – Murmuring and Contesting of Leadership
- Numbers 20 – The Sin of Moses
- Num. 21.4-9 – Healing
- Numbers 22–25 – Balaam, an enigmatic prophet

Hymes' examination leads him to four tentative conclusions. First, it was not until the 1980s that any of the Pentecostal studies examined show any signs of interacting with European or American critical scholarship. Second, he found surprisingly little distinctive Pentecostal-Charismatic interpretations within the writings of the earliest Pentecostals, except for the Balaam narratives. Hymes speculates that some of the themes he sees as ignored receive a greater impetus for study after the advent of the Charismatic movement. Third, most of the attention in these Pentecostal writings was directed to what he calls parish level spiritual insights, specifically dealing with problematic individuals in the local churches or denominations, an emphasis that inhibits additional distinctive interpretations. Fourth, using the discussion of Moses' sin as a case study, one may track the way in

---

[21] David Hymes, 'Pentecostal-Charismatic Reception History of the Book of Numbers,' a presentation to the SPS/SBL Meeting in Boston, MA, 2017.

which typological interpretive models begin to diminish during the 1960s, with harsher criticisms of Roman Catholicism giving way to a more open door approach in the light of the Charismatic Renewal and Pentecostal-Charismatic interaction with critical scholarship.[22]

The Former Prophets

This survey moves next to the Former Prophets and specifically to the recent work of Rick Wadholm Jr. In his monograph devoted to *A Theology of the Spirit in the Former Prophets*, Wadholm devotes a chapter to the reception history in the early Pentecostal periodical literature of the pneumatological texts within the Former Prophets.[23] His extensive examination, covering some fifty-two pages, includes texts from Judges, 1–2 Samuel, and 1–2 Kings. Wadholm treats the periodical literature in chronological order without contextualizing them in a specific stream of the tradition.

Among the results of his analysis, Wadholm highlights seven.

(1) The most prominent issue is the baptism of the Holy Spirit, which is seen to be connected to the activity of the Spirit in the Former Prophets, with Elijah/Elisha looming exceptionally large as a type of Spirit baptism.

(2) All the periodicals give attention to the power of the Spirit and its ability to overcome, enable witness, deliver, prepare, heal, and make provision. Sometimes, Spirit experiences are likened to Spirit experiences of the present, but other times contemporary experiences are seen to be truer Spirit experiences.[24]

(3) In all these journals, prayer is viewed as closely connected to the experience of the Spirit, with Elijah's persistent prayer serving as an example.

(4) Every periodical warns that the Spirit may be lost owing to faithlessness, with Saul as the primary example.

(5) The Former Prophet texts are received as providing an apologetic defense 'of their experiences of the Spirit in such things as dancing and running (*TBM, CGE, WW,* and *BC*) and the various

---

[22] Hymes, 'Pentecostal-Charismatic Reception History of the Book of Numbers', p. 14.

[23] Rick Wadholm, Jr, *A Theology of the Spirit in the Former Prophets: A Pentecostal Perspective* (Cleveland, TN: CPT Press, 2018), pp. 65-117.

[24] Wadholm, Jr, *A Theology of the Spirit in the Former Prophets*, pp. 115-16.

charismatic gifts of the Spirit like speaking in tongues, interpretations, and the prophetic (*CGE, LRE, PE*)'.

(6) Divine love is seen as being an endowment of the Spirit, which required a persistent abiding.[25]

(7) There is a Christological orientation present for interpreting the Spirit, with 'anointing' language especially tied to Saul and David, whilst acknowledging that Jesus offers a better anointing.[26]

The Latter Prophets

Whilst there have been a significant number of reception history studies devoted to the Latter Prophets, interestingly enough they have all concentrated on the Book of Ezekiel and have all been undertaken by female scholars.

The first such exploration came in the form of an article-length study entitled, 'Wesleyan Holiness and Finished Work Pentecostal Interpretations of Gog and Magog Biblical Texts' by Alicia R. Jackson, who is Assistant Professor of Old Testament at Vanguard University.[27] Jackson surveys the Wesleyan Holiness Pentecostal and Finished Work interpretations of the Gog and Magog biblical texts in an attempt to determine the extent to which dispensational eschatological understandings have influenced the interpretations. Whilst this is not necessarily a precise way to gauge the extent of dispensational influence upon interpreters as such, it does provide an opportunity to assess where interpreters depart from the dispensational narrative with regard to these particular texts in Ezekiel and Revelation. Jackson finds a fair amount of diversity when it comes to the interpretation of Gog and Magog across these different interpretive streams. Wesleyan Holiness interpretations consistently followed a non-dispensational approach to these texts, ruling out an embrace of violence, and even going so far as to argue that Gog and Magog might best be understood in parabolic form.[28] Finally, Jackson found that when dispensational eschatology exerted too much influence on the interpretation of these texts the results contradicted a number of

---

[25] Wadholm, Jr, *A Theology of the Spirit in the Former Prophets*, p. 116.

[26] Wadholm, Jr, *A Theology of the Spirit in the Former Prophets*, p. 117.

[27] Alicia R. Jackson, 'Wesleyan Holiness and Finished Work Pentecostal Interpretations of Gog and Magog Biblical Texts', *JPT* 25.2 (2016), pp. 168-83.

[28] Jackson, 'Wesleyan Holiness and Finished Work Pentecostal Interpretations of Gog and Magog Biblical Texts', p. 182.

early Pentecostal core values such as the embrace of pacifism, expectations for Christ's soon return, and evangelistic zeal for the conversion of all nations.[29] Jackson's *Wirkungsgeschichte* analysis concludes with a warning to those in the tradition of the dangers of dispensational eschatology for the Pentecostal tradition and a call for

> the articulation and dissemination of non-dispensational Pentecostal eschatologies that will somehow bridge the gap between the 'Ivory Tower' and the 'Sunday Pulpit,' so that Pentecostal eschatology once again can be defined by hope – hope for redemption and renewal in the power of the Spirit, hope for the inbreaking of Christ's kingdom throughout the world, and hope for the soon coming of our Lord Jesus.[30]

This article was followed up by Jackson's PhD thesis[31] in which she devotes a chapter to Pentecostal interpretations of Ezek. 36.16–39.29 and Rev. 19.11-21 and 20.7-10. In this chapter Jackson does not divide the tradition into two streams as in her earlier work, but traces the interpretations in a chronological fashion. Her work does not focus exclusively on the first couple of decades, but rather upon the Pentecostal periodical literature from the beginning of the movement to the present, as well as influential populist voices throughout the movement's history. In this regard, the survey does not have the same precision, from a *Wirkungsgeschichte* perspective, as her earlier work, but at the same time she casts the net much more broadly in terms of literature that might be used for reception purposes. Thus, her extensive survey follows a bit more in the history of interpretation vein than a reception history one. In this regard, it sits very nicely with her next chapter in which she traces the history of Pentecostal eschatology amongst contemporary scholars. Consequently, it might be thought that here the lines between reception history and history of interpretation blur. Her two primary conclusions from this extensive survey are (1) an amazing lack of attention devoted to the 'two sticks' of Ezek. 37.15-28 and (2) the dispensational eschatology often

---

[29] Jackson, 'Wesleyan Holiness and Finished Work Pentecostal Interpretations of Gog and Magog Biblical Texts', pp. 182-83.

[30] Jackson, 'Wesleyan Holiness and Finished Work Pentecostal Interpretations of Gog and Magog Biblical Texts', p. 183.

[31] Alicia R. Jackson, 'Ezekiel's Two Sticks and Eschatological Violence in the Pentecostal Tradition: An Intertextual Literary Analysis' (PhD thesis, University of Birmingham, 2018), pp. 68–118.

present led interpreters to identify certain contemporary people and nations as enemies of God who are destined for destruction, an eschatological interpretation that she will challenge as not consistent with Pentecostal theology and practice in later chapters.

In her recently published monograph, *Visions of God in Ezekiel: Pentecostal Explorations of the Glory and Holiness of Yahweh*, Amelia Rebecca Basdeo Hill, an instructor in Hebrew and Old Testament at the Pentecostal Theological Seminary, has offered a brief analysis of the early Pentecostal reception history of these themes in Ezekiel.[32] After examining some 90 references in the early Pentecostal periodical literature from 1906 to 1916, she discovered the following interpretive approaches present within this literature.

First, some early Pentecostals followed an allegorical interpretive approach to the book focusing on specific textual details and making allegorical application to the then-contemporary context in which Spirit Baptism was being experienced. Ezekiel's vision of the valley of dry bones (37.1-25), in particular, exemplifies how an allegorical approach results in different interpretations depending upon one's geographical and ecclesial context. For a Pentecostal missionary in 1916, this vision of the dry bones had reference to unbelievers who needed the Spirit of God to breathe into them to transform them into an army, whilst for 1916 contributors in North America the bones refer to the state of certain North American Pentecostal churches in need of the breath of the Holy Spirit to revitalize them.[33] Second, other early Pentecostals took a literal dispensational interpretation to Ezekiel, specifically chs. 38–48. For these Pentecostals the interpretation of these chapters 'was contingent on the current activities of the people of Israel and the Jews' at that time.[34] Third, in addition to these approaches, still other Pentecostals took a historical and doctrinal approach to Ezek. 36.25-27, which made room for the experiences of salvation, sanctification, and Holy Spirit Baptism. On this view, Ezek. 36.25-27 exemplified the 'threefold aspect of cleansing' that was necessary for every Christian believer – 'justification by faith, or the cleansing by blood; sanctification or the cleansing

---

[32] A. Rebecca Basdeo Hill, *Visions of God in Ezekiel: Pentecostal Explorations of the Glory and Holiness of Yahweh* (Cleveland, TN: CPT Press, 2019), pp. 14-17.

[33] Basdeo Hill, *Visions of God in Ezekiel*, pp. 15-16.

[34] Basdeo Hill, *Visions of God in Ezekiel*, pp. 16-17.

by the water of the Word; and the fullness of the Holy Ghost, or purging by fire'.[35]

The third study focused on Ezekiel is the Bangor PhD thesis by Lisa Ward.[36] Chapter four of her study is devoted to the reception history of Ezekiel's visions and the Spirit in early Pentecostal literature. Specifically, Ward wants 'to discover the extent to which early Pentecostals and their spirituality were influenced by the Spirit's activities in the visions of the book of Ezekiel'.[37] The chapter examines the early Pentecostal periodical literature from 1906–23 beginning with the Wesleyan Holiness publications (*The Bridegroom's Messenger* and *The Evening Light/Church of God Evangel*) followed by the Finished Work publications (*The Pentecost, The Latter Rain Evangel*, and *The Bridal Call*). Amongst her conclusions are the following:

(1) Ward concludes that the book of Ezekiel had a direct bearing upon early Pentecostal spirituality and teaching. Specifically, visions fill the pages of the early Pentecostal periodical literature, with the vision reports from Ezekiel being viewed as support for their own experiences. Such experiences would lead to worship and often result in falling prostrate before God, just as Ezekiel experienced before them (Ezek. 1.4-28).

(2) These and other experiences were understood to be the result of Spirit Baptism, with Ezekiel's inaugural vision thought to be a prophecy of Pentecostal Spirit Baptism that was to come.

(3) Numerous testimonies draw upon the Hebrew idiom used by Ezekiel, 'the hand of the Lord', again in support of their own visionary experiences. Though more prevalent in the Wesleyan Pentecostal literature than that of the Finished Work, in both streams 'the hand of the Lord' was understood to be 'an intense spiritual experience that included (1) visionary transportations by the Spirit, (2) hearing angelic voices, (3) seeing Jesus, his glory, heavenly beings, thrones, and specifically for the Wesleyan

---

[35] *LRE* 4.3 (December 1911), pp. 6-8, in Basdeo-Hill, *Visions of God in Ezekiel*, p. 17.

[36] Lisa Ward, 'Ezekiel's Visions, the רוח, the יד־יהוה, and the Affective Language: A Pentecostal Hearing of Ezekiel's Visions' (PhD thesis, Bangor University, 2020).

[37] Ward, 'Ezekiel's Visions, the רוח, the יד־יהוה, and the Affective Language,' p. 68.

Pentecostals, descriptions of overwhelming feelings in the midst of the vision experiences'.

(4) On the whole, the Wesleyan Pentecostal literature seems to include more testimonies of the affective dimensions of their visionary experiences, though Aimee Semple McPherson went so far as to identify the affective language used in Ezekiel's visions as a way to read Ezekiel's vision reports.

(5) Wesleyan Pentecostals associated Ezekiel's visions with cleansing and sanctification, and some emphasized the symbol of water, representing not only the Spirit but also the cleansing of the believer.

(6) Both groups associated 'the hand of the Lord' with manifestations of the Spirit. Both groups also use the Ezekiel text to support the physical manifestations of the Spirit that occurred during their visionary experiences.

(7) The early Pentecostals also had a tendency to approach Ezekiel's vision of the four living beings in the inaugural vision symbolically as either the 'Bride of Christ', or as a way to interpret the four views of Jesus Christ narrated in the four gospels. McPherson would go so far as founding a denomination, The International Church of the Foursquare Gospel, based on her theological interpretation of Ezekiel's inaugural vision of the glory of God.[38]

The Writings

Pentecostal *Wirkungsgeschichte* in the Writings has been confined primarily to the Psalms, with the work of one scholar dominating the terrain to this point. But before moving to an examination of his work, perhaps mention should be made of an earlier piece that, whilst not being a reception history of specific biblical texts within early Pentecostal periodical literature, is actually distinctive in several ways.

In 2011, Narelle Jane Melton, Associate Lecturer in Old Testament at Alphacrucis College, published an article in which she sought to place biblical Psalms of lament into conversation with early

---

[38] Ward, 'Ezekiel's Visions, the רוח, the יד־יהוה, and the Affective Language', pp. 104-107.

Pentecostal attitudes toward and the use of lament.[39] Building off of a previous study in which she demonstrated the connections,[40] she devotes a follow-up article to reflections on this phenomenon. Whilst not technically a reception history piece, Melton makes several significant contributions that are of interest to the reception history endeavor. First and foremost, she expands the field of reference beyond North American early Pentecostal periodical literature. This move is a first fruit that examinations of early Pentecostal literature from around the globe have to bear. Second, she demonstrates a disciplined approach to placing early Pentecostal spirituality into intentional conversation with the biblical text informed by the scholarly community. Third, she demonstrates an integrative approach that makes room for both one's own personal reflection and theological context.

By far, the most extensive work on early Pentecostal reception history of the Psalms comes from Lee Roy Martin, Professor of Hebrew and Old Testament at the Pentecostal Theological Seminary, in his work entitled, *The Spirit of the Psalms: Rhetorical Analysis, Affectivity, and Pentecostal Spirituality*.[41] In this collection of studies, he includes a chapter that examines the early Pentecostal reception history of the Psalms. In the Preface of this volume, Martin offers three reasons for his use of *Wirkungsgeschichtliche*.

First, the *Wirkungsgeschichtliche* study of the early Pentecostal literature aims to correct any previously held misconceptions about the Pentecostal interpretation of the Psalms. Second, the act of engaging with the early literature furthers the researcher's formation as a Pentecostal interpreter as it instills the Pentecostal affections. Third, early Pentecostal approaches to the Psalms can contribute to the ongoing construction of contemporary Pentecostal hermeneutics.[42]

---

[39] Narelle Jane Melton, 'Lessons of Lament: Reflections on the Correspondence between the Lament Psalms and early Australian Pentecostal Prayer', *JPT* 20 (2011), pp. 68-80.

[40] Narelle Jane Melton, 'A Pentecostal's Lament: Is there a Correspondence between the Form of the Biblical Lament Psalms and the early Australian Pentecostal Practice of Prayer?' *Australasian Pentecostal Studies* 12 (2009), pp. 39-72.

[41] Lee Roy Martin, *The Spirit of the Psalms: Rhetorical Analysis, Affectivity, and Pentecostal Spirituality* (Cleveland, TN: CPT Press, 2019).

[42] Martin, *The Spirit of the Psalms*, p. xiii.

Martin makes use of *Wirkungsgeschichtliche* in his study of Psalm 91 and in his chapter devoted to the Psalms in early Pentecostal period-ical literature. He also includes an appendix (C) that consists of a chart listing the Psalms and their frequency of citation collectively in the Wesleyan Holiness periodicals and the Finished Work periodicals. The former category consists of *The Apostolic Faith*, *The Bridegroom's Messenger*, *The Church of God Evangel*, and *The Whole Truth*, whilst the latter category consists of the *Latter Rain Evangel, Pentecostal/Christian Evangel, The Pentecost, Pentecostal Testimony*, and *Word and Witness*. This chart enables one to take in, at a glance, the prominence the Psalter played in the early Pentecostal periodical literature. In a previous ap-pendix (B), Martin identifies the most frequently cited Psalms in the literature in descending order, Psalms 119, 103, 37, and 91, though the two streams of the tradition have different preferences with re-gard to their favorite psalms, it would appear.

In his analysis of Psalm 91 Martin observes:

> The history of effects is viewed somewhat like a 'testimony' of past experiences with the text. As testimony, the examples from effective history are placed into conversation with the text and with contemporary interpreters. The effective history does not govern the contemporary interpretation, but it serves as one voice – 'a great cloud of witnesses' (Heb. 12.1) – within the larger Pen-tecostal community of faith. In this chapter, I will listen to the witness of early Pentecostals regarding Psalm 91 as one element of my interpretation of the psalm.[43]

When turning to the reception of the text, Martin begins with a brief section devoted to the impact of the text upon Jewish and Christian readers generally. Following this, he offers an analysis of the Pentecostal reception of this psalm. According to Martin, the psalm was interpreted in the following ways. First, by far the most extensive reception of Psalm 91 was the way in which it was thought to function as an encouragement to piety and service. This interpre-tation was extensive and far-reaching in both streams of the tradition. Second, and next in importance, Psalm 91 was seen to be a protection against violence. Third, the psalm was also held to be a promise of immunity against disease. This was especially the case during the time

---

[43] Martin, *The Spirit of the Psalms*, p. 48.

of the 1918 Flu Epidemic. Fourth, the psalm was understood, in both streams of the tradition, to be protection against false teaching. Less frequently, Psalm 91 was understood to be a safeguard against heated conflicts, to testify that God functions as mother as well as father, to produce inner peace, and to refer to life in the millennium. Despite an occasional unusual or fanciful interpretation, Martin concludes that the reception of this psalm is consistent with interpretations rooted in an ancient Jewish context.[44]

Martin also includes a chapter entitled 'The Psalms in Early Pentecostal Periodical Literature'. In this chapter he focuses upon the literature appearing between 1906 and 1915, paying attention to the two streams identified earlier, finding 576 references to the Psalms in his survey. Among these he finds that the most popular psalms were: 103 (30x), 119 (24x), 91 (23x), 51 (20x), 34 (18x), 45 (16x), 9 (14x), 23 (14x), 37 (14x), and 107 (12x). In the Wesleyan Holiness periodicals, the most popular were: 103, 91, 9, 34, 37, 45, and 126; and in the Finished Work periodicals: 119, 51, 18, 23, 34, 45, 91, and 103. In addition, Martin identifies the most commonly cited verses as

> Ps. 103.3 (20) 'he healeth all thy diseases'; 9.17 (9) 'the wicked shall be turned into hell'; 45.14-15 (5) 'she shall be brought unto the king ...'; 46.10 (5) 'Be still, and know that I am God: I will be exalted ...'; 107.20 (5) 'He sent his word, and healed them'; 2.8 (4) 'I will give thee the heathen for thine inheritance'; 8.4 (4) 'What is man ... and the son of man ...?'; 42.11 (4) 'Why art thou cast down ...?'; 51.17 (4) 'The sacrifices of God are a broken spirit ...'; 91.10 (4) 'He shall cover thee with his feathers, and under his wings thou shalt trust ...'; 110.3 (4) '... in the day of thy power, in the beauties of holiness ...'; and 119.105 (4) 'Thy word is a lamp unto my feet ...'

Owing to limitations of space, Martin focuses his more in-depth analysis on the *Apostolic Faith*, including the issues published at Azusa Street and those published later in Portland, OR. In these issues he finds 25 references to the Psalms, which he breaks down into five categories based upon the hermeneutical function of the citation. The first category is 'The Psalms as Confirmation of Doctrine'. Amongst the doctrines discussed were divine healing, Hell, the

---

[44] Martin, *The Spirit of the Psalms*, pp. 58-68.

creation of Adam in the image of God, and sanctification. The second category is 'The Psalms as Allegories'. Specifically, these focused on 'royal psalms' or those deemed to be messianic psalms. The third category is 'The Psalms as Analogous to Pentecostal Experience'. In contrast to the allegorical approach, which takes an OT text and brings it forward to a NT context, 'the analogical approach takes the reader's present experience and carries it backward into the Old Testament narrative context'.[45] Treatments of Ps. 66.10 and Psalm 23 are especially noteworthy. The fourth category is 'The Psalms as Affective Argument'. The affective dimension of Spirit Baptism is teased out of Ps. 72.6-7 in considerable detail. The fifth category is 'The Psalms as Assurance and Comfort'. Examples of these psalms of orientation are Psalm 91 and Ps. 37.7. Martin offers the following conclusions with regard to the use of the Psalms in *The Apostolic Faith*.

> First, it is clear that early Pentecostals relied on both Old and New Testament as the Word of God. Second, they emphasized the overall unity of Scripture and downplayed the diversity of Scripture. Third, they utilized intertextuality without reservation. Fourth, their interpretations sometimes followed a rationalist, proof-texting approach; but, at other times, they followed a more literary, narrative, theological approach. Fifth, they appreciated the affective dimension of the Psalter and made wide use of it. Sixth, the early Pentecostal hermeneutic was thoroughly confessional.[46]

Before concluding this survey of the academic study of the early Pentecostal reception of OT texts, perhaps mention should also be made of the SPS paper presented by Chris E.W. Green entitled, '"Treasures Old and New": Reading the Old Testament with Early Pentecostal Mothers and Fathers'.[47] In this study, Green identifies five exemplary early Pentecostal readers – Alice Luce, another writer identified only as 'Deborah', J.H. King, E.N. Bell, and Hattie Barth – and studies their readerly approaches. Green next offers a synopsis of the definitive features of this hermeneutic before moving to a final section that identifies the hermeneutical possibilities that the

---

[45] Martin, *The Spirit of the Psalms*, p. 196.
[46] Martin, *The Spirit of the Psalms*, pp. 208-209.
[47] Chris E.W. Green, '"Treasures Old and New": Reading the Old Testament with Early Pentecostal Mothers and Fathers' (a paper presented to the 41st Annual Meeting of the Society for Pentecostal Studies 2012, Biblical Studies Group, Virginia Beach, VA).

retrieval of first generation Pentecostal spiritual hermeneutics may promise.

Matthew and Mark

Significantly, little has been done at this point with regard to early Pentecostal reception of the Gospel according to Matthew, despite Matthean texts that have proven of great interest to Pentecostals in the early years of the tradition and beyond. With regard to Mark, mention has already been made of the work devoted to Mk 16.9-20.

John

Owing to the considerable overlap that exists between Luke and Acts in early Pentecostal reception, I next turn to the Gospel according to John before taking up the reception of Luke-Acts.

Apparently, the first early Pentecostal reception piece devoted to the Fourth Gospel is a brief study that appears in an article on healing and the atonement that I published in 2005 entitled, 'Healing in the Atonement: A Johannine Perspective'.[48] In this study, I sought to expand the discussion of biblical texts on healing in the atonement beyond consideration of Mt. 8.16-17 and 1 Pet. 2.24 to include the Fourth Gospel. Focusing primarily on Jn 3.14-15 and its place in the structure of the Fourth Gospel, I sought to follow up my own literary and theological analysis of the text by tracing the early Pentecostal reception of this passage. There I found that these earlier voices may be profitably consulted as one discerns one's interpretive way forward. Amongst the study's conclusions is the following on the reception aspect of the text.

> [T]his study has shown that early Pentecostal readings of Jn 3.14-15 can be profitably consulted in the attempt to arrive at an informed understanding of this entire issue. What is perhaps surprising to some is that a number of these readings are more appreciative of the holistic nature of the life, which Jesus brings, than many contemporary readers. Methodologically, such a result suggests not only that *Wirkungsgeschichte* has a contribution to make in the hermeneutical challenge that lies before us, but also

---

[48] John Christopher Thomas, 'Healing in the Atonement: A Johannine Perspective', *JPT* 14.1 (2005), pp. 23-39. This study would later appear in John Christopher Thomas, *The Spirit of the New Testament* (Blandford Forum: Deo Publishing, 2005), pp. 175-89. In this presentation reference will be made to the latter source here mentioned.

that hearing the voices from those who have gone before us in the tradition might be an especially edifying activity.[49]

Though not a *Wirkungsgeschichtliche* study as such, Chris E.W. Green makes a contribution to the early Pentecostal reception of John 6 in particular in the survey of the Lord's Supper in early Pentecostal periodical literature he offers in his extensive study *Toward a Pentecostal Theology of the Lord's Supper: Foretasting the Kingdom*.[50] He finds that, surprisingly enough, John 6 figured into a variety of early Pentecostal reflections on the Lord's Supper in the *Apostolic Faith*, the *Church of God Evangel*, *The Pentecostal Evangel*, and *Confidence*.[51] He concludes:

> John 6.53-56 received special attention, both by those who insisted on the importance of obeying Jesus in sharing the meal and those who claimed Christians were called to 'feast' on Jesus mystically, as a way of life, and not merely ritually. Apparently, most did not regard these as mutually exclusive alternatives, but as parallel dimensions of the sacred.[52]

In her forthcoming PhD thesis entitled, 'Toward a Johannine Pentecostal Theology of Sanctification and Holiness',[53] Karen Holley offers an extensive survey and analysis of this theme in the Fourth Gospel and 1 John. As others before her, Holley traces her reception history along the two streams of the tradition, examining a variety of Johannine texts that relate in one way or another to sanctification and holiness. For the Wesleyan Pentecostal stream, she notes that the topic of sanctification was quite a significant one, for which the Johannine literature played an important role. Amongst her conclusions for the Wesleyan Pentecostal stream are the following. First, John 13–20 was deemed to be foundational for an understanding of sanctification, as these chapters provide a frame of reference for understanding sanctification as a second definite work of grace distinct from salvation and Spirit baptism. Second, these Pentecostals

---

[49] Thomas, *The Spirit of the New Testament*, pp. 188-89.
[50] Chris E.W. Green, *Toward a Pentecostal Theology of the Lord's Supper: Foretasting the Kingdom* (Cleveland, TN: CPT Press, 2012), cf. esp. pp. 74-181.
[51] These are discussed in Green, *Toward a Pentecostal Theology of the Lord's Supper* on pages 86, 113-14, 157, and 170, respectively.
[52] Green, *Toward a Pentecostal Theology of the Lord's Supper*, p. 179.
[53] Karen Holley, 'Toward a Johannine Pentecostal Theology of Sanctification and Holiness' (PhD thesis, Bangor University, forthcoming).

understood the need for believers to participate in their own sancti-fication. Third, these Pentecostals found truths that transcended the divisive issues over the timing of the experience and focused more on the essentials of sanctification. Fourth, 1 Jn 3.6-9 impacted these early Pentecostals with regard to the incongruity of abiding in Jesus and remaining in sin. Fifth, the Johannine literature clearly shaped their understanding of the connection between loving Jesus and fol-lowing his commands.[54]

With regard to the Finished Work Pentecostals, the usage of the Johannine literature was more varied. In the literature before the di-vision over the finished work controversy, Jn 17.16-19 functioned similarly to how their Wesleyan Pentecostal counterparts interpreted the passage, but after the division, this passage and others were inter-preted to mean that Jesus' disciples did not stand in need of sanctifi-cation. First John 4.17 is viewed as proof that the sanctification of the believer was accomplished through the work of Christ on Cal-vary, being concurrent with salvation rather than a separate work from it. First John 1.7 and 3.3 are understood to show that sanctifi-cation is a process, whilst 1 Jn 1.7, 1.9, and 3.5-6 are interpreted to underscore the fact that Jesus' blood deals with sin in the life of the believer. First John 1.8 and 3.8-9 are understood to mean that whilst occasional sin might be committed by the believer, habitual sin is condemned.[55]

Luke and Acts

In turning to Luke-Acts one must begin with the first rate mono-graph that lays out the history of Pentecostal interpretation of Luke-Acts by Martin William Mittelstadt entitled, *Reading Luke-Acts in the Pentecostal Tradition*.[56] This significant volume provides an overview of the interpretation of Acts offered by individual interpreters from Az-usa Street until the time of the volume's publication in 2010. Here one finds an account that is methodologically on its way from history of interpretation to reception history, even if the author is not fully aware of this shift at the time of composition! A proper assessment

---

[54] Holley, 'Toward a Johannine Pentecostal Theology of Sanctification and Ho-liness', pp. 113-14.

[55] Holley, 'Toward a Johannine Pentecostal Theology of Sanctification and Ho-liness', pp. 115-16.

[56] Martin William Mittelstadt, *Reading Luke–Acts in the Pentecostal Tradition* (Cleve-land, TN: CPT Press, 2010).

of this monograph cannot be offered in the space allocated for this study. What might be said is that if there is a monograph length study by a Pentecostal on reception history, Mittelstadt's volume certainly must be considered as the prime candidate for that honor. And yet, given the volume's focus on individual interpreters in this comprehensive accounting of Pentecostals scholarship on Luke-Acts, the work is not often able to offer a reception history of individual biblical texts by early Pentecostals. Perhaps surprisingly, there is a dearth of such reception studies on texts from Luke or Acts, a fact that is almost embarrassing to discover and even more embarrassing to admit!

Ironically, the two pieces that offer a reception of specific texts within early Pentecostalism both focus on the same somewhat obscure text. What is perhaps just as ironic is that both pieces were written at very close to the same time without either author knowing of the other's work. The subject of these two article length studies is Acts 19.11-12, which describes pieces of cloth that had come into contact with Paul's body – apparently inadvertently – through which the sick were healed and those with evil spirits were delivered, a text that gave rise to the practice and use of anointed cloths within early and later Pentecostalism. Not surprisingly, one of these explorations was offered by the aforementioned Martin Mittelstadt, and the other one offered by me.

In 2016 I was asked to contribute to a volume my colleague and good friend Lee Roy Martin was editing on a Pentecostal theology of worship. Having just taught a course on Acts for the first time earlier that year, I was intrigued by this text and its potential power for Pentecostal belief and practice, despite any misgivings about the way in which this practice has been abused by individuals in and around the tradition. In this piece, entitled, 'Toward a Pentecostal Theology of Anointed Cloths' I began with about a ten page reception history of Acts 19.11-12 in early Pentecostal periodical literature through about 1925, offered a narrative reading of this text, provided reflection upon Acts 19.11-12 theologically, and made some suggestions about a few of the significant aspects of possible contemporary practice.[57] With regard to the Pentecostal reception of the practice, I was struck

---

[57] John Christopher Thomas, 'Toward a Pentecostal Theology of Anointed Cloths' in L.R. Martin (ed.), *Toward a Pentecostal Theology of Worship* (Cleveland, TN: CPT Press, 2016), pp. 89-112 (cf. esp. pp. 89-101).

by how widespread the practice was in early Pentecostalism, how self-evident the biblical rationale appeared to these early interpreters, and how quickly theological explanations and even practical theological instructions began to emerge, perhaps the most impressive being those contained in *The Bridal Call*, written by Aimee Semple McPherson. One of the ways the reception portion of this study informs the theological construction portion concerns the way in which this practice functioned communally, where in early Pentecostalism

> communal requests seem to have driven the practice. Significantly, this communal practice does not appear to have been commercialized or commoditized in any way, but was viewed as a ministry of the church or the broader believing community. The various entities simply requested that the sent items be accompanied by a self addressed stamped envelope.[58]

In many ways Martin Mittelstadt's study of Acts 19.11-12 stands nicely alongside my slightly earlier piece, as in the reception portion of the study he focuses primarily on early Canadian Pentecostal periodical literature, thus expanding our knowledge of early Pentecostal reception on this text considerably.[59] The other primary focus of Mittelstadt's contribution is his advocacy for the appropriation of this methodological approach by Pentecostals and the legitimacy of *Wirkungsgeschichte* as a hermeneutical tool.[60] In ways not dissimilar to my own study, Mittelstadt calls for the re-appropriation of the use of anointed cloths amongst contemporary Pentecostals. The fact that these two article length studies were conceived of, researched, and written almost simultaneously, and without knowledge of each other, might be taken as a positive sign of the promise of this hermeneutical approach for the ways in which many of the conclusions reached are so similar.

---

[58] Thomas, 'Toward a Pentecostal Theology of Anointed Cloths', pp. 109-10.

[59] Martin William Mittelstadt, 'Nothing to Sneeze At: Receiving Acts 19:11-12 in the Canadian Pentecostal Tradition', in Riku P. Tupparainen (ed.), *Reading St. Luke's Text and Theology: A Pentecostal Voice. Essays in Honour of Roger Stronstad on his 75th Birthday* (Eugene, OR: Pickwick Publications, 2019), pp. 73-84.

[60] On this call cf. Martin William Mittelstadt, 'Receiving Luke–Acts: The Rise of Reception History and a Call to Pentecostal Scholars', *Pneuma* 40.3 (2018), pp. 367-88.

Paul and 2 Peter

The primary reception work done on Paul (and in this case 2 Peter) to date comes as part of a section in Jeffrey S. Lamp's article entitled, 'New Heavens and New Earth: Early Pentecostal Soteriology as a Foundation for Creation Care in the Present', which includes a section devoted to the early Pentecostal reception of texts related to this theme.[61] Three texts in particular emerge in his survey including Romans 8, 1 Corinthians 15, and 2 Peter 3. After providing examples from a variety of early Pentecostal periodical sources, Lamp offers the following assessment.

> What is striking about this survey ... is that the search term *new earth* led to discussions that reflected primarily on matters of end-time eschatology, but did not preclude participation of the other-than-human aspects of creation in God's soteriological program. While attribution of an ecological motivation for the positions surveyed here would surely be anachronistic, nevertheless this discussion has illustrated that a focus on eschatology need not lead to a position that sees the destruction of the other-than-human created order in the end. Among some early Pentecostals, the whole creation is viewed as an object of God's salvation. The focus on the salvation of the entire created order is one rationale currently cited by Pentecostals to urge care for creation in the present.[62]

Before leaving this portion of the survey, a forthcoming article on Romans 8 by Jesse D. Stone should perhaps be mentioned. Stone, whose forthcoming University of St Andrews PhD thesis entitled 'A Pauline Theology of Pneumatic Prayer', has produced a shorter study called 'Inward Groans and Unknown Tongues', that gives some attention to the early Pentecostal reception of Rom. 8.26.[63] Stone's examination of the reception of this text from 1906–1940 leads him to the following tentative conclusions. First, there was some division of thought on whether or not the 'inarticulate groanings' are to be identified as praying in tongues. While some equate Rom. 8.26 with Eph.

---

[61] Jeffrey S. Lamp, 'New Heavens and New Earth: Early Pentecostal Soteriology as a Foundation for Creation Care in the Present', *Pneuma* 36.1 (2014), pp. 64-80 (see esp. pp. 68-73).

[62] Lamp, 'New Heavens and New Earth', p. 73.

[63] Jesse D. Stone, 'Inward Groans and Unknown Tongues: Romans 8.26 in Early Pentecostal Literature', *JPT* (forthcoming).

6.18 or 1 Cor. 14.14-15, not all interpreters do so. Some would even go so far as to suggest that such 'groaning' may be a separate kind of pneumatic experience altogether. Second, these early Pentecostals seem to have an uncanny ability to detect what are now called 'intertextual echoes', some of which have been picked up on by contemporary scholarship, others of which have not but appear to have a contribution to make to contemporary NT scholarly discussions. Third, these early Pentecostals have a remarkable ability to blend or integrate the horizon of the text with their own horizons, resulting in interpretive insights that might at first glance not appear to be derived explicitly from the text, but on further reflection appear to come from deeper textual connections – places where 'the text sometimes reads their experience, and their experiences ... enable new readings of the text'.[64]

Hebrews
In his forthcoming PhD thesis, 'Hebrews and the Spirit: A Pentecostal Exploration', Jeff Holley includes an extensive chapter tracing the early Pentecostal reception of the pneumatological texts that appear in the Book of Hebrews.[65] This study focuses on the periodical literature of the Wesleyan Pentecostal and Finished Work streams of the tradition that were published within the first decade of the Pentecostal movement, identified as the years 1906–1916.

Amongst the conclusions reached from an assessment of the Wesleyan Pentecostal literature are: (1) Of the seven pneumatological passages in Hebrews, 2.4, 6.4 and 10.15 occurred more frequently than 9.8, 9.14 and 10.29, whilst Heb. 3.7 did not occur at all. (2) Hebrews 2.4 was especially important to these Pentecostals, for it provided a biblical validation of their experience, as well as the signs and wonders that were occurring in their midst. (3) Wesleyan Holiness Pentecostals offered a distinctive interpretation of Heb. 10.15, here finding evidence for an 'experience in which the Holy Spirit would bear witness to the sanctification of the believer characterized ... by joy or by a profound sense of purity and peace ... an experience ... meant to provide confirmation that God had completed the work of sanctification in the life of the believer'. 4) Owing to opposition and

---

[64] Stone, 'Inward Groans and Unknown Tongues'.
[65] Jeff Holley, 'Hebrews and the Spirit: A Pentecostal Exploration' (PhD thesis, Bangor University, forthcoming).

oppression, Wesleyan Holiness Pentecostals understood Heb. 6.4, and to a lesser extent Heb. 10.29, as being of some assistance in understanding 'the sin against the Holy Ghost', owing to their own keen sense of respect and reverence for the Spirit. 5) The term 'Eternal Spirit' in Heb. 9.4 was understood as having reference to the Holy Spirit. This Spirit is understood to anoint Jesus for his work as Sanctifier. 6) 'The Wesleyan-Holiness tradition also recognized that the Spirit had a significant role to play in the process of interpreting Scripture, a role that went beyond mere illumination. The Spirit actually unveiled and interpreted the meaning of scripture as it was being proclaimed, providing fresh and new meaning of the text. This work was a present and ongoing work of the Spirit'.[66]

Amongst the conclusions drawn from the Finished Work tradition are the following:

(1) While all seven pneumatological passages in Hebrews are cited, five receive detailed attention: Heb. 2.4, 6.4, 9.14, 10.15, and 10.29.

(2) Hebrews 2.4 was deemed to validate the occurrence of signs and wonders experienced during Pentecostal worship services. They were thought to have a three-fold purpose: 'a) the exaltation of Christ, b) confirmation that the end of the age was at hand and c) confirmation of the proclaimed Word'.

(3) Appeal was made to Heb. 6.4, and to a lesser extent Heb. 10.29, to understand better 'the unforgivable sin of blasphemy against the Holy Spirit'.

(4) Mention of the 'Eternal Spirit' in Heb. 9.14 was always understood to be having reference to the Holy Spirit. This text was at times thought to make clear the essential unity between Christ and the Spirit in carrying out the complete atoning work of Christ, including sanctification.

(5) The Spirit was thought to have a significant role to play in the process of interpreting Scripture, a role going beyond mere illumination. The Spirit was thought actually to speak through the text in a way that was thought to be a present and ongoing work

---

[66] Holley, 'Hebrews and the Spirit'.

of the Spirit, an essential component of the hermeneutical process.

(6) Rather than as an object to be studied, early Pentecostals approached Scripture as a story to be acted out and to be lived, an understanding that exhibited a strong sense of shared experience with the apostolic generation and with the text. This experience shaped the way in which Scripture was read, interpreted, and applied.

(7) Generally speaking, early Pentecostals in the Wesleyan-Holiness Tradition and the Finished Work Tradition read, interpreted, and utilized the pneumatological texts in the Epistle to the Hebrews in similar ways with one important exception ... Wesleyan-Holiness Pentecostals demonstrated a distinctive interpretation of Heb. 10.15 in that they found evidence there for an experience in which the Holy Spirit would bear witness to the sanctification of the believer. There is no evidence for such an interpretation of Heb. 10.15 in the Finished Work Tradition. This finding should not be surprising owing to 'the differences in the two traditions' positions with respect to the doctrine of sanctification.[67]

1–3 John
With regard to 1–3 John, reference has earlier been made to the pioneering work of Heather Landrus on 3 John 2 – and the response by Mark Roberts – as well as the work of Karen Holley.

The Apocalypse
One of the aspects of the virtual explosion in Apocalypse studies within Pentecostalism is the fact that a number of pieces have appeared that trace the reception of the Apocalypse both amongst early Pentecostals, as well as within the broader church and culture. These contributions include chapter length studies and articles devoted to a *Wirkungsgeschichte* of a variety of issues.

In my commentaries devoted to the Apocalypse, I devoted an extended section of the introduction to 'The Apocalypse and Its Streams of Influence: The History of Effects'.[68] This study includes

---

[67] Holley, 'Hebrews and the Spirit'.
[68] John Christopher Thomas, *The Apocalypse: A Literary and Theological Commentary* (Cleveland, TN: CPT Press, 2012), pp. 51-86 and John Christopher Thomas

sections devoted to: disastrous interpretations of the Apocalypse (including the events around the Anabaptist kingdom established in Münzter in the 1530s, the Tate-LaBianca murders directed by Charles Manson, and David Koresh and the Branch Davidians), the Apocalypse's influence on other Johannine apocalyptic documents ('The Second Apocalypse of John', 'The Apocalypse of John Chrysostom', 'The Third Apocalypse of John', and 'The Coptic Apocalypse of John'), its influence on art (the Catacombs in Rome, *The Trinity Apocalypse*, Hans Memling, *Beatus of Liébana*, Albrecht Dürer, and Jan van Eyck's *The Adoration of the Lamb*), music (Handel's *Messiah* and the Hymns of Charles Wesley), poetry (the *Gawain* Poet, William Blake, and the Azusa Street Pentecostal Brother A. Beck), film (*End of Days* and *The Omega Code*), and commentaries (Victorinus, the Venerable Bede, Joachim of Fiore, and A. Boesak).

The first extensive *Wirkungsgeschichte* of the Apocalypse in the early Pentecostal periodical literature came in the form of a chapter devoted to such in Melissa L. Archer's *'I Was in the Spirit on the Lord's Day': A Pentecostal Engagement with Worship in the Apocalypse*.[69] This 50 page chapter tracks the impact of the worship texts found within the Apocalypse in the Wesleyan Pentecostal and Finished Work periodicals in turn, that appeared in the first decade of the tradition identified as 1906–1916.

> This survey of early Pentecostal literature (1906–1916) reveals that the liturgy of the Apocalypse played a significant role in Pentecostal worship for both Wesleyan-Holiness and Finished Work streams of the tradition. To a large degree, the publications present a unified portrait of the worship of these early Pentecostals and demonstrate that they were clearly influenced in their worship by the Apocalypse in general and by the worship scenes in particular … this study reveals that in their descriptions of worship, both streams had very similar experiences. For both, worship is grounded pneumatologically and christologically. For both, their experience of worship is a real participation in the worship of heaven. The Holy Spirit transforms their worship and even transports them into the heavenly throne room, via the experience of

and Frank D. Macchia, *Revelation* (*THNTC;* Grand Rapids: Eerdmans, 2016), pp. 44-72.

[69] Melissa L. Archer, *'I Was in the Spirit on the Lord's Day': A Pentecostal Engagement with Worship in the Apocalypse* (Cleveland, TN: CPT Press, 2014), cf. pp. 68-118.

being slain under the power of God. Further, the Holy Spirit 'speaks for Himself' the songs of heaven through the saints. The Spirit inspires original songs and poetry which often are based on images and themes found in the Apocalypse. Loud, exuberant music and shouting along with kinesthetic movement, such as leaping, jumping and dancing, are viewed across both branches of the tradition as normative expressions of worship. All of this for early Pentecostals is made possible by the Spirit of God.[70]

Significantly, Archer found that even within the Finished Work tradition, the stream that was uniformly committed to a dispensational eschatological hermeneutical paradigm, when engaging the worship texts of the Apocalypse, these interpreters instinctively allowed their Pentecostal experience to override – at least momentarily – their dispensational commitments, and thought theologically in ways more consistent with their own Pentecostal experience of God.

Archer's monograph was followed in 2016 by an article length exploration on Pentecostal reception by David R. Johnson in a study devoted to 'The Mark of the Beast, Reception History, and Early Pentecostal Literature'.[71] Johnson examines the periodical literature for reception of the mark of the beast in the two streams of the tradition from 1906–1918, which includes issues from the time of World War I. His extensive analysis leads Johnson to some of the following conclusions:

(1) There was a tendency in the Wesleyan-Holiness stream to include non-dispensational and dispensational interpretations alike while the Finished Work stream exhibited a stronger influence of Dispensationalism. However, … the early Pentecostal movement was not monolithic concerning the mark of the beast and neither stream allowed dispensational eschatology to prevent contextual readings of Revelation.

(2) The context of the Great War inspired an abundance of apocalyptic interest among these early Pentecostals, and it is apparent that the Apocalypse influenced the early Pentecostals' reaction to World War I.

---

[70] Archer, *'I Was in the Spirit on the Lord's Day'*, p. 118.
[71] David R. Johnson, 'The Mark of the Beast, Reception History, and Early Pentecostal Literature', *JPT* 25.2 (2016), pp. 184-202.

(3) There were multiple references to the absolute military, political, and economic power being exerted by the nations. Activities by nations participating in war and forcing its citizens to fight were identified with the beast and drafting soldiers was the same as stamping the mark of the beast upon them. The early Pentecostals urged believers against participating in the war. The choice was dualistic: either individuals were of heaven and marked by Christ or were identified with the beast and were marked by him.

(4) Beyond specific references to the Great War, nearly all publications surveyed observed the political, economic, and military aspects of the beast. These keen obviations are prominent features of the beast as described in the Apocalypse.

(5) While the Wesleyan-Holiness stream connected these beast-like qualities to their contemporary world, the Finished Work stream was more reluctant to contextualize any bestial texts without clarifying that it was proleptic of a future reality. Thereby, when addressing the absolute military or political power of the beast in the Finished Work stream, there were two approaches: first, they confined the bestial texts to a future reality during the Great Tribulation; or second, any person, institution, federation, nation, or country that contained beast-like qualities was qualified with the phrases: 'the spirit of the beast' or 'the spirit of the antichrist' that was already present in the world.

(6) The interpretative diversity revealed in this survey of early Pentecostal literature has formed me as a Pentecostal interpreter. The diversity of interpretation found among early Pentecostals creates interpretative space for the Pentecostal community to hear the Word by the Spirit anew. It allows Pentecostals an opportunity to reflect upon the ways in which beast-like qualities are evident in our own context in a way that is true to the ethos of the Pentecostal tradition.[72]

This *Wirkungsgeschichte* piece was followed by another contribution from Johnson in 2018 in the form of an article entitled, 'Reception History, Early Pentecostal Literature, and the Pneumatology of the

---

[72] Johnson, 'The Mark of the Beast, Reception History, and Early Pentecostal Literature', p. 202.

Apocalypse'.[73] Johnson's review reveals a number of details. First, both streams of the early Pentecostal tradition were very attentive to the role of the Holy Spirit in Revelation, with no stark differences in interpretation. Significantly, dispensational thought did not seem to influence their pneumatological interpretations, with common dispensational terminology rarely appearing. Second, the seven Spirits were uniformly interpreted as having reference to the Holy Spirit, with the number seven thought to underscore the completeness of the Spirit. Intertextual connections with Zech. 4.10 and Isa. 11.2-3 were also noted. Third, the Apocalypse was a robust theological well from which early Pentecostals drew upon to understand and explain their own pneumatological experiences 'in the Spirit', functioning as a formative text in many regards. Fourth, the pneumatology of the Apocalypse influenced their process of discernment to identify and discern various false teachings which they encountered. Some even thought that the only way to understand the Apocalypse was to be 'in the Spirit' as was John when he wrote. Fifth, 'these early Pentecostal testimonies offer a renewed look at the pneumatology of the Apocalypse, an aspect … that seems to be overlooked among many contemporary Pentecostal congregations'.[74]

A final contribution to the *Wirkungsgeschichte* of the Apocalypse from David Johnson comes in the form of two chapters – that total over 90 pages – in his recent monograph, *Pneumatic Discernment in the Apocalypse: An Intertextual and Pentecostal Exploration.*[75] These chapters explore the theme of pneumatic discernment in the Wesleyan Pentecostal periodicals and the Finished Work periodicals in successive chapters. As Johnson begins to offer his conclusions about this extensive survey, he starts with some reflection on the impact of the exercise upon him as an interpreter.

> This examination of the early Pentecostal intertexts offers an opportunity to dialogue with the theological heart of the Pentecostal (con)text, while also forming me as a Pentecostal interpreter concerning pneumatic discernment that attunes my ears to hear notes

---

[73] David R. Johnson, 'Reception History, Early Pentecostal Literature, and the Pneumatology of the Apocalypse', *JPT* 27.1 (2018), pp. 53-73.

[74] Johnson, 'Reception History, Early Pentecostal Literature, and the Pneumatology of the Apocalypse', pp. 72-73.

[75] David R. Johnson, *Pneumatic Discernment in the Apocalypse: An Intertextual and Pentecostal Exploration* (Cleveland, TN: CPT Press, 2018), pp. 101-93.

of the Apocalypse in a distinct fashion. As a Pentecostal interpreter, the diverse interpretative spectrum of the early Pentecostal
periodical literature provides space to interpret the (inter)text of
the Apocalypse in a new context, creating space for the Pentecostal community to hear anew.[76]

With regard to the influence of a dispensational eschatological orientation amongst the periodicals, Johnson notes the following:

> Both streams of the early Pentecostal movement reveal a scaling
> interpretative continuum of reading Revelation dispensationally.
> Some of the periodicals such as *The Apostolic Faith* scaled far away
> from dispensational readings. *The Bridegroom's Messenger*, *The Latter
> Rain Evangel*, and *The Church of God Evangel* stood near the center
> of the scale where each publication permitted dispensational and
> nondispensational interpretations to stand together. *The Pentecostal
> Holiness Advocate* and *The Christian/Weekly Evangel* scaled far toward
> the dispensational side that often isolated the text (especially Rev-
> elation 4–22) from the life of the community. This survey con-
> firms a tendency in the Wesleyan-Holiness stream to include non-
> dispensational and dispensational interpretations alike, while the
> Finished-Work stream tended to permit testimonies and articles
> that were dispensational. However, … neither stream of the early
> Pentecostal movement was monolithic and did not allow dispen-
> sational eschatology to control their interpretations of Revelation
> entirely.[77]

With regard to the reception of texts dealing with discernment, Johnson observes that early Pentecostal readers were not only able to pick
up on overt aspects of the text related to this topic, but also outside
of such 'explicit references to pneumatic discernment in Revelation,
the early Pentecostals on numerous occasions commented on the
Spirit as being actively involved in discernment, interpretation, and
decision-making'.[78] Finally, Johnson offers these observations on a
final point of convergence between the two dominant streams of
early Pentecostalism.

---

[76] Johnson, *Pneumatic Discernment in the Apocalypse*, p. 191
[77] Johnson, *Pneumatic Discernment in the Apocalypse*, pp. 191-92.
[78] Johnson, *Pneumatic Discernment in the Apocalypse*, p. 192.

Both streams of the early Pentecostal movement shared in critiquing violent participation in World War I. While both streams appealed to Revelation to address violent action, they differed in
their approaches, which seems to be determined by the extent of
the influence of dispensational eschatology upon them. This can
be seen in interpretations of Revelation 13. On the one hand,
those who scaled away from dispensational thought suggested
that the nations which drafted soldiers were stamping them with
the mark of the beast. On the other hand, those who revealed a
strong presence of dispensational thought did on occasion appeal
to Rev. 13.9-10 but overall avoided any comment on the possibility
that the beast was present in their contemporary context. This
distinction becomes more noticeable when considering that contributors in both streams acknowledged the supreme military and
political power of the beast, but only those who were not captive
to dispensational thought read the bestial texts against World War
I.[79]

And with this, our survey of the canonical lay of the land concludes.

Observations, Implications, and Prospects

In bringing this investigation to a close, I would like to offer the following, somewhat disparate, observations in the light of this study.

(1) It is clear to me that the methodology employed by Kimberly
E. Alexander in her monograph, *Pentecostal Healing*,[80] was revolutionary in the sense that it opened up ways of thinking for scholars
to engage the early Pentecostal periodical literature for biblical reception purposes.

(2) It is interesting to note how much has already been done on
early Pentecostal reception of the Bible and, in some ways, it is
even more fascinating to note what studies and/or subjects are
missing that one would expect to have already been done.

---

[79] Johnson, *Pneumatic Discernment in the Apocalypse*, pp. 192-93.
[80] Kimberly Ervin Alexander, *Pentecostal Healing: Models in Theology and Practice*
(JPTSup 29; Blandford Forum: Deo Publishing, 2006).

(3) There are a remarkable number of pieces that are forthcoming, a promising sign for the future of the discipline.

(4) There is an amazing amount of gender parity amongst the studies surveyed in this study, which bodes well for the future of Pentecostal biblical studies.

(5) Whilst the focus of most of these studies has been early American Pentecostalism, there are signs of some broadening of focus with A.A. Boddy's *Confidence* being utilized by some interpreters and the work of Narelle Melton on Australian Pentecostal publications – not to mention Mittelstadt's examination of the Canadian publications.

(6) While a significant number of pieces focus on the first generation of the tradition broadly defined, several studies have extended the boundaries to other stopping points to include 1940, 1960, and even up to the present. Such movement cannot help but enable assessments and comparisons with the reception of a variety of texts during different periods.

(7) There is a pronounced need for expanding the media focus of the reception field of study to include art, music, poetry, etc. The art of the tradition has only recently begun to be acknowledged and explored. Specific suggestions might include a reception history of the numerous charts found within the tradition on the Book of Revelation – for example the rolling chart of F.J. Lee[81] has never been fully examined – nor has the art work generated in the sphere of Aimee Semple McPherson's influence been comprehensively studied in this way. I believe there is a thesis waiting to be written on the poetry of the early tradition, with Brother A. Beck's work in *The Apostolic Faith* being but one example.

(8) Though not all reception studies divide the periodical literature into Wesleyan Pentecostal and Finished Work Streams, those that do, provide an opportunity for learning more about the tradition than those that do not. When Kimberly Alexander discovered that there were significant differences between Wesleyan Pentecostal and Finished Work views of healing, based in part it would seem on one's view of sanctification, these results called for a

---

[81] Housed in the Dixon Research Center in Cleveland, TN.

reassessment of how uniform early Pentecostal thought was and was not on a variety of issues. Some additional studies confirmed that there were significant theological differences between the streams,[82] whilst other studies indicated that this was not always the case, even when expected.[83] The point here is not to force the streams into different theological understandings, but rather to discover the actual lay of the land, so to speak. It would seem important to appreciate these differences and similarities if not always understanding their *raison d'être*.

(9) There appear to have been three ways in which the method has been utilized to this point. Some studies have treated these voices as a foreground of sorts to the biblical texts, tracing the trajectory of certain texts and/or themes in early Pentecostal literature. Others have privileged voices in the doing of constructive Pentecostal theology as being foundational in some fashion, providing concrete examples of Pentecostal thought and practice. Still others see the reception history enterprise as an opportunity for Pentecostal interpreters to be formed by the testimonies of the tradition, including these ancient voices. As such, these voices are not to be fossilized or thought static, but are to be engaged in the broader project of revisioning Pentecostal faith and practice in the twenty-first century. Obviously, these uses are not mutually exclusive.

In my estimation, for the Pentecostal interpreter, the hearing of the testimonies of the community should not be limited to the contemporary voices of the Pentecostal community, but should be extended by means of *Wirkungsgeschichte* to include the voices of those who have preceded us in discerning their way on this narrative journey.[84] Specifically, I find the voices that come from the first ten to

---

[82] Cf. for example the significant eschatological differences found within the two streams in Larry R. McQueen, *Toward a Pentecostal Eschatology: Discerning the Way Forward* (JPTSup 39; Blandford Forum: Deo Publishing, 2012) and Johnson, *Pneumatic Discernment in the Apocalypse*.

[83] In other studies, where one might have expected to find differing theological emphases, such comparisons reveal more uniformity between the traditions. Cf. esp. Archer, *'I Was in the Spirit on the Lord's Day'* and Green, *Toward a Pentecostal Theology of the Lord's Supper*.

[84] On this approach to biblical studies cf. the seminal work of U. Luz, *Matthew in History* and his *Studies in Matthew* (trans. R. Selle; Grand Rapids: Eerdmans, 2005),

twenty years of the movement to be extraordinarily helpful, as this period represents the heart, not necessarily the infancy, of the movement's spirituality.[85] Hearing these voices provides the Pentecostal interpreter with additional opportunities to discern and reflect upon the Pentecostal identity and ethos, as well as concrete examples of Pentecostal approaches to and interpretations of specific texts. My own experience has been that such encounters with these 'ancient' testimonies have acted as a bridge between the biblical texts and myself, as I have come to realize more and more that they too are part of the community in which I seek to hear what the Spirit is saying to the church.[86] At the same time, I have often been amazed by the clarity and depth of insight into the biblical text, even when compared to various historical critical commentaries on a given passage.[87]

If *Wirkungsgeschichte* is similar to tracing the flow of water from its source down a mountain or hill, then not only does one discover beautiful things as one moves away from the source, but one also understands something of the vastness of the impact of the water itself.[88] There are concrete things to be learned from such interpretive activity. I am happy to be part of this first major monograph devoted to the practice of Pentecostal and Charismatic reception history.

Bibliography

Alexander, Kimberly E., *Pentecostal Healing: Models in Theology and Practice* (JPTSup 29; Blandford Forum: Deo Publishing, 2006).

---

pp. 263-379. Cf. also Heikki Räisänen, 'The Effective "History" of the Bible: A Challenge to Biblical Scholarship', *Scottish Journal of Theology* 45 (1992), pp. 303-24; Kenneth G.C. Newport, *Apocalypse and Millennium: Studies in Biblical Eisegesis* (Cambridge: Cambridge University Press, 2000), as well as the Blackwell Bible Commentaries devoted to this approach edited by John Sawyer, Christopher Roland, and Judith Kovacs.

[85] Steven J. Land, *Pentecostal Spirituality: A Passion for the Kingdom* (JPTSup 1; Sheffield: Sheffield Academic Press, 1993), p. 47, following Walter J. Hollenweger, 'Pentecostals and the Charismatic Movement' in C. Jones, G. Wainwright, and E. Yarnold (eds.), *The Study of Spirituality* (New York: Oxford University Press, 1986), pp. 549-53.

[86] A result in remarkable agreement with Luz's observations about the results of the method, *Matthew in History*, pp. 24-25.

[87] A result which parallels Luz's own experience with a number of so-called 'pre-critical interpreters', *Matthew in History*, pp. 34-35.

[88] I think especially of the difference between the humble origins of the Mississippi River and its increasingly vast size and power as it makes its way south.

Archer, Melissa L., *'I Was in the Spirit on the Lord's Day': A Pentecostal Engagement with Worship in the Apocalypse* (Cleveland, TN: CPT Press, 2014).

Best, Ernest, 'Review', *Journal of Theological Studies* 44.1 (1993), pp. 249-51.

Green, Chris E.W., '"Treasures Old and New": Reading the Old Testament with Early Pentecostal Mothers and Fathers' (a paper presented to the 41st Annual Meeting of the Society for Pentecostal Studies 2012, Biblical Studies Group, Virginia Beach, VA).

—*Toward a Pentecostal Theology of the Lord's Supper: Foretasting the Kingdom* (Cleveland, TN: CPT Press, 2012).

Herron, Robert W., *Mark's Account of Peter's Denial of Jesus: A History of Its Interpretation* (Lanham, MD: University Press of America, 1991).

Hill, A. Rebecca Basdeo, *Visions of God in Ezekiel: Pentecostal Explorations of the Glory and Holiness of Yahweh* (Cleveland, TN: CPT Press, 2019).

Hollenweger, Walter J., 'Pentecostals and the Charismatic Movement' in C. Jones, G. Wainwright, and E. Yarnold (eds.), *The Study of Spirituality* (New York: Oxford University Press, 1986), pp. 549-53.

Holley, Jeff, 'Hebrews and the Spirit: A Pentecostal Exploration' (PhD thesis, Bangor University, forthcoming).

Holley, Karen, 'Toward a Johannine Pentecostal Theology of Sanctification and Holiness' (PhD thesis, Bangor University, forthcoming).

Hymes, David, 'Pentecostal-Charismatic Reception History of the Book of Numbers' (a Presentation to the SPS/SBL Meeting in Boston, MA, 2017).

Jackson, Alicia R., 'Ezekiel's Two Sticks and Eschatological Violence in the Pentecostal Tradition: An Intertextual Literary Analysis' (PhD thesis, University of Birmingham, 2018).

—'Wesleyan Holiness and Finished Work Pentecostal Interpretations of Gog and Magog Biblical Texts', *JPT* 25.2 (2016), pp. 168-83.

Johnson, David R., *Pneumatic Discernment in the Apocalypse: An Intertextual and Pentecostal Exploration* (Cleveland, TN: CPT Press, 2018).

—'Reception History, Early Pentecostal Literature, and the Pneumatology of the Apocalypse', *JPT* 27.1 (2018), pp. 53-73.

—'The Mark of the Beast, Reception History, and Early Pentecostal Literature', *JPT* 25.2 (2016), pp. 184-202.

Jurgensen, Hubert, 'Awaiting the Return of Christ: A Re-examination of 1 Thessalonians 4.13-5.11 from a Pentecostal Perspective', *JPT* 4 (1994), pp. 81-113.

—'Saint Paul et la Parousia: I Thessaloniciens 4, 13-5, 11 dans l'exegesis Modern et Contemporaine', (ThD thesis, Universite dex Science Humaines de Strasbourg, 1992).

Lamp, Jeffrey S., 'New Heavens and New Earth: Early Pentecostal Soteriology as a Foundation for Creation Care in the Present', *Pneuma* 36.1 (2014), pp. 64-80.

Land, Steven J., *Pentecostal Spirituality: A Passion for the Kingdom* (JPTSup 1; Sheffield: Sheffield Academic Press, 1993).

Landrus, Heather L., 'Hearing 3 John 2 in the Voices of History', *JPT* 11.1 (2002), pp. 70-88.

Luz, U., 'A Response to Emerson Powery', *JPT* 14 (1999), pp. 19-26.

—*Matthew in History: Interpretation, Influence, and Effects* (Minneapolis: Fortress Press, 1994), pp. 5-22.

—*Studies in Matthew* (trans. R. Selle; Grand Rapids: Eerdmans, 2005).

Martin, Lee Roy, *The Spirit of the Psalms: Rhetorical Analysis, Affectivity, and Pentecostal Spirituality* (Cleveland, TN: CPT Press, 2019).

McQueen, Larry R., *Joel and the Spirit: The Cry of a Prophetic Hermeneutic* (JPTSup 8; Sheffield: Sheffield Academic Press, 1995).

—*Toward a Pentecostal Eschatology: Discerning the Way Forward* (JPTSup 39; Blandford Forum: Deo Publishing, 2012).

Melton, Narelle J., 'A Pentecostal's Lament: Is there a Correspondence between the Form of the Biblical Lament Psalms and the early Australian Pentecostal Practice of Prayer?' *Australasian Pentecostal Studies* 12 (2009), pp. 39-72.

—'Lessons of Lament: Reflections on the Correspondence between the Lament Psalms and early Australian Pentecostal Prayer', *JPT* 20 (2011), pp. 68-80.

Mittelstadt, Martin W., 'Nothing to Sneeze At: Receiving Acts 19:11-12 in the Canadian Pentecostal Tradition' in Riku P. Tupparainen (ed.), *Reading St. Luke's Text and Theology: A Pentecostal Voice. Essays in Honour of Roger Stronstad on his 75th Birthday* (Eugene, OR: Pickwick Publications, 2019), pp. 73-84.

—*Reading Luke–Acts in the Pentecostal Tradition* (Cleveland, TN: CPT Press, 2010).

—'Receiving Luke–Acts: The Rise of Reception History and a Call to Pentecostal Scholars', *Pneuma* 40.3 (2018), pp. 367-88.

Newport, K.G.C., *Apocalypse and Millennium: Studies in Biblical Eisegesis* (Cambridge: Cambridge University Press, 2000).

Powery, Emerson B., 'Ulrich Luz's Matthew in History: A Contribution to Pentecostal Hermeneutics?', *JPT* 14 (1999), pp. 3-17.

Räisänen, H., 'The Effective "History" of the Bible: A Challenge to Biblical Scholarship', *Scottish Journal of Theology* 45 (1992), pp. 303-24.

Roberts, Mark E., 'A Hermeneutic of Charity: Response to Heather Landrus', *JPT* 11.1 (2002), pp. 89-97.

Schumacher, Steffen G., *The Spirit of God in the Torah: A Pentecostal Exploration* (Cleveland, TN: CPT Press, 2020).

Stone, Jesse D., 'Inward Groans and Unknown Tongues: Romans 8.26 in Early Pentecostal Literature' (PhD thesis, University of St Andrews, forthcoming).

Thomas, John Christopher, 'Healing in the Atonement: A Johannine Perspective', *JPT* 14.1 (2005), pp. 23-39.

—'Pentecostal Theology in the Twenty-First Century', *Pneuma* 20 (1998), pp. 3-19.

—*The Apocalypse: A Literary and Theological Commentary* (Cleveland, TN: CPT Press, 2012).

—*The Spirit of the New Testament* (Blandford Forum: Deo Publishing, 2005).

—'Toward a Pentecostal Theology of Anointed Cloths' in L.R. Martin (ed.), *Toward a Pentecostal Theology of Worship* (Cleveland, TN: CPT Press, 2016), pp. 89-112.

Thomas, John Christopher and Kimberly E. Alexander, '"And the Signs Are Following": Mark 16.9-20–A Journey into Pentecostal Hermeneutics', *JPT* 11.2 (2003), pp. 147-70.

Thomas, John Christopher and Frank D. Macchia, *Revelation* (THNTC; Grand Rapids: Eerdmans, 2016).

Wadholm, Jr, Rick, *A Theology of the Spirit in the Former Prophets: A Pentecostal Perspective* (Cleveland, TN: CPT Press, 2018).

Wall, R.W., 'A Response to Thomas/Alexander, "And the Signs Are Following" (Mark 16.9-20)', *JPT* 11.2 (2003), pp. 171-83.

Ward, Lisa, 'Ezekiel's Visions, the רוח, the יד־יהוה, and the Affective Language: A Pentecostal Hearing of Ezekiel's Visions' (PhD thesis, Bangor University, 2020).

5

'UNTIL I, DEBORAH, AROSE' (JUDGES 4–5): A PENTECOSTAL RECEPTION HISTORY OF DEBORAH TOWARD WOMEN IN MINISTRY

RICK WADHOLM, JR[*]

Prophet and Judge: A Mother in Israel

In the cycles of Israel's rebellions and Yahweh's judgments and de-
liverances found in the book of Judges, one encounters Deborah as
a woman of the Spirit (without the Deborah texts explicitly mentioning the Spirit). In Judges 4–5, Deborah is introduced as the one who
leads Israel, providing prophecies and judgments prior to her leading
Israel (and accompanying Barak) into deliverance from the Canaan-
ites led by General Sisera. A narrative prose account is provided for
this deliverance in Judges 4, with a song sung with prophetic poetic
license by Deborah and Barak in Judges 5 concerning the previous
account. The introduction of Deborah would not only cause pause
to readers (both ancient and contemporary) for gendering issues, but
also as the introduction of how Yahweh would once again deliver his
wayward people from the judgment they have brought upon themselves by his hand. Deborah's tale and song, inspired and inspiring,
capture the imagination of readers and arouse potential for a re-con-
ception of women in ministry, not least surprising among Pentecostal

[*] Rick Wadholm, Jr (PhD, Bangor University, UK) is an independent scholar
based in Ellendale, ND, USA.

communities who have (as is demonstrated below) called for women to preach (sometimes using this synonymously with prophesying). Despite this appropriation of the texts, some early Pentecostals still placed limitations upon women serving in certain ecclesiastical roles.

The prophetic figure of Deborah is often treated as an anomaly among the other judges and concerning women in leadership. Yet it seems that prophetic figures themselves are anomalous, as are positive characters in the book of Judges. If anything, the 'anomaly' of Deborah appears to have been intended to indicate the *very type* of prophetic character necessary to lead Israel well when read against the backdrop of the succeeding judges who show increasing failures in righteousness and ability to lead Israel into continued newness of life. [1] As such, Deborah stands above the sons of Israel. Indeed, she rightfully stands as a mother in Israel. One might even say (albeit anachronistically) she stands as a mother in the Church. Further still, she is often portrayed as the one indicating the very ideal forms of leadership within the Pentecostal tradition/s. It is in this vein that I have attempted to hear Deborah along with the early Pentecostal sisters and brothers to establish a constructive theology of women in ministry. This study is not intended to address directly the issues of women holding any and every ecclesiastical role, but does suggest movements toward such. Instead, I propose that the proclamations of Deborah, as they have been employed by our Pentecostal forebears, serve as an example for modern Spirit-empowered women called to proclaim the full gospel to the whole world. This reading along with those of early Pentecostals is followed by a closer literary and theological reading within the milieu of contemporary biblical scholarship upon these texts as a way of noting similarities and contrasts towards a re-hearing of Judges 4–5 concerning Deborah and women in ministry.

---

[1] V.P. Hamilton, *Handbook on the Historical Books: Joshua, Judges, Ruth, Samuel, Kings, Chronicles, Ezra-Nehemiah, Esther* (Grand Rapids: Baker Academic, 2001), p. 119. Hamilton will specifically describe Deborah as one of two 'exemplary judges'. On Othniel as the 'ideal' judge, see R. Wadholm Jr, *A Theology of the Spirit in the Former Prophets: A Pentecostal Perspective* (Cleveland, TN: CPT Press, 2018), pp. 122-24, 210.

A Pentecostal Reception History of Deborah

In seeking to hear these texts of Judges 4–5 through a Pentecostal reception history (akin to the *Wirkungsgeschichte* I have offered elsewhere regarding other texts),[2] early Pentecostal periodicals were consulted that addressed these texts in relation to the question of women in ministry. Those extant copies which are included here as containing such references include *Confidence* (an independent British periodical connected to A.A. Boddy) and *The Latter Rain Evangel* (Stone Church, Chicago), along with the periodicals of multiple Pentecostal denominations: *The Church of God Evangel* (Church of God), *The White Wing Messenger* (Church of God of Prophecy), *The Pentecostal Holiness Advocate* (Pentecostal Holiness Church), *The Weekly Evangel* and *The Pentecostal Evangel* (Assemblies of God), and *Foursquare Crusader* and *The Bridal Call* (Foursquare Church). The years consulted cover 1914–35. While other periodicals were published in this period (and shortly preceding it), no extant copies contained such references to Deborah toward women in ministry. Further, while there are likely other materials, which may address this issue (sermons, tracts, booklets, books, etc.), none of these were consulted for this study. The periodicals themselves offer comments via submitted articles (often unsigned), prophetic calls, editorials, sermon notes, public debates, meeting notes, and Sunday school lessons. Such an approach as is offered here not only allows but encourages readers to hear early Pentecostal engagement between biblical text (Judges 4–5) and contemporary context. However, it misses the many unpublished and no longer extant published voices of early Pentecostals (notably of the early Majority World, African American, Latino, and Oneness Pentecostal fellowships).

Confidence
Speaking at the Sunderland Convention in England in 1914, a 'Pastor Paul' of Berlin shared about a 'Woman's Place in the Church'. Using Deborah as an example, he contended that despite the Apostle Paul's concern for women not to lead men, that sometimes 'if there are not men, the Lord would take a Deborah, because there [*sic*] Barak was unable to come with Deborah'.[3] This argument was used by Pastor

---

[2] Wadholm, *A Theology of the Spirit*, pp. 65-118.
[3] Pastor Paul, 'Woman's Place in the Church', *Confidence* 7.11 (November 1914), pp. 208-209, 212-14 (209).

Paul in order to contend that the German Pentecostal congregations were on 'Bible lines'. Mentioning that women are overly dictated by the heart rather than by the head as men, he argued that women should be permitted to exercise in the church every gift given by God, but without exercising authority over a man.[4] Pastor Paul clarified that he believed women were teachers within small 'assemblies' in Corinth, but were not permitted to teach in the 'church' gathering that included all of the assemblies of Corinth.[5]

The Latter Rain Evangel

At a camp meeting on June 30, 1932, J.N. Hoover emphatically defends women's call to the task of preaching, using Deborah as an exemplar. This leads him to proclaim that Jesus led 'woman up and out of the clutch of cruel and selfish men' and gave 'her a public and conspicuous place in the great and blessed work of Christianity'.[6]

Church of God, Cleveland, Tennessee

Numerous editorials in these periodicals addressed the issue of women preaching and serving in ordained and/or pastoral ministry as a point that was regularly being addressed to Pentecostal ministers and publications. The Church of God includes several such pieces. The Sept. 11, 1915 editorial in *The Church of God Evangel* makes use of Deborah as one of numerous examples of women 'preaching' in the Scriptures and thus counters an argument against women being permitted to preach (though still withholding the office of pastor).[7]

Several *Evangel* articles include references to Deborah as justification for women in ministry. The editor of *The Church of God Evangel* in 1935 issued a prophetic call based on Deborah's example for women to be called to mission's work stating, 'Women have a work and ministry as well as the men'.[8] Mrs Gann, 1928, affirmed the prophetic and preaching ministry of women as Deborah did in her own day,[9] and E.C. Clark, 1935, contended from Scripture for the right of women to preach, using Deborah as an OT example. He says,

---

[4] Pastor Paul, 'Woman's Place in the Church', p. 213.

[5] Pastor Paul, 'Woman's Place in the Church', p. 214.

[6] J.N. Hoover, 'Women Preachers – Is it Scriptural?', *LRE* 24.11 (August 1932), pp. 7-9 (9).

[7] 'Editorial', *CGE* 6.37 (September 11, 1915), pp. 1, 4. The editorial was likely authored by S.W. Latimer.

[8] Editor, 'Missions', *CGE* 26.37 (November 16, 1935), p. 7.

[9] Mrs A. Gann, 'Woman's Work', *CGE* 19.48 (December 8, 1928), p. 3.

The gospel itself may be freely administered by the Holy Spirit thru [*sic*] men or women and there seems to be no difference in a sense in their calling. However, as a general rule, the government of the Church has been placed in the hands of the elders and deacons. ... I trust this argument will commend itself unto your conscience and that you will allow that God has as much right to use the women to dispense the Word of Jesus Christ as He had to use the mouth of a dumb ass to restrain a disobedient prophet.[10]

Church of God of Prophecy

The White Wing Messenger, the official organ of the Church of God of Prophecy, includes two submitted articles in 1929–1930 that briefly tied Deborah to the issue of women in ministry. Mrs Larkin Taylor points to Deborah as one of many women in Scripture empowered by the Spirit to preach and prophesy, even if things were out of 'divine order' by having a 'woman judge over them'.[11] A briefer comment is offered by Stanley R. Ferguson who lists Deborah immediately alongside Barak as a 'judge' as an example of 'men' whom God called.[12]

Pentecostal Holiness Church

The Pentecostal Holiness Advocate includes several submitted articles and one editorial on Deborah's ministry. R.B. Hayes, in 1918, contends for women preaching as a sign of the outpoured Spirit and being 'red hot for God'.[13] He argues that only when churches 'backslide and compromise and tone down' are women elbowed out of the pulpit by men more convinced of formalizing doctrine and creeds. He argues further that women have always been empowered by the Spirit to preach (and prophesy); his reading of the Scriptures leads him to mark Deborah as a prime example. W. Egioff, 1927, contends that Deborah was only raised up as a judge because 'there could not be found a man of valor in the Lord'.[14] Paul F. Beacham, 1930, provides an editorial with answers to multiple questions regarding the ordination of women, women as pastors, and biblical support for

---

[10] E.C. Clark, 'Women Preachers', *CGE* 26.10 (May 4, 1935), p. 5.
[11] Mrs L. Taylor, 'Women Preachers', *WWM* 6.6 (March 23, 1929), p. 4.
[12] S.R. Ferguson, 'Touch Not God's Anointed', *WWM* 7.16 (August 2, 1930), pp. 1, 4 (4).
[13] R.B. Hayes, 'Women Preaching', *PHA* 2.11 (July 11, 1918), p. 6.
[14] W. Egioff, 'Ruth', *PHA* 11.10 (July 7, 1927), pp. 2-4 (2).

deaconesses.[15] He makes use of Deborah in his defense of the question of ordination by also appealing to Scripture sanctioning women to ministry and the absence of biblical censure of women to ministry. Then he follows by naming women who were ministers in formal senses – including Deborah – and among the prophetesses and precursors of Joel's prophecy employed by Peter on the Day of Pentecost.[16]

Assemblies of God

Within the Assemblies of God, numerous editorials and Sunday School lessons deliberated over Deborah in relation to women in ministry. E.N. Bell, editor of *The Weekly Evangel*, answers the question in September 1916: 'Has a woman the Bible right to be pastor over an assembly of Apostolic Faith saints? If so, explain 1 Tim. 2:12.'[17] Bell argues that women are to be permitted to serve as pastors in a 'temporary' fashion if there is 'no man at that place' who is 'prepared' to take the pastorate. He cries out, 'If God will raise up now some Deborah who can give rest and peace to the Pentecostal people for forty years (as the Biblical account concludes), I will only praise Him and leave God to attend to His own business'. In a 1921 response to a similar question regarding women in ministry, Bell neither supports nor denies women the right to administer communion or water baptism, but makes use of Deborah as an example of a woman doing what a man failed to do and thus explains women only carrying out such functions if no man is present and capable of doing so.[18] Likewise, A.P. Collins in February 1917 thanks God 'for the Deborahs in the Pentecostal work', even as he notes such are raised up because 'there are no men whom God can use'.[19] H.C. Ball, in a 1934 issue of *The Pentecostal Evangel*, testifies that since no men were answering the call to carry the gospel to Cuba so two women – H. May Kelty, missionary to Argentina and the border of Mexico, and Anna Sanders, missionary to Mexico – were answering the call to go as 'in the days of Deborah, [when] there was no man to judge Israel'.[20]

---

[15] P.F. Beacham, 'Editorial', *PHA* (August 7, 1930), pp. 9-10.

[16] Beacham, 'Editorial', p. 9.

[17] E.N. Bell, 'Editorial', *WE* 155 (September 2, 2016), p. 8.

[18] E.N. Bell, 'Questions and Answers', *PE* 374-375 (January 8, 1921), p. 10.

[19] A.P. Collins, 'Pentecostal Bible Course', *WE* 175 (February 3, 1917), p. 13.

[20] H.C. Ball, 'The Gospel in Foreign Lands', *PE* 1073 (November 10, 1934), pp. 18-19 (18).

Pentecostal Use of the International Sunday School Lesson of July 1933

The summer of 1933 saw multiple of the periodicals that were following the biblical texts provided as an International Sunday School lesson[21] pertaining to Deborah and found ways of potentially addressing the question of women in ministry. Myer Pearlman, in *The Pentecostal Evangel*, notes in the Sunday school lesson on Deborah that while priesthood was determined by numerous criteria (including gender), the prophetic office was for whomever received the filling of the Spirit of God.[22] That same week, the Sunday school lesson in *The Church of God Evangel* covering Deborah never broaches the specific subject of women preaching, but does refer to Deborah as 'only a feminine prophet' who would have found being a 'handmaiden of the Lord or a housekeeper' as being more 'in keeping with her domestic life'.[23] The same subject covered in the *Foursquare Crusader* emphasizes that God chose to 'speak through a woman' and that Deborah was a woman whose 'appointment by God was generally recognized by the people'.[24] The manuscript of a sermon (likely influenced by this Sunday school text) published on July 27, 1933, by S.A. Bishop (Assistant General Superintendent of the Pentecostal Holiness Church) on the text of Deborah's song in Judges 5 issues a call to action heeding the words of Deborah as she cursed those who did not respond to the call to arms. While this sermon does not specify a call for women to answer, it also does not deny such.[25] It would seem that these four periodicals discussing this particular text from the Sunday School curriculum were ambiguous (at best) regarding women in pastoral leadership, but all of them proclaimed some need for women to respond, as Deborah had before them, to the empowering call of the Lord to preach or prophesy.

Foursquare Church

Not surprisingly, the publications of the Foursquare Church founded by Sister Aimee Semple McPherson have the most to say with regard

---

[21] On the origin and history of the International Sunday School lessons (though this volume does not include the particular lesson for this year), see E.W. Rice and J. McConaughy (eds.), *Handbook on the Origin and History of the International Uniform Sunday-School Lessons* (Philadelphia: American Sunday-School Union, 1922).

[22] M. Pearlman, 'The Sunday School Lesson', *PE* 1006 (July 8, 1933), p. 19.

[23] 'Sunday School Lesson', *CGE* 24.19 (July 8, 1933), p. 12.

[24] 'International Sunday School Lesson', *FC* (July 5, 1933), p. 6.

[25] S.A. Bishop, 'Our Weekly Sermon', *PHA* 17.13 (July 27, 1933), pp. 2-3, 9-11.

to women in ministry and connecting this call to Deborah. An un-named article reporting the British crusades of McPherson in 1928 states, 'Immense auditoriums have failed to house the crowds that flocked to the standard raised for God by this modern Deborah'.[26] Another anonymous article in the June 1933 issue of *The Bridal Call Foursquare* compares McPherson to Deborah as a woman to lead many to victory in these last days, noting that 'God has again chose [*sic*] a women [*sic*] to be among the greatest of His leaders'.[27] Accord-ing to the article, McPherson did not seek a place of leadership nor greatness in the public, but only 'an earnest love for souls and a sin-cere desire to serve … when the call of God came'.[28]

McPherson proclaimed at a baccalaureate sermon in January 1930 that the end was near, and thus, the work of the last days must com-mence with everyone contributing to the work. She beckons for there to be 'room for both the servant and the handmaiden' as calling men and women both to this work. As she commends the many men who have carried forward the gospel (likening them to the saints of Scrip-ture), she furthers this commendation with a call to all of her sisters,

> Go on with the Word of God! God has used the womenfolks! As I look back into those other days, I remember Miriam and the sweet music of her timbrel and how God used her. He used Deb-orah too, as she went forth with flaming banners, leading her troups [*sic*], conquering and triumphant. She was a real leader, a statesman, a politician, and a devout follower of Jehovah … Marching! Marching! Those precious women of yesterday! Tramp! Tramp! Tramp! An unbroken, steady line of heroic womanhood! It was not only yesterday that the Lord used women, He has used them since time began and is still using them, praise the Lord![29]

In 1932, McPherson answers naysayers who might question whether women ought to serve as preachers, 'If the Lord allowed Deborah to lead an army' then women must indeed join in the last

---

[26] 'London Paper Announces Sister's Coming Visit', *FC* (September 19, 1928), pp. 1, 5 (5).
[27] '… and Your Daughters', *BCF* 17.1 (June 1933), pp. 11, 19 (11). The article indicates it was sent as a letter to the journal.
[28] '… and Your Daughters', p. 11.
[29] A. Semple McPherson, 'The Servants and the Handmaidens', *BC* (Feb 1930), pp. 5-6, 32.

day harvest as kingdom workers.[30] In a 1934 article titled 'Little Women', McPherson points to Deborah as one of many women in Scripture who demonstrated the place of women 'in politics, in economics, and in the church'.[31]

The focus upon Deborah as 'mother'[32] is offered numerous times in the Foursquare literature pointing to the leading, directing, and teaching function for women to contribute toward the life of the church. One author in May 1930 considers Deborah as 'a mother in Israel' worthy of inclusion for a study outline of 'Honored Mothers'.[33] Similarly, a Sunday school lesson in the July 16, 1930 issue of the *Foursquare Crusader* specifically covers Deborah as the lesson topic. The writer proposes that God is only looking for those who by faith

---

[30] A. McPherson Hutton, 'The Harvest Is Ended', *FC* 7.8 (December 7, 1932), pp. 1-2 (2).

[31] A. Semple McPherson, 'Little Women', *FC* 8.35 (June 13, 1934), pp. 2-4, 8.

[32] I was unable to locate any direct correlation between the language of 'mother' in relation to Deborah and the traditionally African American Pentecostal churches' titular use of 'mother' for leading women within the movement (Church of God in Christ, Pentecostal Assemblies of the World, the Church of Our Lord Jesus Christ, and Mt. Calvary Holy Church of America). 'Mother' Lizzie Woods Robinson served just such a leading role with this title from 1911–45 in the Church of God in Christ, see http://www.cogic.org/womensdepartment/about-us/former-general-supervisors/mother-lizzie-robinson/ (accessed January 9, 2019). It is unclear what Scriptures might have informed the African American Pentecostal tradition toward such language, though the potential connection to Deborah in Judges 5 offers itself as one of many possible texts which may have been used. It was suggested to me in a personal email (January 9, 2019) from Revd Dr Jane Caulton that the title 'Mother' may in fact date back to the days of US slavery as a title indicating 'compassion and wisdom' that seemed to her to be 'a social term adopted by the church'. She indicated the following resources with regard to 'the development of the social construct of church mothers': A. Butler, 'Church Mothers and Migration in the Church of God in Christ', in B.B. Schweiger and D.G. Matthews (eds.), *Religion in the American South: Protestants and Others in History and Culture* (Chapel Hill: University of North Carolina Press, 2004), pp. 195-218; A. Butler, *Women in the Church of God in Christ: Making a Sanctified World* (Chapel Hill: University of North Carolina Press, 2007); C.T. Gilkes, '"Together in Harness": Women's Traditions in the Sanctified Church', *Signs* 10.4 (1985), pp. 678-99; C.T. Gilkes, 'The Role of Women in the Sanctified Church', *Journal of Religious Thought* 43.1 (1986), pp. 24-41; C.T. Gilkes, 'The Roles of Church and Community Mothers: Ambivalent American Sexism or Fragmented African Familyhood?', *Journal of Feminist Studies in Religion* 2.1 (1986), pp. 41-59; C.E. Hardy, 'Fauset's (Missing) Pentecostals: Church Mothers, Remaking Respectability, and Religious Modernism', in E.E. Curtis and D.B. Sigler (eds.), *New Black Gods* (Bloomington: Indiana University Press, 2009), pp. 15-23; J.W. Peterson, 'Age of Wisdom: Elderly Black Women in Family and Church', in Jay Sokolovsky (ed.), *The Cultural Context of Aging: Worldwide Perspectives* (Westport, CT: Bergin & Garvey, 1990), pp. 213-28.

[33] N.H.C., 'Honored Mothers', *FC* 4.24 (May 7, 1930), p. 5.

will believe his Word and who join themselves to him, and in doing so, be empowered for the work of redemption.[34] The lesson indicates at one point that Deborah was chosen because there 'was no man among the people of Israel that God could have used to be Judge over His people, so He chose a woman'.[35] The point of the lesson is given at the end: 'There have been great and noble women who have done noble things for God in heathen lands. God can use girls as well as boys to help spread the gospel'.[36] In a 1933 Mother's Day message by Charles H. Babcock, Deborah prayed, as mother of Israel, and those prayers 'transformed the nation from cowards to heroes'.[37]

The ascription of leadership to Deborah as part of an overall contention for women in ministry is also found numerous times in Foursquare literature. J.C. Kellogg contends that the prophecy of Joel concerning the Spirit poured out upon women to prophesy and preach is being fulfilled in his day as a sign of the soon coming of the Lord.[38] As one of many evidences, he points to Deborah as one of the 'women leaders' of Scripture. Quoting A.B. Simpson, Kellogg notes 'It is too late in the day to question the public ministry of women. The facts of God's providence and the fruits of God's Spirit are stronger than all our theological fancies.'[39] In choosing characters to offer studies to highlight, the *Foursquare Crusader* in 1932 focuses upon Deborah as 'a national leader' in a multi-week series where she is described among Abraham, Joseph, Moses, Deborah, Ruth, Samuel, Saul, David, and Solomon. Of note, the author selected Deborah and Ruth to highlight when numerous men could have been named in such a list.[40] *The Bridal Call Foursquare* in July 1933 notes how women the likes of Deborah have led the way in the work of God, often when 'men have failed to complete their obligation to God in service'.[41] These women are thus compelled to carry the good news everywhere it is not being preached.

---

[34] 'Sunday School Lesson', *FC* (July 16, 1930), p. 7.
[35] 'Sunday School Lesson', p. 7.
[36] 'Sunday School Lesson', p. 7.
[37] C.H. Babcock, 'The Supreme Value of Motherhood', *BCF* 16.12 (May 1933), p. 7; similarly, see Babcock, 'Enthronement of Motherhood', *FC* 12.31 (May 17, 1933), pp. 2, 8 (8).
[38] J.C. Kellogg, 'The Sign of the Outpouring of the Spirit and Women in Prophecy Is Shown in the Word of God', *FC* (May 4, 1932), p. 3.
[39] Kellogg, 'The Sign', 3.
[40] 'Bible Characters', *FC* 6.40 (July 20, 1932), p. 8.
[41] 'Woman's Ministry in Serving the Lord', *BCF* 17.2 (July 1933), p. 8.

Rheba Crawford, Assistant Pastor at Angelus Temple, responded in an April 1934 public debate regarding women preaching, '[W]oman has climbed up into a pulpit and into a place of joint leadership, not because man has given her a helping hand, but because her capacity for understanding and devotion to a cause has made of her a fit minister to be used in the service of the King'.[42] Sister Aimee took up the challenge of her opponents at the debate to indicate that it was Deborah who acted in faith as a prophetess, which she repeatedly claims as indicating specifically the act of preaching.[43] Crawford's and McPherson's responses serve as the headline news for the April 1934 issue: 'Foursquare Program Proves Women Should Preach Gospel'.[44]

Finally, a sermon in December 1934 by Rheba Crawford points to Deborah as one of several examples for women who take leadership not 'to honor herself', but because Deborah was 'a Mother in Israel' and could not but act on behalf of those suffering.[45] Deborah demonstrates a woman not seeking self-aggrandizement, but the betterment of her community, and a woman who stands for righteousness. Crawford closes her sermon with the call, 'There is a place in the Kingdom for the woman after God's own heart. There is a work in the kingdom for such women, for he has said, "In the latter days my handmaidens shall prophesy (preach)." May God touch us and make us women after His own heart!'[46]

Receiving their Testimonies

Our Pentecostal mothers and fathers have offered their teachings and testimonies regarding women in ministry by their own hearing of Deborah: judge, prophet, and mother. The extant early literature reveals three key features. First, early Pentecostals were regularly assailed from many sides not to allow women to preach. However, they persisted and employed Deborah as a testimony to endorse women empowered by the Spirit to do just that. This endorsement required

---

[42] 'Should Women Preach the Gospel? (Debate Held in Angelus Temple)', *FC* 8.26 (April 11, 1934), pp. 1-2, 4, 7-8 (2).

[43] 'Should Women Preach the Gospel?', pp. 7-8.

[44] 'Should Women Preach the Gospel?', p. 1.

[45] R. Crawford, 'Women on Trial', *BCF* (December 5, 1934), pp. 4, 15, 19 (15).

[46] Crawford, 'Women on Trial', p. 19.

an interpretation (sometimes implicit, sometimes explicit) of prophecy equated as preaching. Second, the endowment of the Spirit upon women to preach and prophesy was deemed a testimony to signal the soon return of Jesus and thus a latter rain outpouring of the Spirit in preparation for the last harvest before the Day of the Lord. This eschatological element gave empowerment toward encouraging and calling for women to respond to the Spirit in preaching and carrying forward the mission of God to the ends of the earth. Third, the issue of 'leading' was contentious, at times treating the judging function of Deborah as only a witness to women to do ministry in general or to do it only until such a time as a man fitted to such ministry should be raised up. Others saw in Deborah a woman leading a nation (as judge and especially 'mother') in transformation toward redemption as a call to take up the tasks at hand (including the likes of the right to vote, prohibition, care for the poor, and missions). Still others included within their reading of Deborah's story as empowerment to plant churches and persist in pastoring them, even as they did so, confessing that perhaps this was never an ideal, nor that women desired to attain to such, but feeling the compulsion of the enabling Spirit to do so.

Arise, O Deborah!: A Literary Reading

While it remains beyond this work to hear the full texts of Judges 4–5, the key claims pertinent to the early Pentecostal literature can be found in the narrative of Judg. 4.4–5 regarding Deborah's role as prophet and judge, and then in the poetry of Judg. 5.7b regarding Deborah arising as a 'mother in Israel'. As such, these three verses are commented upon briefly toward a Pentecostal appreciation of women in ministry. These three terms – prophet, judge, mother – describe the role and function of Deborah and are each taken up by the early Pentecostals toward understanding the role and function of women in ministry (as noted in the early Pentecostal reception section). However, while we have heard the early Pentecostal voices, we should also remain attuned to hearing yet further toward the orientation of these texts: both biblical and Pentecostal. Toward this end, the texts are engaged via a literary and theological approach that seeks to hear these texts in their canonical locations, as those which are heard by the Church and specifically toward a Pentecostal hearing in light of the foregoing early Pentecostal reception history.

Arise, Prophet and Judge: A Tale to Tell

> Now Deborah, a female prophet, a fiery woman,[47] judged Israel at that time and she was seated under the Palm of Deborah between Ramah and Bethel in the hill (country) of Ephraim and the sons of Israel came up to her for judging (Judg. 4.4–5).[48]

Following the lead of Tammi J. Schneider,[49] the flow of the text introducing Deborah places the emphasis upon her being *a woman* and being *a prophetess* over and against her familial relationship.[50] Schneider also highlights the leading function of Deborah prior to military leadership in contrast to the other named judges.[51] In these ways, Deborah stands above her supposed peers. She stands above the other judges in several distinct ways. Deborah is the only judge in the Book of Judges that is actually described as specifically 'judging' (שׁפט Judg. 4.4).[52] This feature should not be quickly dismissed. While others might be described as being raised up to deliver Israel, only Deborah is described as carrying on the judicial function in her ongoing care of the tribes prior to their military deliverance. Further, Deborah as prophetess holds a unique role among the judges of Israel as one attuned personally to hearing from and speaking for Yahweh. 'While other judges talk to God or about God, Deborah is the one judge

---

[47] There is some debate about the meaning and sense of 'Lappidoth'. While the most natural reading of this prose section appears to be the sense that Deborah is the 'wife of [a man named] Lappidoth', it is questioned that her husband is never named elsewhere in the prose section and never appears in the poetry of ch. 5. The alternate reading suggests she was a 'woman of torches' or a 'fiery woman'. On which, see S.E. Haddox, 'Gendering Violence and Violating Gender in Judges 4–5', *Conversations with the Biblical World* 33 (2013), p. 75.

[48] All translations are my own unless otherwise noted.

[49] T.J. Schneider, *Judges*, (Berit Olam Studies in Hebrew Narrative and Poetry, Collegeville, MN: Liturgical Press, 2000), pp. 65-67.

[50] This is akin to the introductory descriptors for Othniel and Ehud previously in Judges that highlight particulars about them prior to familial connections.

[51] Schneider, *Judges*, p. 68.

[52] M.J. Boda, 'Recycling Heaven's Words: Receiving and Retrieving Divine Revelation in the Historiography of Judges', in M.J. Boda and L.M. Wray Beal (eds.), *Prophets, Prophecy, and Ancient Israelite Historiography* (Winona Lake, IN: Eisenbrauns, 2013), pp. 43-67 (50); a point which R. Nelson seems to have missed, see Nelson, *Judges: A Critical and Rhetorical Commentary* (New York: Bloomsbury, 2017), p. 78.

who speaks for God'.[53] Again, this should not be quickly dismissed. Numerous prophetic figures (including angelic beings) appear in the text providing words from Yahweh, but Deborah is the sole judge also functioning explicitly as a prophet, and she also appears as the first named prophet after Moses. While one 'from among your brothers' (Deut. 18.15) was expected, it is a sister who arises as 'mother' in Israel.[54] Thus, the reader encounters Deborah seated above the others as one who will arise on behalf of Israel.

It has, however, become commonplace to somehow dismiss the unique function of Deborah simply because no man was available to fill the roles of judge and prophet in those days. However, the text never states such, despite the tendencies of interpreters (mostly male) to read such into the text. By way of two examples among OT commentators, Bruce Waltke summarizes, 'God raised a woman to lead Israel because the Israelite men were cowards and declined leadership'.[55] According to Trent Butler, in Judg. 5.7, Deborah arose 'when all looked hopeless and no masculine leaders stepped forward'.[56] It appears for some men that the Spirit's choice was the will of the LORD specifically because of her personal usefulness rather than others' failure to be useful. They seem more intent on deriving this choice as a second-best option, demonstrating a clear gendered bias in their readings.

However, other readers show a penchant for receiving the self-witness of the Spirit toward a better hearing of such texts.[57] The

---

[53] Hamilton, *Handbook on the Historical Books*, p. 119.
[54] L.R. Martin, *Judging the Judges: Pentecostal Theological Perspectives on the Book of Judges* (Cleveland, TN: CPT Press, 2018), p. 41.
[55] B.K. Waltke and C. Yu, *An Old Testament Theology: An Exegetical, Canonical, and Thematic Approach* (Grand Rapids: Zondervan, 2007), p. 600; similarly, T.C. Butler, *Judges* (Word Biblical Commentary 8; Grand Rapids: Zondervan, 2009) claims, 'The emphasis on her gender points to the lack of men to fill such roles', p. 94.
[56] Butler, *Judges*, p. 139.
[57] Even the ninth-century Rabanus Maurus has discerned the testimony of the Spirit above a gendered preference or prerequisite. Rabanus seems to interrupt his allegorical reading of Judges at one point to state:

> … although there were many men who were judges in Israel, of no one of them is it said, as it is said of Deborah, that he is a prophet. In this issue, even the literal meaning offers no small encouragement to the sex of women and it challenges them not to despair because of the weakness of their sex, since they are able to become capable of the gift of prophecy. Let them know and believe

Spirit gives testimony of the Spirit's choice to lead. This happens regardless of tribe (Benjamin, Ephraim, Dan, or Judah), regardless of family (smallest of families or son of a prostitute), regardless of gender, and regardless of personal regard for holiness (Gideon, Jephthah, or Samson). Among these many (ignoble) sons of Israel, a Spirit-ed mother (prophesying and judging) is sought for guidance from the LORD, for decisions, and for a call to take arms against enemies.

Arise, Mother in Israel: A Song to Sing

Judges 5.7b: 'Until I, Deborah, arose // I, a mother in Israel, arose'.[58] While there is a notable absence of the phrase 'the LORD raised up a judge' with regard to Deborah (Othniel: Judg. 3.9; Ehud: Judg. 3.15) in the narrative account of ch. 4, the Song of Deborah in Judg. 5.7b specifically says Deborah 'arose as a mother in Israel'.[59] According to Butler, 'Deborah uses the title ['mother'] to underline her authority and leadership in an Israel sadly lacking in authoritative leaders'.[60] This would be so throughout the period of the judges where leadership seemed always lacking and thus 'men' doing 'whatever they thought was right in their own eyes' (Judg. 17.6; 21.25). One might argue the 'male gaze' predominates in Scripture with few exceptions, but here in the Song of Deborah is just such a place where the

---

that this grace is given according to purity of mind rather than according to the differentiation of the sexes.

This is as cited in M.A. Mayeski, '"Let Women Not Despair": Rabanus Maurus on Women as Prophets', *Theological Studies* 58 (1997), pp. 237-53 (238). At least Rabanus has picked up on the testimony of the individual capabilities (spirit), but falls short of noting the testimony of the Spirit's own choice: gifts of prophesying and judging.

[58] I am following the BHS text (along with the Syriac and Targums) against some other Hebrew manuscripts which do not read in the first person singular. This is also against the third person readings of LXXᴬ, LXXᴮ, and the Old Latin. For some discussion of the LXX witnesses see Butler, *Judges*, p. 117. I have translated as a first person ending while Natalio Fernández Marcos has argued for an emended Hebrew text against the MT, see N.F. Marcos, *Judges* (Biblia Hebraica Quinta 7; Deutsche Bibelgesellschaft), p. 56.

[59] Also noted in Hamilton, *Handbook on the Historical Books*, pp. 119-20.

[60] Butler, *Judges*, p. 140. Butler again seems to suggest by the rhetoric of his comment here that there were no men who were taking the authority that was theirs and thus was left to the leadership of a woman.

mother in Israel is directing the gaze of the men and calling for Israel not simply to do whatever is right in their own eyes.[61]

A number of literary suggestions have been made about Deborah's sung title of 'mother in Israel'. P.C. Craigie compares the Ugaritic descriptions of Anat as warrior goddess with her male warrior assistant specifically pointing to Deborah as 'mother in Israel' as comparable to the Ugaritic title holding a sense of 'progenitress of the people'.[62] J. Cheryl Exum claims that 'mother in Israel' functions comparably to the language in Judges of 'God of Israel'.[63] Though not specifically pointing to this similarity, both Lee Roy Martin and Bruce Herzberg trace the comparable descriptors shared between Deborah and Moses.[64] Herzberg gives detailed notes of specific numerous comparisons between Moses and Deborah as judges, prophets, military leaders, and providing victory songs. Herzberg states, 'Neither song nor story betrays any sense that Deborah's position is inappropriate or dangerous to the social order, that patriarchy is under siege, or – and this is the key element – that anything very unusual is happening'.[65] He goes on to claim, 'It seems highly likely to me that Deborah was seen as … the Moses of her time'.[66]

While these literary links might frame a potential historical literary (and theological) connection for the original audience, a nearer literary connection ought to be noted in the contrast of the two mothers mentioned in Judges 5: the mother of Israel and the mother of Sisera.[67] Perhaps in the literary echoing of these two mothers, readers might also see one mother who simply tends to home (often seen as the woman's place) looking longingly out her window to see her son return from doing what men do. This mother would then stand in stark contrast with the prophetic mother of Israel who leads her sons into battle as one declaring the word of the LORD to them (as

---

[61] C.J. Sharp, *Irony and Meaning in the Hebrew Bible* (Bloomington: Indiana University Press, 2009), p. 86.

[62] The Ugaritic *ybmt.limm* is used ten times by his count, P.C. Craigie, 'Deborah and Anat: A Study of Poetic Imagery (Judges 5)', *Zeitschrift für die alttestamentliche Wissenschaft* 90.3 (1978), pp. 374-81 (376-77).

[63] J.C. Exum, 'Mother in Israel', in Letty Russell (ed.), *Feminist Interpretation of the Bible* (Philadelphia: Westminster Press, 1985), pp. 73-85.

[64] Martin, *Judging the Judges*, pp. 42-44; and B. Herzberg, 'Deborah and Moses', *Journal for the Study of the Old Testament* 38.1 (2013), pp. 15-33.

[65] Herzberg, 'Deborah and Moses', p. 32.

[66] Herzberg, 'Deborah and Moses', p. 33.

[67] Butler, *Judges*, p. 129.

showing what women might, or even should, do). Thus, Deborah's role as mother in Israel 'seems to be one of calling her children [to] stand up for themselves, mustering them into a battle against oppressors'.[68] This is precisely the call issued within the early Pentecostal periodicals for women, like Deborah, to arise by the empowerment of the Spirit and to lead many into the full gospel salvation of the Lord. For Pentecostals, the use of Deborah as a Spirit-ed woman leading the charge to victory as evidence of the outpoured Spirit and soon-coming King stands in contrast to the reading of many contemporary scholars, who seem more intent on locating Deborah within their reconstructed histories than in her serving as an exemplar and witness for the contemporary community of God's people.

Arise, Mothers of the Church

Contributors to the various Pentecostal periodicals provided diverse voices. Some of these voices (like the scholars noted above) contended for women to respond like Deborah when men could not be found to lead the mission of the church. Others saw the testimony of Deborah as a straightforward and clarion call for women to respond to the Spirit and do what the Lord desired for the advancement of the kingdom of God, and as witness to Jesus' soon return. Notably, many of the early Pentecostals showed preference for women not pastoring (as noted by the few who mention such), but *with one voice* they *all* called for women to preach and prophesy, to carry forward the mission of God throughout the nations. It seems necessary to restore such clarity in light of what the Spirit is doing among our daughters to raise up mothers of the church, and to see the nations brought into the light of that soon-coming kingdom.

As many of the early Pentecostals saw in Deborah the call to respond as preachers of the gospel, they likewise could not but hear the words of Ps. 68.11: 'The LORD giveth the word: the women that publish the tidings are a great host' (ASV). The singularity of the witness of Deborah among the many sons of Israel would find a fulfillment in the great host of women publishing the tidings of the soon-coming King Jesus.[69] Indeed, the 'account of Deborah accentuates

---

[68] Haddox, 'Gendering Violence and Violating Gender in Judges 4–5', p. 71.

[69] Nelson, *Judges*, p. 116. Perhaps we might note as Richard Nelson contends that the author of Psalm 68 'knew Deborah's Song' by allusions and motifs shared between them. This seems to have been realized at some level by the early

God's readiness to send his Spirit upon women and "men" to bring about God's plans and purposes (cf. Gal. 3.28)'.[70] May we join our testimony with that story of judge and prophet, that song of a mother in Israel, and declare, 'Arise! Preach! Prophesy! Lead on!'

Bibliography

Boda, Mark J., and Lissa M. Wray Beal (eds.), *Prophets, Prophecy, and Ancient Israelite Historiography* (Winona Lake, IN: Eisenbrauns, 2013).

Butler, Anthea, *Women in the Church of God in Christ: Making a Sanctified World* (Chapel Hill: University of North Carolina Press, 2007).

Butler, Trent C., *Judges* (Word Biblical Commentary, 8; Grand Rapids: Zondervan, 2009).

Craigie, P.C., 'Deborah and Anat: A Study of Poetic Imagery (Judges 5)', *Zeitschrift Für Die Alttestamentliche Wissenschaft* 90.3 (1978), pp. 374-81.

Curtis, Edward E., and Danielle B. Sigler (eds.), *New Black Gods* (Bloomington: Indiana University Press, 2009).

Gilkes, C.T., 'The Role of Women in the Sanctified Church', *Journal of Religious Thought* 43.1 (1986), pp. 24-41.

—'The Roles of Church and Community Mothers: Ambivalent American Sexism or Fragmented African Familyhood?', *Journal of Feminist Studies in Religion* 2.1 (1986), pp. 41-59.

—'"Together in Harness": Women's Traditions in the Sanctified Church', *Signs* 10.4 (1985), pp. 678-99.

Haddox, S.E., 'Gendering Violence and Violating Gender in Judges 4–5', *Conversations with the Biblical World* 33 (2013), pp. 67-81.

Hamilton, Victor P., *Handbook on the Historical Books: Joshua, Judges, Ruth, Samuel, Kings, Chronicles, Ezra–Nehemiah, Esther* (Grand Rapids: Baker Academic, 2001).

Herzberg, B., 'Deborah and Moses', *Journal for the Study of the Old Testament* 38.1 (2013), pp. 15-33.

Martin, Lee Roy, *Judging the Judges: Pentecostal Theological Perspectives on the Book of Judges* (Cleveland, TN: CPT Press, 2018).

Mayeski, M.A., '"Let Women Not Despair": Rabanus Maurus on Women as Prophets', *Theological Studies* 58 (1997), pp. 237-53.

Moore, Rickie D. and Brian N. Peterson, *Voice, Word, and Spirit: A Pentecostal Old Testament Survey* (Nashville: Abingdon Press, 2017).

Pentecostals who made such connections (albeit perhaps not through such critical methodology).

[70] R.D. Moore and B.N. Peterson, *Voice, Word, and Spirit: A Pentecostal Old Testament Survey* (Nashville: Abingdon Press, 2017), p. 78.

Nelson, Richard D., *Judges: A Critical and Rhetorical Commentary* (New York: Bloomsbury, 2017).

Rice, Edwin W. and James McConaughy (eds.), *Handbook on the Origin and History of the International Uniform Sunday-School Lessons* (Philadelphia: American Sunday-School Union, 1922).

Russell, Letty M., (ed.), *Feminist Interpretation of the Bible* (Philadelphia: Westminster Press, 1985).

Schneider, Tammi J., *Judges* (Berit Olam Studies in Hebrew Narrative and Poetry, Collegeville, MN: Liturgical Press, 2000).

Schweiger, Beth B., and Donald G. Matthews (eds.), *Religion in the American South: Protestants and Others in History and Culture* (Chapel Hill: University of North Carolina Press, 2004).

Sharp, C.J., *Irony and Meaning in the Hebrew Bible* (Bloomington: Indiana University Press, 2009).

Sokolovsky, Jay (ed.), *The Cultural Context of Aging: Worldwide Perspectives* (Westport, CT: Bergin & Garvey, 1990).

Wadholm Jr, Rick, *A Theology of the Spirit in the Former Prophets: A Pentecostal Perspective* (Cleveland, TN: CPT Press, 2018).

Waltke, Bruce K., and Charles Yu, *An Old Testament Theology: An Exegetical, Canonical, and Thematic Approach* (Grand Rapids: Zondervan, 2007).

6

TRULY OUR SISTER?: PENTECOSTAL READINGS OF MARY[1]

LISA P. STEPHENSON[*]

In 1981 the topic of Mary was the designated focus of discussion during the ninth international ecumenical dialogue between Roman Catholics and Pentecostals.[2] The following year, Pentecostal scholar and ecumenist Jerry Sandidge published his reflections on points of agreement and disagreement between Roman Catholics and Pentecostals. In his introduction, Sandidge notes

> there is a great dearth of material written by Pentecostals about Mary. Outside of some discussion centered around the Christmas story and the virgin birth of Jesus, and a few lines about Mary at the wedding of Cana, there is practically nothing on the subject. There are comments by Pentecostals criticizing Roman Catholic charismatics for their veneration of Mary in prayer meetings and conferences. So, it could almost be said that Pentecostals have no

---

[1] The title of the chapter is a play on Elizabeth Johnson's book, *Truly Our Sister: A Theology of Mary in the Communion of Saints* (New York: Continuum, 2003). Whereas Johnson's move is one of lowering Mary from her high accord in Catholicism so that she is situated alongside fellow Catholics as a sister, I am trying to raise Mary up from her general neglect in Pentecostalism so that she is situated alongside fellow Pentecostals as a sister.

[*] Lisa P. Stephenson (PhD, Marquette University) is Professor of Systematic Theology at Lee University, Cleveland, TN, USA.

[2] Jerry L. Sandidge, *Roman Catholic/Pentecostal Dialogue (1977–1982): A Study in Developing Ecumenism* (New York: Peter Lang, 1987).

'view' or 'theology' of Mary, unless it would be negative terms, i.e., those things which are *not* believed about her.[3]

I wish to challenge Sandidge's claim that there is no view or theology of Mary among Pentecostals. That is, while Sandidge is right that there is a great dearth of material written by Pentecostals on Mary, a Pentecostal view of Mary does exist, even if not robust. Therefore, in this essay I examine how various Pentecostals have portrayed Mary, the Mother of Jesus; to do so, I employ a grassroots sampling of Pentecostal periodicals.[4]

My survey of this literature reveals little surprise concerning Pentecostal disdain for Catholic Mariology. Having said this, Pentecostals also affirm Mary in significant ways. The reason for this seemingly bipolar treatment by Pentecostals is rooted in their underlying concern that Catholic Mariology has strayed away from the teachings of Scripture. As one author quips, 'Mariolatry gets no encouragement from Christ's own words'.[5] But at the same time, Charles Conn, a prominent leader in the Church of God (Cleveland, TN), notes:

> It is a pity that the life story of one so precious as Mary should become encumbered with unnecessary and unscriptural legends and myths – suppositions and fabrications that rob her of her warm humanness and realness ... her life needs no further embellishment to make her one of the greatest persons to ever live.[6]

---

[3] Jerry L. Sandidge, 'A Pentecostal Response to Roman Catholic Teaching on Mary', *Pneuma* 4.2 (Fall, 1982), pp. 33-42 (34).

[4] For research on this topic, I utilized the digital collections of the Consortium of Pentecostal Archives (www.pentecostalarchives.org). The periodicals range in date from the beginning to the end of the twentieth century. They are primarily representative of Pentecostal denominations and voices within North America, including several of the largest Pentecostal denominations in that region (e.g., Assemblies of God, Church of God, and Foursquare). Due to the limitations of the search engine, I used the search terms 'Mother Mary' and 'Virgin Mary' to find pertinent articles. In no way does this research exhaust the data, but it does provide a window into Pentecostals' views on the subject, even from leading denominational figures like Charles Conn (Church of God) and Aimee Semple McPherson (Foursquare).

[5] 'The Pulse of a Dying World', *LRE* 22.5 (February, 1930), p. 17; H.C. Ball, 'Revival Work Among the Mexicans', *PE* 903 (June 20, 1931), p. 2; J.C. Kellogg, 'Modern Women in Prophecy', *FC* 6.33 (June 1, 1932), p. 3; 'Passing and Permanent: Newsbriefs from the Christian Perspective', *PE* 2067 (December 20, 1953), p. 7; Ghaly Ibrahim, 'Around the World with Missions: Egypt', *WWM* 32.2 (October 2, 1954), p. 3.

[6] Charles W. Conn, 'God's Favorite Woman', *CGE* (December 13, 1947), p. 14.

Predictably, then, when Pentecostals do focus positively on Mary, their efforts are aimed at uncovering what Rolf McPherson, son of Aimee Semple McPherson, terms the 'true portrait' of Mary by attending to the 'native naturalness of Scripture'.[7] While a 'true' or 'native' Pentecostal portraiture of Mary may be an impossibility, a basic portrait emerges. I turn now to what Pentecostals affirm about Mary and attempt to piece together a Marian mosaic using their varied depictions. Though Pentecostal claims are not always lengthy treatises, taken together they form an intriguing depiction of Mary that indicates Pentecostals do have a theology of Mary.

Mary: The Woman from Nazareth

References to Mary are found in all four Gospels and the book of Acts.[8] Though these texts do not provide many descriptive characteristics about who Mary was or what she was like, Pentecostals have not been shy to supply details. Some Pentecostals found the need to comment on Mary's embodiment. With respect to Mary's physical strength and stature, she is consistently depicted to be small and weak. She is referred to as 'little Mary', who has 'little sandaled feet' that move softly, she is a 'drooping flower' with a 'little form', a 'wee little mother-to-be'.[9] She has 'frail, womanly strength'.[10] With respect to her physical beauty, Pentecostals differ on whether she was considered attractive or not. One author, in trying to emphasize that the reason God chose Mary was because she was humble and lowly, goes so far as to infer from this that there were certainly other women more beautiful than she (because apparently, for this author, beauty and humility are mutually exclusive!).[11] However, Aimee Semple McPherson (henceforth Sister Aimee) disagrees with this assessment

---

[7] Rolf K. McPherson, 'Think on These Things: The Virgin Mary's Place in History,' *FM* 19.12 (December 1947), p. 12. This piece appears again almost verbatim seven years later by the same author: 'The Virgin Mary: Her Position in the Church,' *FM* 27.12 (December 1954), pp. 2, 9-10.

[8] The following are references to Mary in the Gospels and Acts: Mt. 1.16, 18-25, 2.1-23; Mk 3.20-21, 31-35; Lk. 1.26-56, 2.1-52; Jn 2.1-11, 19.25-27; Acts 1.14-15, 2.1-21.

[9] Aimee Semple McPherson, 'Footsteps of Destiny', *BCF* 8.7 (December 1929), pp. 5-8, 29.

[10] Charles W. Conn, 'Unto You', *CGE* 38.42 (December 20, 1947), p. 11.

[11] Alpheus Noseworthy, 'The Savior Which is Christ the Lord', *PHA* 27.32 (December 16, 1943), p. 4.

and claims that the name 'Mary' itself is beautiful and blessed, and men still love for their mother, wife, or sweetheart to bear that name.[12] She imagines Mary with 'great, dark wonderful eyes that glowed so tenderly'.[13] Rolf McPherson shares this view with a different twist. When trying to answer why Mary was chosen to be Christ's mother, he reasons that Mary must have been attractive because Jesus had to look at her for thirty years![14]

Some Pentecostals highlight Mary's economic situation by noting her poor status. When elaborating on what this hardship must have meant for Mary, one author depicts Mary as an unassuming woman living in a meager house, wearing plain clothing, owning very little, and forced to take up the menial tasks of everyday life.[15] Sister Aimee describes Mary packing for the trip to Bethlehem, specifically noting that there was little to pack because she is of a simple, frugal family. And, when it was time to embark on the journey, Sister Aimee imagines Joseph lamenting his lack of earthly goods, 'Oh! ... I wish I had a beautiful chariot in which to take her, that she might rest. Oh, I wish I had money! I never needed much money before, but I wish I had it now. I wish I had a more beautiful home for her. But there is nothing but this little ass to bear her.'[16]

Finally, several Pentecostals create a domestic picture of Mary that echoes certain twentieth-century cultural expectations about the proper sphere for women. Rolf McPherson places Mary in her home when Gabriel visits. He describes Mary as 'quietly engaged in her domestic duties, offering the sacrifice of her daily task'.[17] Charles Conn not only locates Mary in the home, but also infers her personality: 'God favors a girl of quiet and gentle mien [which] is attested by the fact that He sought the mother of His Son in the sanctuary of her

[12] Aimee Semple McPherson, 'Here Comes the Bride', *FC* 13.16 (October 4, 1939), p. 3.
[13] Aimee Semple McPherson, 'Footsteps of Destiny,' p. 6.
[14] Rolf McPherson, 'Think on These Things: The Virgin Mary's Place in History', p. 12; *idem*, 'The Virgin Mary: Her Position in the Church', pp. 2, 9-10.
[15] Bert Edward Williams, 'The Birth of Christ was on This Wise: When God Bestowed Honor on the Poor', *LRE* 25.3 (December 1932), p. 3; and Noseworthy, 'The Savior Which is Christ the Lord', p. 4. Williams and Noseworthy's pieces are almost identical, including the subdivisions, so it is likely that either both were dependent upon the same external source or Noseworthy copies from Williams.
[16] McPherson, 'Footsteps of Destiny', pp. 5-6.
[17] McPherson, 'Think on These Things: The Virgin Mary's Place in History', p. 12; *idem*, 'The Virgin Mary: Her Position in the Church', pp. 2, 9-10.

home, and not in some house of frolic. The capricious, flippant, gig-gling, light-headed type of girl is never a favorite in the court of heaven.'[18] And Sister Aimee surmises that because Mary has come to the home of Joseph, a transformation has taken place 'under the touch of her woman's hand', and that she is responsible for creating a different atmosphere there.[19]

Mary: A Virtuous Woman

Faith and Faithfulness

Numerous Pentecostals point to Mary's many admirable traits. She is a woman of great faith and enduring faithfulness. Conn claims that Mary's 'boundless faith' is one of her most striking qualities.[20] In her dramatic Christmas play, Sister Aimee demonstrates that Mary's faith is extolled and depicted in a very favorable light, particularly in con-trast to Zacharias and Joseph. Because Pentecostals view Mary as a paragon of faith, when faced to account for the questions Mary asks Gabriel (Lk. 1.29, 34), a variety of explanations are suggested. One author understands her response to be an 'expression of inward per-plexity'.[21] Rolf McPherson points out that Mary's response is an at-tempt to understand the *means* of the task at hand, rather than an expression of astonishment.[22] And yet another author finds within Mary's 'simple' and 'artless' question, a sincerity that demonstrates her simplicity and open heartedness.[23]

Mary's faith translates into faithfulness at Jesus' crucifixion. Pen-tecostals note that in contradistinction to the disciples who fled or Peter who followed at a distance, Mary remained at the cross (Jn 19.25-27).[24] Her fidelity would not allow her to leave his side. Once again, Charles Conn:

> the steadfastness of Mary was perhaps her greatest virtue. She held on; she stayed, not only when the warm winds of eager youth

---

[18] Conn, 'God's Favorite Woman', p. 3.

[19] McPherson, 'Footsteps of Destiny', p. 5.

[20] Conn, 'God's Favorite Woman', p. 3.

[21] Raymond Becker, 'The Virgin Birth: Fact or Fallacy?', *FM* 35.12 (December 1962), p. 3.

[22] McPherson, 'Think on These Things: The Virgin Mary's Place in History', p. 12; *idem*, 'The Virgin Mary: Her Position in the Church', pp. 2, 9-10.

[23] Charles Wm. Walkem, 'Perplexing Problems', *FM* 21.6 (June 1949), p. 15.

[24] Doris L. Cox, 'The Woman's Place', *WWM* 30.10 (January 31, 1953), p. 4.

were blowing, but through blasting tempests of hopelessness and despair, and finally through the doldrums of loneliness, of weakness, of helplessness. No up-and-down experience was in her heart, no vicissitudes ever occurred in her spiritual life. After the cruel death of her son, most mothers would have quit, or, at least, ceased an active part in religious work. But not constant Mary. On the day of Pentecost she was still with the followers of her son … Regardless of the shock of seeing Jesus crucified, her stout heart kept beating for God.[25]

Humility, Obedience, and Diligence

Pentecostals frequently describe Mary to be a humble young woman, generally connecting this characteristic with God's choosing of her for the task of bearing forth Christ.[26] Sister Aimee contrasts Mary's obedience with Eve's disobedience, saying, 'And Mary the Virgin – God's lovely handmaiden. "Blessed art thou among women!" Eve, sinless and pure, disobeyed God, but Mary bowed to God's will and said, "Be it according to thy will!" Mary, the mother of our Lord! Thou art favored among women!'[27] Noted Pentecostal Holiness minister and leader Paul Beacham looks to Mary as a model for any contemporary Christian seeking to experience the fullness of the blessing of the Gospel. Mary 'took God at His word' and she allowed God's will to be worked in her life; Mary responded in complete submission to God and, thus, completely consecrated her body, soul, and spirit.[28] Conn further notes that Mary's obedience was not only exemplified with her role in the birth of Jesus, but also with her involvement in the miracle at Cana. The obedience she gave to the Father, she also gave to the Son of God.[29] Following Gabriel's visit to Mary, the Gospel of Luke says that Mary 'hurried' to Elizabeth's

---

[25] Conn, 'God's Favorite Woman', pp. 11, 14; 'International Sunday School Lesson: Adult Department', *FC* 5.4 (December 17, 1930), p. 10.

[26] Williams, 'The Birth of Christ was on This Wise', p. 3; Noseworthy, 'The Savior Which is Christ the Lord', pp. 4, 9; 'Junior Sunday School Lesson: The Song of Jesus' Mother', *FC* 2.26 (December 25, 1935), p. 7.

[27] Aimee Semple McPherson, 'The Rising Star', *FC* 14.12 (December 1942), p. 25.

[28] Paul F. Beacham, 'The Song of Mary', *PHA* 32.33 (December 16, 1948)*,* p. 3; McPherson, 'Think on These Things: The Virgin Mary's Place in History', p. 12; *idem*, 'The Virgin Mary: Her Position in the Church', pp. 2, 9-10.

[29] Conn, 'God's Favorite Woman', p. 11.

home (Lk. 1.39). One author interprets this swiftness of Mary as indicative of her diligence.[30]

Disciplined Spirituality

Pentecostals often portrayed Mary as a woman of disciplined character because of her knowledge of the scriptures and her meditative habits. Both the Annunciation and Magnificat serve as windows into Mary's spiritual life. Reflecting on the announcement from Gabriel to Mary, Rolf McPherson surmises that Mary was not surprised at all by the angelic message because she was versed so well in scripture. Consequently, instead of coming as shock, the idea came 'rather as a familiar thought and with a heavenly naturalness'.[31] With respect to the Magnificat, Conn states that this response demonstrates 'Mary's ability to effectually praise God [and] is a worthy gauge of her deep piety'.[32] It also demonstrates for some Pentecostals that Mary's heart was filled with the rich treasures of scripture.[33] Beacham marvels at Mary's 'unusual acquaintance with the scripture' and notes that she must have had these truths stored up in her heart.[34] Moreover, given that Mary is a woman and traditionally would not have been as well-versed in scripture as a man, Sister Aimee suggests that the reason Mary knew so much scripture by heart is because there were many times when she would sneak off to the synagogue where the scrolls were open and read them![35]

Several Pentecostals understand the scriptural descriptions of Mary 'treasuring up' and 'pondering' as events were unfolding in her life (Lk. 2.19) to indicate that she was a thoughtful young woman who engaged in meditative habits.[36] One author contrasts the response of the crowd who 'wondered' (Lk. 2.18) with the response of Mary who 'pondered' (Lk. 2.19), positing Mary as a model for Christians today.[37] Conn claims that Mary

---

[30] John Howard, 'Spiritual Myopia, or Short-sighted Christianity', *PHA* 34.27 (November 2, 1950), p. 4.

[31] McPherson, 'Think on These Things: The Virgin Mary's Place in History', p. 12; *idem*, 'The Virgin Mary: Her Position in the Church', pp. 2, 9-10.

[32] Conn, 'God's Favorite Woman', p. 11.

[33] 'Adult Sunday School Lesson: A Mother's Son', *FC* 2.26 (December 25, 1935), p. 5.

[34] Beacham, 'The Song of Mary', p. 3.

[35] McPherson, 'Footsteps of Destiny', p. 6.

[36] McPherson, 'Footsteps of Destiny', p. 8.

[37] Elmer Gottschalk *et al.*, 'The Birth of Jesus', *FC* 14.12 (December 1942), p. 23.

spent much of her time in reverent meditation and musing on God's righteousness, Person, and Word. Religion to her was not a perfunctory task to be performed regularly, but it was an inner experience that never grew old, that never relaxed hold on her heart and mind ... Still quiet and reticent, she mused within her own heart and confided to her own spirit the wondrous grace of God.[38]

He states further that it was not just initially that we see the meditative habits of Mary, but again when Mary and Joseph found Jesus in the temple discoursing with the rabbis (Lk. 2.51).[39]

Related to Mary's spiritual stature, Pentecostals regard Mary as a woman of purity. At times this descriptor is employed in a spiritual sense, but at other times this descriptor hints at some sort of sexual quality. Once again, Williams describes Mary's life to be as 'spotless as the lilies that blossom in the woodland. Her heart was as pure as the dewdrop which sparkles in the morning sun.'[40] And Sister Aimee claims that the name 'Mary' itself is a type of purity because it means 'chosen of God'.[41] Conn concludes that because Mary had God's favor she must have been doubly pure, both spiritually and physically:

> No doubt she was adverse to the frivolous coquettishness that many girls used to win favor with the male gentry of their day. Mary did not seek the favor of men, and probably did not have it, but the purity of her heart and mind won for her the attention and favor of God. Then what matter was it to her if she was not highly popular? What did it matter if she did not have a waiting list of suitors? She had found the favor of God! Her fame was not in the mouths of ribald men, in street-corner jesting – but her name was known in heaven and whispered among the angels.[42]

Gendered Virtues

While at times Mary's virtues are held up as a paradigm for Christians, there were other occasions when some Pentecostals employed their gender stereotypes to color their depiction of Mary or circumscribe

---

[38] Conn, 'God's Favorite Woman', p. 11.

[39] Conn, 'God's Favorite Woman', p. 11.

[40] Williams, 'The Birth of Christ was on This Wise: When God Bestowed Honor on the Poor', p. 3; Noseworthy, 'The Savior Which is Christ the Lord', p. 4.

[41] McPherson, 'Here Comes the Bride', pp. 3, 5.

[42] Conn, 'God's Favorite Woman', p. 3.

her to a role model for women alone. For example, Conn depicts Mary as a woman of 'discretion' because after she had spent three months with Elizabeth, she returned home quietly and kept her secret to herself, not even telling Joseph. Mary did not 'gossip', even though what she was keeping to herself was true.[43] Moreover, other authors infer from the reference to Mary 'keeping' and 'pondering' things in her heart (Lk. 2.19) that she must have been a woman of a 'quiet tongue', who did not 'talk about everything and everybody', and 'never falsely accused another'.[44]

Still another Pentecostal reduces Mary's virtues of purity, holiness, faith, and love to lessons of chastity and obedience. Not only are her virtues reduced to these two traits, but they are then relegated as exemplary only for women, while Christ – who is also described with similar virtues – serves as a model for all Christians.[45]

Mary: Not 'The Mother' but 'A Mother'

One of the more touching portraitures of Mary by Pentecostals are those describing Mary's role as a mother. However, Pentecostals distinguish clearly between Mary as 'a mother' in contrast to Mary as the 'mother of God'. The former, they believed, is an accurate title for Mary's role in Jesus' incarnate life, while the latter is a claim to posit Mary as responsible for Jesus' divinity. To illustrate this, one author states, 'Christ's deity does not come from his mother. *Mary is never called the mother of God*.'[46] Another maintains that rather than being the 'mother of God', Mary was the 'mother of Jesus' because Mary only gave birth to Christ's *humanity*, whereas his *divine sonship* has always existed. Jesus as the Son of God could not have been 'born' via Mary, only 'given'.[47] Finally, another author says, 'Mary did not produce God. She was merely the vehicle through which the human body of our Lord was to come'.[48] To reiterate this claim, some Pentecostals highlight the connection between Mary and the humanity of Christ

---

[43] Conn, 'God's Favorite Woman', p. 11.

[44] E.S. Williams, 'The Birth of the King', *PE* 2014 (December 14, 1952), p. 10; 'Godly Mothers in the Church of God', *WWM* 24.9 (April 26, 1947), pp. 1, 4.

[45] Will Shead, 'Marriage by the Word of God', *CGE* 33.37 (November 28, 1942), p. 8.

[46] Walkem, 'Perplexing Problems', p. 15. Italics are original.

[47] Kellogg, 'Modern Women in Prophecy', p. 8. Italics are original.

[48] Williams, 'The Birth of the King', p. 10.

when referring to his genealogy by saying, 'In Joseph He was the legal Heir …; in Mary, the *human* Sacrifice; in the Holy Ghost, Immanuel; in Joseph, the Son of David; in Mary, the Son of *man*; in the Holy Ghost, the Son of God; in Joseph, Heir of Israel (Matt. 21.38); in Mary, Heir of the *world* (Rom. 4.1); in the Holy Ghost, Heir of all things (Heb. 1.2)'.[49]

Despite the varied descriptions of Mary as 'mother', Pentecostals do not hesitate to put her in a preeminent place among mothers everywhere, recognizing her as the most beloved among them.[50] And because of Mary's good example, motherhood everywhere is honored and lifted up.[51] As a mother, Mary is depicted by Pentecostals as a good example for other mothers by means of the way in which she cared for Jesus. When Jesus was lost in Jerusalem, Mary and Joseph were troubled and concerned for his welfare, and when they found Jesus, it is Mary's reproof to him that is recorded. Some authors suggested that Mary was integral to the development of Jesus' teaching and training as he was growing up. As his mother, Mary was fully invested in Jesus' ministry and offered assistance in every way possible. She was with Jesus when he performed his first miracle and she informed him that there was no longer any wine at the marriage feast. After this event she continued with him to Capernaum.[52] On one occasion, the Gospels report that Mary was standing outside along with Jesus' brothers calling for him. Rolf McPherson interprets this event as Mary calling Jesus home so that he would not tax himself beyond his strength. Her summons was viewed as a self-sacrificial act of love, thoughtfulness, and care for Jesus' wellbeing and not her own.[53]

Finally, Mary's motherhood is on display as an example of her tremendous suffering.[54] On an Easter journey to Jerusalem, Sister Aimee recounts her being moved to tears as she reflected upon the

[49] D.M. Panton, 'Born of a Virgin', *PE* 2172 (December 25, 1955), p. 4. A similar form of this statement appears earlier: S.A. Jamieson, 'The Virgin Birth of Our Lord Jesus Christ', *PE* 518 (October 20, 1923), p. 8. Italics added.
[50] Aimee Semple McPherson, 'Mothers of the Bible', *FC* 4.24 (May 7, 1930), p. 6.
[51] 'Godly Mothers in the Church of God', p. 1.
[52] 'Godly Mothers in the Church of God', pp. 1, 4.
[53] McPherson, 'Think on These Things: The Virgin Mary's Place in History', p. 12; *idem*, 'The Virgin Mary: Her Position in the Church', pp. 2, 9-10.
[54] S.W. Latimer, 'There is Born a Savior', *CGE* 20.42 (December 21, 1929), p. 3; 'Godly Mothers in the Church of God', pp. 1, 4; McPherson, 'Mothers of the Bible', p. 6.

agony that Mary must have experienced as a witness to the events of the cross.[55] Similarly, Conn captures the agony and turmoil of this event for Mary by saying,

> The pain of heart and soul she endured at the crucifixion of Jesus is indescribable. She compelled her aged, spent body to follow the infamous procession that prodded Him onward to His death. On and on she ran, groaning at every step for her son. How gladly she would have substituted her frail, joyless body on that cross so that He might not suffer so. With perfect love she could have felt the spikes pierce her hands and have the thorny crown mat her locks – if that would spare Him.[56]

Mary: A Pentecostal Sister

In addition to all that Pentecostals have noted about Mary, some are especially attuned to the work of the Spirit in her life. Given the over-shadowing of the Spirit upon Mary to form Jesus within her womb, Sister Aimee positions Mary as an example of a person who allowed a 'godly life' to be formed within because she submitted herself to the Spirit of God. Just like Mary, 'so we of today need the manifestation of the Spirit of God that a godly life may be formed within us'.[57] Another author understands Mary's conception of Jesus to be a lesson in allowing the Spirit to make alive the 'Word' in our life in order for it to become a reality. Mary serves as a model for this process and response when she said, 'Be it unto me according to Thy Word'.[58] Though Mary could not understand what was happening, her faith connected with the power of the Spirit was all that was needed to accomplish the work of God in her life.[59] If this was sufficient for Mary, then it should be sufficient for us today!

Following Gabriel's visit to Mary, Luke records that Mary 'hurried' to Elizabeth's home. One author interprets this swiftness of Mary to

---

[55] Aimee Semple McPherson, 'Give Me My Own God', *FM* 24.6 (June, 1951), p. 15.

[56] Conn, 'God's Favorite Woman', p. 11.

[57] Aimee Semple McPherson, 'Latter Day Rain from Heaven: "Drops" by Sister', *BCF* 23.32 (October, 1932), p. 2; Aimee Semple McPherson, 'Jesus Christ the Baptizer', *FM* 21.11 (November, 1949), p. 13.

[58] M.B., 'Emmanuel: "God with Us"', *Confidence* 7.12 (December, 1914), p. 232.

[59] Conn, 'God's Favorite Woman', p. 3.

indicate Mary's diligence, which then leads to a move of the Spirit. The author says,

> The word diligence means haste, and is used by Luke in Ch. I, verses 39–41 and describes the eager swiftness with which the Virgin Mary went to Elizabeth after the angel had spoken that wonderful message. Subsequently, Elizabeth was filled with the Holy Ghost. Do you see, dear reader, what you can do for others by your diligence? Let us excite and engage grace and holiness.[60]

For another author, the Magnificat itself testifies to the Spirit's work in Mary's life beyond the initial overshadowing. It is proof that she was speaking under the 'direct inspiration' of the Spirit when she uttered forth her song.[61]

After Jesus' death and resurrection, Mary is also present for the second overshadowing of the Spirit, this time on the Day of Pentecost. A.A. Boddy, a leading pioneer of Pentecostalism in Britain, notes that before the Day of Pentecost, Mary and some of the other women who were with her continually met to have 'little prayer meetings' that the disciples would sometimes join. Presumably during one of these 'little prayer meetings', the Spirit was then poured out.[62] Another author draws attention to the fact that Mary was in the Upper Room tarrying with all the others for the baptism of the Holy Spirit. In so doing, Mary acknowledges her equal need for the Spirit and receives the same experience.[63] In a more imaginative piece, Sister Aimee recounts a scene right before the event of Pentecost that involves Mary and some of the disciples. When the narrator of the story asks Mary where she is going, Mary replies that she is headed to the Upper Room to wait for the promise of the Father. The narrator then retorts that surely the holy Mother of Jesus does not need the coming of the Spirit, but Mary states emphatically that even she needs the Spirit in her life. The narrator concludes: 'Then, Oh Virgin Mary, if you, even you, need this experience, surely I and all the world (no matter how devoted and clean, through the word that has been

---

[60] Howard, 'Spiritual Myopia, or Short-sighted Christianity', p. 4.
[61] Chas S. Price, 'High Lights in the Life of Peter', *LRE* (October 1926), p. 3.
[62] A.A. Boddy, 'They Two Went On', *LRE* (October 1912), p. 5.
[63] H.T. Spence, 'Quizzing the Pope', *PHA* 34.29 (November 16, 1950), p. 1.

spoken to us, no matter how rich our Christian experience), also need this Holy Spirit for which you are all seeking so earnestly!'[64]

Conclusion

In sum, Pentecostal depictions of Mary offer a rich and textured mosaic, a stark contrast to the bleak assessment of Jerry Sandidge. These Pentecostals consistently present Mary in a favorable light and see her as a model of Christian faith and discipleship – even if, at times, this model reflects more of a twentieth-century Pentecostal than a first-century Jewish woman. The lack of historical congruence, however, does not remove the fact that Pentecostals identify Mary as a figure worthy of bearing these traits and this role. Among them, Mary receives such accolades as the 'most blessed of all women',[65] one who lived a 'beautiful, unblemished, exemplary life',[66] 'one of the greatest women that we have any account of',[67] and the 'connecting-link between earth and heaven'.[68] As both the mother of Jesus upon whom the Holy Spirit overshadowed and a participant present in the Upper Room on the Day of Pentecost, Pentecostals see in Mary a paradigmatic sister with whom they can identify. For, truly, she is our sister!

Bibliography

Johnson, Elizabeth, *Truly Our Sister: A Theology of Mary in the Communion of Saints* (New York: Continuum, 2003).
Sandidge, Jerry L., 'A Pentecostal Response to Roman Catholic Teaching on Mary', *Pneuma* 4.2 (Fall 1982), pp. 33-42.
—*Roman Catholic/ Pentecostal Dialogue (1977–1982): A Study in Developing Ecumenism* (New York: Peter Lang, 1987).

---

[64] Aimee Semple McPherson, 'The Holy Spirit', *BC* 7.2 (July 1923), pp. 6-7. Several times McPherson notes that Mary, the Mother of God, who had already been overshadowed by the Holy Spirit, was among those in the Upper Room waiting for the Spirit to descend. See Aimee Semple McPherson, 'Pentecost on Trial', *FC* 11.37 (March 9, 1938), p. 3; *idem*, 'Baptism of the Holy Spirit and Its Place in the Church', *FC* 12.39 (March 22, 1939), p. 8.

[65] Will Shead, 'Marriage by the Word of God', *CGE* 33.37 (November 28, 1942), p. 8.

[66] Conn, 'God's Favorite Woman,' p. 14.

[67] Latimer, 'There is Born a Savior,' p. 3.

[68] McPherson, 'Think on These Things: The Virgin Mary's Place in History,' p. 12; *idem*, 'The Virgin Mary: Her Position in the Church,' pp. 2, 9-10.

7

UNIVERSALIZING THE PENTECOSTAL COMMISSION: A RECEPTION HISTORY OF MARK 16.17-18

CLAYTON COOMBS[*]

Introduction: Pentecostal Appropriation of Mark 16.17-18

> And these signs shall follow those who believe. In my name they will cast out demons. They will speak in new tongues. They will pick up snakes with their hands and if they drink any deadly thing it will not hurt them at all. They will lay their hands on the sick and they will recover (Mk 16.17-18).

This bold declaration has long been a source text for Pentecostal preaching and practice. Pentecostals, in spite of the growing critical consensus to athetize the pericope in which this promise is found, have largely continued to declare and believe it.[1] And while it is true that certain isolated groups have used this passage in a way that has damaged people (not to mention the reputation of the broader Pentecostal body), the reception history of Mk 16.17-18 demonstrates that Pentecostals are the unwitting heirs of an interpretive tradition

---

[*] Clayton Coombs (PhD, Wheaton College) is Academic Dean, Planetshakers College, Melbourne, Australia.

[1] It is important to establish at the outset that my observations concerning Pentecostal understanding and appropriation of Mk 16.17–18 in this chapter are primarily concerned not with the academic discourse, but rather with preaching and practice at the popular level.

that both expects and experiences miraculous manifestations of the Spirit on the basis of it. This study analyses a selection of significant citations of Mk 16.17-18 from the second through the early fifth century. It will aim for breadth rather than depth to determine what, if any, consistent patterns of interpretation or significant discontinuities may emerge over these early centuries of the church. Reception history is found to be an insightful interpretive lens through which to view this contentious passage, as it protects its place in the canon on the one hand and guards against an overly literal interpretation on the other; indeed, some refreshing and unexpected interpretive possibilities emerge.

Pentecostal hermeneutics can be described as literal, but not in a slavishly fundamentalist way. It is spiritual, but not in a spiritualist or gnostic way. It is freely allegorical, but not in a liberal way, and thoroughly intertextual, though sometimes only in an intuitive way. It is experiential, but not in a hedonistic way. An exploration of Mk. 16.17-18 will demonstrate this assessment. While we may at times, despite our protestations to the contrary, allow our experience to recalibrate our expectations in a way that better nuances our interpretation, we will always insist that Scripture, correctly understood should govern our experiences rather than the other way round. If this explanation seems hopelessly imprecise and frustratingly nonspecific, it is because Pentecostal hermeneutics (at its best) is an endeavour guided by the Holy Spirit. It is a process that draws us closer to and makes us dependent on him, rather than on theory and method.[2]

Mark 16.17-18 presents a fascinating problem for Pentecostal interpretation, and as such is an important case study for understanding its internal logic. This paper begins with a brief demonstration of early Pentecostal hermeneutics, using Mk 16.17-18 as a case study, and then proceeds to a reception history of this passage in the second through fifth centuries.

---

[2] Elsewhere I have characterized this as 'a hermeneutic of intimacy rather than … mastery'. See Clayton Coombs, 'Reading in Tongues: The Case for a Pneumatalogical [*sic*] Hermeneutic in Conversation with James K. Smith,' *Pneuma* 32.2 (2010), pp. 261-68.

Early Pentecostal Understanding and Appropriation of Mark 16.17-18

One of the key catalysts for the early Pentecostal movement was the persistent prayer for the manifestation of tongues, the 'baptism of the Holy Spirit', that these early Pentecostals believed was promised in Scripture.[3] That Mk 16.17 was used as a source text for this expectation is instructive. Reverend Alexander A. Boddy of Sunderland, England, lists the NT texts that bear upon this practice at the beginning of his article entitled 'Speaking in Tongues. Is this of God?' His list is as follows: Mk 16.17, Acts 2.4, 17, 18; 10.44-46; 19.6, 1 Cor. 12.8-10, 13 [presumably v. 1], 14.2, 4, 5, 39.[4] Boddy records the testimony of a Geo. E. Beady, who encountered the power of the Holy Spirit in a meeting at Shrewsbury under the ministry of Smith Wigglesworth and his wife. Beady witnessed numerous people experiencing God's power in that meeting, but he did not himself receive the baptism of the Holy Spirit until sometime later. Writes Beady:

> Since that time (over 9 months ago) I have been continuously pleading the Blood and praying for the Baptism of the Holy Ghost *with signs following* [emphasis supplied]. About the middle of last week God wonderfully impressed upon my mind John xvi., 7. Then it came to me that the Comforter (Holy Ghost) was still in the world and all I needed was to be thoroughly cleansed from sin, plead the Blood of Jesus, and in mighty faith accept God's promises. So from early morning I claimed God's promises and continuously pleaded '*the precious Blood of Jesus*,' [emphasis original] until about 1 p.m. in the afternoon, when there came such a strong inspiration to go upstairs; so, saying nothing to anyone, I went by myself and knelt down by the bedside, still pleading '*the precious Blood of Jesus*,' [emphasis original] until suddenly the Holy Ghost

---

[3] Indeed, this is my own experience. I would not have continued to pray earnestly for the baptism of the Holy Spirit as evidenced by speaking in tongues for nearly two years until I received, unless I had been convinced that such was an inalienable promise of Scripture. For the record, I remain convinced.

[4] Alexander A. Boddy, 'Speaking in Tongues: Is This of God?', *Confidence* 8 (1908), pp. 9-10. See also p. 15 where the 'Copy of Minute Regarding the Gift of Tongues' from Kilsyth is recorded including: 'At this present time all the office-bearers, with two exceptions, have received their Pentecost and are speaking in tongues, all according to the Scriptures, as recorded in Mark 16–17 [*sic*], Acts 2, 10, 19, also 1 Cor. 12, 13, 14 chapters'.

came upon me, and I found myself glorifying God in an unknown tongue as the Spirit gave utterance. Hallelujah to Jesus![5]

Beady, along with many others, took the promise that signs, including speaking in tongues, would follow believers (from Mk 16.17) literally, and prayed persistently on that basis until he received. In the same edition of *Confidence*, a testimony from A. Murdoch is recorded from Kilsyth which, like Beady's testimony, relates speaking in tongues to the expectation of signs following:

It would do your heart good to see nearly 100 YOUNG MEN and maidens in the upper room on Sabbath night all praying, sometimes nearly all in tongues. I say it to the Glory of Jesus. I don't think you could see the like of it in all Scotland, and this has continued for over eight months, and is the result of Pentecost. Dear brother, I believe the Gospel is to be preached in these days of scepticism and pleasure living with the Power of the Holy Ghost *and Signs following* [emphasis supplied] … Since writing you last, we have had people from different parts of Scotland who have received the Baptism of the Holy Ghost and Signs following, viz., the New Tongue.[6]

In an early edition of *The Apostolic Faith*, the publication of the Azusa Street Revival, is found a piece which acknowledges the text critical problem with the Markan ending and urges Jesus' 'last words' (Mk 16.15-18) to be taken seriously. Of the five signs mentioned, the application here is *only* to speaking in other tongues:

Many of the dear holiness people are rejecting the last words of Jesus in the last chapter of Mark, beginning at the fifteenth verse:

'And He said unto them: Go ye into all the world and preach the Gospel to every creature. He that believeth and is baptized shall be saved; but he that believeth not shall be damned. And these signs shall follow them that believe; in my name shall they cast out devils; they shall speak with new tongues; they shall take up serpents and if they drink any deadly thing, it shall not hurt them; they shall lay hands on the sick and they shall recover'.

---

[5] Geo. E. Beady, 'Pontesford', *Confidence* 8 (November 15, 1908), pp. 11, 13.
[6] A. Murdoch, 'Kilsyth', *Confidence* 8 (November 15, 2008), pp. 14-15.

Why do they reject these verses? Because Dr. Godbey, in his commentary and translation, has left them out. Why did he leave them out? Because they were not in the Sinanitic [*sic*] manuscript from which he translates. It was a manuscript found in later years in a mission on Mount Sinai. The man who found the manuscript, a German by the name of Tischendorf, said that some sheets of it had already been thrown into a receptacle for kindling wood. In this or some other way, a part may have been lost from that manuscript.

However this may be, we feel sure that these are the words of Jesus. The writer herself, being a great admirer of Bro. Godbey, was for some time influenced by his views in regard to the last words of our Lord as given above. But since being in these Holy Ghost meetings, and hearing these same words given again and again by the Spirit in unknown tongues and interpreted, all doubt has been swept away in regard to them. Besides they are proved true before our eyes. We have thrown all doubts to the winds and taken to our hearts the whole word of Jesus. Dear friends, do not let any man riddle your Bible for you or cut out any part of it. You need the whole. Hallelujah for the Word.[7]

Two issues later, the *Apostolic Faith* circular was subtitled 'Pentecost with Signs Following'.[8] In this issue, there appears a short article by 'Mother Wheaton' entitled 'Signs Shall Follow'.

Jesus said in Mk 16.17, 18, 'These signs shall follow them that believe: In my name shall they cast out devils; they shall speak with new tongues; they shall take up serpents; and if they drink any deadly thing, it shall not hurt them; they shall lay hands on the sick and they shall recover.' He told them to, 'Go ye therefore and teach all nations, teaching them to observe all things whatsoever I have commanded you.' What did this mean? It meant to preach healing, preach casting out of devils, preach that these signs shall follow them that believe, preach all the doctrine of Jesus. If they had preached only a part of the Gospel, would the signs have followed? These signs shall follow them that believe – not them that

---

[7] 'Shall We Reject Jesus' Last Words?', *AF* 1.2 (October 1906), p. 3.
[8] 'Pentecost with Signs Following: Seven Months of Pentecostal Showers. Jesus, Our Projector And Great Shepherd', *AF* 1.4 (December 1906), p. 1.

doubt or believe a part, but those that are simple enough and honest enough to believe every word of Jesus. We must believe it all,
for if only a part is true, or if anything is changed in His commis-
sion of the Gospel to the world, it would not be a perfect Gospel.
So a return to the full Gospel brings a return of the signs following them that believe.[9]

Here we see an interpretive trend that permeates much of the early
Pentecostal commentary on this passage. Where the promise of the
following signs is not merely used as a 'proof text' for the gift of
tongues, it is used *mainly* to support healing and exorcism, but *not* to
argue for picking up snakes and drinking poison. Important work already done in the early Pentecostal reception of Mk 16.17–18 largely
bears out this observation. Indeed, John Christopher Thomas and
Kimberly Alexander, in speaking of the importance of the promise
of signs following to the early Pentecostal movement, themselves
only mention the first second and fifth sign:

> ... These Pentecostals, who understood themselves to be *apostolic*,
> restoring the faith of the New Testament church, were experienc-
> ing manifestations and phenomena delineated in the Mk 16.9-20
> passage. In addition, they were urgently preaching the Pentecostal
> message everywhere they went. It should be expected, then, that
> they would identify with this particular commissioning text, which
> including preaching, speaking in tongues, healing the sick and ex-
> orcising demons.[10]

Almost all of the examples they offer likewise mention the fulfillment
of only the first second and fifth sign. The same is the case in a section of Alexander's book, *Pentecostal Healing*, that also deals with the
'signs following' promise.[11]

Thomas and Alexander do discuss (at some length) an exception
to the trend I am observing in which A.J. Tomlinson (apparently
alone) advocated for the taking up of snakes and drinking of poison
as tests of faith. He even went so far as to report testimony of where

[9] Mother Wheaton, 'Signs Shall Follow', *AF* 1.4 (December 1906), p. 2.
[10] John Christopher Thomas and Kimberly E. Alexander, '"And the Signs Are
Following": Mark 16.9-20 – A Journey into Pentecostal Hermeneutics', *JPT* 11.2
(2003), pp. 147–70 (p. 150).
[11] Alexander, Kimberly E. Alexander, *Pentecostal Healing: Models in Theology and
Practice, Pentecostal Healing* (JPTSup 29; Leiden: Brill, 2006).

this faith did not apparently work. Such was the case with the story of V.A. Bishop who died following a failed attempt at demonstrating the fourth sign in a revival service.[12] Alexander seems to indicate that the Church of God in general, may have followed Tomlinson in his hyper-literal reading of the sign list.[13]

A couple of additional exceptions to this trend are worth noting. The first appears in *The Pentecost* from February 1910, in which a lady submits a testimony of her husband's recovery from food poisoning and she (or more likely the editor of the publication) includes the 'drinking poison' promise from Mk 16.18 at the conclusion to the testimony.[14]

A second is found in a teaching on the signs in the *Pentecostal Holiness Advocate* in 1917. In answer to the question 'Is it Scriptural for the Lord to put His power on Spirit-filled people to handle snakes?' the author provides a lengthy answer concerning the signs. His conclusion concerning snakes:

> The New Testament gives us several instances of speaking in new tongues, of healing the sick, and of casting out demons, but only one of taking up a viper, and that one was accidental. (Acts 28:3-6) There were benefits that resulted from this action (Acts 28:7-10), but they were not the primary end sought. In other words, Paul did not purposely pick up the snake in order to bless the people of that island. If he had done so, the result would have been idolatry. (Acts 28:6.) If Jesus had meant that the taking up of serpents should be purposely practiced in the church, we feel sure that we would have some account somewhere of its practice.

> To show further that the promise is only for the protection of the believer, read Luke 10.19: 'Behold, I give unto you power to tread on serpents and scorpions, and over all power of the enemy.' This is practically the same thing as Mark 16.18, but for what purpose is such power given? Is it for the benefit of others? Is it just to display 'power'? Can there be no practical result? Read on, 'And nothing shall by any means hurt you.' No other reason than this is

---

[12] See Thomas and Alexander, '"And the Signs Are Following"', p. 154.
[13] Alexander, *Pentecostal Healing: Models in Theology and Practice*, *Pentecostal Healing*, pp. 104–106. Note that she focuses almost exclusively in this section on *The Church of God Evangel* between 1917 and 1921.
[14] Mrs J.C. Ament, 'Healing from Poison', *TP* 2.3 (February 1910), p. 3.

assigned for such action. To purposely take up a serpent and rely on this promise would be to 'tempt God.' (Matt. 4.7.)[15]

Early Pentecostal interpretation then employed a literal herme- neutic. And yet it was also intertextual, allowing the meaning of a word or principle in one verse or passage, to be calibrated by its usage elsewhere in the Canon. This intuitive intertextuality is delightfully demonstrated in Hattie Barth's rich theological reflection on the sign promise:

> Are we to cast out devils in His name? Satan will be bound the thousand years. Are we to drink deadly poison without hurt? Thorns, weeds, poisonous plants shall no more infest the ground. Are we to take up serpents? The suckling child shall play on the hole of the asp and the weaned child shall put his hand on the cockatrice den. Are we to heal the sick? When Jesus comes, 'the inhabitant shall not say, 'I am sick.' Are we to overcome this age, all sin, sickness, death, and be caught up to meet him in the air without dying? He must reign, till he hath put all enemies under His feet. The last enemy that shall be destroyed is death. Do we begin now to speak with other tongues of men and of angels, and have the gifts of interpretation? The time is coming when the old curse given at Babel shall be lifted, and the inhabitants of the earth shall be no more divided, but shall have knowledge of His power, and be one people with God. Do we have knowledge of His power and taste of the glories of the age to come? 'The earth shall be filled with the knowledge of the glory of the Lord, as the wa- ters cover the sea'.[16]

Pentecostals did not take their understanding of tongues from a single verse. The Pentecostal expectation of the initial evidence of

---

[15] G.F. Taylor, 'Question Box', *PHA* 2.3 (May 10, 1917) pp. 11-13 (13).

[16] Hattie Barth, *The Bridegroom's Messenger* 2.34 (March 1909), p. 4 cited in Thomas and Alexander, '"And the Signs Are Following"', p. 153. At the risk of missing some of the richness, Barth reads Mk 16.17–18 in the context of at least the following: Rev. 20.1–6; 21.3; Gen 3.18; 11.1–9; Isa. 11.8; 33.24; 1 Thess. 4.17; 1 Cor. 15.25–26; 13.1; 12.10; Heb. 6.4; and Hab. 2.14. The association between the fourth sign and Isa. 11.8–9 that Barth identifies helps us to understand why this sign has been taken as a promise of protection in general. For a contemporary Pentecostal interpretive alternative, note the intriguing suggestion of Robert Men- zies, *Speaking in Tongues: Jesus and the Apostolic Church as Models for the Church Today* (Cleveland, TN: CPT Press, 2016), pp. 74–78. Menzies reads the fourth (and the fifth) sign as a reference to Job 20.16.

speaking in tongues was famously derived from five passages in the book of Acts – or possibly three passages in spite of the other two – so the passages must be read together. It is this intertextuality that permits us (apparently along with the early Pentecostals) to wonder if the promise that believers would not suffer any ill effects from drinking 'a deadly thing' might be speaking about something other than what it apparently says, for while we readily find three of the five signs fulfilled in the book of Acts, and rightly wonder whether the account of Paul shaking off a snake into the fire in Acts 28 might be taken for fulfilment of a third, [17] we search in vain for the fulfilment of the poison promise. As demonstrated above, most early Pentecostals took this promise to refer to the promise of protection in general, to grant believers confidence even in the face of spiritual or physical attack. This early intuition is still in evidence. It was indeed the view of a Pentecostal missionary I have known personally for years who, when asked whether he was nervous that he might get sick from eating certain of the local foods, replied simply, 'I never worry about it. My Bible says that if I were to drink even deadly poison it would not hurt me a bit, so I don't need to fear unwashed hands or strange food. I just thank God for it and eat it in faith.'

This brings us to the curious dialectic between theology and experience in Pentecostal thought. As is well known, the pre-Azusa Street revivalists set themselves to pray in earnest for the charism of tongues because of their biblical conviction that this was the initial evidence of the Baptism of the Holy Spirit. And yet their understanding of what they were praying for shifted in response to their experience when it became clear that what they had received was glossolalia, rather than the xenolalia that they had expected. [18] On the one hand, if someone wished to argue that Pentecostals place a priority on experience over theology (as is often asserted both from within and without), one would need to look no further than this adjusted expectation. On the other hand, the instinct behind the initial prayer is held as evidence of the priority of theology over

---

[17] Not surprisingly, as Thomas and Alexander, "'And the Signs Are Following'", point out, Tomlinson rejected this event as a fulfillment of the third sign on the basis that it was accidental.

[18] See Allan Anderson, *An Introduction to Pentecostalism* (Cambridge, MA: Cambridge University Press, 2004), p. 34. This notwithstanding the testimony concerning Agnes Ozman who, it was reported, spoke in Chinese.

experience. The reality is that it has always been a bit of both.[19] Given the tension between the fervent and persistent prayer for tongues which they had not yet experienced on the one hand, and the pivot on the nature of the tongues when they had experienced them on the other, the apparent hermeneutical inconsistency of the Pentecostal intuition on the promise of immunity to poison is easier to understand. Tucked away in the back of their minds is the possibility that it ought to be taken literally, and thus reserved for if and when somebody ever tried to actually poison them, and yet one might wonder whether it might be better applied to protection in general. This is partly because the plenitude of scriptural references to snakes has already suggested an allegorical interpretation for the third sign, and partly because of the paucity of poison drinking testimonies. Pentecostals allow their experience to recalibrate their expectation because unlike the other four signs, this sign of immunity to poison is entirely absent from the book of Acts (and indeed the rest of Scripture). So while intertextuality and allegory suffice for the promise of picking up snakes – also mercifully lacking in the experience of most – the presence of several occurrences of protection from persecution in Acts (e.g. Acts 12.1-19), and many other miraculous manifestations of the Spirit's power, allow for other possibilities. This perhaps explains the instinct to substitute the signs or supplement the list with things that actually are happening. Such seems to have been the instinct behind the interpretation of a prominent Australian Pentecostal, Brian Houston, in a sermon entitled 'What's following you?'[20] based on Mk 16.17-18. The premise of the sermon was biblically sound; Jesus promised that signs would follow the preaching of the gospel. However, Houston freely substituted the five scriptural signs with other manifestations of God's favour such as influence, prosperity, and a good reputation.

---

[19] Douglas Jacobsen, *Thinking in the Spirit: Theologies of the Early Pentecostal Movement* (Bloomington: Indiana University Press, 2003), p. 5.
[20] Brian Houston, 'What's Following You?', sermon, Hillsong Church, Australia, 1998.

The Traditional Reception of Mark 16.17-18 between the Second and Fifth Century

The question at hand concerns the extent to which Pentecostal appropriation of Mk 16.17-18 resembles that of the patristic interpreters? Are the hermeneutical moves that we intuitively make validated or challenged by the history of interpretation before us? How do the experiences of the interpreters affect their interpretation, and what are their intertextual instincts? Specifically, can the expectation of signs following, and in particular the sign of tongues, be substantiated from earlier ages of the church? To what extent can the catholicity of Pentecostal interpretation be supported? The material presented below is selected from a broader pool of citations to reflect the views of interpreters in both the East and the West, writing in both Greek and Latin, spanning several centuries of the church. The time period quite deliberately straddles the fourth century, from which are the great Alexandrian codices that call these very verses into question, in order to demonstrate the continuity of reception and interpretation and bracket out the text critical discussion of the authenticity of the passage in which they are found.[21]

Irenaeus and Hippolytus

Irenaeus of Lyon was born c. 130 CE to Christian parents in Smyrna. He rose to leadership as an adult and flourished in the second half of the second century as the Bishop of Lyon. In order to understand Irenaeus' citation of Mk 16.17-18, we need first to understand that tongues and prophecy are often conflated in Patristic thought, or as Morton Kelsey has put it, 'glossolalia became lumped into a single category with prophecy'.[22] Kelsey offers as evidence the following

---

[21] Note the omission of any material from Eusebius, whose evidence features in the modern text critical debate about Mk 16.9-20. This is also deliberate. The text critical discussion is beyond the scope of the present paper. Not only has it been thoroughly dealt with in numerous publications since Tischendorf's discovery of Codex Sinaiticus in 1844, but I have dealt at length with the evidence of Eusebius in Coombs, *A Dual Reception: Eusebius and the Gospel of Mark* (Minneapolis: Fortress Press, 2016), see in particular Chapter 4. In many ways the text critical discussion is tangential to the endeavor of reception history, though in this case it can never be entirely divorced from it. For this reason also, the supposed non-reception of Origen (for a thorough treatment of this see Chapter 3) is also beyond the scope of the present work.

[22] Morton Kelsey, *Tongue Speaking* (New Jersey: Double & Co, 1964), pp. 34-36.

two quotes from Irenaeus which I reproduce in full here. The first comments,

> Neither, for a like reason, would he [Peter] have given them baptism so readily, had he not heard them prophesying when the Holy Ghost rested upon them. And therefore did he exclaim, 'Can any man forbid water, that these should not be baptized, who have received the Holy Ghost as well as we?'[23]

Here Irenaeus cites the story of the conversion of Cornelius' household and Peter's subsequent report in Acts 10, however, as Kelsey points out, he has substituted prophecy for tongues in the quote.

In the second passage Kelsey cites, Irenaeus overtly and intentionally links tongues with prophecy.

> [F]or the perfect man consists in the commingling and the union of the soul receiving the spirit of the Father, and the admixture of that fleshly nature which was moulded after the image of God. For this reason does the apostle declare, 'We speak wisdom among them that are perfect,' terming those persons 'perfect' who have received the Spirit of God, and who through the Spirit of God do speak in all languages, as he used Himself also to speak. In like manner we do also hear many brethren in the church, who possess prophetic gifts, and who through the Spirit speak all kinds of languages, and bring to light for the general benefit the hidden things of men, and declare the mysteries of God ...[24]

It is evident from this quote that Irenaeus believed the gift of tongues referred to xenolalia, meaning earthly languages unlearned by the speaker, but understood by the hearer as in Acts 2. He seems to indicate that such could be witnessed in the church, but nevertheless broadens the application of tongues to inspired speech in general.

With this in mind, then, another reference to the promise of accompanying signs appears as part of a broader argument Irenaeus is making against heretical teachers and 'wonder workers'. He suggests that these practitioners are in fact charlatans performing the signs, which they do either by the power of demons or by trickery.

---

[23] Irenaeus, *Against Heresies* III.XII.15 (ANF 1.436), quoted in Kelsey, *Tongue Speaking*, p. 35.

[24] Irenaeus, *Against Heresies* V.VI.1 (ANF 1.531), quoted in Kelsey, *Tongue Speaking*, p. 36.

But if they claim that even the Lord did (miracles) in the same way – by sleight of hand – we point them to the prophetic books, from which we will demonstrate that all of the things (that he did) were predicted concerning him and most assuredly happened, and that He is the only Son of God. And this is why in his name, those who are truly his disciples, who receive grace from him, accomplish (miracles) which benefit the rest of mankind, each one according to the gift that s/he received from him. Indeed some drive out demons most assuredly and truly, with the result that those who have been cleansed from the vile spirits frequently come to faith and are added to the church. Others have foreknowledge of the future and visions and prophetic utterances, others cure those suffering variously with sickness by the imposition of hands, and they are restored to health. Indeed even the dead have been raised, as I have said, and they lived many years among us (after being raised). And what else? It is impossible to specify the number of gifts that the church receives throughout the whole world from God in the name of Jesus Christ who was crucified under Pontius Pilate, and (which the church) exercises every single day for the help of the nations, neither deceiving any, nor extorting any money from them. For just as (the church) received freely from God, it also ministers freely.[25]

Here we have a reasonably unambiguous reference to Mk 16.17-18, where the first, second, and fifth signs are mentioned in order. Furthermore, it is clear from the way Irenaeus uses this passage that

---

[25] Irenaeus, *Adverses haereses*, 2.32.4 (SC 294.340-42). Translation is mine. The Latin is: 'Si autem et Dominum per phantasmata huiusmodi fecisse dicunt, ad prophetica reducentes eos, ex ipsis demonstrabimus omnia sic de eo et praedicta esse et facta firmissime et ipsum solum esse Filium Dei. Quadpropter et in illius nomine qui uere illius sunt discipuli, ab ipso accipientes gratiam, perficiunt ad | beneficia reliquorum hominum, quemadmodum unusquisque accepit donum ab eo. Alii enim daemonas excludunt firmissime et uere, ut etiam saepissime credant ipsi qui emundati sunt a nequissimis spiritibus et sint in Ecclesia; alii autem et praescientiam habent futurorum et uisiones et dictiones propheticas; alii autem laborantes aliqua infirmitate per manus impositionem curant et sanos restituunt; iam etiam, quemadmodum diximus, et mortui resurrexerunt et perseuerauerunt nobiscum annis multis. Et quid autem? Non est numerum dicere gratiarum quas, per uniuersum mundum Ecclesia a Deo accipiens, in nomine Christi Iesu crucifixi sub Pontio Pilate per singulos dies in opitulationem gentium perficit, neque seducens aliquem, neque pecuniam ei auferens : quemadmodum enim gratis accepit a Deo, gratis et ministrat'. This section is also attested in Greek in Eusebius, *hist.eccl* 5.7.1-5 (LCL 153.450-54).

these signs did not merely function as a theological affirmation but were indeed being experienced in his ecclesial community. Conspicuous by their absence then are the third and fourth sign, that those who believe would 'pick up snakes in their hands and if they drink any deadly thing it will not hurt them a bit'. Curiously though, in the place of these signs, which presumably were not happening in the church around Irenaeus, he substitutes the (frankly more impressive) miracle of the raising of the dead. And while there is no indication that this is a *common* occurrence in Irenaeus' church, it is nevertheless common enough to be well known. It would have been easy to investigate and disprove. Neither was it a unique occurrence as Irenaeus speaks of *plural* dead who had been raised. Reflecting on his hermeneutic, he is literal enough to interpret the occurrence of miraculous healings and exorcism as fulfilment of Mk 16.17-18. However, he seems to allow his interpretation to be calibrated by his experience, or at the very least his observation of God's Spirit at work in the church in his own day. Furthermore, his interpretation of the signs passage is sufficiently broad that he feels no need to insist upon snake handling and immunity from poison while freely substituting the resurrection of the dead as a fulfilment of the promise that signs would follow those who believe.

I have argued at length elsewhere[26] that Hippolytus exhibits demonstrably similar tendencies to Irenaeus in his citations of Mk 16.9-20. Hippolytus cites Mk 16.17-18 and deals with it and its implications in detail. A literal interpretation of these promises is in evidence, which indicates a situation in the church where these sorts of things are both expected and experienced. Indeed, the concern for Hippolytus in the passage in which the sign list is referred to, is that the signs and gifts of the Spirit should not elevate a person above their God-ordained authority. The Markan signs are conflated in Hippolytus with the gifts of the Spirit, and their purpose is to point unbelievers to faith.

Aphrahat

Aphrahat, 'the Persian Sage', ministered in the first half of the fourth century in a region located in present-day Iraq. Aphrahat's use of Mk 16.17-18 serves only to substantiate points already made further. Given the tendency evident in both Irenaeus and Hippolytus to

---

[26] Coombs, *A Dual Reception*, pp. 65-74.

interpret the sign list broadly, and Irenaeus' omission of the third and fourth sign without explanation, it is interesting that Aphrahat's quote of Mk 16.17-18 simply omits the third and fourth signs:

> And again He said thus – This shall be the sign for those that believe; they shall speak with new tongues and shall cast out demons, and they shall lay their hands on the sick and they shall be made whole.[27]

The tendency to omit the third and fourth sign emerges as a common theme across different centuries and regions. One can only assume that the experience of the third and fourth signs were not sufficiently common in the Church and that if the interpreter were not inclined to allegorise, simply broadening the list of signs or omitting altogether were the only options.

Augustine

Of course, Augustine's usage of the passage in question is of little consequence in the text critical debate over the authenticity of the passage. Augustine writes during the late fourth to the early fifth centuries, a period after the publication of the 'earliest and most reliable manuscripts' of the early fourth century. Furthermore, Augustine, though his works are saturated in Scripture, reads and most frequently quotes from the Vulgate, which includes Mk 16.9-20 without comment. Augustine is significant for at least two reasons. On the one hand, Augustine is a vocal opponent of the notion (which clearly, given the polemical nature of some of his commentary, survived to his day in certain parts of the Church) that the manifestation of speaking in tongues was necessary to substantiate that a person had received the Holy Spirit – in this regard, perhaps we may (anachronistically) call him a 'cessationist'. On the other hand, Augustine clearly anticipated – indeed had observed and participated in—miraculous manifestations of the Spirit's power such as physical healing, financial provision, and the exorcism of demons.

First, to Augustine's understanding of the cessation of the gift of tongues.

> Suddenly, you see, there came a sound from heaven, as if a fierce gust were bearing down; and there appeared to them divided

---

[27] Aphrahat, *Demonstrations*, sec. 1.17, http://www.newadvent.org/fathers/370101.htm (accessed February 19, 2019).

tongues as of fire, which also settled upon each of them; and they began to speak in tongues, as the Spirit gave them to utter (Acts 2.2–4). That gust, that puff, did not puff them up, but quickened them instead; that fire did not burn them up, but stirred them up instead. There was fulfilled in them what had been prophesied so long before: There are no dialects, no words, whose voices may not be heard; so that from then on, scattering to preach the gospel, they might do what follows: Their sound has gone forth to all the earth, and their words to the ends of the world (Ps 19.3–4).

What else, after all, was the Holy Spirit foreshadowing, by endowing with the tongues of all nations people who had only learned the one tongue of their own nation (that's what he chose at that time to indicate his presence by), but that all nations were going to believe the gospel; so that first each of the faithful, later on, though, the very unity of the Church, should speak in all languages? What have they got to say to that, these people who refuse to join and be incorporated into the society of Christians, which is bearing fruit and growing in all nations? Can they possibly deny that even now the Holy Spirit comes upon Christians? So why does nobody now, either among us or among them, speak in the tongues of all nations – which was then the sign of his coming – if not because what was then being signified is now being fulfilled? Then, you see, each single believer was speaking in all languages; and now the unity of believers is speaking in all languages. And so even now all languages are ours, since we are members of the body in which they are to be found.[28]

Again from the same sermon series:

Isn't the Holy Spirit being given nowadays, then, brothers and sisters? Anyone who thinks that, isn't worthy to receive it. It certainly is given nowadays. So why is nobody speaking with the tongues of all nations, as people spoke who were filled with the Holy Spirit at that time? Why? Because what that signified has been fulfilled.[29]

---

[28] Saint Augustine, Sermon 269, John Rotelle (ed.), *The Works of Saint Augustine: A Translation for the 21st Century*, III (trans. Edmund Hill; Brooklyn, NY: New City Press, 1993), pp. 283-84.

[29] Saint Augustine, Sermon 267, *The Works of Saint Augustine*, sec. 3.

As if that were not emphatic enough, this one from his sermon series on 1 John:

> In the first days the Holy Spirit fell upon the believers [those who believe], and they spoke in tongues that they hadn't learned, as the Spirit gave them to speak. *These signs* were appropriate for the time. For it was necessary that the Holy Spirit be signified thus in all tongues, because the gospel of God was going to traverse all tongues throughout the earth. That was the sign that was given, and it passed. Is it expected now of those upon whom a hand is imposed, so that they may receive the Holy Spirit, that they speak in tongues? Or, when we imposed our hand upon those infants, was any one of you paying attention to see if they would speak in tongues? And, when he saw them not speaking in tongues, was there any one of you with a heart so perverse as to say, 'They didn't receive the Holy Spirit, for, if they had received him, they would be speaking in tongues in the same way as happened then?' If, therefore, there is no testimony now by way of these miracles to the presence of the Holy Spirit, how does anyone know that he has received the Holy Spirit?
>
> Let one question one's heart. If a person loves his brother, the Spirit of God is abiding in him.[30]

This passage is of particular importance to the present study because it demonstrates clearly Augustine's intertextual instinct on the gift of tongues. He is recounting the story of Acts 2 (in a sermon on 1 John!) but his wording seems to be influenced by Mk 16.17-18. The italicized text in the citation above reveals verbal correspondence between the Vulgate of Mk 16.17-18 and Augustine's Latin. This passage is also important because Augustine clearly sees the interpretive difficulty that was caused by the fact that the Church lacked the experience of speaking in tongues in the early fifth century (or did they? See below). He sees the inconsistency of interpretation and seeks to mitigate it.

Augustine clearly understands the gift of tongues to have been temporary, but not because miraculous gifts and manifestations of the Spirit are temporary. Augustine sees tongues as temporary

---

[30] Saint Augustine, 'Homilies on the First Epistle of John', *The Works of Saint Augustine*, sec. 6.10.

because their purpose had been fulfilled when the gospel reached the then-known world. We may perhaps see in this theological account of the gift of tongues a desire to reinterpret based on experience (or lack of experience) because Augustine, like others before him, interpreted the promise of tongues as xenolalia.

This is not to say that Augustine disbelieved miracles in general. Augustine clearly believed in, and had personally experienced, miracles.[31] In his *City of God*, Augustine gives an extended account of the various miracles that were occurring in and around the churches in North Africa. This chapter was written in response to Augustine's frustration that the many miracles that were occurring were going unreported and uncelebrated. He recounts numerous miracles of physical healing, of miraculous financial provision, and of release from demonic oppression. In the very first of these, Augustine himself was among a group of friends that prayed fervently for one of their number who was about to undergo a particularly painful and risky surgery. As the patient was prepared for the surgery he wept loudly and cried out to God for healing while all his friends prayed in agreement. Before the first incision was made the physician examined again and found that the presenting condition had been completely healed. It is a particularly moving passage, and I commend it to Pentecostal readers; Augustine includes a further healing account apparently effected through the relics of the saints (though it should be noted that there seems to be a parallel of exactly this type of miracle in 2 Kings 13). It will be equally fascinating to Pentecostal readers that Augustine actually gives an account of what is almost certainly glossolalia though Augustine does not describe it as tongues, but rather 'jubilation'. Elsewhere he explains jubilation as follows:

> Ye already know what it is to make a joyful noise (to 'jubilate') [Latin: *Jam nostis quid sit jubliare*]. Rejoice and speak. If ye cannot express your joy, shout ye [Latin: *Si quod gaudetis loqui non potestis, jubilate*]; let the shout manifest your joy [Latin: *gaudium vestrum exprimat jubilatio*], if your speech cannot.[32]

Augustine further explains the practice of 'jubilation' thus:

---

[31] For this see in particular Augustine, *City of God* 22.8 in entirety.

[32] Augustine, *On the Psalms* XCVIII.4 vol. 8, Nicene and Post Nicene Fathers: Second Series (Peabody, MA: Hendrickson, 1996), p. 481. For the Latin see Augustine, *Enarratio in Psalmum* XCVIII (PL 37.1254).

I am about to say what ye know. One who jubilates, uttereth not words, but it is a certain sound of joy without words: for it is the expression of a mind poured forth in joy, expressing, as far as it is able, the affection, but not compassing the feeling. A man rejoicing in his own exultation, after certain words which cannot be uttered or understood, bursteth forth into sounds of exultation without words, so that it seemeth that he indeed doth rejoice with his voice itself, but as if filled with excessive joy cannot express in words the subject of that joy ... Those who are engaged at work in the fields are most given to jubilate; reapers, or vintagers, or those who gather any of the fruits of the earth, delighted with the abundant produce, and rejoicing in the very richness and exuberance of the soil, sing in exultation; and among the songs which they utter in words, they put in certain cries without words in the exultation of a rejoicing mind; and this is what is meant by jubilating.[33]

To summarise thus far, Augustine clearly believed and had experienced miracles including physical healing and the casting out of demons. He believed in tongues, but since he understood the promise of tongues to refer to xenolalia, and since he had no experience of this in the fifth century (despite his apparent experience of glossolalia), he read the promise of tongues as a theological affirmation about the nature of the Church rather than an enduring requirement for a particular manifestation.

Given his easy turn to a less 'literal' interpretation,[34] it is hardly surprising to find the following appropriation of the promise of immunity from poison:

The Lord, however, foretold concerning His faithful followers, that even if they should drink any deadly thing, it should not hurt them (Mark 16:18). And thus it happens that they who read with judgment, and bestow their approbation on whatever is commendable according to the rule of faith, and disapprove of things

---

[33] Augustine, 'On the Psalms' vol. 8, *Nicene and Post Nicene Fathers: Second Series* (Peabody, MA: Hendrickson, 1996), p. 488.

[34] It is important to note that Augustine would not characterize this as a 'spiritual' interpretation, but rather a 'literal' one. For him, the 'literal' meaning of a passage of Scripture is the 'intended' meaning, whether or not the meaning that the Holy Spirit intends corresponds to what we might consider to be a 'literal' reading.

which ought to be reprobated, even if they commit to their memory statements which are declared to be worthy of disapproval, they receive no harm from the poisonous and depraved nature of the sentences.[35]

Though this may seem like the kind of free allegorization of which Augustine is sometimes accused, he should be given credit for at least addressing the issue of the interpretation of the fourth sign! But this is not mere fanciful allegorization. Augustine's method, as always, is intertextual – one cannot help but think of Hattie Barth's intertextual allegorization at this point. Noting that 'drinking' in Scripture is often symbolic of imbibing of a person's soul/spirit is the key that allows him to interpret 'drinking poison' as reading the books of a particular heretic – hence imbibing of his spirit – and yet not being harmed in the process.

Discussion

There are undoubtedly similarities and indeed continuities between Pentecostal interpretation of the promise that signs would follow those who believe and the interpretation of the Church between the second and fifth centuries. First, Pentecostal interpretation seems internally inconsistent when it insists on the expectation of the literal sign in the case of exorcism, tongues, and healing on the one hand, while diminishing, broadening, omitting or allegorizing the third and fourth signs. And yet somewhat surprisingly, such interpretation is entirely consistent with Patristic interpretation of this passage. Furthermore, as the Patristic treatment of the promise of the signs demonstrates, what appears on the surface to be an inconsistent interpretation is in fact shown to be consistent because it relies on the principle of intertextuality. Since the promise of tongues, healing, and exorcism are found elsewhere in the NT, and since they are frequently practiced by the NT Church, these may be taken as promised literally. However, since the same cannot be said for the third and fourth signs, other interpretations may be sought.

Second, the Early Church tended to honor Scripture above experience, a trait that also characterizes and should characterize

---

[35] Augustine, *On The Soul and Its Origin*, sec. 23.17 http://www.newadvent.org/fathers/15082.htm (accessed February 25, 2019).

Pentecostals. However, in several of the examples cited, the Early Church allowed a greater place for their theology to be altered by their experience and while, as noted above, this possibility is not entirely excluded in Pentecostal interpretation, it seems that we may be a little more stubborn in contending for what Scripture promises than were the early churches. Particularly, it seems, as time went on.

Third, the Early Church tended to follow a 'literal' hermeneutic when it came to promises of miraculous manifestations of the Holy Spirit's power. Ironically, it is this 'literalist' default that leads Augustine to 'theologize away' (if I may!) the gift of tongues. He comes to the same conclusion as Pentecostal interpreters, at least initially: the book of Acts teaches that the initial evidence of the baptism of the Holy Spirit is speaking in other tongues. However, he cannot sustain the tension between this conclusion and the reality that he neither witnesses nor experiences this phenomenon.

A critical difference is revealed in the extent of depth of the intertextuality of the Early Church. In this regard, Pentecostals certainly have something to learn and can be challenged by our forebearers that better interpretations will arise to the extent that we continue to saturate ourselves in Scripture. A related difference is the ease and confidence with which the Early Church spiritualized/allegorized. This will concern some Pentecostals. It should not. For as Augustine's interpretation demonstrated, allegory done well is simply intertextuality.

To return to the question of whether and to what extent the basic features of Pentecostal biblical interpretation and experience can be traced in the Church of the second to fifth century, the answer is unequivocally yes. And despite the lamentable characteristic of some contemporary Pentecostals to rush to celebrate novelty (and thus tolerate heresy), this should encourage us greatly. If what we have is truly and entirely new, that is to say, if our interpretation of Scripture (to apply generally what has been demonstrated more narrowly in this study) has truly never occurred to any generation of the Church between the book of Acts and 1901, then it is almost certainly wrong and, worse than that, dangerous. On the other hand, if what we believe and expect and teach, and encourage and strive and pray diligently for *can* be found in the intervening centuries, then what we have is what we have claimed since the 'beginning': a restoration of important New Testament truths. Not only is the type of supernatural Christianity that we advocate for, expect, and experience justified; the literalist, intuitive, intertextual, experiential hermeneutic that leads us to do so is not unique, but rather an important retrieval from our spiritual forbears. This conclusion both demonstrates the continuity of Pentecostal-type experience and expectation beyond the book of Acts, and also contributes to establishing the essential catholicity of the global Pentecostal movement.

Bibliography

Anderson, Allan, *An Introduction to Pentecostalism* (Cambridge, MA: Cambridge University Press, 2004).

Alexander, Kimberly E., *Pentecostal Healing: Models in Theology and Practice* (JPTSup 29; Leiden: Brill, 2006).

Aphrahat, *Demonstrations*. Accessed February 19, 2019. http://www.newadvent.org/fathers/370101.htm.

Augustine, *On the Soul and Its Origin*. Accessed February 25, 2019. http://www.newadvent.org/fathers/15082.htm.

—*Homilies on the First Epistle of John* (ed. Daniel Doyle and Thomas Martin; trans. Boniface Ramsey; *The Works of Saint Augustine: A Translation for the 21st Century*, III; vol. 14, Brooklyn, NY: New City Press, 2008).

—*On the Psalms* (ed. Philip Schaff and Henry Wace; trans. Alexander Roberts and James Donaldson; *Nicene and Post Nicene Fathers*, Second Series, vol. 8: Peabody, MA: Hendrickson, 1996).

—Sermon 267 (ed. John Rotelle; trans. Edmund Hill; *The Works of Saint Augustine: A Translation for the 21st Century*, III; vol. 7, Brooklyn, NY: New City Press, 1993).

—Sermon 269, (ed. John Rotelle; trans. Edmund Hill; *The Works of Saint Augustine: A Translation for the 21st Century*, III; vol. 7, Brooklyn, NY: New City Press, 1993).

Coombs, Clayton, *A Dual Reception: Eusebius and the Gospel of Mark* (Minneapolis: Fortress Press, 2016).

—'Reading in Tongues: The Case for a Pneumatalogical [*sic*] Hermeneutic in Conversation with James K. Smith', *Pneuma* 32.2 (January 1, 2010), pp. 261-68.

Houston, Brian, 'What's Following You?' (Sermon, Hillsong Church, Australia, 1998).

Jacobsen, Douglas, *Thinking in the Spirit: Theologies of the Early Pentecostal Movement* (Bloomington: Indiana University Press, 2003).

Kelsey, Morton, *Tongue Speaking*, (NJ: Double & Co, 1964).

Menzies, Robert P., *Speaking in Tongues: Jesus and the Apostolic Church as Models for the Church Today* (Cleveland, TN: CPT Press, 2016).

Thomas, John Christopher, and Kimberley E. Alexander, '"And the Signs Are Following': Mark 16.9-20 – A Journey into Pentecostal Hermeneutics', *Journal of Pentecostal Theology* 11.2 (2003), pp. 147–70.

8

A LINKING OBJECT'S PRESENCE IN ABSENCE: A PRAXIS FOR MOURNING FROM LUKE-ACTS

PAMELA F. ENGELBERT*

It was the fall of 2012 when the visitor entered the 82-year-old widower's home. An astute observer may have noted that the calendar near the door displayed June 2010. Since this was the first of many monthly visits, the awkward tension was evident between the visitor, a minister, and the old farmer. After all, what did a Pentecostal minister, who was raised in an educated home in a university city, have in common with a retired, German wheat farmer with a grade-school education? The elderly gentleman had lost his wife over two years before – June of 2010, one week prior to their 57th wedding anniversary. It took a few months of regular visits for the retired farmer to speak of the calendar with the minister: 'I guess I have never changed that calendar – it was my wife's'. And for the first time, the visitor gained a precious entrance into the widower's grief. In these few words, it was learned that the older man was attempting to remain present with his wife in her absence through an item that belonged to her, which may be referred to as a linking or transitional object.

In reflecting on a pastoral response to an open window into an old widower's grieving soul, how do we as Pentecostals respond? Many Pentecostals are aware of the various victorious Pentecostal

---

* Pamela F. Engelbert (PhD, Luther Seminary) is an independent Assemblies of God scholar from Colorado and adjunct instructor for various institutions in the United States and abroad.

replies that may attempt to impel the man out of his grief, such as 'You need to move on as your wife is in a better place' or 'She is free from all her suffering, so you should rejoice'. While these, or similar responses, may urge someone out of sorrow and grief and into joy and victory, they fail to meet the widower in his place of grief and to seek to connect with him in the place where he is attempting to keep his absent wife present. By drawing from the concept of presence-absence as portrayed in grief theory's linking or transitional objects, I propose that a foundation for a Pentecostal response to grief may be enhanced by exploring the theme of presence-absence in Luke–Acts, a highly regarded text for Pentecostal theology. This practical theological study endeavors to contribute to the Pentecostal response to mourners in which one is not only present to the mourner, but also upholds a genuine Pentecostal understanding of Spirit-Christology; I do so by drawing from the Lukan theme of presence-absence, and connecting it with grief theory's linking or transitional objects. This will be accomplished in four movements: (1) by exploring the reception history of Lk. 24.13-35 in a study of early Pentecostals' interpretation; (2) by putting forth the theme of presence-absence of the divine in Luke–Acts; (3) by examining the concept of linking or transitional objects in grief; and (4) by showing how the giving of the Spirit is a theological transitional praxis of presence.

Pentecostal Reception of Luke 24.13-35

In my attempt to contribute a theological praxis of how Pentecostals respond to mourners, it may be helpful to uncover a reception history of Lk. 24.13-35 by studying the interpretations of early Pentecostals.[1]

---

[1] I searched among multiple digital collections via iFPHC.org by completing a word search of all years and all countries using the words 'Emmaus' or 'emmaus', which provided 180 and 191 publications, respectively. Documents included in the search were: *Apostolic Faith* (Alvin, TX); *Apostolic Faith* (Azusa Street); *Apostolic Faith* (Portland, OR); *Apostolic Messenger*; *Assemblies of God Heritage*; Assemblies of God Ministers Letter; *Blessed Truth*; *The Bridegroom's Messenger*; *Christ's Ambassadors Herald*; Church Directory General Council; COGIC (White) Roster; *Confidence*; *Discipline* (CHC); *El Evangelio Pentecostal* (eliminated since I do not speak Spanish); *Gospel of the Kingdom*; *Household of God*; *La Luz Apostolica* (eliminated since I do not speak Spanish); *Latter Rain Evangel*; *Maran-atha*; *Meat in Due Season*; Ministers Directory General Council; Minutes (CHC); Minutes General Council; *The Pentecostal Evangel*; *Pentecostal Herald*; *Pentecostal Testimony*; *Petals from the Rose of Sharon*; *Popular Gospel*

I chose this pericope because of its pronounced demonstration of the themes of grief-mourning and presence-absence while aiming to ask, 'What has this text meant to Pentecostals?' I found this inquiry challenging as I experienced my own grief on two counts. First, I experienced feelings of frustration, annoyance, and dismay as to how Pentecostals had interpreted the Scriptures. I identified with Martin Mittelstadt's words regarding contemporary readers' inclination 'to believe they should view this intervening period [which Mittelstadt refers to as that era "between original authors and current readers"] as an obstacle to avoid'.[2] These are my thoughts exactly! Second, this inquiry became more complicated when I experienced feelings of loss in relation to my father, who died in 2017. This is justifiable when one realizes that the articles, which were written by early Pentecostals, exhibited a tenor that my father savored in his listening of sermons. Despite these challenges, I attempted to be present in my own feelings of grief in the absence of both the presence of mystery in early Pentecostal interpretations, and of my father's own person in an embodied form. Simultaneously, I endeavored to unearth nuggets of fresh understanding in relation to Pentecostal reception history by striving to remain open. In researching digital documents on the website of the Flower Pentecostal Heritage Center, I perused 118 Pentecostal publications from 1909 through 1969 in which articles of various lengths referred to the story of the two men on the road to Emmaus. These articles are not from academic journals but include grassroots poems, sermons, and writings composed by lay people and ministers. Since time does not permit me to provide a complete listing of the various interpretative threads of Lk. 24.13-35, I highlight two themes that are relevant to this paper: grief and the second advent. The book of Luke is also the only book in the NT to be written with a sequel, namely, the Acts of the Apostles. Because Luke wrote Acts as the necessary sequel to his first account, Luke's two-volume history about the origin and the spread of Christianity (Luke–Acts), though separated in the canon, is the longest narrative in the NT.

Truth; Present Truth; Refleks; The Pentecost; Whole Truth; Word and Witness; Wort und Zeugnis (eliminated since my German is inadequate). I draw from 118 documents from the years 1909 through 1969, including duplicate printings, which either used a portion of the story or the whole story found in Luke 24.

2 Martin W. Mittelstadt, 'Receiving Luke–Acts: The Rise of Reception History and a Call to Pentecostal Scholars', *Pneuma* 40 (October 2018), pp. 367-88.

Concerning the first theme of grief, many articles address the sorrow, discouragement, and sadness of the two disciples on the Emmaus road (24.14-16, 21). *Confidence*, an early British Pentecostal periodical, includes an anonymous poem called 'Along the Road to Emmaus', in which the first stanza speaks of the disciples' grief:

VANQUISHED.
Along the road of grief and disappointment,
Of morning promise lost in early gloom;
Their footsteps echo to the bitter message,
The One they trusted lay in rock-hewn tomb.
Along the road of an offended sorrow,
Of Faith and Hope awakened but to die;
How could their tearful eyes behold the vision,
How see, that while they talked, 'The Lord drew nigh.'[3]

In a similar vein, *The Weekly Evangel* (later called *The Pentecostal Evangel*) offers a devotional thought to be read on Wednesday of that particular week: 'Ah, yes, we too have walked that Emmaus way – hearts crushed and disappointed like those two disciples. And our blinded eyes "of knowledge" have failed to recognize the Glorious One who drew near, and walked with us.'[4] One common method of interpretation was to utilize a component of the story as an illustration for a theme of an article. For instance, in *Maran-atha* in 1931, an article focuses on the Song of Solomon when Philip Wittich writes:

But the deepest lesson for Bridesouls is to even lose confidence in their own self, to be stripped of everything that seems like a comfort and stay in the natural; – **all alone**, – then He will appear to be **our all in all**! When the two disciples on their journey to Emmaus expressed their loneliness and sorrow: '**but we hoped that it was He should redeem Israel**' – then the lonely Christ joined them and turned their sadness into joy (bold in the original).[5]

---

[3] 'Along the Road to Emmaus', *Confidence* 9.1 (January 1916), p. 3.

[4] Mrs A.R. Flowers, 'Daily Portion from the King's Bounty', *WE* 203 (August 18, 1917), p. 7.

[5] Philip Wittich, 'The Song of Solomon', *Maran-atha* 8.3-4 (September/October 1931), pp. 11-12.

An additional article in *The Latter Rain Evangel* centers on Joseph when it states, 'Joseph was cast into prison and forgotten. Jesus was buried, and even His own little flock despaired that He would ever redeem Israel. You remember when the Lord appeared to two walking from Jerusalem to Emmaus how sad they were as they told Him of the recent happenings.'[6]

Frequently, I detected in my research the authors connecting the disciples' grief to some issue residing in the disciples, such as something they did or failed to do. J. Bashford Bishop contends that while Jesus longs to make himself known, people who are too focused on their trials fail to recognize his presence:

> Jesus wishes to make Himself known to us in the daily circumstances of life. If, however, we are taken up with our trials and sorrows – our eyes upon ourselves; if we fail to count on His sure Word of promise, then we shall fail to recognize His presence, and thereby miss the joy and comfort which His presence brings.[7]

The Apostolic Faith (Portland, OR) argues that the two men's fear and doubt demonstrated that they were not completely sanctified; however, when Jesus sanctified them, they believed all that Jesus said.[8] J. Calvert Jeays links the disciples' sadness with unbelief:

> If they had believed what He had said they would not have been sad ... Their hearts were full of unbelief and they did not know their Lord, though he was walking just beside them. We have been like that at times, unbelief has blinded our eyes. 'In whom the god of this world hath blinded the minds of them which believe not.'[9]

---

[6] Philip Wittich, 'Jesus Pictured in the Life of Joseph: Man Meant Evil, God Meant Good', *LRE* (October 1925), p. 21.

[7] J. Bashford Bishop, 'Sunday School Lesson: The Walk to Emmaus – Lesson for March 24', *PE* 1349 (March 16, 1940), p. 10; also published as 'Fellowship with the Risen Christ: Sunday School Lesson for April 14, 1968', *PE* 2813 (April 7, 1968), p. 14. A similar theme is seen in 'The Shaking of the Nations', as the two disciples on the Emmaus road are described as an example of people who look at their own problems, wondering if God cares; see 'The Shaking of the Nations', *PE* 1366 (July 13, 1940), p. 1; an article in *TBM* also speaks of being so worried that believers fail to recognize that Jesus is with us. Beulah Watters, 'Jesus Himself Drew Near', *TBM* 43.3 (December 1952), pp. 1-2.

[8] 'The Heart Is Cleansed from Doubts', *AF* 68 (1929), p. 3.

[9] J. Calvert Jeays, 'Jesus Himself', *PE* 524 (January 12, 1924), p. 2.

However, this same article points out Jesus' way of responding to the disciples: '[N]otice the attitude of Jesus. Some people might have done a war dance around them and scolded. Jesus walked with them, inquired into it, and chided so gently … Jesus knew all about it, but He wanted His disciples to tell Him.'[10] On a related subject, other writers assert that the disciples' reasoning in v. 15 cannot discern spiritual truth. For instance, R.J. Carlson comments about the disciples reasoning together: 'Unsanctified reasoning without the presence of the Lord will not help us, for it fails to comprehend the plan of God'.[11] Such reasoning means that when believers center on their own plans, they fail to see Jesus when he comes close to them. In contrast, D.H. McDowell believes that since the men were discussing Jesus, it engendered his presence. He writes, 'Meditation about holy things always brings the presence of the Lord. We may not always have light on the subject, but the meditation will always bring the presence of the Lord.'[12]

An additional theme concerning the second advent is seen particularly among writers prior to 1947, underscoring the absence of Jesus and the presence of the Spirit in today's world. Some authors implicitly point to Jesus' current absence by emphasizing that believers are waiting for the second advent. Horace W. Houlding interprets the eating of the bread in Luke 24 as the Lord's Supper, which was interrupted when the two disciples recognized Jesus. In like manner, current disciples of Jesus are on pause between the eating of the bread and the drinking of the cup until that day that they receive the cup from the hands of Jesus Christ.[13] G. Campbell Morgan perceives that in the same way Jesus suddenly appeared to the two on the road, so Jesus will unexpectedly appear 'in order to the carrying out His

[10] Jeays, 'Jesus Himself', p. 2.
[11] R.J. Carlson, 'Taking Christ to the People', *PE* 2264 (September 29, 1957), p. 3; A similar interpretation was made by E.S. Williams, 'Sunday's Lesson', *PE* 1922 (March 11, 1951), p. 10. Similarly, M.L. Grable writes how the disciples 'supposed' who Jesus was and states, 'How easy it is for men to defeat their own progress in the Lord because of closed minds and their *supposing* they could do nothing' (italics in original); see M.L. Grable, 'My Favorite Scripture: The Lord Opened My Understanding', *PE* 2876 (June 22, 1969), p. 7.
[12] D.H. McDowell, 'The Preeminent Christ', *PE* 575 (December 6, 1924), p. 4. A similar theme is seen in 'Jesus Himself Drew Near', *WE* 225 (February 2, 1918), p. 4.
[13] Horace W. Houlding, 'Waiting for the Cup, or the Interrupted Supper', *TBM* 6.124 (January 1, 1913), p. 3.

purposes'.[14] William B. McCafferty comments that Jesus promised his disciples that they would see him again after his death, which is seen as the disciples traveled on the road to Emmaus; thus, believers, too, shall see him again since they live because Jesus lives.[15]

Still others underline not only the absence of Jesus but also the presence of the Holy Spirit. Uldine Utley in 'School Days' speaks of the Spirit coming to teach Christ-followers in Jesus' absence. In the same way the two disciples on the Emmaus road required a teacher to explain about the Messiah in the Scriptures, contemporary disciples need a teacher, whom Jesus has already given.[16] Similarly, Harry J. Steil writes of Jesus informing his disciples that they would no longer see him; however, Jesus, having anticipated their doubts, sent them the Holy Spirit.[17] One article not only speaks of the second advent but also the presence of the Spirit today, who explains about Jesus' coming:

> They had had doubts as to His being the Redeemer of Israel, but all their doubts vanished as Christ expounded and explained unto them in all the Scriptures the things concerning Himself and His first advent. There are plenty who are willing to put doubts into the seeker's mind concerning His coming again. They say, 'Where is the promise of His coming?' But if you are concerned about His coming, the Holy Spirit will unfold the Scriptures to you. Christ explained the first advent, and by His Spirit He is ready today to unfold and explain to you the promises concerning His second coming.[18]

Having explored two basic themes that may be detected in the Pentecostal reception history of Lk. 24.13-35, I draw attention to several points of interest. Concerning the theme of grief, early Pentecostals demonstrate that they are not in denial of the disciples' grief and discouragement when they openly speak of the disorientation of

---

[14] G. Campbell Morgan, 'The Coming Revelation of the Lord Jesus Christ', *WE* 232 (March 23, 1918), p. 5.

[15] William B. McCafferty, 'I'll See You Again', *PE* 1667 (April 20, 1946), pp. 6-7.

[16] Uldine Utley, 'School Days', *Petals from the Rose of Sharon* 3.9 (September 1927), p. 3.

[17] Harry J. Steil, 'I Will Not Leave You Orphans', *PE* 1145 (April 18, 1936), p. 5.

[18] 'A Glimpse of Things to Come', *PE* 1607 (November 16, 1946), p. 4.

these two disciples. Such an acknowledgment invites grieving Pentecostals to take that which is inward (grief) and make it outward
(mourning).[19] Some early Pentecostals even reference how Jesus invited the disciples to mourn through outward sharing of their grief,
which grief studies see as an avenue for healing. Nonetheless, writers
frequently indicate that the disciples' grief is the reason for the two
disciples' failure to recognize Jesus. That is to say, several writers assert that unbelief, fear, doubt, or human reasoning foster an inability
to see Jesus. It is important for Pentecostals to be aware of how early
Pentecostals have received this story as it may influence how contemporary Pentecostals 'receive' the grief stories of others today. On the
one hand, current Pentecostals may receive a mourner's story of grief
by acknowledging its depth and difficulty. On the other hand, as Pentecostals receive the story, they may attempt to propel individuals
from their grief by using principles, such as 'Meditate on Jesus, and
the sorrow will turn to joy', which may only contribute to, not ame-
liorate, mourners' grief. It behooves Pentecostals to be aware of their
Pentecostal heritage and the previous patterns of relating to others,
as these historical patterns are powerful, engendering a tendency toward repetition. Such awareness will assist in guarding against detri-
mental proclivities of Pentecostalism.[20]

In contrast to an abundance of articles that underscore the theme
of grief, the ones that highlight the second advent are fewer in number. These latter articles emphasize the presence-absence dynamic of
this pericope, be it directly or indirectly. This dynamic particularly
emerges in reference to Jesus' second coming, concerning the writers
who encouraged continued belief during this time of Jesus' absence.
It is this dynamic of presence-absence to which I now turn by putting
forth a theme of presence-absence in the broader context of Luke–
Acts.

---

[19] I am drawing from grief counselor Alan W. Wolfelt for these definitions; see
*Understanding Your Grief: Ten Essential Touchstones for Finding Hope and Healing Your
Heart* (Fort Collins, CO: Companion Press, 2003), p. 22.
   [20] I am referring to Murray Bowen's theory of family system, which holds that
a family system is a multigenerational emotional unit. It has patterns of relating
(emotionally reacting) to one another that are passed down from generation to
generation.

Presence–Absence in Luke–Acts

Typically, Pentecostals uphold the presence of God – the divine encounter – as a theme in Luke–Acts. However, if one considers that the Gospel of Luke stresses the presence of Jesus Christ on earth and that the majority of Acts highlights the actions of the church while Jesus is bodily absent, then the collocation of Luke with Acts juxtaposes Jesus' presence with absence. Furthermore, readers of the text (both original and contemporary) continue to experience the physical absence of Jesus while Luke–Acts (particularly Luke) puts forth the presence of Jesus.[21] As such, the argument could be made that through the reading of the text amidst Jesus' absence, the Lukan corpus forms a theme of presence alongside absence.

At the beginning of the Third Gospel, Luke quickly launches into the dynamic of presence and absence. Chapter one tells of an old woman, who is beyond child-bearing years, becoming pregnant following an angel's prediction made to her husband. Such an account of God opening a womb may call to mind for a Jewish reader other similar stories, such as Abraham and Sarah (Genesis 17); the pregnancy of Hannah (1 Samuel 1); or the birth of Samson to a childless couple (Judges 13). In each of these incidents, the divine becomes potently present when a prediction of a birth of a son is fulfilled. On the heels of a prediction of a son is to be born to an older, married couple, Luke places the account of another prediction being made by the same angel: a son is to be born to an unmarried woman and much younger woman in the absence of sexual relations. That is, the Holy Spirit has come upon her, and once again God is encountered. Divine presence is then noted when Elizabeth's baby leaps within her during Mary's visit, after which Elizabeth, filled with the Holy Spirit, prophesies (Lk. 1.42-46). The chapter closes as Zechariah, who had lost his ability to speak and perhaps hear (v. 64), is also filled with the Holy Spirit and prophesies after declaring in writing that his son is to

---

[21] Jonathan Knight writes,

Jesus … is both present and absent for the readers. He is present in the text and present through His Spirit in every act of worship whenever the Gospel is read. Yet the presence of Jesus also draws attention to his continued absence because he has yet to return from heaven to act as the eschatological judge (9:26). Part of the Gospel's function is to make the absent Jesus present by the repetition of his life and words.

Jonathan Knight, *Luke's Gospel* (London: Routledge, 1998), p. 148.

be called 'John' (vv. 59-67). Thus, divine presence in this Lukan chapter is profoundly noticed while contemporary readers are experiencing Jesus' physical absence on the earth. One could say that Luke purposely directs his reader's attention to the presence of the divine in Luke–Acts in order that they 'may know for certain the things [they were] taught' (1.4) amidst divine bodily absence.

However, Luke not only intensely emphasizes divine presence while readers experience divine absence, but he also clearly underscores Jesus' absence while he is present on the earth within the text itself. Space does not permit me to note each instance of divine presence and absence in Luke–Acts. Instead, I have formulated two broad categories of presence-absence, of which I include a limited number of sub-themes with examples of each. These categories are: *prior to the resurrection* and *after the resurrection*. I begin with *prior to the resurrection* under which I have chosen to highlight four sub-themes of Jesus' absence as being: (1) an intratextual prelude; (2) a deliberate withdrawal; (3) in connection to authority; and (4) in association with Jesus' return. By emphasizing these themes of Jesus' absence in Luke–Acts, readers of the Third Gospel may find a point of identification as they strive to believe in Jesus the Christ in light of Jesus' physical absence.

An *intratextual prelude* is the first theme and instance of Jesus' absence amidst his physical presence on earth, which is in Lk. 2.41-51. On a visit to Jerusalem during the Passover feast, Luke records that the 12-year-old Jesus accompanies his parents to this celebration; however, unbeknownst to Mary and Joseph, Jesus remains in Jerusalem while they travel home. By the time it is recognized that Jesus is not among those traveling in the caravan and by the time they find him, three days have passed. By referring to this theme as an 'intratextual prelude', I am drawing from Stefan Alkier, who writes, 'The three days connect this episode intratextually to the resurrection story'[22] in which Jesus is dead for three days. However, as Alkier points out, unlike the childhood incident, Jesus, or one could say his body, cannot be as easily located in a frantic search for him following

---

[22] Stefan Alkier, 'Ways of Presence and Modes of Absence in the Gospel of Luke – Or: How Scripture Works', in Ingolf U. Dalferth (ed.), *The Presence and Absence of God: Claremont Studies in the Philosophy of Religion, Conference 2008* (Tübingen, Germany: Mohr Siebeck, 2009), p. 49.

the resurrection.[23] That is, after the resurrection, humans cannot will themselves to vanquish Jesus' physical absence on the earth since he appears randomly at his own will. I revisit this theme below in an exploration of Jesus' presence-absence after the resurrection.

A deliberate withdrawal is the second theme of Jesus' absence in the Third Gospel in which Jesus purposefully disconnects himself or withdraws from the people.[24] Two such occasions are noticed in Luke 4: (1) during Jesus' forty day temptation in the wilderness (vv. 1-2); and (2) his journeying to a 'deserted place' (v. 42). In the latter, the crowds attempt to force Jesus to stay with them, but he insists that he must preach the good news to others (vv. 42-44). It may be viewed as a tacit signal to Luke's readers that Jesus' physical presence on earth will not always remain. Alkier concurs, 'His presence at one location will not endure; he will remain only for the time he needs to preach and teach the good news and the kingdom of God. After that his absence is necessary because he must be present also at other places in order to do his duty.'[25]

The third theme of Jesus' absence appears *in connection to authority.* Such an occasion is seen in ch. 7 when a centurion's servant is ill (vv. 1-10). The centurion recognizes that Jesus has the authority to heal from a distance, so he insists that Jesus simply speaks a word to heal the slave. Jesus, who discerns the centurion's belief in who Jesus is, heals *in absentia.*[26] In Acts, Luke stresses to readers this same theme when they read of Christ-followers operating under the authority of Jesus' name after the ascension – namely, in the bodily absence of Jesus. To borrow words from Luke 7, Jesus' disciples in Acts go here and there, ministering under the authority of the name of Jesus in his corporeal absence. The aforementioned theme continues to be

---

[23] Alkier, 'Ways of Presence and Modes of Absence in the Gospel of Luke', p. 49. He also writes, '[I]n Luke 24 the absence of Jesus cannot be surmounted by walking to the tomb. The resurrected body cannot be found like the body of the absent young Jesus at a special location in the empirical world'.

[24] Additional instances of Jesus withdrawing from the people include Lk. 5.16, which informs the reader that Jesus 'frequently withdrew to the wilderness and prayed', and 6.12, which speaks of Jesus going to a mountain to pray.

[25] Alkier, 'Ways of Presence and Modes of Absence in the Gospel of Luke', p. 49.

[26] I speak more extensively about a similar incident in John 4 and also the understanding of presence in absence and absence in presence; see Pamela F. Engelbert, *Who Is Present in Absence? A Pentecostal Theological Praxis of Suffering and Healing* (Eugene, OR: Wipf & Stock, 2019).

underscored a few verses later when John the Baptist inquires if Jesus is the Christ or if they should expect another (vv. 18-19). Rather than rebuking John, Luke rehearses Jesus' deeds and points towards Jesus' authority;

> At that very time Jesus cured many people of diseases, sicknesses, and evil spirits, and granted sight to many who were blind. So he answered them, 'Go tell John what you have seen and heard: The blind see, the lame walk, lepers are cleansed, the deaf hear, the dead are raised, the poor have good news proclaimed to them' (Lk. 7.21-22).

Such an inquiry by the imprisoned John, who is unable to be present physically with Jesus, could serve as inspiration for readers to maintain belief in Jesus Christ and his authority.[27] This theme of persistent belief during Jesus' absence is re-emphasized in Acts when believers are being persecuted during Jesus' bodily absence (e.g. Peter and John heal a lame man in the authority of Jesus' name and are persecuted in Acts 3–4).[28] Lest Christ-followers forget about their own finitude, a pericope in Luke 9 functions for readers as a reminder of their dependence on Jesus' authority while he is absent (vv. 28-42). In this story, Jesus is physically absent from nine disciples while he climbs a mountain with three disciples and experiences God's glory. During his absence, the nine are unable to deliver a demonized boy, whom Jesus sets free upon his return.

A fourth theme of Jesus' absence is *in association with Jesus' return*, which also signifies Jesus' upcoming corporeal absence.[29] One indicator that Jesus will not continue to be physically present appears in Luke 5, when Jesus informs the Pharisees as to the reason his disciples do not fast: 'But those days are coming, and when the bridegroom is taken from them, at that time they will fast' (5.35). In writing

---

[27] Darrell Bock implies this; he associates John with Theophilus. Darrell Bock, *The NIV Application Commentary: Luke* (Grand Rapids: Zondervan, 1996), p. 210.

[28] The theme of absence *in connection to authority* is also seen in 9.1-9 when Jesus sends his disciples out alone, giving them authority to heal and cast out demons, and again in ch. 10 in the sending out of the 72.

[29] Additional instances of this sub-theme of his return are in Lk. 12.35-48 when Jesus communicates through parables concerning his bodily absence and his return, requiring the necessity to be ready, and in ch. 21 when Jesus predicts his return, conveying his upcoming physical absence from the earth.

about Pentecostal theology concerning Jesus' presence in the Lord's Supper, Christopher Stephenson comments about Lk. 5.33-35 in which presence and absence appear:

> To the extent that fasting often accompanied mourning, there is nothing surprising in Jesus' assertion that the time of the bride-groom's *presence* — a time of joy and feasting — is not the time for fasting. The shock is in his claim that the bridegroom will depart, during which time his followers will fast in his *absence* (italics in original).[30]

In Luke 22, Jesus continues to underscore his upcoming absence as well as the future fullness of the kingdom at the institution of the Lord's Supper (vv. 14-20). Stephenson speaks of this presence-absence dynamic when he writes about a Pentecostal understanding of Jesus' presence in communion:

> [I]n the Last Supper passages from the Synoptic Gospels, the context of the meal is not Jesus' *presence* but his *absence*. Jesus is preparing his disciples for his departure, and they will thereafter eat the meal in his remembrance because he will not be present with them in the meal until he eats it again with them in the kingdom of God (Mt. 26.29; Mk. 14.25; Lk. 22.16) (italics in original).[31]

In Lk. 5.35 and 22.14-20, the bridegroom's absence leads to the bride's participation in fasting and the Lord's table. The aforementioned four sub-themes of Jesus' absence, then, may serve as encouragement for Luke's readers to continue to believe while being unable to physically see Jesus.

Having briefly outlined four sub-themes of Jesus' absence *prior to the resurrection*, I now turn to the category *after the resurrection*, under which I have chosen to center on three sub-themes of the presence-

---

[30] Christopher A. Stephenson, *Types of Pentecostal Theology: Method, System, Spirit* (Oxford: Oxford University Press, 2013), p. 123.

[31] Stephenson, *Types of Pentecostal Theology*, p. 123. Luke additionally includes an interesting notation about Jesus being absent from Galilee when he sails across the Sea of Galilee (8.26); however, when Jesus returns, Luke is careful to say that the crowd welcomes him as the people are waiting for him (8.40).

absence of Jesus' body.[32] By the end of Luke 23, readers are well-informed of the theme of presence-absence. It is at this point, however, that a shift transpires in how Jesus' presence and absence is experienced. This shift is magnified by the text's use of the word 'now' (δε in 24.1). The women's honoring of the Sabbath (23.55-56), which is succeeded by *now*, gives the sensation of a literary pause in the story. This pause and the aforementioned shift are significant in that they allude to a type of preparation for the upcoming corporeal absence of Jesus in the majority of Acts. Alkier also refers to this shift when he writes that the 'prophesied absence of Jesus [see Lk. 5.34-35] does not work the same way as the absence of the man Jesus before his death on the cross'.[33] Luke provides three accounts of this variance in presence-absence of Jesus' body, which include: (1) the women and Peter who go to the tomb, witnessing the absence of Jesus' body (Lk. 24.1-12); (2) the mourning of the absence of Jesus' body while Jesus is present (Lk. 24.13-35); and (3) the eventual absence of Jesus' body in the ascension (Lk. 24.50-53; Acts 1.9-11).

The verses immediately preceding the first account of variance in presence-absence (Lk. 24.1-12) are significant for the understanding of presence-absence of Jesus' body. According to Luke, the women see not only the tomb but also how Jesus' body is laid in it; thus, while the body is present, there is an absence of Jesus. At this point, the women expect the body to remain. Once a dead body is placed, it does not have the capacity to move itself, which is an implicit understanding of the women in Lk. 24.1 as they bring spices to anoint Jesus' body.[34] However, although they encounter the absence of Jesus' body, the angels inform them of the presence of a living Jesus (vv. 5-

---

[32] This idea of the tension of presence-absence of Jesus' body in Luke–Acts is drawn from Luke Timothy Johnson's *Living Jesus: Learning the Heart of the Gospel* (San Francisco: HarperSanFrancisco, 1999).

[33] Alkier, 'Ways of Presence and Modes of Absence in the Gospel of Luke', p. 51.

[34] Alkier, 'Ways of Presence and Modes of Absence in the Gospel of Luke', p. 51, states, '[T]he living know where the dead body is: He is in the grave … The empirical logic of death lets them think that he cannot move, because the death takes away the body's ability to move. He must be present in the tomb because the dead body is no longer able to choose his absence and go away.' Joel B. Green also makes a similar observation that since they saw where the body was laid, the women in returning to the tomb, 'can hardly expect anything other than an undisturbed corpse'; see Green, *The Gospel of Luke* (Grand Rapids: Eerdmans, 1997), p. 837.

6), thereby his bodily absence signifies his presence. Luke Timothy Johnson comments on the angels' words:

> [T]he women visiting the tomb are told that they are mistaken in their quest: 'Why do you seek the Living One among the dead?' (24.5). It is clear from this response that Jesus' body is no longer where it had been, but this absence is explained on the basis of his being 'the Living One' who cannot be constrained even by death.[35]

The reader is to note that, according to Luke, the women do not experience the bodily presence of Jesus.[36] Peter also encounters the absence of a body as indicated in that he 'saw only the strips of linen cloth' (v. 12). As Alkier asserts, Peter longs to believe, but he, too, embraces the 'empirical logic of death', which holds that if one is dead, one's body is where people place it; Peter, then, must see in order to believe (24.34).[37] Thus, in this resurrection incident Jesus' body is absent with suggestions that he is somehow present.

The next account is a type of a transitional pericope (Lk. 24.13-35) in that it makes known Jesus' bodily presence but not in the same way as it had been previously. The reader may recall that earlier in Luke, prior to the resurrection, Jesus is present on the earth, so he potentially could be found by searching for him. Then after the resurrection in the first account of the variance of presence-absence, the reader has just seen how Jesus' body remains absent with only indications of his presence. In the upcoming third account, the focus is on Jesus' ascension (Lk. 24.50-53 and Acts 1.9-11), which means that he is bodily absent on the earth while he is present at the right-hand of God the Father. However, in this scene, Jesus' body is present and also absent, but not in the same way it was previously. It is as if at this point in reading Luke–Acts that the reader's exploration of the variation of presence-absence deepens.[38] Johnson explains,

---

[35] Johnson, *Living Jesus*, p. 21.

[36] Johnson, *Living Jesus*, p. 21, writes, 'The women, however, are given no immediate vision of Jesus as alive'.

[37] Alkier, 'Ways of Presence and Modes of Absence in the Gospel of Luke', pp. 51-52.

[38] Johnson, *Living Jesus*, p. 21, comments, 'The appearances in Luke 24:13–49 are obviously a mode not of Jesus' absence but of his presence to his followers. He moves about him as he had before – yet, as we have seen, not *really* as before.

His presence to them now is both more powerful and more allusive, more dramatic and more mediated. Though he is 'really' present in his body, that body has a transfigured quality that enables him to be present in different places to different people (24.31-34).[39]

A deeper dive into presence-absence of Jesus emerges in v. 13 with the strong, emphatic transitional words of καὶ ἰδοὺ ('now behold'). Another feature of this account is the disciples' experience of grief amidst Jesus' absence. This grief is seen not only in Luke's description of the two disciples being sad (v. 17b) but also in indications of their confusion and disappointment, other emotions that may be identified as grief. Additionally, the curiosity communicated by Jesus (vv. 17, 19) signifies a space for the disciples to express their grief. Yet, at the same time, Jesus exhorts them to believe, pointing towards the maintaining of their faith during Jesus' absence even amidst grief. The reader may recall that this is not the first time Luke implies grief and belief in tension. Earlier I mentioned about the bride fasting (mourning) in the absence of the bridegroom (5.33-35); fasting in and of itself is a praxis of both faith and mourning. That is to say, grief and faith may not be mutually exclusive; instead, belief amidst grief expresses an authentic faith. The subject of fasting in the absence of the bridegroom moves me toward the final account: Jesus' bodily absence from the earth.

After being bodily present to his followers by walking with them and eating with his disciples, Luke writes of Jesus' ascension, his bodily absence as seen in Lk. 24.50-53 and Acts 1.9-11. As Darrell Bock notes, the two accounts are linked in that Luke includes a summary of the more detailed account in Acts. Additionally, Bock detects that Luke highlights the disciples 'return to the Temple, where Luke's story began with Zechariah'.[40] For me, these two events are in stark contrast to each other: the account at the beginning emphasizes divine presence, while the account at the end stresses divine bodily absence. Such absence through the removal of Jesus' body, as Johnson

---

Jesus is not present in the way he had been when he walked and talked with them in Galilee' (italics in original).

[39] Darrell Bock also agrees that this pericope deepens the discussion of the resurrection; see Bock, *The NIV Application Commentary: Luke*, p. 614.

[40] Bock, *The NIV Application Commentary: Luke*, p. 622.

writes, is 'preparation for another mode of his presence'[41] – namely, the presence of the Holy Spirit. Bock perceives that the theme of the Spirit in the Lukan corpus is to reassure 'Theophilus that though the Messiah is dead and seemingly absent, he is present in the gift and presence of the Spirit he has sent'.[42] The presence of the Spirit serves as a connection with Jesus while also serving as a reminder of Jesus' bodily absence on the earth. In the midst of Jesus' current physical absence and the presence of the Spirit, Luke offers a promise of Jesus' return in the same manner that he departed (Acts 1.11). As Jonathan Knight asserts:

> Jesus in Luke is thus a character who disappears. His absence gives the story its meaning: Jesus for the readers is the Lord who journeys from earth to heaven (9.51). The heavenly Lord makes his presence felt whenever Jesus the character is mentioned. His enthronement is a symbol that he is waiting to return to earth to effect the visible climax of the kingdom of God (22.69; cf. Acts 7.56).[43]

The presence of the Spirit is experienced, then, in a transitional period. That is, the giving of the Spirit becomes a *link*, joining believers to Jesus' presence in his absence, until the day when God's kingdom will be established on the earth. This is the hope of Christ-followers, as Knight writes, 'At this return [of Jesus], it is implied, absence will yield before presence and the eschatological hopes which the Gospel creates will be satisfied'.[44] Seeing the giving of the Spirit as a type of link invites me to consider grief theory's concept of linking or transitional objects as a way to continue examining presence-absence.

Linking or Transitional Objects in Grief

I have briefly explored Pentecostal reception of the two men on the Emmaus road in which the discussion of the disciples' grief and the subject of Jesus' second coming was underscored. This was followed

---

[41] Johnson, *Living Jesus*, p. 21.

[42] Darrell Bock, 'Luke, the Gospel of', in Joel B. Green and Scot McKnight (eds.), *Dictionary of Jesus and the Gospels*, (Downers Grove, IL: InterVarsity Press, 1992), p. 505.

[43] Knight, *Luke's Gospel*, p. 148.

[44] Knight, *Luke's Gospel*, p. 149.

by highlighting an overview of presence-absence in Luke–Acts in which Luke makes a shift in the presence of Jesus on earth and provides the Spirit as a link to a future of being in the fullness of Jesus' presence. I now turn to the concept of linking, or transitional objects in grief theory. The term 'transitional object' first appeared in a theory unrelated to grief, in the work of Donald W. Winnicott. According to Margaret Gibson, Winnicott developed the concept of 'transitional object' from his research on childhood development and the concepts of separation and attachment. As children develop, they learn that they and their caregivers are not one and the same, but that they are separate from their caregivers. Such a realization of this separation means that the caregiver is not always present, causing children to learn to navigate through 'the existential anxiety of absence'; thus, children seek for ways to enable themselves to negotiate this process of differentiation,[45] one of which is the selection of a *transitional object*. Winnicott defines a *transitional object* as an object (often a soft object such as a blanket) that becomes of significant value to a child to protect the child 'against anxiety', namely during times of sleep, loneliness, or sadness. According to Winnicott, it is equally important that the transitional object is representative of the primary caregiver while also not being the actual caregiver. In other words, Winnicott perceives both 'difference and similarity' between the caregiver and the object chosen by the child. Both 'difference and similarity' symbolized in a transitional object help children navigate from the perception that the primary caregiver is merged with them to relating to the caregiver as one who is separate from them.[46] Such separateness means that the caregiver is not always present; therefore, transitional objects provide the necessary calming effect in place of, or in the absence of, the caregiver. In speaking of Winnicott's theory, Gibson writes, 'Transitional objects express the anguish and militate against the [caregiver's] absence as a primary figure and corporeal site of absence and loss'.[47]

---

[45] Margaret Gibson, 'Melancholy Objects', *Mortality* 9.4 (Nov 2004), pp. 287-88, doi: 10.1080/13576270412331329812.

[46] D.W. Winnicott, 'Transitional Objects and Transitional Phenomena – A Study of the First Not-Me Possession', *International Journal of Psycho-Analysis* 34 (1953), pp. 91-92.

[47] Gibson, 'Melancholy Objects', p. 288.

The term 'transitional objects' also eventually came to be used in relation to grief. As in child development, objects may assist the bereaved during the absence of significant others – that is, their death. Death produces an absence where there once was presence. Gibson artistically writes of the impact of such an absence:

> No longer present in their physical being, the deceased socially and corporeally transform to the status of non-being, and through burial, non-visibility and non-contact … The ongoing absence of the deceased in their bodily being is one of the profound existential shocks of bereavement and the desire for their bodily return is a powerful fantasy in the early months of death … The transitional nature of human corporeal existence is both compensation for and replaced by representation and objects.[48]

As such, these objects help bridge the gap between presence and absence, to create a sense of presence in the absence of the deceased, as well as to provide comfort to the bereaved. But, according to Judith M. Simpson, these objects remind one of the deceased's absence. Simpson writes that one of the more common types of objects selected is an article of clothing, which holds the smell and shape of the wearer, allowing the griever 'to re-establish contact with those who have died'. Such objects serve to generate memories, which grievers attempt 'to control' by enjoying the 'presence of the deceased without suffering the harsh reminder of loss'.[49] As Gibson says, humans 'grieve with and through objects' so that 'death vacates as well as raises the meaning and value of objects' even though the objects cannot be a substitute 'for the person themselves'. When individuals keep objects of the deceased, Gibson describes it as 'a way of reclaiming and rehousing the remains of a life now gone'.[50] They provide a sense of presence in the bodily absence, or as Simpson says, 'It [transitional objects like clothes] forces upon our consciousness "the presence of absence"'.[51]

---

[48] Gibson, 'Melancholy Objects', p. 291.
[49] Judith. M. Simpson, 'Materials for Mourning: Bereavement Literature and the Afterlife of Clothes', *Critical Studies in Fashion & Beauty* 5.2 (2014), pp. 253-70 (253-55), https://doi.org/10.1386/csfb.5.2.253_1.
[50] Gibson, 'Melancholy Objects', pp. 296-97.
[51] Simpson, 'Materials for Mourning', pp. 254-55.

One of the pioneers in creating an understanding of the use of objects in grief was Vamik D. Volkan. It was in observing pathological grievers that Volkan developed his theory of *linking objects*, which he viewed as a 'variation' of the transitional object in Winnicott's theory.[52] By studying patients who experienced complicated grief in which they remained stationary in their grief process, Volkan noticed that they chose 'an inanimate object – a symbolic bridge (or link) to the representation of the dead person – to use in a magical way'.[53] According to Volkan, the linking object represents parts of both the bereaved and the deceased. As a representation of the deceased, the bereaved are able to maintain an illusion of being in control of the life of the deceased – to either bring to life or to 'kill' it. This means that the linking object helps the bereaved to control that space where they connect with the deceased. It is in this space of connection that the bereaved are desiring 'to restore and finally resolve the ambivalence that characterized' the relationship they had with the deceased when the deceased lived.[54]

According to Volkan, linking objects are inanimate items that are chosen soon after the person dies. The linking object is not used as it was intended, such as the wearing of a bracelet, but rather it is kept hidden in a safe place where the bereaved may be able to retrieve it at will or choose to avoid it for extended periods.[55] As such, it is unlike Winnicott's transitional object, which the child usually clutches or sees it at all times.[56] Since there are numerous objects that may become linking objects, Volkan found that linking objects may be ascribed to one of the five categories: (1) property of the deceased which was used regularly, such as a shirt; (2) a gift given by the deceased to the bereaved prior to their death, such as a watch from a husband to his wife; (3) an item that had been used by the dead to extend his/her sensory faculties, such as glasses to extend vision; (4) a true to life likeness of the deceased, such as a photograph; and (5) an item that was readily available when the bereaved learned of the

---

[52] Vamik D. Volkan, *Linking Objects and Linking Phenomena: A Study of the Forms, Symptoms, Metapsychology, and Therapy of Complicated Mourning* (New York: International Universities Press, 1981), pp. 102-103.

[53] Volkan, *Linking Objects and Linking Phenomena,* p. 20.

[54] Volkan, *Linking Objects and Linking Phenomena,* p. 20.

[55] Volkan, *Linking Objects and Linking Phenomena,* p. 103.

[56] Volkan, *Linking Objects and Linking Phenomena,* pp. 373-74.

death or viewed the body, which Volkan says could be a 'last minute object'.[57] These linking objects, then, are used to 'absorb … some of the conflicts pertaining to the work of mourning' so that 'the pain … of the usual work of mourning is not felt'.[58]

While Volkan perceives linking objects as strictly pointing towards pathological grief in that the pain of mourning is avoided, others use the terms 'transitional objects' and 'linking objects' interchangeably in the area of grief, viewing them as an important part in the healing process. For instance, grief counselor Alan D. Wolfelt describes transitional objects as 'belongings of the person who died', which provide 'comfort' to the mourner. He perceives that the objects generate 'a sense of security', which will be taken away if the objects are removed too quickly; thus, it is not until mourners have reconciled the loss into their lives (that is, integrated it) that they are in a place to choose to dispose or keep the objects. For Wolfelt, transitional objects are distinct from shrines. A shrine 'keeps everything just as it was after the death', which 'only prevents acknowledging the painful new reality that someone' who was loved 'has died'. For Wolfelt, the distinction in grief between transitional objects and a shrine is that the former assists in healing while the latter hinders healing.[59]

As I studied these theories in connection to the story of the grieving widower above, I would suggest that his calendar, unmoved since

---

[57] Volkan, *Linking Objects and Linking Phenomena,* p. 104.

[58] Volkan, *Linking Objects and Linking Phenomena,* p. 373.

[59] Alan D. Wolfelt, 'You're Not Going Crazy – You're Grieving!', Center for Loss & Transition (article), December 14, 2016, https://www.centerfor-loss.com/2016/12/youre-not-going-crazy-youre-grieving/ (accessed November 20, 2018). This tends to be a cultural issue, for erecting such a shrine in the West is viewed as unhelpful, but in Japan it is standard behavior; see Gabrielle Syme, 'Bereavement', in Colin Feltham and Ian Horton (eds.), *The SAGE Handbook of Counseling and Psychotherapy* (London: SAGE, 2nd edn, 2006), p. 385. An additional type of object discussed in the area of grief, but not germane to this paper, is a *melancholy object*. Gibson refers to 'melancholy objects', which are 'objects that have been central to grieving, and particularly, the memory of grieving'. These objects, for Gibson, were once transitional objects, which negotiated 'the void of the death and an irreversible absence'. A melancholy object becomes 'a reminder of the loss of grief as an intensive pervasive state of being'. An example Gibson provides is a deceased husband's sweater that the wife wore for many weeks. The woman states she has kept the sweater, but it is packed away, and while she has no intention of throwing it out, she would not wear it again. Gibson's discussion on melancholy objects is based on interviews conducted between 2002 and 2003 with 30 Australian men and women between the ages of 30 and 75 who had experienced bereavement. Gibson, 'Melancholy Objects', pp. 285-99.

June 2010, served as a linking or transitional object. Since it was his wife's possession, it produced a sense of her presence for the retired farmer in that she turned the monthly page of the wall calendar. At the same time, the calendar reminded him of her absence in that the month being shown was the month she had died. She no longer was growing older with him. She no longer was turning the pages on the calendar. Time on earth had ceased for her and in some ways, it had for him too. In essence, he was frozen in time, at that point in his life when his wife had died. It is here through the linking or transitional object that a Pentecostal may connect with a mourner, and it is to this I now turn.

The Giving of The Spirit as Transitional Praxis of Presence

Thus far, I have examined how Luke's Emmaus account, specifically the grief and the presence-absence of Jesus, was received by early Pentecostals. I then emphasized the theme of the presence-absence of Jesus as seen in the corpus of Luke, noting how today's Christ-followers live in the bodily absence of Jesus with the Spirit as a connection (link) to Jesus as well as implicitly pointing towards what is to come. I explored the use of linking and transitional objects during grief to provide both the presence of the deceased and a reminder of the deceased's absence. I now turn to how Pentecostal caregivers, both lay and ordained, may formulate a theological transitional praxis by using the theme of presence-absence in Luke–Acts in combination with grief theory's linking or transitional objects. This will be accomplished in four movements by: (1) clarifying the meaning of the word praxis; (2) determining how the Spirit is dissimilar to a linking or transitional object; (3) asserting how the Spirit is similar to a linking or transitional object; and (4) demonstrating how the Spirit serves as a type of theological transitional praxis of presence in which Pentecostals participate.

What is *praxis*?[60] This word is not to be confused with the application of theology so that action serves theology, making theology a priority over action. Instead, drawing from the work of Ray S.

---

[60] For a more expanded explanation of practical theology and praxis, see Engelbert, *Who Is Present in Absence?*, ch. 1.

Anderson and Andrew Root, I define *praxis* as 'truth in action'.[61] In other words, humans know God through God's acts of ministry; thus, beliefs are formed about God through God's action. God, who is truth, acts by giving the Son, who embodies truth, making Jesus' being an act of ministry. In this sense, God's praxis (truth in action) is the giving of the Son as Jesus embodies God's act of ministry. Humans know God loves them through God's giving of the Son (Jn 3.16); thus, God's action declares this truth.

In like manner, the Son, as the Baptizer, gives his followers the Spirit after he ascends to the right hand of the Father. In the same way, Christ-followers encounter God through God's action; they experience Jesus, during his time of absence, through the giving of the Spirit. The release of the Spirit declares to believers that they are not alone and helpless like orphans. The giving of the Spirit offers Christ-followers hope that signifies this is not all there is or ever will be in that the giving of the Spirit is an act of ministry that points toward the eschaton, the time when God will be fully present in all of creation. The giving of the Spirit provides believers with a taste of God's presence while they wait for Jesus' second coming. The giving of the Spirit, then, is Jesus' praxis declaring who Jesus is and his promise for the future. The giving of the Spirit is a theological transitional praxis that is truth in action.

With this understanding of theological praxis, I turn now to how the Spirit is contrasted and compared to grief theory's linking or transitional objects. First and foremost, unlike a linking or transitional object, which is inanimate, the Spirit is a living person. The Spirit has a will, emotions, and an ability to act. For example, in Acts the Spirit encourages (9.31), predicts (11.28), sends (13.4), prevents (16.6), comes (19.6), compels (20.22), warns (20.23), appoints (20.28), and speaks (28.25) in acts of ministry. Additionally, while a linking object is in only one place at a time, the Spirit is omnipresent while simultaneously abiding in each Christ-follower. Unlike linking objects, which signify for the mourner a power over the deceased (to kill it or make it come to life), Christ-followers do not have power over the Spirit or

---

[61] See Ray S. Anderson, *The Shape of Practical Theology: Empowering Ministry with Theological Praxis* (Downers Grove, IL: InterVarsity Press, 2001); Ray S. Anderson, *The Soul of Ministry: Forming Leaders for God's People* (Louisville, KY: Westminster / John Knox Press, 1997); and Andrew Root, *Christopraxis: A Practical Theology of the Cross* (Minneapolis: Fortress, 2014).

over Jesus through the Spirit. Instead, Christ-followers are given life by the Omnipotent One and will be judged by the one who has conquered death and who is the Judge of the living and the dead. While the linking object signifies a desire to heal an ambivalent relationship with the deceased, the giving of the Spirit indicates that reconciliation has already occurred between humanity and the divine. Furthermore, the presence of the Spirit is the actual presence of the divine whereas the object is only a representation of the person who has died. An additional dissimilarity includes Jesus' decision to give Christ-followers the Spirit, whereas the bereaved choose which object becomes the transitional or linking object.

Although there are many dissimilarities between grief theory's linking or transitional objects and the giving of the Spirit, there are several similarities that I believe assist Pentecostals in forming a theological transitional praxis of presence. As in the case of a linking object not being the actual person who has died, the Spirit is not identical to Jesus. Miroslav Volf, in writing of the triune Godhead, reminds readers that although in each divine person the other two persons mutually dwell, they do so without each one losing distinctiveness; the reason Volf mentions this is because persons who dissolve in each other cannot exist in each other.[62] As the linking object is dissimilar to the person, so is the Spirit's omnipresence dissimilar to the bodily presence of Jesus prior to the resurrection, which was unable to be two places at once. Moreover, as a linking object points to the person who has died, the Spirit also points to the Son, glorifying the Son. As a linking or transitional object is representative of the deceased, the Spirit also is representative of a future in which Jesus will return and God's kingdom will be fully established. Thus, the giving of the Spirit provides believers with a sense of Jesus' presence in a similar fashion that the transitional object provides a sense of presence of the deceased to the bereaved. At the same time, the giving of the Spirit reminds believers that Jesus is not physically present in a similar fashion to the transitional object, reminding the mourner that the deceased is absent. As a result, the church fasts and takes communion in the bridegroom's absence, which are acts that involve mourning, implicitly declaring the absence of the bridegroom, Jesus

---

[62] Miroslav Volf, *After Our Likeness: The Church as the Image of the Trinity* (Grand Rapids: Eerdmans, 1998), p. 209.

Christ. These actions by the bride are reminders that Christ-followers are unable to see Jesus clearly in much the same manner that the mourner is unable to see and experience the deceased except through the chosen object. Additionally, this object provides a comforting presence to the bereaved like the Spirit, who is the Comforter; and offers comfort to Christ-followers. However, it is to be clearly stated that the comfort the object gives is passive in that it is unable to actively offer comfort, unlike the Spirit, whose very being is comfort. The giving of the Spirit, then, becomes a praxis, truth in action, as the Spirit is moving among Christ-followers and dwelling in them, serving as a reminder to them of the absence and presence of Jesus.

With such similarities between grief's linking or transitional objects and the giving of the Spirit from which Pentecostals may draw, the Pentecostal has a place of identification with a mourner, which may generate a praxis of presence. The Pentecostal's emphasis on Spirit Christology and on the corporeal absence of Jesus offers a unique understanding to those mourners who are grieving the absence of their loved ones while simultaneously utilizing linking or transitional objects to sense the deceased's presence. Since Pentecostals stress the power and presence of the Spirit and long for the coming of the Lord, Pentecostals have an understanding of longing for the presence of the one who is absent. Such an understanding has the potential to foster an empathic connection with those who are mourning, a willingness to be present to them in a similar manner that the Spirit is present to believers as they wait and long for Jesus' coming. In this way, the coming or giving of the Spirit becomes an invitation to participate in the ministry of Jesus Christ in the power and presence of the Spirit by going to those who mourn and by being present with them. As the giving of the Spirit gives believers a taste of the fullness of Jesus' presence that is to come, so also does a linking object provide a taste of presence of their loved one to the bereaved. Yet, not only does the linking or transitional object remind a mourner of the deceased's presence, but also their absence. With that being said, unlike the bereaved who know what it is to have been physically with the deceased, believers do not fully know what it is to physically be with Jesus. Thus, while Pentecostals are being pulled toward a future through the use of their imaginations and the Spirit's presence as hope for future fulfillment, the bereaved are being pulled toward a past that they once shared with their loved one while simultaneously being pulled toward a future without the loved one.[63] Thus, as the giving of the Spirit provides comfort in the now and hope for a future, so also may Pentecostals participate in this ministry by being present with the mourner, providing comfort for today and hope for a future amidst a transition of integrating a loss into one's life.

Conclusion

I have argued for a Pentecostal theological transitional praxis of being present to those who are mourning the loss of a significant other. I began by exploring how Pentecostals have received the story of the two men on the road to Emmaus, a story that highlights grief and the presence-absence of Jesus. While early Pentecostals acknowledged the grief of the two men, many also attributed the lack of recognition of Jesus to their grief, disappointment, and doubt. Such a reception is indicative of ongoing patterns of how Pentecostals may receive the stories of mourners today; thus, I suggest a correction is in order in the receiving of grief stories. Other early Pentecostals highlighted the presence-absence dynamic of Jesus while speaking of waiting for Jesus' second coming and the current presence of the Spirit. In underscoring the latter, I accentuate a strength of Pentecostals – their emphasis on longing for the Savior amidst Jesus' absence – in order that Pentecostals would draw from this strength by identifying with mourners; the purpose of such identification is to kindle within them a reception of grief stories that enables them to be alongside the bereaved in a similar manner the Spirit is to believers. Through such presence, as with the Spirit's presence, Pentecostals assist in mitigating the bereaved's pain amidst the absence of a significant other.

I turned toward the theme of presence-absence in Luke–Acts, a vital foundation for Pentecostal theology, which examined two categories of the presence-absence of Jesus: *prior to the resurrection* and *after the resurrection*. I traced how Jesus' absence prior to the resurrection

---

[63] One understanding of grief and mourning is called *dual process* in which the bereaved move back and forth, remembering the past and planning for a future. In the beginning, one may spend more time remembering and less time planning for a future without the significant other; however, as one continues in the grief process, one's remembering will give way to thinking more about the future.

could be overcome by actively seeking him. In the latter category, I focused on a variance of presence-absence of Jesus' body as it was absent (not seen by the women and Peter); as it was present and absent (on the Emmaus road); and as it was absent (the ascension). After the ascension, the Spirit becomes present in the transition of waiting for Jesus to return. The theme of presence-absence, then, serves as an encouragement to readers to continue to believe, during this time of transition, during the bodily absence of Jesus.

This section was followed by an examination of grief theory's linking or transitional objects. These objects are inanimate, which are chosen soon after the death of the significant other. These objects provide a sense of the deceased's presence for the mourner as well as a reminder of the deceased's absence. Linking or transitional objects may be unhealthy or healthy. In terms of the former, linking objects keep a mourner from grieving the loss of the person while the latter assist bringing about healing on the grief journey.

In the final section, I combined linking and transitional objects with the presence of the Spirit in the absence of Jesus to formulate a Pentecostal, theological transitional praxis of presence. I tracked several similarities, namely, the giving of the Spirit likened to a linking or transitional object in that in Jesus' absence, the giving of the Spirit provides a sense of Jesus' presence while reminding believers that Jesus is bodily absent. It is here in this space that Christ-followers participate in acts that contain elements of mourning: fasting and the taking of communion. Such actions seek to bring a sense of Jesus' presence in his absence through the Spirit's presence; thus, they contain both grief and faith by recognizing Jesus' absence and being pulled toward a future of being fully in his presence.

Since Pentecostals are actively mourning in this transitional period in which they have been given the Spirit, this ongoing activity becomes a place of connection to the mourner who longs for the deceased's presence in their absence. As such, it becomes a place of participation in a ministry of presence. In like manner that the giving of the Spirit in Jesus' physical absence brings a taste of Jesus' presence that generates comfort, Pentecostals may participate in the Spirit's ministry by being present to mourners, generating strength, support, and healing. As Pentecostals wait and grieve prior to Jesus' second coming, and as the giving of the Spirit ministers Jesus' presence to them during this transitional time, so Pentecostals, too, may abide with mourners during their transitional period of reconciling their loss with their hope for complete reconciliation (healing) of all creation.

I began with a story of a Pentecostal minister visiting an elderly widower who had lost his wife. This story demonstrates the power of being present in that as the minister made his monthly visits, the retired farmer eventually spoke of a linking or transitional object, the 2010 calendar, a reminder of his wife's death in June of that year. As the visits continued, the minister noted to himself on one particular occasion that the calendar had been replaced. No longer was the year 2010 serving to generate the widower's wife's presence and absence. Instead, the absence of the object indicated movement in the 80-some-year-old's grief journey, which was portrayed in a renewed interest in other activities. Someone's becoming present to him, participating in the Spirit's ministry, allowed him to be present to his grief, engendering movement towards the reconciliation of his loss.

Bibliography

Aikier, Stefan, 'Ways of Presence and Modes of Absence in the Gospel of Luke – Or: How Scripture Works', in Ingolf U. Dalferth (ed.), *The Presence and Absence of God: Claremont Studies in the Philosophy of Religion, Conference 2008* (Tübingen, Germany: Mohr Siebeck, 2009) pp. 41-56.

Anderson, Ray S., *The Shape of Practical Theology: Empowering Ministry with Theological Praxis* (Downers Grove, IL: InterVarsity Press, 2001).

—*The Soul of Ministry: Forming Leaders for God's People* (Louisville, KY: Westminster / John Knox Press, 1997).

Bock, Darrell., 'Luke, the Gospel of', in Joel B. Green and Scot McKnight (eds), *Dictionary of Jesus and the Gospels* (Downers Grove, IL: InterVarsity Press, accordance edn, 1992).

—*The NIV Application Commentary: Luke* (Terry Muck (ed.); The NIV Application Commentary Series; Grand Rapids: Zondervan, 1996).

Engelbert, Pamela F., *Who Is Present in Absence? A Pentecostal Theological Praxis of Suffering and Healing* (Eugene, OR: Wipf & Stock, 2019).

Gibson, Margaret, 'Melancholy Objects', *Mortality* 9.4 (Nov 2004), pp. 285-99. doi: 10.1080/13576270412331829312.

Green, Joel B., *The Gospel of Luke* (The New International Commentary of the New Testament; Grand Rapids: Eerdmans, 1997).

Mittelstadt, Martin W., 'Receiving Luke–Acts: The Rise of Reception History and a Call to Pentecostal Scholars', *Pneuma* 40 (October 2018), pp. 367-88.

Johnson, Luke Timothy, *Living Jesus: Learning the Heart of the Gospel* (San Francisco: HarperSanFrancisco, 1999).

Knight, Jonathan, *Luke's Gospel* (London: Routledge, 1998).

Root, Andrew, *Christopraxis: A Practical Theology of the Cross* (Minneapolis: Fortress, 2014).

Simpson, Judith M., 'Materials for Mourning: Bereavement Literature and the Afterlife of Clothes', *Critical Studies in Fashion & Beauty* 5.2 (2014), pp. 253-70.

Stephenson, Christopher A., *Types of Pentecostal Theology: Method, System, Spirit* (Oxford: Oxford University Press, 2013).

Volf, Miroslav, *After Our Likeness: The Church as the Image of the Trinity* (Grand Rapids: Eerdmans, 1998).

Volkan, Vamik D., *Linking Objects and Linking Phenomena: A Study of the Forms, Symptoms, Metapsychology, and Therapy of Complicated Mourning* (New York: International Universities Press, 1981).

Winnicott, D.W., 'Transitional Objects and Transitional Phenomena – A Study of the First Not-Me Possession', *International Journal of Psycho-Analysis* 34 (1953), pp. 91-92.

Wolfelt, Alan D., 'You're Not Going Crazy – You're Grieving!', Center for Loss & Transition (article), December 14, 2016, https://www.centerfor-loss.com/2016/12/youre-not-going-crazy-youre-grieving/ (accessed November 20, 2018).

9

How Long Shall We Tarry?: A Reception History of Luke 24.49 in Early Pentecostal Testimonies

Daniel D. Isgrigg[*]

Before Jesus ascended into heaven, he instructed his disciples to 'Tarry ye in the city of Jerusalem until ye be endued with power from on high' (Lk. 24.49; Acts 1.4 KJV). Drawing from these words, 'tarrying' became a uniquely Pentecost ritual whereby believers developed the practice of actively lingering for the impartation of the Spirit. As Wolfgang Vondey comments, 'The entire tone of Pentecostal worship has been described at times as "one of waiting"'.[1] There are a number of empirically based studies focused on the reception of the Spirit that document a number of variables surrounding reception of the Spirit.[2] However, there has yet to be a study related to the amount of time Pentecostals spent tarrying before they received the baptism

---

[*] Daniel D. Isgrigg (PhD, Bangor University, UK) is Assistant Professor and Director of the Holy Spirit Research Center, Oral Roberts University, Tulsa, OK, USA.
[1] Wolfgang Vondey, *Pentecostal Theology: Living the Full Gospel* (London: Bloomsbury T&T Clark, 2017), p. 62.
[2] For example, see Aaron T. Friesen, *Norming the Abnormal: The Development of the Doctrine of Initial Evidence in Classical Pentecostalism* (Eugene, OR: Pickwick Publications, 2013); Mark J. Cartledge, *Charismatic Glossolalia: An Empirical – Theological Study* (Burlington, VT: Ashgate, 2002).

in the Spirit in light of Jesus' command to wait until you have been endued with power from on high (Lk. 24.49).[3]

This essay will investigate the methodology of tarrying for the baptism in the Holy Spirit as expressed in the testimonies recorded throughout the thirteen existing issues of *The Apostolic Faith* (1906–1908) of the Azusa Street Mission. In order to extract the 'ordinary theology'[4] expressed by this diverse cross-section of early Pentecostals, this study will engage in a history of reception of how Pentecostals received Jesus' command to 'tarry' and how that reception shaped the expectation of the early Pentecostal's experience of receiving the baptism in the Holy Spirit.[5] Of the hundreds of testimonies in *The Apostolic Faith*, 80 have been identified that specifically mention the amount of time the subject 'tarried', or waited, before receiving the baptism.[6] From this population, each testimony was documented according to the following variables: the stated amount of time before reception took place, the location and context of their reception, and any expressed barriers to receiving.[7] Based on these variables, this

---

[3] The closest investigation of the Pentecostal experiences can be found in Cecil M. Robeck Jr, *Azusa Street Mission & Revival: The Birth of the Global Pentecostal Movement* (Nashville: Nelson Reference & Electronic, 2006), pp. 177-86, who devotes considerable time to describing Spirit baptism experiences at the Azusa Street Mission. However, he limited himself to a 'quick analysis of a half-dozen' of the hundreds of testimonies as a demonstrative sample.

[4] Jeff Astley, 'The Analysis, Investigation, and Application of Ordinary Theology', in Jeff Astley and Leslie J. Francis (eds.), *Exploring Ordinary Theology* (Farnham, Surrey: Ashgate, 2013) defines 'ordinary theology' as 'the theological beliefs and processes of believing that find expression in the God-talk of those believers who have received no scholarly theological education'. Similarly, Mark J. Cartledge, Jeff Astley, Leslie J. Francis, *et al.*, *Testimony in the Spirit: Rescripting Ordinary Pentecostal Theology* (Farnham, Surrey: Ashgate, 2010), p. 16, assert that Pentecostal ordinary theology expresses the 'common sense expertise' of those who had experienced the Spirit.

[5] Reception History will be used in two ways in this piece. First, as a hermeneutical approach to Pentecostal literature that explores how early Pentecostals received the scriptural edict to 'tarry' found in Luke 24 and Acts 1. Second, it will be used in an experiential sense as a historical account of how Pentecostals 'received' the baptism in the Spirit.

[6] Tarrying is a synonym for 'waiting' in this study. Many, but not all, of the accounts use the term 'tarry' to describe their experience. Therefore, the individual accounts were selected based on the single criteria of whether a length of time was mentioned in relationship to receiving the baptism in the Holy Spirit.

[7] The gender balance of this population was surprisingly equal, representing forty men and forty women. The ages of the seekers were not a significant detail in most of the testimonies, although several testimonies of children as young as 11

study will seek to identify patterns concerning the role tarrying played in reception of the Spirit by early Pentecostals.[8]

Origin of Tarrying

Like many Pentecostal spiritual practices, tarrying has its roots in African spirituality.[9] David Daniels refers to the practice of tarrying as 'the core of African American Pentecostal spirituality'.[10] Tarrying originated within slave communities in the American South where, unrestrained by the European sensibilities of order and control that characterized the religion of slave owners, slaves found solace in secret meetings where there was emotional singing, shouting, and dancing in what was called the 'ring shout'. This dynamic act of communal lingering and praying invited worshippers into a transformational experience with God through the Spirit.[11] As one ring shout participant testified, 'At camp-meeting there must be a ring here, a ring there, and a ring over yonder, or sinners will not get converted'.[12] As Daniels points out, the elements of active waiting on God, patterned

---

years old were included. There was little information that would indicate the race of the seekers outside those who may have been notable in history.

[8] Rather than a formal empirical study using quantitative analysis, this study is a rudimentary qualitative survey of only expressed phenomenon. One obvious limitation of a study like this is that these testimonies are naturally limited to those who had testified to having achieved the goal of receiving Spirit-baptism. This study cannot account for the totality of experiences since the voices of those who had not yet received are not accounted for and some may have been omitted because they did not conform to the intended outcome. It is possible that this study does not sufficiently account for any editorializing out of testimonies or of those who would never send a 'testimony' since they did not experience the intended outcome for these publications.

[9] Walter J. Hollenweger, *Pentecostalism: Origins and Developments Worldwide* (Peabody, MA: Hendrickson, 1997), pp. 18-19, argues that Pentecostalism inherited from African spirituality the elements of orality in liturgy, narrative theology, testimony, and participatory worship. See also Walter J. Hollenweger, 'The Black Roots of Pentecostalism', in Allan H. Anderson and Walter J. Hollenweger (eds.), *Pentecostals after a Century* (JPTSup 15; Sheffield: Sheffield Academic Press, 1999), pp. 33-44; Estrelda Alexander, *Black Fire: One Hundred Years of African American Pentecostalism* (Downers Grove, IL: InterVarsity Press, 2011).

[10] David D. Daniels III, '"Until the Power of the Lord Comes Down": African American Pentecostal Spirituality and Tarrying', in Clive Erricker and Jane Erricker (eds.), *Contemporary Spiritualties: Social and Religious Contexts* (London: Continuum, 2001), pp. 173-91 (175).

[11] Daniels, '"Until the Power of the Lord Comes Down"', p. 175.

[12] Albert L. Raboteau, *Slave Religion: The 'Invisible Institution' in the Antebellum South* (Oxford: Oxford University Press, 1978), p. 69.

repetition of praise words, and fervent prayer until the 'power of the Lord come down' became the basis for the practice of tarrying.[13] As a son of former slaves, it is not surprising that the tarrying service was one of the essential elements William Seymour employed in the upper room especially designated to initiate seekers into the Pentecostal experience at the Azusa Street Mission.[14]

Receiving Jesus' Command to Tarry

Tarrying for the Pentecostal experience was more than an element of Pentecostal spirituality; it was an apostolic standard set by Jesus himself. At the Azusa Mission, those who were saved and sanctified were instructed using Jesus' command to 'tarry' until they received 'power from on high'.[15] For Seymour, the command to tarry was proof that the Pentecostal baptism in the Spirit was differentiated from the holiness experience of sanctification.[16] He comments,

> Jesus said, 'Tarry ye.' For what? For a work of grace? No, for He had said before He went down into the grave, 'Ye are clean.' He got all the fears and doubts out of His church before He went back to bright glory. So after He had ascended to the Father, all they had to do was to praise God till the comforter came.[17]

---

[13] Daniels, "'Until the Power of the Lord Comes Down'", p. 178.

[14] Robeck Jr, *Azusa Street Mission & Revival*, p. 160. 'At Azusa Mission', *AF* 1.8 (May 1907), p. 2, Seymour comments, 'When the altar call is made on Sunday, the seekers for Pentecost pass upstairs and seekers for justification and sanctification remain below. Souls receive Pentecost right along at the altars. Some get saved and sanctified.'

[15] Despite the ubiquitous use of the term 'tarrying' in the reports and testimonies, nearly all the references to Jesus' command came in the form of exhortations by William Seymour *AF* 1.4 (December 1906), p. 1; 'The Enduement of Power', *AF* 1.4 (December 1906), p. 2; W.J. Seymour, 'Counterfeits', *AF* 1.4 (December 1906), p. 2; *AF* 1.4 (December 1906), p. 3; William J. Seymour, 'The Baptism with the Holy Ghost', *AF* 1.6 (February/March 1907), p. 7.

[16] William J. Seymour, 'Two Works of Grace and the Gift of the Holy Ghost', *AF* 1.1 (September 1906), p. 3; Whereas it is often said that Holiness Pentecostals had three works of grace (salvation, sanctification, baptism in the Spirit), Seymour had a different way of referring to it. He says, 'Sanctification is the second and last work of grace, but the baptism in the Spirit is a gift of power'. 'The Enduement of Power', *AF* 1.4 (December 1906), p. 2. Seymour says, 'They were not to tarry in Jerusalem till He should pour out His blood upon them, but tarry for the promise of the Father'.

[17] *AF* 1.10 (September 1907), p. 3.

On the one hand, the work of grace of sanctification came with an inner 'witness of the Spirit', which did not require tarrying; it required faith.[18] Tarrying for the Holy Ghost, on the other hand, was God's responsibility that required the recipient to be subject to God's timing and his sovereignty.[19] The act of receiving was not in the control of the seeker, therefore it required 'waiting on God'.[20] They used the terms 'tarrying for the baptism' synonymously with 'waiting on God'.[21]

Tarry Until the Evidence Comes

What is clear about each of these testimonies in *The Apostolic Faith* is that the concept of tarrying was contingent upon the doctrine of speaking in tongues as evidence. For the seeker, the 'Bible evidence' of speaking in tongues verified the apostolic pattern and served as sign to the seeker that their wait was over.[22] As one seeker testified, 'I have not the baptism with the Holy Ghost because I have not the gift of tongues, the evidence of Pentecost'.[23] This sign was particularly important in the experiences of those who had prolonged periods of waiting. For example, Glen A. Cook had several experiences where he was 'under the power' for hours at a time, yet remained unconvinced that he was baptized in the Spirit because he lacked the

---

[18] 'New Tongued Missionaries for Africa', *AF* 1.3 (November 1906), p. 3, illustrated one Azusa attendee's conversation with the Lord. 'The Spirit said to me as plainly as a voice, "How did you receive your justification? How did you receive your sanctification?" I said, Lord, by faith. He then said, "Receive me".'

[19] Daniels, '"Until the Power of the Lord Comes Down"', p. 179.

[20] Note the way *AF* 1.4 (December 1906), p. 1, expresses it. 'Companies of Christians in many places were waiting on God, tarrying for the baptism with the Holy Ghost.'

[21] 'Praying for the Holy Ghost', *AF* 1.2 (October 1906), p. 3; 'Filled with God's Glory', *AF* 1.7 (April 1907), p. 4; 'In Fort Worth Tex.', *AF* 1.7 (April 1907), p. 8.

[22] *AF* 1.2 (October 1906), p. 1; 'Ask What Ye Will', *AF* 1.2 (October 1906), p. 3; 'Pentecost in Toronto', *AF* 1.5 (January 1907), p. 4; 'Pentecost in the Middle States', *AF* 1.6 (February/March 1907), p. 3; 'What Pentecost Did for One Family', *AF* 1.6 (February/March 1907), p. 7; 'Holiness Preacher Who Received Pentecost', *AF* 1.6 (February/March 1907), p. 7.

[23] 'Baptized in Minneapolis', *AF* 1.4 (December 1906), p. 4. Similarly, 'Holiness Preacher Who Received Pentecost', *AF* 1.6 (February/March 1907), p. 7, testified, 'I then began to tarry and pray night and day, and did not stop until I was wonderfully baptized with the Holy Ghost, and He gave me the blessed evidence which always follows, which is the speaking in tongues'.

apostolic evidence.[24] In fact, Seymour himself warned against seekers confusing dramatic experiences such as falling under the power with the Pentecostal baptism. He notes, 'We have been running off with blessings and anointings with God's power, instead of tarrying until Bible evidence of Pentecost came'.[25]

While many seekers described receiving Pentecost as 'glorious' and 'wonderful', for those with prolonged tarrying experiences, this process was not always blessed. Louis Osteberg described his nine months of tarrying as 'torturous' because each service left him feeling 'as far away as ever before'.[26] Arthur B. Shepherd recalled that his weeks of tarrying were 'tedious in the extreme, but God's grace was sufficient'.[27] Mrs James Hebdon became discouraged to the point of almost giving up because as she testified, 'over fifty times I arose from the altar to face the world without my enduement of power'.[28] In most of these cases, the seekers were encouraged to 'pray through' until they got the victory.[29] As Seymour reminded seekers, '[Jesus] did not say how long they were to tarry, but He did say, "until ye be endued"'.[30]

The emphasis on speaking in tongues as the confirming sign of reception inevitably led to believers seeking tongues instead of the baptism. Seymour warned, 'Dear loved ones, do not seek for tongues, but seek for the baptism with the Holy Ghost … Then He will manifest His power in the demonstration of speaking or singing in tongues, just as the Holy Ghost chooses.'[31] Seymour was right to be concerned that tongues would become a hindrance for seekers. This

---

[24] G.A. Cook, 'Receiving the Holy Ghost', *AF* 1.3 (November 1906), p. 2. Other examples are found in, 'Pentecost in the Middle States', *AF* 1.6 (February/March 1907), p. 3; 'A Chicago Evangelist's Pentecost', *AF* 1.6 (February/March 1907), p. 4; 'Pentecostal Testimonies', *AF* 1.6 (February/March 1907), p. 8.

[25] *AF* 1.1 (September 1906), p. 2.

[26] 'Filled with God's Glory', *AF* 1.7 (April 1907), p. 4. In the midst of sharing his frustration with friends, Osterberg describes, 'I was like a man grasping at straws'. But with his friends' prayers he was able to believe again and 'little by little I felt the power fall. To make a long story short, I was soon speaking in other tongues.'

[27] 'Pentecostal Testimonies', *AF* 1.6 (February/March 1907), p. 8.

[28] 'Found the Pearl of Great Price', *AF* 1.6 (February/March 1907), p. 4.

[29] 'Pentecost in Pueblo, Colo', *AF* 1.5 (January 1907), p. 4. Tom Hezmalhalch encouraged those who were seeking for sanctification and baptism who did not 'get through' to be encouraged 'to go on until they had the victory'.

[30] *AF* 1.4 (December 1906), p. 3.

[31] *AF* 1.12 (January 1908), p. 3.

was illustrated by 'Sister Mead', who despite having Seymour and Florence Crawford personally praying for her for several weeks, became extremely disappointed because she had not yet spoke in tongues. Sister Mead admitted that tongues became a 'stumbling block' from the enemy and a tool 'to get me discouraged, telling me this baptism was not for me'. Once she got over her preoccupation with tongues she was able to receive 'in simplicity' and faith. Only then did the tongues follow as a sign.[32]

Because of the overemphasis on tongues, some came with a resistance to speaking in tongues. But this too could become a hindrance. One sister who came to the mission admitted she 'did not want tongues', but after she prayed through, 'God baptized her like all the rest'.[33] Although Seymour was cautious on tongues, he did recognize tongues were a legitimate part of the apostolic pattern. Seekers were encouraged to continue to tarry until the evidence came, no matter how long.

> Don't stop because you do not receive the baptism with the Holy Ghost at the first, but continue until you are filled … Many people today are willing to tarry just so long, and then they give up and fail to receive their personal Pentecost that would measure with the Bible.[34]

The need for endurance in waiting was sometimes expressed as a 'battle' that seekers would need to press through until they received the victory by 'getting through' to the baptism.[35]

---

[32] 'New Tongued Missionaries for Africa', *AF* 1.3 (November 1906), p. 3. Sister Mead navigated through her disappointment when the Spirit showed her that she should receive the Spirit the same way she received salvation and sanctification: 'by faith'.

[33] 'Testimonies', *AF* 2.13 (May 1908), p. 1.

[34] *AF* 1.4 (December 1906), p. 3. An almost exact statement was also included in W.J.S., 'Letter to One Seeking the Holy Ghost', *AF* 1.10 (September 1907), p. 3.

[35] Tom Hezmalhalch, 'Pentecost in Pueblo, Colo', *AF* 1.5 (January 1907), p. 4, commented, 'others who were seeking for sanctification and baptism and did not get through, were encouraged to go on until they had the victory'. See also *AF* 1.5 (January 1907), p. 1; 'A Businessman's Testimony of Pentecost', *AF* 1.5 (January 1907), p. 4; *AF* 1.8 (May 1907), p. 3.

How Long Shall We Tarry?

According to the biblical 'pattern' of tarrying, Jesus told the disciples they would be baptized in the Holy Spirit 'in a few days' (Acts 1.5). In reality, the disciples tarried for ten days before they received. What is interesting is that the majority of the testimonies followed similar trajectories in that 62 out of 80 (77.5%) reported receiving in about a week.[36] M.L. Ryan expressed the expectation that one would receive the Spirit in a similar amount of time when he testified, 'I had my mind made up that I must seek for the Pentecostal Baptism at least one week before receiving it. To my utterable surprise and joy the power fell upon me at once.'[37] Ryan's 'surprise' that the Pentecostal baptism was immediately available suggests that at some level he was influenced by the expectation that waiting was part of the process of receiving.

Seymour certainly did not believe receiving the baptism in the Spirit was an inherently prolonged process, despite his own experience of leading others into the experience before he himself received.[38] He insisted that anyone could receive 'this day or this night'.[39] He expected that the properly prepared seeker should have 'no trouble in receiving the Pentecostal baptism'.[40] He commented, 'You do not have to strain your mind in order to receive the Holy Ghost, but just believe the Word of Jesus and the Lord pours the Holy Ghost into your heart just as freely as you breathe'.[41] To some degree, the testimonies confirm this point as 45 of 80 (56%) received immediately or within the same day. Therefore, in Seymour's understanding, Jesus' command to tarry was seen more so as a command to follow the apostolic pattern than it was a statement of how long one must wait before the fullness of the Spirit was available.

---

[36] For example, 'Pentecost in Washington', *AF* 1.5 (January 1907), p. 4, records the testimony of Mrs K.E. Andrews who 'after tarrying six days I received the same enduement or power that Jesus promised to His disciples'.

[37] 'Bro. Ryan Receives His Pentecost', *AF* 1.3 (November 1906), p. 3.

[38] 'Pentecost with Signs Following', *AF* 1.4 (December 1906), p. 1. Seymour conducted cottage meetings when he arrived in Los Angeles. Seymour himself did not receive until three days after the first person in those meetings received.

[39] 'Tarry in One Accord', *AF* 2.13 (May 1908), p. 3.

[40] William J. Seymour, 'The Baptism with the Holy Ghost', *AF* 1.6 (February/March 1907), p. 7. This is an interesting comment considering his own delay in receiving the Spirit.

[41] *AF* 1.8 (May 1907), p. 1.

It is interesting to note that the percentage of people who received quickly was higher during the first year of the revival. From September to December of 1906, 86% of the testimonies (18 of 21) claimed to have received the Spirit either immediately or in the first few days.[42] Consequently, for much of the first year of the paper (1906), there were few admonitions from Seymour to encourage those who were 'still waiting'. It was not until mid-1907 that Seymour began to address those who were experiencing a prolonged season of tarrying.[43] Seymour even wrote to 'those still seeking' to see Jesus' command to tarry as a call to endure as long as it takes.[44] In addition to admonitions for believers to endure, in 1907 and 1908 the paper also focused more on providing instructions for those still waiting than on individual testimonies of those who had received. Although it is hard to say with certainty, this could suggest that as time went on the instances of immediate receiving were waning and the number of people who were still in the process of seeking were increasing.[45]

Where Shall We Tarry?

The Azusa Street Mission was arguably the nexus of the greatest revival in modern history. Seekers were known to come from hundreds or even thousands of miles to seek for the baptism in the Holy Ghost.[46] One might assume that the revival at the Azusa Street Mission made it easier for individuals to be filled with the Spirit, but the

---

[42] The three exceptions were testimonies by three Holiness ministers. Each had prolonged experiences that they described as frustrating. 'Filled with God's Glory', *AF* 1.7 (April 1907), p. 4; *AF* 1.2 (October 1906), p. 1; 'New Tongued Missionaries for Africa', *AF* 1.3 (Nov 1906), p. 3. All the rest were within days of beginning their seeking of baptism and most were immediate.

[43] William J. Seymour, 'The Baptism with the Holy Ghost', *AF* 1.6 (February/March 1907), p. 7; *AF* 1.8 (May 1907), p. 1; W.J.S. 'Letter to One Seeking the Holy Ghost', *AF* 1.9 (September 1907), p. 3.

[44] W.J.S. 'Letter to One Seeking the Holy Ghost', *AF* 1.10 (September 1907), p. 3.

[45] This is seen as the Sept 1906 and Oct 1906 issues contained far fewer individual testimonies. Reports were given of various revivals, but I recorded no personal testimonies by individuals giving details about the length of time they sought the baptism in the Spirit in either of these issues. Since there are no copies of November and December available, it is unclear if this pattern continued.

[46] 'What Pentecost Did for One Family', *AF* 1.6 (February/March 1907), p. 7, tells the story of R.J. Scott who 'traveled 3,200 miles to Azusa with his family' because they were hungry for God. Cf. 'Came 3,000 Miles for His Pentecost', *AF* 1.4 (December 1906), p. 3.

testimonies may suggest otherwise. Of the 80 testimonies in the *Apostolic Faith*, less than half (35) were from Seymour's Mission. Of these Azusa testimonies, 74% received in a week or less of seeking, which is 3% less than the average for the entire sample (77%). This suggests that visiting the Azusa Street Revival did not necessarily increase their likelihood of receiving the baptism in the Holy Spirit without prolonged tarrying. They were just as likely, if not more, to receive the baptism at another Pentecostal mission. This reality was not a surprise to Seymour, who believed what was happening at the mission was only a small part of what God was doing around the world.[47] He believed that anyone, anywhere, could receive the baptism in the Spirit if 'two or three are gathered in His name and pray for the baptism of the Holy Ghost'.[48]

As for the specific environment, the stories of where people received varied highly. A preacher from Minneapolis reported, 'Most of those who received the baptism in the Spirit are prostrated on the floor. Some received it while sitting in a chair or standing on their feet.'[49] One 'very old sister' simply walked into the Azusa Mission and began to shake hands with the saints when 'the power fell on her and she was baptized with the Holy Ghost'.[50] However, a number of testimonies indicated that reception was not limited to Pentecostal services at all. Seymour notes, 'People receive the baptism with the Holy Ghost while about their work. One sister received hers while she was baking a cake.'[51] Another received while going about doing 'domestic work' at her home.[52] Bro. Otto Braulin of Minneapolis received his Pentecost while 'reading the paper'.[53] Bro. Hebden received his Pentecost one morning while quietly meditating on the Word of the Lord and 'not thinking of the baptism'.[54] And one received the baptism with the Holy Ghost 'on the Santa Fe train running forty miles an hour, and ten more after him received the same gift'.[55]

---

[47] *AF* 1.8 (May 1907), p. 3, notes, 'Azusa Mission is not the head of this movement; we are a body of missions with Christ as the Head. All glory to God.'

[48] 'Tarry in One Accord', *AF* 2.13 (May 1908), p. 3.

[49] 'In the Last Day', *AF* 1.9 (June 1907), p. 1.

[50] 'Hundreds Baptized in the South', *AF* 1.6 (February/March 1907), p. 3.

[51] *AF* 1.6 (February/March 1907), p. 1.

[52] *AF* 1.8 (May 1907), p. 1.

[53] 'Baptized in Minneapolis', *AF* 1.4 (December 1906), p. 4.

[54] 'Pentecost in Toronto', *AF* 1.5 (January 1907), p. 4.

[55] *AF* 1.4 (December 1906), p. 1.

While location did not seem to be a significant factor in Pentecostal reception of the Spirit, there is some evidence that the time of day was a factor, as over 77% of those that mention the time of day reported receiving the baptism at night.[56] However, these numbers could be misleading, considering that these Pentecostal missions often had multiple services per week, most of which were in the evening.[57]

Who Shall Tarry?

The greatest variable in the amount of time spent tarrying was ordinal in nature, referring to the type of person who was seeking the Pentecostal experience.[58] The subjects in these testimonies self-identified based on three classifications: 18 unsaved/unbelievers, 12 pastors/ministers, and 50 other undesignated believers. Of these three groups, unbelievers and 'back sliders' [*sic*] seemed to be the least likely to have to 'tarry' before they received the baptism. Of the eighteen testimonies by unbelievers, 77% received on the same day and all but one (94.4%) received in less than a week.[59] Unbelievers also had a fairly uniform experience in that all but one testified to progressing through the three distinct stages of salvation, sanctification, and

---

[56] *AF* 1.2 (October 1906), p. 1; 'New Tongued Missionaries for Africa', *AF* 1.3 (November 1906), p. 3; *AF* 1.4 (December 1906), p. 3; 'Baptized in Minneapolis', *AF* 1.4 (December 1906), p. 4; 'San Francisco and Oakland', *AF* 1.4 (December 1906), p. 4; 'Speeding to Foreign Lands', *AF* 1.5 (January 1907), p. 3; 'A Businessman's Testimony of Pentecost', *AF* 1.5 (January 1907), p. 4; 'Pentecost Falling, in San Francisco', *AF* 1.6 (February/March 1907), p. 2; 'Pentecost in the Middle States', *AF* 1.6 (February/March 1907), p. 3; 'Pentecostal Testimonies', *AF* 1.6 (February/March 1907), p. 8; 'Pentecost in San Francisco', *AF* 1.7 (April 1907), 4. *AF* 1.8 (May 1907), p. 1; 'Testimonies', *AF* 2.13 (May 1908), p. 1.

[57] For example, *AF* 1.5 (January 1907), p. 4, records that in Toronto there was a Monday Bible study, all day Wednesday prayer meeting, Friday healing service, and Sunday morning and Sunday evening worship service. The Azusa Street Mission held services seven days a week and three times a day. Robeck, *Azusa Street Mission & Revival*, pp. 135-36.

[58] Cartledge, *Charismatic Glossolalia*, p. 132.

[59] The sole testimony of over a week was of a businessman who 'wandered into a meeting' and was saved. This businessman's prolonged time of tarrying, 60 days, was consistent with his other experiences, which included over a month and a half of seeking sanctification. 'A Businessman's Testimony of Pentecost', *AF* 1.5 (January 1907), p. 4.

baptism in the Holy Spirit.[60] The uniformity of these testimonies is likely due to Seymour's conviction that believers must progress through the proper order of Pentecostal experiences.[61]

The second group, those simply identified as already saved and/or sanctified, occupied the majority of testimonies (62%). Of these fifty testimonies, 76% tarried under a week for their baptism and 48% received either immediately or the same day. Although the majority received in under a week, there were 24% who had to tarry for an extended time and gave reasons for the delay. For some, it was spiritual opposition that prevented them from receiving. For example, Arthur B. Shepherd, who waited 'weeks' to be filled, commented, 'Satan seemed to exhaust his resources in opposing me, and the weeks of waiting were tedious in the extreme'.[62] Levi Upton attributed his nine days of waiting as 'some of the darkest conflict with the devil that I ever experienced'.[63] Still others, while a small number, recognized that the issue rested with their own sin issues of pride and unbelief. One sister had to get alone in her room and pray until she got 'the idols out' of her heart.[64] Myrtle K. Shideler struggled because 'pride was not all out of my heart'.[65] However, most of those who had sin issues also resolved them and received the very same day.

The group of individuals who had to tarry most often were those who identified as ministers. Of the 12 minister testimonies, only 58% received in under a week, compared to 77% of the entire sample. This is of note because one might assume that ministers who accepted the doctrine would have the least hindrances to receiving. However, a minister's prior doctrinal belief, especially coming from

---

[60] *AF* 1.5 (January 1907), p. 4, records the testimony of a sick woman who came in for healing and within 'about half an hour' was baptized in the Spirit. Nora Wilcox, 'In Denver, Colo.', *AF* 1.8 (May 1907), p. 1, tells of a demonized woman who was saved, sanctified, and Spirit-baptized 'inside an hour'. 'Pentecost in New York', *AF* 1.4 (December 1906), p. 4, records that a paralyzed man in New York was 'reclaimed', sanctified, and filled with the Holy Ghost in 'thirty minutes'. 'Testimonies', *AF* 2.13 (May 1908), p. 1, tells of a burglar who wandered into a service and was saved, sanctified, and water-baptized in the ocean, and the same afternoon was baptized in the Holy Spirit.

[61] 'Praying for the Holy Ghost', *AF* 1.2 (October 1906), p. 3; William J. Seymour, 'The Baptism with the Holy Ghost', *AF* 1.6 (February/March 1907), p. 7.

[62] 'Pentecostal Testimonies', *AF* 1.6 (February/March 1907), p. 8.

[63] 'Holiness Bible School Leader Receives Pentecost', *AF* 1.6 (February/March 1907), p. 5.

[64] 'Testimonies', *AF* 2.13 (May 1908), p. 1.

[65] 'Received Her Pentecost', *AF* 1.5 (January 1907), p. 3.

the Holiness tradition, seemed to be a factor that led to a prolonged amount of time tarrying. As a Spirit-filled Nazarene pastor noted, 'To get a fellow that has been preaching twenty years to see that he has not received the baptism, when he has been preaching all the time that he had it, and then to get him to turn seeker, is a hard job'. [66] In fact, several Holiness preachers who were unconvinced that the baptism in the Spirit was a separate experience came to the Azusa Mission as skeptics. [67] For example, Glen A. Cook originally came to Azusa Mission to condemn the movement; however he was quickly convinced and later testified it took five weeks to lay down his 'pre-conceived ideas' and become 'absolutely empty'. [68] For Cook, each of his experiences in those five weeks had the potential of bringing him to the fullness, but he had to fight through his hesitance. He explains, 'I believe I would have spoken in tongues then, if I had remained in the hands of the Lord long enough'. Cook's experience suggests that for some ministers, the internal doctrinal struggles added to the length of their tarrying experience, perhaps directly in relation to breaking through to speak in tongues. This struggle may also have been an issue for William H. Durham, who sought for over two weeks at the Azusa Mission before he received, perhaps because of his own internal struggle with the Holiness sanctification doctrine. [69]

Despite this increased length of tarrying among ministers, there were several notable leaders of the early Pentecostal movement who received with little or no tarrying. For example, when J.H. King heard about the baptism in the Holy Spirit from G.B. Cashwell, he searched the Scriptures for two days and on the third day he received his Pentecost. [70] Similarly, A.J. Tomlinson heard about the baptism from Cashwell in an evening meeting and the very next Sunday he received

---

[66] *AF* 1.2 (Oct 1906), p. 1.

[67] Robeck, *Azusa Street Mission & Revival*, pp. 90-92.

[68] G.A. Cook, 'Receiving the Holy Ghost', *AF* 1.3 (November 1906), p. 2.

[69] 'A Chicago Evangelist's Pentecost', *AF* 1.6 (February/March 1907), p. 4. Durham initially reported here that he had received sanctification and then was filled with the Holy Spirit. Later he contradicted this testimony claiming, 'I had never believed that sanctification and baptism in the Holy Spirit were one and the same thing'. *Pentecostal Testimony* 2.1 (January 1912), p. 4. This reversal was instrumental in the finished work controversy with Seymour in 1912, in which Durham came out vocally against the Holiness doctrine of sanctification and even tried to take over leadership of the Azusa Street Mission.

[70] Douglas Jacobsen (ed.), *A Reader in Pentecostal Theology: Voices from the First Generation* (Bloomington: Indiana University Press, 2006), p. 111.

the Holy Spirit and spoke in tongues.[71] This was also true of both William Seymour and Charles H. Mason, who also preached and led others into the baptism before they received. William Seymour began holding cottage meetings after arriving in Los Angeles in April 1906 and almost immediately people began to receive the baptism, but Seymour himself did not receive until three days later.[72] C.H. Mason had already been preaching the baptism in the Spirit to his people, but upon arriving at Azusa Street Mission he received the baptism in the Holy Spirit in the first meeting he attended.[73]

Conclusion

Having looked at the history of the reception of the baptism in the Spirit found in *The Apostolic Faith*, a number of conclusions can be drawn.

First, early Pentecostals received Jesus' command to 'tarry' as an invitation to pursue the baptism in the Spirit rather than a statement about the duration of time required before one could receive. Although the practice of tarrying was fully embraced, in general they believed that the Spirit was immediately available to seekers. This interpretation was confirmed in that 77% of seekers had a relatively short period of waiting, having received within a week of their initial seeking experience. The other 23% had to tarry longer than others, but only 10% of the sample tarried three weeks or more. This statistic suggests that for most early Pentecostals, tarrying was not a prolonged experience.

Second, the phenomenon of speaking in tongues was essential to the concept of tarrying because it was the necessary signal that the tarrying process was complete. No matter how powerful one's experience with the Spirit, seekers were encouraged to continue to tarry

---

[71] A.J. Tomlinson, 'The Work at Cleveland, Tenn.', *TBM* 1.7 (February 1, 1908), p. 4.

[72] 'Pentecost with Signs Following', *AF* 1.4 (December 1906), p. 1; Gaston Espinoza, *William Seymour and the Origins of Global Pentecostalism* (Durham, NC: Duke University Press, 2014), p. 55.

[73] C.H. Mason, 'Tennessee Evangelist Witnesses', *AF* 1.6 (February/March 1907), p. 7. The details are somewhat unclear in this testimony, but he insinuated that he received during his first meeting. He notes, 'As I arose from the altar and took my seat, I fixed my eyes on Jesus, and the Holy Ghost took charge of me. I surrendered perfectly to Him and consented to Him. Then I began singing a song in unknown tongues, and it was the sweetest thing.'

until they had received the 'Bible evidence'. On the one hand, this proved a great comfort because 'evidence' confirmed the Spirit's presence in those who were seeking. It provided the empirical evidence needed to verify that they had received the gift they were seeking. But, on the other hand, for those who had prolonged experiences, the lack of ability to speak in tongues led to discouragement. For many, this was an agonizing reality. Yet, within the community, the encouragement to keep seeking provided the support needed to endure. It was also clear that being a seeker without getting preoccupied with glossolalia proved a formidable challenge. The longer one sought, the easier it was to focus on speaking in tongues rather than receiving the Holy Spirit. In these cases, a change in location from the altar to another less public context often eased the anxiety and allowed the seeker to receive more easily. This suggests that, for some, revivalistic environments may actually hinder reception. Furthermore, the instances of those who received in isolation, though not as frequent as communal environments, were no less dramatic than those in revivalistic contexts.

Third, this study points out that early Pentecostals did not see sin as a major hindrance to receiving the Spirit. Only a small number identified particular issues, mostly pride and unbelief, before they could receive the baptism. For the majority, there was seemingly no fault in the seeker for the prolonged process. I found this particularly interesting considering the Holiness *via salutis* in which sanctification is often required before receiving the Spirit. However, prior doctrinal belief and pride was found to be a significant factor, especially for ministers from Holiness backgrounds. The fact that ministers seemed to have the most difficulty receiving, while unbelievers seemed to walk seamlessly through the *via salutis* into an immediate Spirit baptism experience, demonstrates that prior beliefs and expectations were at some level obstacles to receiving the Spirit immediately. Some ministers experienced internal conflicts over accepting the truth that they had not already 'received the Spirit'. This reality would undoubtedly require humility for ministers to admit that they were outside the company of the initiated. This concept was certainly true for Bro. Rosa who said, 'I was too proud as a minister of the Gospel to humble myself in a lowly mission and let ladies pray over me for the gift of the Holy Ghost, and I had in my mind what people would think of me'.[74] I believe this point is informative to the minister and lay-person alike. Whatever hunger there may be for experiences with God, it must be accompanied by humility.

Perhaps the most instructive element of this study was that despite the effectiveness of the Azusa Street Mission in introducing the world to the Pentecostal experience, those who attended the services at the revival were not necessarily at a significant advantage to receiving the baptism in the Spirit. The percentage of those who received immediately or the same day outside Azusa was similar to those who received inside. This data suggests that the true power of the tarrying meetings for early Pentecostals was not the hallowed location or how long they waited; it was the hunger engendered within a supportive communal environment.[75] This should be instructive to Pentecostals in this day when tarrying services have become uncommon in Pentecostal churches.[76] As Margaret Poloma has documented, only a small percentage of believers today receive the baptism in the Spirit outside of communal experiences.[77] The primary reason is that in order for 'non-glossolalics' to become initiated into the Spirit-filled life, they must be exposed to atmospheres in which there is a communal practice of glossolalia and encouragement for believers to seek the baptism. This is what the Azusa Street Mission and all the other missions provided for believers. Therefore, the practice of tarrying for the baptism in the Holy Spirit is just as needed today as it was a century ago; not because it is a prolonged process, but because there is always a new generation that needs the encouragement and spaces to seek a Pentecost of their own.

---

[74] *AF* 1.2 (Oct 1906), p. 1.

[75] William W. Menzies and Robert W. Menzies, *Spirit and Power: Foundations of Pentecostal Experience* (Grand Rapids: Zondervan, 2000), p. 23, comment, 'Believers seeking the baptism in the Spirit were brought into "tarrying meetings" where a cluster of Spirit-baptized believers would gather around the candidate, furnishing a supportive context in which the individual could seek God for the blessing'.

[76] Margaret M. Poloma, *The Assemblies of God at the Crossroads: Charisma and Institutional Dilemmas* (Knoxville, TN: University of Tennessee Press, 1989), pp. 40-42.

[77] Poloma, *The Assemblies of God at the Crossroads*, p. 191, documents that in her congregational sample, only 20% of those in the congregation had received the Spirit while alone. She also notes that the vast majority of these experiences were at emotionally and spiritually charged environments such as altar services, revivals, or camp services (41).

Bibliography

Astley, Jeff and Leslie J. Francis (eds.), *Exploring Ordinary Theology* (Farnham, Surrey: Ashgate, 2013).

Cartledge, Mark J., Jeff Astley, Leslie J. Francis, *et. al*, *Testimony in the Spirit: Rescripting Ordinary Pentecostal Theology* (Farnham, Surrey: Ashgate, 2010).

Erricker, Clive and Jane Erricker (eds.), *Contemporary Spiritualties: Social and Religious Contexts* (London: Continuum, 2001).

Espinoza, Gaston, *William Seymour and the Origins of Global Pentecostalism* (Durham, NC: Duke University Press, 2014).

Hollenweger, Walter J., *Pentecostalism: Origins and Developments Worldwide* (Peabody, MA: Hendrickson, 1997).

Jacobsen, Douglas (ed.), *A Reader in Pentecostal Theology: Voices from the First Generation* (Bloomington: Indiana University Press, 2006).

Menzies, William W. and Robert W. Menzies, *Spirit and Power: Foundations of Pentecostal Experience* (Grand Rapids: Zondervan, 2000).

Poloma, Margaret M., *The Assemblies of God at the Crossroads: Charisma and Institutional Dilemmas* (Knoxville, TN: University of Tennessee Press, 1989).

Raboteau, Albert L., *Slave Religion: The 'Invisible Institution' in the Antebellum South* (Oxford: Oxford University Press, 1978).

Robeck Jr, Cecil M., *Azusa Street Mission & Revival: The Birth of the Global Pentecostal Movement* (Nashville: Nelson Reference & Electronic, 2006).

Vondey, Wolfgang, *Pentecostal Theology: Living the Full Gospel* (London: T & T Clarke, 2017).

10

RECEIVING THE LIVING WATER: JOHN 4 AND JOHN 7 IN EARLY PENTECOSTAL LITERATURE

MATTHEW A. PAUGH*

I trace the genesis of this project back to 2003. In a class on Pentecostal and Charismatic movements at the Assemblies of God Theological Seminary, Gary B. McGee charged us to read Agnes Ozman's reflection on the events of January 1, 1901. On that day in Topeka, KS, Ozman became the first to speak in tongues at Bethel Bible School under Charles Parham's tutelage. With a clear nod to Jn 7.38, she described her experience in these words: 'It was as if rivers of living water were proceeding from my innermost being'. Here was a key person in American Pentecostal lore who used Johannine language to encapsulate what she later referred to as 'the baptism according to Acts 2:4 and 19:1-6'.[1] I began to wonder if early American

---

* Matthew A. Paugh (DMin, Wesley Theological Seminary) is the pastor of St. Paul's United Methodist Church in Oakland, MD, and an instructor for the Methodist Theological School in Ohio Course of Study Program.

[1] Agnes Ozman (LaBerge), 'The Gift of the Holy Spirit', in Rosemary Skinner Keller and Rosemary Radford Ruether (eds.), *In Our Own Voices: Four Centuries of American Women's Religious Writing* (Louisville, KY: Westminster / John Knox Press, 1995), pp. 234-36. Shortly thereafter, I heard George O. Wood, who was then interim pastor at Central Assembly of God, relate the story of Pentecostalism's beginnings in Springfield, MO. He told the story of Rachel Sizelove and her 1913 vision of a 'sparkling fountain' emanating from Springfield in all directions until the 'whole land was deluged with living water'. See Rachel Sizelove, 'A Sparkling Fountain for the Whole Earth', *Word and Work* 56.6 (June 1934), p. 1.

Pentecostals commonly alluded to Johannine terms, specifically 'living water', to communicate the meaning of their spiritual encounters.

Several years later, John Christopher Thomas and his doctoral students at the Centre for Pentecostal Theology in Cleveland, TN, introduced me to the concept of *Wirkungsgeschichte*, or the 'history of effects'. Understanding how various communities have read a text can yield insights into how that community impacts present interpretation, and bring additional layers of meaning to contemporary theological formulations.[2] After seeing this method in action, I realized a 'history of effects' approach could fuse my interest in biblical studies and Pentecostal history.

In what follows, I seek to trace how early American Pentecostals interpreted 'living water' in John 4 and 7. To accomplish this, I shadow the methodology first employed by Kimberly E. Alexander that examines periodicals during the movement's first decades.[3] My inquiry focuses on Pentecostal literature between the years 1906 and 1920. Like other interpreters, I concentrate on these early years based on Steven J. Land's contention that they represent the theological 'heart' of Pentecostalism.[4] Following my survey of teachings, editorials, sermons, and testimonies, I offer some initial observations and implications for contemporary Pentecostal theology.

In the wake of Alexander's proposal that Wesleyan-Holiness and Finished-Work Pentecostals present distinct understandings of healing, I divide my analysis into these two broad categories. In simple

---

[2] In calling for a Pentecostal *Wirkungsgeschichte*, John Christopher Thomas '"What the Spirit Is Saying to the Church" – The Testimony of a Pentecostal Working in New Testament Studies', in Kevin Spawn and Archie T. Wright (eds.), *Spirit & Scripture: Examining a Pneumatic Hermeneutic* (London: Bloomsbury T&T Clark, 2012), pp. 115-29 (118), likens the biblical text to 'a source of water with the goal of the interpreter being to trace where the water flows'.

[3] Kimberly Ervin Alexander, *Pentecostal Healing: Models in Theology and Practice* (JPTSup 29; Blandford Forum: Deo Publishing, 2006). Others who have followed this approach include Larry R. McQueen, *Toward a Pentecostal Eschatology: Discerning the Way Forward* (JPTSup 39; Blandford Forum: Deo Publishing, 2012); Chris E.W. Green, *Toward a Pentecostal Theology of the Lord's Supper: Foretasting the Kingdom* (Cleveland, TN: CPT Press, 2012); and Melissa L. Archer, *'I Was in the Spirit on the Lord's Day': A Pentecostal Engagement with Worship in the Apocalypse* (Cleveland, TN: CPT Press, 2015).

[4] Steven J. Land, *Pentecostal Spirituality: A Passion for the Kingdom* (JPTSup 1; Sheffield: Sheffield Academic Press, 1993), p. 47; see also Walter J. Hollenweger, 'Pentecostals and the Charismatic Movement', in Cheslyn Jones, Geoffrey Wainwright, and Edward Yarnold (eds.), *The Study of Spirituality* (Oxford: Oxford University Press, 1986), pp. 549-53.

terms, these two Pentecostal streams have divergent conceptions of sanctification. For Wesleyan-Holiness Pentecostals, sanctification represents a definite second work of grace; for the Finished-Work Pentecostals sanctification occurs concurrently with justification at conversion.[5]

Introduction to the Biblical Texts

Water flows throughout the Fourth Gospel, but two texts focus on 'living water'.[6] In John 4, Jesus informs the Samaritan woman that if

---

[5] This study represents a simplified explanation of a complicated soteriological issue. The 'Finished Work Controversy' rose to the surface in 1910. William H. Durham began to preach against sanctification as a second work of grace because he held that the work of Christ on the cross finished the work of salvation. See Richard M. Riss, 'The Finished Work Controversy', in Stanley M. Burgess and Eduard M. Van Der Maas (eds.), *The New International Dictionary of Pentecostal and Charismatic Movements* (Grand Rapids: Zondervan, rev. and exp. edn, 2002), pp. 638-39. As Larry R. McQueen, *Toward a Pentecostal Eschatology: Discerning the Way Forward* (JPTSup 39; Blandford Forum: Deo Publishing, 2012), p. 144, points out, however, the Finished-Work doctrine was evident well before Durham in some Pentecostal literature. Regardless, the Wesleyan-Holiness outlook continued to be embraced by denominations such as the Church of God (Cleveland, TN), the Pentecostal Holiness Church, and the Church of God in Christ; the Finished-Work position was adopted by groups such as the Assemblies of God and the Foursquare Church. In general terms, the Wesleyan-Holiness stream conceives of a fivefold gospel (Jesus as Savior, Sanctifier, Baptizer in the Holy Spirit, Healer, and Coming-King), while the more baptistic and Reformed Finished-Work stream espouses a fourfold gospel (Jesus as Savior, Baptizer in the Holy Spirit, Healer, and Coming-King).

[6] In addition to the two texts under consideration, water appears in the narration of John's baptizing (Jn 1.26; 3.23); Jesus' transformation of water into wine (2.6); Jesus' announcement to Nicodemus of the need to be born of water and the Spirit (3.5); the healing of an invalid at the pool of Bethesda (5.7); Jesus' walking on the sea (6.16-20); the man born blind who washes in the pool of Siloam (9.7); Jesus' washing of the disciples' feet (13.5); and the piercing of Jesus' side (19.34). In light of the surprising frequency of water imagery, R. Alan Culpepper, *The Anatomy of the Fourth Gospel* (Minneapolis: Fortress Press, 1983), pp. 192-95, refers to water as 'a dominant motif and expanding core symbol' and suggests that it has 'the most varied associations of any of John's symbols'. For additional treatments of water symbolism in John's Gospel, see Craig R. Koester, *Symbolism in the Fourth Gospel: Meaning, Mystery, Community* (Minneapolis: Fortress Press, 2nd edn, 2003), pp. 175-206; Larry Paul Jones, *The Symbol of Water in the Gospel of John* (JSNTSup 145; Sheffield: Sheffield Academic Press, 1997); Wai-Yee Ng, *Water Symbolism in John: An Eschatological Interpretation* (Studies in Biblical Literature 15; New York: Peter Lang, 2001); J. Joubert, 'Johannine Metaphors/Symbols Linked to the Paraclete-Spirit and their Theological Implications', *Acta Theologica* 27 (2007), pp. 83-103; and Rhonda G. Crutcher, *That He Might Be Revealed: Water Imagery and the Identity of Jesus in the Gospel of John* (Eugene, OR: Pickwick Publications, 2015).

she had asked, he would have granted her 'living water'. Since 'living water' could refer to 'flowing water' or 'running water', the woman takes Jesus' offer literally. She protests that Jesus does not even have a bucket to get water from the deep well. The woman's misunderstanding gives Jesus an opening to expound on 'living water'. Distinguishing the water he offers from ordinary water, Jesus declares, 'Whoever drinks from the water that I will give will never thirst again' (4.14 NIV). Jesus goes on to describe it as a 'well of water' that springs up within a person and produces eternal life. In this interaction, 'living water' symbolizes the new life of which 'Jesus is the giver and source'.[7]

The Johannine Jesus returns to the concept of 'living water' on the last day of the Feast of Sukkoth in Jn 7.37-39.[8] Jesus cries out, 'Let anyone who is thirsty come to me, and let the one who believes in me drink'. John connects Jesus' cry with a scriptural quotation, but he does not identify the text: 'Out of his belly shall flow rivers of living water'. Among several interpretative dilemmas, a crux issue concerns from whose belly the 'rivers of living water' comes.[9] It could refer to Jesus' belly or the believer's belly. Craig R. Koester

---

[7] Culpepper, *Anatomy*, p. 192. Jocelyn McWhirter, *The Bridegroom Messiah and the People of God: Marriage in the Fourth Gospel* (Society for New Testament Studies Monograph Series 138; Cambridge: Cambridge University Press, 2004), pp. 21-44, draws attention to the bridegroom imagery in this passage. The image flows out of John's identification of Jesus as the bridegroom (3.24) and the Old Testament texts echoed by the well scene in chapter 4 (e.g. Gen. 24.10-27; 29.4-12; Exod. 2.15-22).

[8] For the background of the water pouring ceremony at the Feast of Sukkoth, see Joseph R. Greene, 'Integrating Interpretations of John 7:37–39 into the Temple Theme: The Spirit as Efflux from the New Temple', *Neotestamentica* 47 (2013), pp. 333-53.

[9] In addition to the question of whose belly is in view, two other key interpretative challenges concern the text's proper punctuation (i.e. does 'the one who believes in me' go with what comes before it or what comes after it?) and the identification of what Scripture Jesus has in mind. Scholars put forth a multitude of possible sources. On these matters, see Juan B. Cortés, 'Yet Another Look at Jn 7:37–38', *Catholic Biblical Quarterly* 29 (1967), pp. 75-86; Gordon D. Fee, 'Once More – John 7:37–39', *Expository Times* 89 (1977/78), pp. 116-18; Dale C. Allison Jr, 'The Living Water (John 4:10–14, 6:35c, 7:37–39)', *St. Vladimir's Theological Quarterly* 30 (1986), pp. 143-57; Martinus J.J. Menken, 'The Origin of the Old Testament Quotation in John 7:38', *Novum Testamentum* 38 (1996), pp. 160-75; Joel Marcus, 'Rivers of Living Water from Jesus' Belly (John 7:38)', *JBL* 117 (1998), pp. 328-30; Michael A. Daise, '"If Anyone Thirsts, Let That One Come to Me and Drink": The Literary Texture of John 7:37b–38a', *JBL* 122 (2003), pp. 687-99; John Christopher Thomas, *The Spirit of the New Testament* (Blandford Forum: Deo Publishing, 2005), pp. 163-66.

suggests that the ambiguity points to 'a primary and secondary level of meaning'. On one level, 'his' refers to Jesus as the source of living water. But on another level, 'his' indicates the believer, from whom 'a well of water' springs up (see Jn 4.13-14).[10] As Willard M. Swartley posits, 'the life-giving water originates from Jesus and flows out from believers'.[11]

But John then makes a proviso: 'Now this he said about the Spirit, which those who believed in him were to receive; for as yet the Spirit had not been given, because Jesus was not yet glorified' (7.39). This statement makes clear that the 'living water' refers to the Spirit and that Jesus' glorification exists as a precondition for the Spirit's conferral. In John's Gospel, Jesus' glorification culminates in his crucifixion, resurrection, and ascension.[12] Jesus' promise in John 7 anticipates both Jn 19.34, where water flows from Jesus' side on the cross, and Jn 20.22, where the risen Jesus breathes the Holy Spirit on his disciples.

Living Water in Wesleyan-Holiness Voices

With this background from the evangelist John's 'living water' texts established, I turn now to early Pentecostal reflections on 'living water'. The analysis begins with Wesleyan-Holiness Pentecostal periodicals. Publications include *The Apostolic Faith, The Bridegroom's Messenger,* the *Church of God Evangel,* and *The Pentecostal Holiness Advocate.*

The Apostolic Faith
Between the years 1906 and 1908, *The Apostolic Faith,* an offshoot of the Azusa Street revival, chronicled the growth of the burgeoning Pentecostal movement and provided teaching from its leaders. William J. Seymour published the periodical and penned many of its articles. For Seymour, 'living water' symbolizes 'the baptism with the Holy Ghost'. He utilizes the image to outline a Wesleyan-Holiness

---

[10] Koester, *Symbolism,* p. 14.

[11] Willard M. Swartley, *John* (Believers Church Bible Commentary; Harrisonburg, VA: Herald Press, 2013), p. 203.

[12] Raymond E. Brown, *The Gospel according to John XIII–XXI: A New Translation with Introduction and Commentary* (AB; Garden City, NY: Doubleday, 1970), p. 951, emphasizes that 'the whole process of glorification' includes 'the hour' of the passion, death, resurrection, and ascension'. See also Gary M. Burge, *The Anointed Community: The Holy Spirit in the Johannine Tradition* (Grand Rapids: Eerdmans, 1987), pp. 136-37.

Pentecostal order of salvation. In an exhortation entitled 'Receive Ye the Holy Ghost', Seymour delineates the process for seeking Spirit baptism. The 'first step' requires 'the pardoned sinner' to become 'a child of God in justification'. The 'next step' includes 'the second work of grace', that is, sanctification. With 'a clear knowledge of justification and sanctification', believers can receive 'the baptism with the Holy Ghost'. In Seymour's *ordo salutis,* justification and sanctification result in 'brooks and streams of salvation flowing in our souls'. But, says Seymour, 'we can have the rivers'. The 'rivers of living water' refer to the Spirit being 'poured out upon all flesh', so that 'all races, nations, and tongues are receiving the baptism with the Holy Ghost'.[13]

The baptism with the Holy Ghost comes to those who hunger and thirst for God. After commencing his 'Letter to One Seeking the Holy Ghost' with Jesus' blessing upon those who hunger and thirst for righteousness (Mt. 5.6), Seymour contends, 'The Lord Jesus is always ready to fill the hungry, thirsty soul, for He said …, "He that believed on Me as the scripture hath said, out of his innermost being shall flow rivers of living water".' For Seymour, 'the rivers of living water' correspond to the 'promise of the Father' (Lk. 24.49) and 'power' to witness (Acts 1.8).[14]

Seymour continues this trajectory in exploring Jesus' encounter with the Samaritan woman in John 4. The woman left her 'old water pot on the well' and 'ran away' to share the news of salvation. Seymour connects the woman's witness to Spirit baptism: 'The baptism with the Holy Ghost gives us power to testify to the risen, resurrected Saviour'. Having received 'rivers of living waters', believers can go forth 'in the mighty name of Jesus to the ends of the earth and water dry places … until these parched, sad, lonely hearts are made to rejoice in the God of their salvation'. Conceived as living water, Spirit

---

[13] William J. Seymour, 'Receive Ye the Holy Ghost', *AF* 1.5 (January 1907), p. 2. William J. Seymour, 'The Holy Ghost Foreshadowed', *AF* 1.4 (December 1906), p. 2, suggests that the baptism in the Holy Ghost was foreshadowed in the OT tabernacle (Exod. 25); the tabernacle design corresponds to the order of salvation. Seymour differentiates between sanctification and Spirit baptism by using images of streams and rivers: 'In the Holy Place we had the streams of salvation, but in the Holy of Holies, we have the rivers'.

[14] William J. Seymour, 'Letter to One Seeking the Holy Ghost', *AF* 1.9 (June 1907), p. 3.

baptism makes the believer a conduit that shares God's salvation with others.[15]

Seymour takes up the theme of believers as channels of living water in his typological reading of Genesis 24. In the Genesis narrative, Abraham sends a servant to seek a wife for his son Isaac, and the servant returns home with Rebecca. Although Genesis does not name the servant, Seymour follows a tradition that designates the servant as 'Eliezer'. In Seymour's reflection, 'Eliezer (meaning "God's helper") is a type of the Holy Spirit, and Isaac is a type of Christ'. Eliezer sought a bride for Isaac in the same way that the Spirit seeks a bride for Christ. Focusing on Rebecca's deed of drawing water for Eliezer's camels (Gen. 24.20), Seymour declares that 'when we have the mighty Spirit in our hearts … we are ready for watering the whole entire world with the precious well of salvation in our heart … O may all of Christ's waiting bride be filled with the rivers of living water that they may water the thirsty parched hearts with the rivers of salvation'.[16]

Along with the emphasis on living water flowing out to others, other authors use the imagery to point to the personal benefits of Spirit baptism. For example, an unattributed article asserts, 'If you pray in the Spirit, you will strike the spring of living water and it will bubble up in you and you never get tired praying'.[17] In addition, living water also emphasizes power. The September 1907 edition proclaims, 'O to have that well of water springing up to everlasting life'! Out of this well the believer derives 'power with God, not only to tread on serpents and scorpions, to drink any deadly thing and it shall not hurt

---

[15] William J. Seymour, 'River of Living Water', *AF* 1.3 (November 1906), p. 2. Seymour also alludes to John 4 in 'The Salvation of Jesus', *AF* 1.12 (January 1908), p. 4: 'Jesus says, "He that drinketh of this water shall never thirst". This is the water of life that runs through the ceaseless ages of eternity', *AF* 1.11 (October–January 1908), p. 4, confirms the order of sanctification, then baptism in the Holy Spirit: 'The most wonderful thing a man or woman can receive after being sanctified is the outpouring of the Holy Ghost in their heart. He is fire and rivers of salvation in you [*sic*] inmost being.' The article then goes on to discuss OT prophecies that compare the outpouring of the Spirit to water; these include Ps. 72.6-7; Isa. 32.15 and 44.3.

[16] William J. Seymour, 'Rebecca; Type of the Bride of Christ – Gen. 24', *AF* 1.6 (February–March 1907), p. 2.

[17] 'Prayer', *AF* 1.12 (January 1908), p. 3.

you, but to cast out demons and lay hands on the sick and they shall recover' (see Mk 16.18).[18]

A final reflection on 'living water' takes readers to the end of John's Gospel. Alluding to the soldier's piercing of Jesus' side following his death (Jn 19.34), an anonymous writer observes, 'Out of His side flowed Blood and water. That Blood represents cleansing and the water the baptism with the Holy Ghost. The rivers of living water which Jesus promised flowed out of His side.'[19] For this author, the cross fulfills Jesus' words in Jn 7.38-39.

The Bridegroom's Messenger

G.B. Cashwell, dubbed 'the apostle of Pentecost in the South' began publishing *The Bridegroom's Messenger* in 1907.[20] In two January 1908 editorials, Cashwell equates 'rivers of living water' with 'the baptism of the Holy Ghost'. On January 1, he decries preachers who mock the Pentecostals: 'Slandering and making light of this blessed experience will not do for us who have found this blessed peace of God that flows like rivers of living water'.[21] Two weeks later, Cashwell makes the connection between the 'rivers of living water' and Spirit baptism unmistakable:

> Does the power of the baptism rest upon you? Has the stream of God's eternal love and salvation been turned into your life, and is it not flowing like 'rivers of living water'? If this is not your experience, go to the Saviour and tell him you want the promise spoken of in the 4th chapter of John to the woman at Jacob's well, and on the last day of the feast in the 7th chapter of John. When you get in earnest enough He will come in and will have the same effect and give the same evidences that He did on the day of Pentecost and down through the days of the apostles.[22]

If Cashwell sees Spirit baptism as the fulfillment of the Johannine 'living water' passages, A.S. Worrell uses the image to emphasize the need for further growth beyond Spirit baptism. He observes that with

---

[18] *AF* 1.10 (September 1907), p. 4.

[19] *AF* 1.10 (September 1907), p. 2.

[20] H. Vinson Synan, 'Cashwell, Gaston Barnabas', in Stanley M. Burgess and Gary B. McGee (eds.), *Dictionary of Pentecostal and Charismatic Movements* (Grand Rapids: Zondervan, 1988), pp. 109-10.

[21] G.B. Cashwell, 'Editorials', *TBM* 1.5 (January 1, 1908), p. 1.

[22] G.B. Cashwell, 'Editorials', *TBM* 1.6 (January 15, 1908), p. 1.

'a whole-hearted walk with God, and unreserved obedience to the word of God, and to all the admonitions of the Holy Spirit', the baptism in the Holy Spirit 'may grow better' and 'increase in power, so that what was "water" may grow into a "well of water", and the well may become "rivers of living water"'.[23]

In a similar vein, C.E. Kent presents a meditation on Hos. 6.3. According to Kent, Spirit baptism changes the believer's longings and affections. As this happens, Hosea's prophecy comes to fruition; the Lord 'shall come to us as the rain, as the latter and the former rain'. Quoting Jn 7.38, Kent implies that 'the rivers of living water' have been poured out to indicate that the 'Latter Rain is falling; the time is very short; soon will come the Bridegroom'.[24]

Like Kent, Elizabeth A. Sexton, who became editor of *The Bridegroom's Messenger* in mid-1908, seeks to prepare readers for Christ's coming in the 'latter rain' season. The Pentecostal baptism provides a means to experience the Holy Spirit's 'latter rain showers'. But only those who 'press on' will live in a constant state of 'readiness for the rapture'. Drawing on Ezekiel 47, Sexton stresses the need for readers to go 'deeper' in their knowledge of God: 'Like Ezekiel's vision, we see by faith a stream of living water proceeding from the throne; it has risen until it cannot be passed over ... The abundant latter rain shall bring a freshet of living water'.[25]

In a similar exhortation, Sexton challenges readers to live as 'palm tree Christians'. Quoting Ps. 92.12, she describes how palm trees receive nourishment from 'rivers' and 'sweet springs of water'. Noting that 'water is used in the word of God to symbolize the Holy Spirit', Sexton demonstrates that 'the godly ... flourish by the rivers of

---

[23] A.S. Worrell, 'Wonderful Times Coming', *TBM* 1.8 (February 15, 1908), p. 4. For more on A.S. Worrell, see Michael Kuykendall, 'A.S. Worrell's *New Testament*: A Landmark Baptist-Pentecostal Bible Translation from the Early Twentieth Century', *Pneuma* 29 (2007), pp. 254-80. A.S. Worrell, *Full Gospel Teachings* (Louisville, KY: Charles T. Dearing, 1900), pp. 53-54, describes his conversion to Pentecostalism: 'I realized, at that time, the opening up of *the well of living water* IN *me*, whose blissful flow has never since subsided. This occurred on the night of the *10th of August, 1891*' (emphasis original).

[24] C.E. Kent, 'If We Follow On', *TBM* 1.9 (November 1, 1908), p. 2.

[25] E.A. Sexton, 'Following On to Know', *TBM* 2.42 (July 15, 1909), p. 1.

"living water"'. The Holy Spirit enables believers to grow in 'upright-ness of character' and to stand strong even amid persecution.[26]

Maintaining the connection between water and the Holy Spirit, Sexton uses another editorial to explain how 'rivers of living water' point backward to Eden and forward to 'the New Jerusalem'. Once believers have the Pentecostal experience, they can swim in God's 'ocean of love'. Remarkably, even now, the Christian can be 'im-mersed in', 'drink of', and 'swim in' the New Jerusalem's 'river of water of life' (Rev. 22.1-5).[27]

Although they still connect 'living water' to Spirit baptism, two authors emphasize John's comment that 'the Spirit was not yet given, because Jesus not was not yet glorified' (Jn 7.39). E.M. Stanton as-serts, 'The Lordship of Jesus Christ was the condition of the bestow-ment of the Holy Spirit by the Father'. According to Stanton, just as Jesus' enthronement heralded the Spirit's outpouring on Pentecost (Acts 2.33), so believers must enthrone Jesus in their hearts in order to receive the baptism in the Holy Spirit.[28] Along the same lines, Mrs C.G. Bayless quotes Jn 7.38-39 and writes,

---

[26] E.A. Sexton, 'Palm Tree Christians', *TBM* 2.43 (August 1, 1909), p. 1. This article was reprinted in *TBM* 11.205 (July 1918), p. 4. R.L. Stewart, 'The Palm Tree Christian', *PHA* 3.46 (March 11, 1920), pp. 2-3, presents a sermon that is clearly based on Sexton's article. It follows the same flow of thought and, in many cases, the same wording; however, there is no acknowledgment to Sexton.

[27] E.A. Sexton, 'River of Water of Life', *TBM* 3.48 (October 15, 1909), p. 1. Over the next decade, Sexton's periodical featured numerous references to living water in connection with the baptism of the Holy Ghost. H.M. Barth, 'Signs of a Revival', *TBM* 5.120 (November 1, 1912), p. 1, suggests that, through the baptism, God satisfies believers' souls 'with living water from the wells of salvation'. In 'The Baptism of the Holy Ghost', *TBM* 7.142 (October 15, 1913), p. 1, an unidentified author argues that 'Jesus spoke of the baptism as rivers of living water'. E.L. Moore, 'Holy Ghost in Last Days', *TBM* 8.164 (November 1, 1914), p. 4, equates Jesus' promise that 'out of his being shall flow rivers of living water' with the 'promise of the Father' in Lk. 24.29 and Acts 2.33. E.A. Sexton, 'Baptism of the Holy Ghost', *TBM* 13.225 (September 1920), p. 4, contends, 'Our Lord Jesus Christ refers to the blessed baptism of the Holy Ghost in John 7:38, 39'. See also William F. Manley, 'Glad Tidings', *The Household of God* 3.11 (November 1907), p. 1, who speaks about his Spirit baptism experience: 'I needed to acknowledge to God that I have never truly known what the true baptism of the Holy Ghost is, such as is recorded in John 7:37, 38, where mention is made of "rivers of living water." I may have a had a little of "the well of water" experience (John 4:14), but oftentimes I get very dry, and a mere existence instead of living abundant with the result. But, glory to God, now its fulness of life is reality'.

[28] E.M. Stanton, 'The Holy Spirit', *TBM* 10.190 (January 1, 1917), p. 4. See also E.M. Stanton, 'The Baptism with the Holy Spirit', *TBM* 13.222 (April/May 1920), p. 4.

Jesus was glorified, was at the right hand of the Father, from whence He poured out 'that Holy Spirit of Promise', and the people in amazement both saw and heard and were convinced that God in POWER was with these people. So in the personal experience of believers, Jesus must be GLORIFIED, given first place in the heart and life before He can 'seal with that Holy Spirit of Promise'.

In Bayless's exposition, the Holy Spirit's seal is 'the baptism of the Holy Spirit'.[29]

Church of God Evangel

In 1910, A.J. Tomlinson established *The Evening Light and Church of God Evangel,* which he would later shorten to *The Church of God Evangel,* to serve as the official periodical of the Church of God (Cleveland, TN).[30] Though it tends to feature more testimonies, the *Evangel* provides relevant teaching on living water. In a teaching designed to instruct believers on 'how to receive the Baptism of the Holy Ghost', W.F. Hesson suggests that one of the conditions includes thirst: 'You must be THIRSTY. "If any man thirst let him come unto me and drink."'[31] Like Hesson, Sam C. Perry believes that Jn 7.37-39 refers to Spirit baptism. He writes, 'Jesus likens the Spirit-baptized believer's experience to "rivers of living water". Rivers of life, light, love, grace and power flowing direct from the throne of God is the portion of those who possess the life more abundant.' The life-giving flow of this river leads to several consequences, including spiritual illumination, an upright walk, fruitfulness, and praise of God.[32]

For Tomlinson, one of the consequences of Spirit baptism involves abandoning one's self to Jesus 'for better or worse'. In Tomlinson's view, Jesus loves 'a soul that thirsts to drink of His Spirit'. Drinking of the Spirit causes one to dwell in the 'springs of living

---

[29] Mrs C.G. Bayless, 'The Seal', *TBM* 13.222 (April/May 1920), p. 4. Interestingly, Bayless also uses John's two references to 'living water' to differentiate between salvation and Spirit baptism. The 'well of water springing up unto everlasting life' in Jn 4 'is the water of life given in salvation, but when He baptizes or immerses in the Holy Spirit there are "rivers of living water", an overflow supply'. In Bayless' view, 'the Overflow gives us the Bible evidence', that is, speaking with tongues.

[30] Harold D. Hunter, 'Tomlinson, Ambrose Jessup,' in Stanley M. Burgess and Eduard M. Van Der Maas (eds.), *The New International Dictionary of Pentecostal and Charismatic Movements* (Grand Rapids: Zondervan, 2002), pp. 1143-45.

[31] W.F. Hesson, 'Seeking the Baptism', *CGE* 5.23 (June 6, 1914), pp. 4-5.

[32] Sam C. Perry, 'Some Spiritual Results', *CGE* 5.35 (August 29, 1914), p. 6.

water', where there exists a 'life-giving flow that invigorates the soul' and 'braces it up' amid life's uncertainties.[33]

The Pentecostal Holiness Advocate

The Pentecostal Holiness Advocate, the official organ of the Pentecostal Holiness Church, featured letters and testimonies for readers as well as Sunday School lessons by G.F. Taylor, the denomination's General Superintendent, and sermons from pastors and evangelists. F.M. Britton offers one such sermon based on Jn 7.37-39. He unequivocally states that 'the rivers of living water is the Baptism of the Holy Ghost'. Through 'the indwelling of the Holy Ghost in Pentecostal fulness', the Spirit continually 'abides' and 'flows out of' the believer. Britton uses water imagery to differentiate the various works of grace. In conversion, one receives 'the cup of salvation'. In sanctification, 'you get water in more abundance'; it is '"a well of living water", but not the river'. The river comes in the baptism of the Holy Spirit.[34]

Several articles emphasize that no one could receive Spirit baptism until after Jesus' glorification. R.B. Beall contends that the Pentecostal baptism represents 'the climax of Christian experience' and proves Jesus' exaltation.[35] For Taylor, the baptism in the Holy Spirit 'establishes a relationship between man and God such as he has never had before … It is the glorified Jesus coming back to dwell in us.'[36] After seeing Jesus' living water promise fulfilled in Acts 2.4, C.F. Noble conflates Jn 7.39 and Acts 2.33: 'Thus spake He of the Holy Ghost which they that believe on Him should afterwards receive for

---

[33] A.J. Tomlinson, 'Get Closer to God', *CGE* 10.35 (August 30, 1919), p. 1.

[34] F.M. Britton, 'The Indwelling Spirit', *PHA* 1.5 (May 31, 1917), pp. 2-3. This sermon was reprinted in *PHA* 3.30 (November 20, 1919), pp. 4-5. Britton also examines possible scriptural precedents for Jesus' promise of living water. He explores Ps. 36.8-9; 46.45; 65.9; Isa. 35.6-7; 43.19; 44.3; 53.1; 58.1; 66.12; and Jer. 31.12. In the end, Britton asserts that these do not represent all the Scriptures that Jesus had in mind. The 'well of water' as a metaphor for salvation is also presented by A.L. Sisler, 'Thirsting for Living Water', *PHA* 3.23-24 (October 2, 9, 1919), pp. 5-6; and S.W. Sublett, 'The Church', *PHA* 4.19 (September 9, 1920), pp. 2-4.

[35] R.B. Beall, 'The Holy Spirit as a Person', *PHA* 1.3 (May 17, 1917), pp. 2-4. W.H. McCurley, 'The Baptism of the Holy Ghost,' *PHA* 1.23 (October 4, 1917), p. 2, makes the same point: 'And we read in John 7:39 that the Holy Ghost was not yet given, for Jesus was not yet glorified. This is a declarative sentence that Jesus must be glorified before the Holy Ghost could be given'.

[36] G.F. Taylor, 'The Baptism of the Holy Ghost', *PHA* 1.38 (January 17, 1918), p. 9. See also G.F. Taylor, 'Sunday School Lesson', *PHA* 4.22 (September 30, 1920), p. 4.

the Holy Ghost was not given for Jesus was not yet glorified, but He is now on the right hand of God and has shed forth this which ye now see and hear'.[37]

Wesleyan-Holiness Testimonies

Testimonies represent a prominent feature of Wesleyan-Holiness Pentecostal periodicals. Readers throughout the United States and the world wrote to tell about their experiences in the fledging movement. Numerous accounts use 'living water' imagery to capture aspects of their stories.

In *The Apostolic Faith,* an unnamed individual writes, '"He that believeth on me, as the scripture hath said, out of his belly shall flow rivers of living water"'. We took that to mean sanctification, but since we have received the Pentecost, we see what the rivers of living water mean. It is the Lord preaching His own sermons and singing His own songs and prophesying.'[38] Maggie Geddis depicts her experience in a similar manner: 'Last Sunday I was given the proof that I had the gift of tongues … and ever since then the tongues are there just bubbling up like a spring of living water'.[39]

While Maggie Geddis focuses on tongues, Mrs F.M. Britton highlights Jesus' promise that the Samaritan woman 'would not thirst anymore'. Britton had experienced salvation and 'entire sanctification', yet she still possessed 'a hunger and thirst'. She began to seek the 'fullness of the Holy Ghost'. During a prayer service, the 'Comforter came in to abide forever'. The Spirit 'testified' and 'sang' through her 'in unknown languages'. 'All thirst was gone', writes Britton, 'every vacancy was filled'.[40]

Like Mrs Britton, Carrie Judd Montgomery expresses thirst for God. In her testimony that begins by quoting Jn 7.37-39, she indicates that she had 'been thirsting for the fullness of the Holy Sprit's

---

[37] C.F. Noble, 'Questions Answered', *PHA* 3.23-24 (October 2 and 9, 1919), p. 4.

[38] *AF* 1.1 (September 1906), p. 4.

[39] Maggie Geddis, 'Found the Pearl of Great Price', *AF* 1.6 (February–March 1907), p. 4. Additionally, Geddis reports, 'The Holy Spirit has also given me the power to write five foreign languages'.

[40] Mrs F.M. Britton, 'Mrs. Britton's Testimony', *TBM* 1.5 (January 1, 1908), p. 3. In *AF* 1.4 (December 1906), p. 1, an interpretation of a message in tongues connects to the thirst theme and stresses that one must ask for the Spirit: 'Open your heart and receive the Spirit. I will give good gifts to My children. Blessed are they that trust Me. O drink of the living waters. Believe in Me. O believe in Me, and ye shall find everything ye ask for.'

presence and power' for some time. In her 'thirsty' state, Montgomery sought God and had an experience 'so sacred that John 7:37-39 seemed to be verified' to her, but she 'stopped short'. But Montgomery grew thirstier 'for the rivers of living water'. She reflects, 'I knew I had tiny streams, but not rivers'. Finally, after a period of tarrying, Montgomery began 'to speak in an unknown tongue'. She recalls, 'The rivers of living water flowed through me and divine ecstasy filled my soul'.[41]

Testimonies that draw on 'living water' to describe Spirit baptism abound in *The Bridegroom's Messenger*. From Orlando, J.H. Sackett declares, 'the blessed abiding Comforter came in and testified in tongues for Himself ... I have now, this moment, that well of living water in me and it runs over'.[42] After narrating his Pentecostal experience in Athens, GA, B.F. Duncan challenges readers: 'Brother, sister, if there is a hungering and thirsting in your soul, ... come to the fountain to drink 'till you are filled and satisfied. Jesus stood and cried saying, "If any man thirst, let him come unto me and drink". John 7.37. I know what it is to hunger and thirst ... I know what it is to be filled with the Holy Ghost.'[43]

---

[41] Carrie Judd Montgomery, 'Ye Shall Be Witnesses unto Me', *TBM* 2.32 (February 15, 1909), p. 3. This was a reprint of Montgomery's account of her Pentecostal experience from *Triumphs of Faith*. In 'A Testimony in Tongues', *AF* 1.8 (May 1907), p. 2, the thirst motif is picked up in an interpretation of a message in tongues that contrasts 'living water' with worldly enticements: 'He found me thirsting for Him, but drinking of that which the world and the churches try to give to the people to satisfy them; but now I am drinking of the living waters and find refreshing for my spirit'.

[42] J.H. Sackett, 'To the Messenger', *TBM* 1.9 (March 1, 1908), p. 3. In the same edition, Mrs B.L. Hill Blake, 'A Letter from Sister Blake', *TBM* 1.9 (March 1, 1908), p. 2, proclaims, 'Oh, how wonderfully sweet to have the blessed abiding Comforter, the Holy Ghost to guide us into all truth, and as a well of water springing up into everlasting life'. In similar terms, Mrs Harry E. Rollins, 'Orlando, Fla.', *TBM* 1.13 (May 1, 1908), p. 3, testifies, 'It was not very long before the Holy Ghost came in and witnessed for Himself and filled my soul with the living water'. G.L. Watson, 'Turkey Creek, Fla.', *TBM* 1.15 (June 1, 1908), p. 3, recounts his experience of the baptism of the Holy Spirit and writes, 'I praise Him for great joy and peace in my soul, for this well of living water springing up into everlasting life'.

[43] B.F. Duncan, 'Athens, Ga.', *TBM* 3.60 (April 15, 1910), p. 3. Similarly, W.F. McDade, 'Pentecostal Revival at Dahlonega, Ga.', *TBM* 4.87 (June 1, 1911), p. 2, relates how 'the audience expressed their desire for the living water of life'; as a result, many were 'baptized with the Holy Ghost, with Bible evidence of speaking in tongues'. Mrs Eben P. Batchelder, 'Ruskins, Ala.', *CGE* 7.20 (May 13, 1916), p. 2, also shares Jn 7.38-39 with readers to encourage them 'to be baptized with the Holy Ghost'.

While there are numerous references to 'living water' in testimonies of one's initial Spirit baptism experience, Emma Simpson uses the metaphor to emphasize that the baptism of the Holy Spirit 'is just a gateway to a deeper life'. In *The Church of God Evangel,* she tells how God has opened up a 'fountain of living water' to sustain the believer's spiritual life. As she drinks from this fountain, Simpson travels throughout the country to 'carry the glad tidings of salvation' in 'word and song'.[44]

While most letters and testimonies came in from the United States, the 'living water' was not limited to a single country; international reports indicate that the water flowed throughout the world. From South Africa, J.O. Lehman writes, 'If we stand true to God …, rivers of living water will flow'.[45] Writing from Hong Kong, Lillian Garr prays that her home would be a welcoming place for missionaries to receive preparation to 'mark out to the weary souls where a … spring of living water' can 'be found'.[46] While ministering in the Bahamas, R.M. Evans testifies that the Spirit continued to propel him: 'If we stop and nurse ourselves the "rivers of living water" will become stagnant pools of bickering self-conceit'.[47]

Finished-Work Voices

The publishers of the early Finished-Work Pentecostal periodicals espoused a 'two-stage' work of grace consisting of justification and baptism in the Holy Spirit. Like their 'three-stage' Wesleyan-Holiness

---

[44] Emma Simpson, 'A Testimony', *CGE* 5.39 (September 26, 1914), p. 8. For Simpson, this 'fountain of living water' flows through 'the true Church of God'. 'No person need ever tell me that the Church of God is wrong', she writes.

[45] J.O. Lehman, 'From Brother J.O. Lehman', *TBM* 3.66 (July 15, 1910), p. 2.

[46] Mrs L. Garr, 'From Sister Garr', *TBM* 4.94 (September 15, 1911), p. 4. Earlier in the year, Lillian Garr, 'From Sister Garr', *TBM* 4.89 (July 1, 1911), p. 2, reported, 'Jesus is magnified! … not only in other tongues as the Spirit gives utterance, but with a full heart so that rivers of living water proceed from within.' Four years earlier, Bro. and Sis. Garr reported numerous people being baptized in the Holy Spirit; in summary, they wrote, 'Rivers of living water are flowing'. See 'The Work in India', *AF* 1.9 (June 1907), p. 1.

[47] R.M. Evans, 'Nassau, N.P, Bahama Islands', *The Evening Light and Church of God Evangel* 1.7 (June 1, 1910), pp. 5-6. See also Mary C. Norton, 'Sister Mary C. Norton's Letter', *TBM* 6.136 (July 1, 1913), p. 1; Max Wood Moorhead, 'Brother Max Wood Moorhead's Letter', *TBM* 5.117 (September 1, 1912), p. 4; and Florence L. Bush and S. Anna Bush, 'Jerusalem, Palestine', *TBM* 7.146 (December 15, 1913), p. 3.

counterparts, Finished-Work publications also reflect extensively on 'living water'. The following survey examines the *Latter Rain Evangel, The Pentecostal Evangel* (also known as *The Christian Evangel* and *The Weekly Evangel*), and *The Bridal Call*.

Latter Rain Evangel

Beginning in 1908, the *Latter Rain Evangel* emanated from the Stone Church in Chicago, IL. In October 1908, Pastor William H. Piper called a convention at the Stone Church to bring unity to the expanding Pentecostal movement. In his convention address, Gilbert E. Farr examines the purpose of tongues. According to Farr, 'when we get so near God that He can control every muscle of our being, our tongue, too, and just let the heavenly message flow through us, it is like rivers of living water flowing from the throne of God, and you feel you are … brought into the very presence of God'.[48]

Harry E. Long sought to explain not just tongues, but the meaning of Pentecost 'according to the Scripture'. For his biblical text, he chose Jn 7.37-39. The theme throughout Long's reflection involves 'living water'. He traces OT precedents for Jesus' promise of rivers of water. After reviewing Isaiah's prophecies that 'pre-figured Pentecost', Long identifies Jesus as the 'Source of the water'.[49] According to Long, 'One of the results of … this mighty river of living water that has come into your inmost being is that we pray in the Holy Ghost'.[50]

For Charles F. Hettiaratchy, 'the rivers' do not refer to tongues, but to the fruit of the Christian life. He proclaims, 'It should not be an effort to bring forth fruit. It is a spontaneous flowing out. "Out of you shall flow rivers of living water".'[51] Hettiaratchy identifies this fruit as love: 'When the love of Christ constrains you, when Christ is in you it will flow out of you and you cannot help it … Then shall

---

[48] Gilbert E. Farr, 'Jesus the Way, the Truth and the Life. Unity with Each Other Only in Him. Utility of Speaking in Tongues', *LRE* 1.2 (November 1908), pp. 18-20.

[49] Long examines Isa. 12.4; 44.3; and 55.1.

[50] Harry E. Long, 'Pentecost According to the Scripture: Rivers of Living Water Flowing from Within', *LRE* 11.10 (July 1919), pp. 2-5.

[51] Charles F. Hettiaratchy, 'Crucifixion of the Self Life: Reckon Yourself Dead', *LRE* 2.7 (April 1910), pp. 7-11 (11).

flow out of us rivers of living water, a spontaneous flowing; it is no effort to love' (see 2 Cor. 5.4).[52]

Similarly, Elizabeth Sisson uses Johannine imagery to emphasize that Christians should be 'riverbeds' for God's love. She declares,

> Jesus has said out of the believer 'shall flow rivers of living water'. He did not say a river, one mighty Mississippi or Amazon. He did not say two rivers, or two hundred ... Perhaps Jesus could not in truth limit it to 'out of him shall flow one thousand Amazons'. So he has left it *un*limited. Eternally LOVE's channel – 'that the love wherewith Thou hast loved Me, may be in them, and I in them'.[53]

According to Sisson, one becomes a 'riverbed' through fervent prayer: 'If a few of us get deeply gripped by the grace of God with soul-travail for this present bleeding suffering world, we shall be river-bed for the waters of His salvation to flow through upon them'.[54] Sisson builds on this concept in a message on Ezekiel's vision of the river from the temple (47.1-12). After establishing that the river brings life, she notes that 'the marshes thereof shall not be healed' (47.11). 'What is the matter with the marshy places'? she asks. Then, she answers, 'They let the water in, but they do not let the water *through*'. She explains,

> Jesus said it should be in us a 'well of water springing up into everlasting life', but He said it should be in us as rivers if we continued to believe on Him. You see we are a riverbed in the salvation arrangement, something to receive God and let Him pass through.[55]

Maria B. Woodworth-Etter also emphasizes the idea that Christians are channels. She writes, 'If those who come to the Lord will be filled as ... on the day of Pentecost we will have streams of living water rushing through us and flowing to the very ends of the earth'. Here she joins Jn 7.38 to Acts 1.8. She goes on to connect the John

---

[52] Charles F. Hettiaratchy, 'But the Greatest of These Is Love', *LRE* 2.8 (May 1910), pp. 9-12 (11).
[53] Elizabeth Sisson, 'Life of the First Resurrectionists', *LRE* 3.7 (April 1911), pp. 16-18 (18; emphasis original).
[54] Elizabeth Sisson, 'Call to Prayer: Zech. 10:1', *LRE* 7.7 (April 1915), pp. 5-7 (6).
[55] Elizabeth Sisson, 'Blessings from Under the Threshold: The Vision of the Holy Waters', *LRE* 4.9 (June 1912), pp. 12–14.

passage to Acts 2.1-4: 'Now when Pentecost came … suddenly the Spirit as a cyclone came and filled the whole building, a great tidal wave of power was turned upon them and they were all filled with living water'. In her retelling of the Pentecost story, Woodworth-Etter replaces the words 'Holy Spirit' in Acts 2.4 with 'living water'.[56]

C.H. Schoonmaker relates an experience that happened as he interceded for unreached people. 'A flood-tide of divine fullness' came upon him, and he received 'a fresh witness' in his heart 'that the reason Jesus said, "Out of them shall flow rivers of living water," was because He knew … there are multitudes of souls that are utterly dry and have no spiritual moisture whatever. They are parched and must be watered by the overflow in us.'[57]

A.W. Frodsham takes yet another angle on the 'living water'. He stresses that when Jesus spoke in Jn 7.37-39, he 'was not yet glorified'. But Pentecost demonstrated that Jesus 'had reached the very throne of God, and received gifts for men, even the rebellious. He led captivity captive' (see Eph. 4.8). In the same way, according to Frodsham, contemporary tongues speech confirms Jesus' glorification. He exclaims, 'Oh it is wonderful to think I have the witness within of the glorification of Christ'.[58]

Christian Evangel

The *Christian Evangel,* which was later renamed *The Weekly Evangel* and then *The Pentecostal Evangel,* became the official publication of the Assemblies of God when it formed in 1914. Most allusions to 'living water' in its pages refer to Spirit baptism. In an article explaining the experience, E.N. Bell connects Jn 7.38-39 to Mk 16.17 to emphasize that the Pentecostal baptism comes to those who believe. Just as

---

[56] Maria B. Woodworth-Etter, 'Blasphemy against the Holy Ghost: God's Cyclone of Power a Great Leveler', *LRE* 5.11 (August 1913), pp. 19-22.

[57] C.H. Schoonmaker, 'God's Estimate of a Heathen Soul. What Is Yours?', *LRE* 10.2 (November 1917), pp. 13-17 (13-14). See also Adolf Nordell, 'The Holy Spirit in Missions', *LRE* 11.1 (October 1918), pp. 20-23.

[58] A.W. Frodsham, 'Speaking Sacred Secrets in the Holy Place: Spiritual Stones Become Priceless Diamonds thru the Illumination of the Word', *LRE* 7.7 (April 1915), pp. 2-4 (4). Elizabeth Sisson, 'Finish the Job Now: "Invest in Victory Liberty Bonds"', *BC* 3.2 (July 1919), p. 10, makes a similar point. After using the image of liberty bonds to illustrate Acts 2.4, she writes, 'That never-to-be-forgotten day of Pentecost was the hour these bonds were first issued. They could not be issued before, because Jesus "was not yet glorified," (John 7:39) but that happy hour, Jesus "being by the right hand of God exalted … shed forth this" which they now saw and heard. (Acts 2:33.).'

Mark's miraculous signs 'follow them that believe', so Jesus promises 'rivers of living water' to 'he that believeth on me'. According to Bell, the disciples had the Spirit '*with* them', but 'not *in* them' prior to Pentecost, but on that day recorded in Acts 2, Jesus fulfills his word to 'pour forth rivers of living water'.[59]

J.W. Welch communicates the view that salvation precedes Spirit baptism by differentiating between 'the well and the river'. He contends that one must first drink of the 'well of water' Jesus gives for 'personal salvation'. Then, the believer can 'get RIVERS FOR OTHERS and for yourself as well'. First comes salvation, and then Spirit baptism, 'the overflow of salvation'. Welch is clear: 'You must have the well experience before you have the river'.[60]

In addition to using Jn 7.37-39 to teach belief as a prerequisite for Spirit baptism, the *Evangel* applies the text to illustrate the necessity of thirst on the experience. In one of Bell's regular question and answer columns, a reader asks, 'How can one receive the baptism with the Spirit?' Bell replies, 'by thirsting and believing', and he cites Jn 7.37-39 and Mk 16.16-17.[61]

J. Roswell Flower moves the conversation from requirements for obtaining Spirit baptism to the results of receiving the experience. For him, 'The Spirit-filled life is like a great river'. After all, 'Scripture hath said, out of his inward parts shall FLOW rivers of living water'.

---

[59] E.N. Bell, 'Baptism with the Spirit with Speaking in Tongues', *WE* 84 (April 3, 1915), pp. 3-4 (emphasis original). In his exposition of the baptism of the Holy Ghost, Andrew D. Urshan, 'The Baptism of the Holy Ghost', *WE* 205 (September 1, 1917), p. 5, also employs Jn 7.37-39 to argue that the Spirit comes following belief. He writes, 'We must be true believers in order to receive the gift of the Holy Spirit; for our Lord said: "they that believe on Him should receive the Holy Spirit."'

[60] J.W. Welch, 'The "Much More" of Latter Rain to Come', *WE* 229 (March 2, 1918), p. 5. J. Narver Gortner, 'A Few More Good Tidings from the Council', *PE* 312 (November 1, 1919), p. 3, makes the same point with a story about boring a well in the Dakotas.

[61] E.N. Bell, 'Some Important Questions Answered', *CE* 282 (April 5, 1919), p. 3. Bell's reply also includes repentance, water baptism, obedience, prayer, and tarrying as necessary steps to receive Spirit baptism. In contrast to criteria for Spirit baptism, 'Burnt to Ashes: What Led Up to the Welsh Revival', *CE* 53 (August 8, 1914), p. 3, focuses on conditions for revival. Humility is essential. The article uses the symbol of dust to make the point: 'God must have dust to convey the living water. We are too mighty, dear people. God cannot use so many Christians. They are not small enough to carry the water to the thirsty land.'

Quoting Eph. 5.20, Flower maintains that 'a continual life of thanks-giving' is part and parcel of the Spirit-filled life.[62]

In his 1917 New Year's message, Welch also focuses on the results of Spirit baptism in a meditation on Jn 7.38. Identifying Ezek. 47.1-12 as the possible Scripture Jesus had in mind when he promised rivers of living water, Welch suggests that the 'living water' points to various consequences of Spirit baptism including 'a consistent walk', a Holy Spirit-controlled 'prayer life', 'strength of character', and 'utter abandonment to the Spirit of God'. Then, Welch asserts that power for service and witness also follows Spirit baptism:

> The baptism of the Holy Spirit is not given for ourselves, in order that we may have a good time; it does not speak of rivers flowing *into* him that believeth, but *from* him, out of his innermost being. This shows that he must first have drunk deeply of that Living Water to satisfy his own thirst; and then from that filled and satisfied soul proceeds the blessed overflow– the rivers going in every direction upon the dry and parched ground.[63]

Like Welch's reference to Ezekiel, many writers seek to elucidate the OT antecedents of living water. In a feature called the 'Pentecostal Bible Course', Arch P. Collins declares that 'the Lord Jesus Christ is the center of all revealed truth'. He then unpacks how the Book of Exodus points to Jesus. When he comes to Exodus 17, Collins identifies the rock in the wilderness as 'a type of Christ'.[64] Moses struck this rock, and out came water to satisfy the Israelites' thirst. Alice E. Luce asserts that 'the stream of living water' flowed from the rock. Drawing on 1 Cor. 10.4 and the hymn 'Rock of Ages', Luce contends that Jesus 'came as the Saviour, to die for our sins, as the

---

[62] J. Roswell Flower, 'Be Filled with the Spirit', *WE* 197 (July 7, 1917), p. 8 (emphasis original).

[63] J.W. Welch, 'The Ever-Deepening River: A New Year's Message', *WE* 171 (January 6, 1917), pp. 4-5, 9 (emphasis original). Andrew D. Urshan, 'The Gracious Dealings of God Misunderstood', *WE* 181 (March 17, 1917), p. 6, makes a similar observation. Through the Spirit, Christ works 'through you bursting with the rivers of living water upon needy souls around you'.

[64] Arch P. Collins, 'Pentecostal Bible Course', *WE* 170 (December 23, 1916), p. 13. See also Andrew Urshan, 'Thirsting after God', *WE* 161 (October 21, 1916), p. 6; and Welch, 'Much More', p. 5. Cf. J.T. Boddy, 'Rivers of Living Water', *PE* 334 (April 3, 1920), p. 4, who compares Jesus not to the Rock, but to Moses.

Smitten Rock, from whose cleft flowed the life-giving River of the Spirit's fulness'.[65]

Luce penned a regular *Evangel* column called 'Pictures of Pentecost in the Old Testament'. In one column, she associates 'streams in the desert' with living water (Isa. 35.6). She summarizes God's promise in Isaiah 35 with these words: 'What was once sterile and arid ... may become a very garden of the Lord, when watered by the Rivers of Living Water'. Focusing eschatologically, Luce argues for both a literal and a spiritual fulfillment of Isaiah's promise. The literal fulfillment will come 'when the Lord Jesus sets up His throne on this earth', but the spiritual realization comes 'in every individual believer who crowns' Jesus as King and 'submits entirely to His sway'.[66]

In Joel 2, Luce sees another picture of Pentecost. Unsurprisingly, she understands God's promise to pour out the Spirit as a reference to Spirit baptism (Joel 2.28-29). According to Luce, the Spirit-filled 'soul becomes the overflowing soul and from the innermost depths of a being that has been baptized (i.e. immersed) in the Holy Spirit, flow forth the Rivers of Living Water'. Luce discusses the results of Spirit baptism, which include not only speaking in tongues, but also 'preaching fearlessly the full Gospel', living together in 'unity', 'bearing one another's burdens', 'signs and wonders', and 'persecution'.[67]

The Bridal Call

The famed evangelist Aimee Semple McPherson began publishing *The Bridal Call* in 1917 to spread her Pentecostal teaching and to share testimonies and healing stories. In a teaching entitled 'The Work of

---

[65] Alice E. Luce, 'Rock of Ages', *PE* 372 (December 25, 1920), pp. 5-6. A.L. Fraser, '"Here a Little and There a Little": A Sunday Morning Meditation', *LRE* 7.11 (August 1915), pp. 8-11 (10), also uses this imagery. After establishing that the 'Rock is Christ', he writes, 'Hiding in that blessed Rock, we don't have to go out, even for a drink of water, for the Rock has been smitten and the living water flows forth from its very heart'.

[66] Alice E. Luce, 'Pictures of Pentecost in the Old Testament: Deserts Changed to Gardens. Isaiah 35', *WE* 201 (August 4, 1917), p. 4. C. Rowe, 'Good Word from Tampa, Fla.', *WW* 12.8 (August 1915), p. 3, also sees the 'living water' in healing: 'the rivers of water are flowing so freely that souls who are sin-sick are being healed by his stripes'. E.N. Bell published *WW* from about 1911 through 1915; after the establishment of the Assemblies of God, the publication merged into *WE* at the beginning of 1916.

[67] Alice E. Luce, 'Pictures of Pentecost in the Old Testament: Devastation and Deliverance. Joel 2', *WE* 212 (October 27, 1917), p. 6. Luce also uncovers images of Pentecost in the historical books; see Alice E. Luce, 'Prayer for the Watersprings', *CE* 246 (June 29, 1918), pp. 4-5.

the Holy Spirit', McPherson turns to living water terminology to describe glossolalia. She explains, 'When the Holy Ghost comes in to abide He takes control of body, soul, and spirit; that out of our innermost being there flows forth rivers of living water'. McPherson emphasizes that the Spirit takes over the tongue, 'the unruly member'. She describes how the Holy Spirit causes the believer's tongue to spill out in 'wells and rivers of praise that … gush forth in uncontrollable ecstatic glory and thanksgiving'.[68]

Apart from tongues, McPherson draws on living water language to explain the gift of prophecy. In an exposition of 1 Corinthians 14, McPherson defines prophecy as 'a direct inspired message given by the Spirit'. She suggests that such 'inspired' speech comes not through learned knowledge, but through connection with the Spirit: 'Insomuch that out of our innermost beings (not out of our heads), shall flow rivers of living water'. Prophecy represents 'an involuntary flowing forth in streams of beautiful language and teachings of which the Spirit Himself is the author'.[69]

In other contexts, McPherson employs living water to discuss the consequences of Spirit baptism. For example, she focuses on the Apostle Peter to demonstrate that Spirit baptism brings courage. Speaking from Peter's perspective on Pentecost, she writes that the Holy Spirit 'has taken fear away and put a holy boldness within my heart and words within my mouth, insomuch that out of my innermost being flow forth rivers of living water'.[70]

---

[68] Aimee Semple McPherson, 'The Work of the Holy Spirit: Dispensationally and Personally and from Conviction to Baptism', *BC* 1.3 (August 1917), pp. 1-2.

[69] Aimee Semple McPherson, 'That Fourteenth Chapter of First Corinthians', *BC* 3.11 (April 1920), pp. 4-9 (7).

[70] Aimee Semple McPherson, 'Baptism of the Holy Spirit', *BC* 2.12 (May 1919), pp. 4-7 (5). Interestingly, McPherson lists the reference for these words from Peter as Acts 4.13. The article was reprinted in *The Pentecostal Herald* 5.4 (September 1919), pp. 1-2. *The Pentecostal Herald* was published by George Brinkman. In December 1919, Brinkman donated the paper to the newly formed Pentecostal Assemblies of the USA, which eventually became the Pentecostal Church of God. Aimee Semple McPherson, 'Baptism of the Holy Spirit', *BC* 3.12 (May 1920), pp. 3-5 (5), stresses that Spirit baptism begins 'a new life of union, fellowship, praise, worship, prayer, love and service'. She describes this new existence as 'a life where out of your innermost being there flows forth rivers of living water' that empower believers to become witnesses 'to the uttermost parts of the earth'.

Finished Work Testimonies

Like their Wesleyan-Holiness Pentecostal counterparts, Finished-Work Pentecostals submitted letters and testimonies to periodicals to share news of God's work in their lives. Such testimonies include reports of evangelistic services, missionary endeavors, personal salvation experiences, receptions of Spirit baptism, and visions. Readers frequently reference 'living water' to frame their testimonies.

In some cases, the 'living water' becomes what petitioners seek in their quest for Spirit baptism. Mrs W.W. Davis recalls how she heard a preacher speak on Jn 7.38, so she 'began seeking the Lord' for the 'river of living water'. She 'waited on the Lord' for two years before she received the 'latter rain baptism'.[71] Like Davis, Mary M. Bodie had reached a point of spiritual drought. She prayed daily 'for the rivers of living water which Jesus promised them who believe in Him'. Shortly thereafter, she went to a Pentecostal meeting and, after tarrying, received the baptism in the Holy Spirit. In Bodie's words, the Holy Spirit 'brought the longed-for rivers of living water'.[72]

Bodie's description of her experience in terms of 'living water' mirrors Gerard A. Bailly's portrayal. Bailly recalls how he heard about 'the tongue movement' when some friends 'found the secret' of 'the hidden springs as in John 7:38, 39'. Bailly's thirst intensified, and when he received the baptism of the Holy Spirit, God made him 'wholly pliable'. 'For about two hours', writes Bailly, the Spirit 'led me through physical motions, loud crying, joyous laughter, holy song and heavenly vision, breaking up the depths, letting the pent-up springs burst forth in rivers through my soul'.[73]

Other contributors clarify through the living water symbolism that believers must function as conduits of God's grace. Alma E. Doering, for example, chronicles a conference in Mulheim, Germany. She relates that Revd and Mrs Polman traveled from Holland to share

---

[71] Mrs W.W. Davis, 'The Holy Spirit upon a Life Twenty-Five Years Ago: Putting Out the Fleece', *LRE* 8.6 (March 1916), p. 21. Pastor Thomas B. Barrett, the Norwegian Pentecostal leader, similarly indicates that he sought 'the blessing' of Jn 7.37-39 when he began seeking 'the full Pentecost'; see B.F. Lawrence, 'Apostolic Faith Restored: Pastor Barrett and the Work in Europe', *WE* 135 (April 15, 1916), pp. 4-5 (4).

[72] Mary M. Bodie, 'My Testimony to the Full Gospel', *TP* 1.12 (November 1, 1909), pp. 2-3.

[73] Gerard A. Bailly, 'Diversities of Operations But the Same Spirit: Tidings from the Great Neglected Continent', *LRE* 1.10 (July 1909), pp. 22-24. See also Elmer B. Hammond, 'Waang Kong, China', *WW* 8.10 (December 20, 1912), p. 7.

about the baptism of the Holy Spirit based on Jn 7.38. 'We need but drink and praise and the rivers will flow', writes Doering. But she cautions, 'The Church has not been called to be a reservoir but rather a channel; not a circle but a center; not a warehouse but a distribution center'.[74]

Observations and Implications

This survey of selected early-twentieth-century Pentecostal literature demonstrates that both Wesleyan-Holiness and Finished-Work streams conceived of 'living water' overwhelmingly, but not exclusively, in terms of the Holy Spirit. In particular, 'the rivers of living water' provided a vocabulary for Pentecostals to describe their otherwise ineffable experience of the baptism in the Holy Spirit. This language helped them to express Spirit baptism as something that came from outside themselves and took control of their very being.

In this regard, many early Pentecostals connect the 'rivers of living water' to speaking in tongues. They experience tongues as a 'bubbling over'; it is something within themselves they cannot suppress. In numerous testimonies, Pentecostals use the 'rivers' metaphor to emphasize that it was not their words that came forth. Instead, the Holy Spirit 'spoke through' them or 'sung through' them. In Spirit baptism, Pentecostals surrender the agency of their tongues and allow the Spirit to direct their speech. That Jesus describes the rivers arising from the 'innermost being' helped Pentecostals depict the visceral, even mystical, nature of their experience.[75]

But speaking in tongues did not represent the 'be all and end all' of Spirit baptism. Pentecostals employ 'living water' to describe the multidimensional nature of this phenomena. An intensified prayer life; praise and worship; power to testify, heal, and drive out demons; Christlike longings and affections; upright character; strength to endure persecution; knowledge of God's love; joy; thanksgiving; peace;

---

[74] Alma F. Doering, 'Gleanings from Mulheim, Germany', *LRE* 5.3 (December 1912), pp. 9-11.

[75] G.F. Taylor, *The Spirit and the Bride: A Scriptural Presentation of the Operations, Manifestation, Gifts and Fruit of the Holy Spirit in his Relation to the Bride with Special Reference to the Latter Rain Revival* (Dunn, NC, 1907), p. 25, writes, 'The Baptism of the Spirit brings an invisible manifestation of living water (John 7:37–39), and a visible or external manifestation of tongues (Acts 2:3, 4)'.

Christian unity; and signs and wonders all come with the 'rivers of living water'.

Pentecostal experience was not only about what happened within the believer; it impacted what happened through the believer. In this sense, the 'rivers of living water' metaphor hits on one of Pentecostalism's fundamental tensions, that is, the tension between the Sprit's inward work in the believer and the Spirit's outward propulsion of the believer in witness and mission. 'Living water' gives Pentecostals an apt image for this tension because it allows Jesus to function as the water source and the believer to serve as a conduit of the water. That is to say, Jesus gives the 'living water' to the believer and transforms the believer in such a way that the 'living water' now overflows from the believer's life to impact others.

While the 'living water' language captures the tension of the Spirit's work in and through the believer, it also embodies the paradoxical nature of thirst in early Pentecostalism. On the one hand, as epitomized in Jesus' summons directed to 'anyone who is thirsty' (Jn 7.37), thirst exists as a precondition for receiving the baptism in the Holy Spirit. Frequent references to tarrying and ardent prayer in testimonies demonstrate the posture of one who longs for the 'living water'. These same testimonies suggest that, in Spirit baptism, Jesus satisfies the seeker's thirst. On the other hand, Pentecostals live in a perpetual state of thirst. Inhabiting a condition of holy discontent, they long for deeper experiences of the Spirit. Spirit baptism signifies a gateway, but after the initial experience, believers have more depths to plumb. For this reason, the early Pentecostals often emphasized that Jesus promised not just '*a* river', but 'river*s*' of 'living water'; the supply proves unlimited and inexhaustible.

Unsurprisingly, a key difference between the Wesleyan-Holiness and the Finished-Work streams concerns their use of 'living water' in relation to sanctification. 'Living water' encapsulates the divine work of grace in both streams, and representatives from both streams differentiate between the 'wells' and 'rivers'. For several Wesleyan-Holiness teachers and their three-stage process, the 'wells' of John 4 become a metaphor for what the believer experiences in sanctification, but the 'rivers' of John 7 represent what comes in Spirit baptism. Only the sanctified soul can receive the 'rivers'. When they distinguish the 'wells' from the 'rivers', Finished-Work Pentecostals tend to distinguish between conversion and Spirit baptism. For the

Finished-Work proponents, belief functions as the basic condition to receive the baptism in the Holy Spirit.

Apart from this one evident difference between the streams, Wesleyan-Holiness and Finished-Work Pentecostals interpret 'living water' along similar lines, and this interpretation extends to their understanding of the realization of Jesus' words in Jn 7.37-38. Besides one notable exception that sees the fulfillment of Jesus' living water promise in Jn 19.34 when a soldier pierced Jesus' side, most Pentecostals contend that Jesus poured out the 'rivers of living water' on the day of Pentecost (Acts 2). Remarkably, apart from the Jn 19.34 reference, none of the literature surveyed looked for the fulfillment of Jesus' promise in the Fourth Gospel itself.[76] I expected to uncover at least some references to Jesus' breathing of the Spirit on Easter evening (Jn 20.22). This lacuna calls for an early Pentecostal reception history of this so-called 'Johannine Pentecost'.

Despite the lack of reference to Jn 20.22, early Pentecostal interpretation of 'living water' demonstrates what Kenneth J. Archer has labeled the 'Bible Reading Method'.[77] Using this hermeneutic, Pentecostals interpret Scripture in light of Scripture and harmonize the biblical story. Within the NT, Pentecostals especially tie 'living water' to Acts 2.[78] Woodworth-Etter exemplifies this approach to Scripture by replacing 'Holy Spirit' with 'living water' in Acts 2.4 so that 'they were all filled with living water'.[79] Similarly, several writers conflate Jn 7.39 with Acts 2.33, so that it becomes clear that Jesus pours out the Spirit after his glorification at the Father's right hand. While it could be argued that John's 'living water' texts in John 4 and 7 deserve a place alongside Acts 2 for early Pentecostal interpretation of Spirit baptism, at the very least this study should lead to a re-examination of the contention that the early Pentecostals based their theology of

---

[76] For the Jn 19.34 reference, see *AF* 1.10 (September 1907), p. 2, and *AF* section above.

[77] Kenneth J. Archer, *A Pentecostal Hermeneutic: Spirit, Scripture and Community* (Cleveland, TN: CPT, 2009). It is also clear that the early Pentecostals read the Scriptures through the prism of their Spirit baptism experience. There is a dialectic between their experience and Scripture; one informs the other.

[78] Notably, 'living water' is also tied to Mk 16.17-18, which has been called 'the "litmus test"' for early Pentecostal's evaluation of fulfillment of 'the apostolic mandates given by Jesus'; see Thomas and Alexander, '"And the Signs Are Following"', pp. 147-70.

[79] Woodworth-Etter, 'Blasphemy', p. 20.

Spirit baptism 'almost exclusively on the Gospel of Luke and the Acts of the Apostles'.[80]

The early Pentecostals also turned to the OT to gain understanding of the Spirit's work. Spurred by Jesus' statement that 'the scripture' had spoken of 'rivers of living water' (Jn 7.38), they combed the Hebrew Scriptures to uncover the source of this promise, and as they did, the Pentecostal readers saw 'living water' oozing from the pages of their Bible. Their treatment of 'living water' reveals that the early Pentecostals read the OT Christologically. The words of Collins bear repeating: 'the Lord Jesus Christ is the center of all revealed truth'.[81] As early Pentecostals examined the OT, they expected to find Jesus in all the Scriptures, and they considered these passages in light of Christ.[82] Reading the Bible backwards, they understood OT characters, events, and objects to foreshadow Jesus.

If Jesus' statement that 'the scripture' spoke of 'living water' pushed Pentecostals to search the OT, John's remark that 'the Spirit had not been given because Jesus had not yet been glorified' drove them to consider Christ's ascension (7.39). Many early Pentecostal interpreters see John's comment as a reference to Jesus' exaltation at God's right hand and connect it to Peter's Pentecost sermon (Acts 2.33). Several teachers take this a step further to argue that individual believers must enthrone or glorify Jesus in their own lives in order to receive the gift of the Spirit. Either way, the baptism of the Holy Spirit provides the evidence that Jesus has ascended to his heavenly throne. Moreover, through Spirit baptism – others contend – the ascended Christ comes to dwell in believers. Finally, for a few, Jn 7.39 provides an argument for subsequence. Although they believed before Pentecost, the disciples do not receive the Spirit until Pentecost, and their example becomes the model for Pentecostal experience. All of this points to the need for a full-orbed Pentecostal theology of

---

[80] Walter J. Hollenweger, *The Pentecostals* (Peabody, MA: Hendrickson, 1972), p. 336. See, for example, Montgomery, 'Ye Shall Be Witnesses', p. 3; in her testimony of receiving Spirit baptism, it is not Acts 2.4 that is 'verified' to her, but Jn 7.37-39. Similarly, when Long, 'Pentecost', p. 2, seeks to explain 'Pentecost according to the Scripture', he turns to John 7, not Acts 2.

[81] Collins, 'Pentecostal Bible Course', p. 13.

[82] In some cases, this means that they read the OT typologically; for example, see the reading of the Gen. 24 well scene in Seymour, 'Rebecca', p. 2, and the reading of the Exodus 17 rock in Luce, 'Rock of Ages', pp. 5-6.

the ascension. Such an inquiry appears poised to bring further depth to contemporary Pentecostal understandings of Spirit baptism.

In addition to implications for ascension theology, 'living water' impacts eschatology. For the early Pentecostals, 'living water' infers both a realized and a future eschatology. In one sense, several early interpreters suggest that, through the baptism in the Holy Spirit, believers drink from the water that flows from God's throne. Even now, Spirit-baptized Christians partake of the 'river of the water of life' (Rev. 22.1). At the same time, the present Pentecostal experience represents only a foretaste of the waters that will surge when the Bridegroom returns and establishes his kingdom on earth.[83] An analysis of Pentecostal readings of Revelation 22, the waters of New Jerusalem, and the invitation of the Spirit and the bride to 'take the water of life as a gift' (22.17) would represent a helpful companion and comparison for the present study.[84]

From an eschatological perspective, the early Pentecostals also link 'living water' to the latter rain outpouring. As D. William Faupel maintains, the latter rain motif provided a conceptual framework for Pentecostals to explain their reception of the Spirit.[85] Centered on God's promises to provide Israel with the early and the latter rain needed for harvest, the latter rain motif understood Pentecost to have brought the early rains, and now, in the early twentieth century, God poured out the latter rain to signal an end-times harvest in anticipation of Jesus' soon return. Thus, for some interpreters in both the Wesleyan-Holiness and Finished-Work streams, the latter rain brings the living water. In the newspapers, a Pentecostal reflection on 'living water' often grows out of consideration of OT texts employed to develop the Latter Rain motif; such texts include Hos. 6.3, Joel 2.23, and Zech. 10.1. The Pentecostal outpouring meant that God gave 'rivers of living water' in the baptism of the Holy Spirit to indicate that the season of the latter rain had arrived.

---

[83] See Luce, 'Deserts Changed', p. 4.

[84] For a consideration of early American Pentecostal eschatology and a constructive 'way forward', see McQueen, *Pentecostal Eschatology*. In connection with Revelation 22, bridal imagery appears in several of the articles surveyed above; on this trope, see Dale M. Coulter, 'The Spirit and the Bride Revisited: Pentecostalism, Renewal, and the Sense of History', *JPT* 21 (2012), pp. 298-319.

[85] D. William Faupel, *The Everlasting Gospel: The Significance of Eschatology in the Development of Pentecostal Thought* (JPTSup, 10; Sheffield: Sheffield Academic Press, 1996), pp. 32-36.

Conclusion

This study of the Johannine 'living water' passages and their 'history of effects' in Wesleyan-Holiness and Finished-Work periodicals has revealed that this metaphor captured the imagination of early Pentecostals. They used John's symbol to describe their experience with the Spirit and to grasp the implications thereof. The early Pentecostal utilization of the 'living water' motif suggests that they drew not only on Acts, but also on the Fourth Gospel to develop their pneumatological outlook. Exploring treatments of 'living water' during this formative phase of the movement provides insight into Pentecostal biblical interpretation whereby adherents elucidate Scripture in light of Scripture and read the OT through a Christological lens. The image also gives Pentecostals language to exploit key tensions in their spirituality such as the Spirit's work both *in* and *through* the believer, the simultaneous fulfillment and intensification of spiritual thirst, and realized and future eschatology. These insights challenge contemporary Pentecostals to continue to contemplate 'living water' in the Johannine texts and its implications for Pentecostal spirituality and theology.

Bibliography

Alexander, Kimberly E., *Pentecostal Healing: Models in Theology and Practice* (JPTSup 29; Blandford Forum: Deo Publishing, 2006).

Allison Jr, Dale C., 'The Living Water (John 4:10-14, 6:35c, 7:37-39)', *St. Vladimir's Theological Quarterly* 30 (1986), pp. 143-57.

Archer, Kenneth J., *A Pentecostal Hermeneutic: Spirit, Scripture, and Community* (Cleveland, TN: CPT Press, 2009).

Archer, Melissa L., *'I Was in the Spirit on the Lord's Day': A Pentecostal Engagement with Worship in the Apocalypse* (Cleveland, TN: CPT Press, 2015).

Brown, Raymond E., *The Gospel according to John XIII-XXI: A New Translation with Introduction and Commentary* (AB; Garden City, NY: Doubleday, 1970).

Burge, Gary M., *The Anointed Community: The Holy Spirit in the Johannine Tradition* (Grand Rapids: Eerdmans, 1987).

Cortés, Juan B., 'Yet Another Look at Jn 7:37-38', *Catholic Biblical Quarterly* 29 (1967), pp. 75-86.

Coulter, Dale M., 'The Spirit and the Bride Revisited: Pentecostalism, Renewal, and the Sense of History', *JPT* 21 (2012), pp. 298-319.

Culpepper, R. Alan, *The Anatomy of the Fourth Gospel* (Minneapolis: Fortress Press, 1983).

Daise, Michael A., '"If Anyone Thirsts, Let That One Come to Me and Drink": The Literary Texture of John 7:37b-38a', *JBL* 122 (2003), pp. 687-99.

Fee, Gordon D., 'Once More – John 7:37-39', *Expository Times* 89 (1977/78), pp. 116-18.

Faupel, D. William, *The Everlasting Gospel: The Significance of Eschatology in the Development of Pentecostal Thought* (JPTSup 10; Sheffield: Sheffield Academic Press, 1996).

Green, Chris E.W., *Toward a Pentecostal Theology of the Lord's Supper: Foretasting the Kingdom* (Cleveland, TN: CPT Press, 2012).

Hollenweger, Walter J., *The Pentecostals: Charismatic Movement in the Churches* (Peabody, MA: Hendrickson, 1972).

—'Pentecostals and the Charismatic Movement', in Cheslyn Jones, Geoffrey Wainwright, and Edward Yarnold (eds.), *The Study of Spirituality* (Oxford: Oxford University Press, 1986), pp. 549-53.

Hunter, Harold D., 'Tomlinson, Ambrose Jessup', in Stanley M. Burgess and Eduard M. Van Der Maas (eds.), *The New International Dictionary of Pentecostal and Charismatic Movements* (Grand Rapids: Zondervan, 2002), pp. 1143-45.

Keller, Rosemary Skinner and Rosemary Radford Ruether (eds.), *In Our Own Voices: Four Centuries of American Women's Religious Writing* (Louisville, KY: Westminster / John Knox Press, 1995).

Land, Steven J., *Pentecostal Spirituality: A Passion for the Kingdom* (JPTSup 1; Sheffield: Sheffield Academic Press, 1993).

Marcus, Joel, 'Rivers of Living Water from Jesus' Belly (John 7:38)', *JBL* 117 (1998), pp. 328-30.

Menken, Martinus J.J., 'The Origin of the Old Testament Quotation in John 7:38', *Novum Testamentum* 38 (1996), pp. 160-75.

McWhirter, Jocelyn, *The Bridegroom Messiah and the People of God: Marriage in the Fourth Gospel* (Society for New Testament Studies Monograph Series 138; Cambridge: Cambridge University Press, 2004).

McQueen, Larry R., *Toward a Pentecostal Eschatology: Discerning the Way Forward* (JPTSup 39; Blandford Forum: Deo Publishing, 2012).

Riss, Richard M., 'The Finished Work Controversy', in Stanley M. Burgess and Eduard M. Van Der Maas (eds.), *The New International Dictionary of Pentecostal and Charismatic Movements* (Grand Rapids: Zondervan, rev. and exp. edn, 2002), pp. 638-39.

Swartley, Willard M., *John* (Believers Church Bible Commentary; Harrisonburg, VA: Herald Press, 2013).

Synan, H. Vinson, 'Cashwell, Gaston Barnabas', in Stanley M. Burgess and Gary B. McGee (eds.), *Dictionary of Pentecostal and Charismatic Movements* (Grand Rapids: Zondervan, 1988), pp. 109-10.

Taylor, G.F., *The Spirit and the Bride: A Scriptural Presentation of the Operations, Manifestation, Gifts and Fruit of the Holy Spirit in his Relation to the Bride with Special Reference to the 'Latter Rain Revival'* (Dunn, NC, 1907).

Thomas, John Christopher and Kimberly Ervin Alexander, 'And the Signs Are Following': Mark 16.9-20 – A Journey into Pentecostal Hermeneutics', *JPT* 11 (2003), pp. 147-70.

Thomas, John Christopher, *The Spirit of the New Testament* (Blandford Forum: Deo Publishing, 2005).

—'What the Spirit Is Saying to the Church" – The Testimony of a Pentecostal Working in New Testament Studies', in Kevin Spawn and Archie T. Wright (eds.), *Spirit & Scripture: Examining a Pneumatic Hermeneutic* (London: Bloomsbury T&T Clark, 2012), pp. 115-29.

Worrell, A.S., *Full Gospel Teachings* (Louisville, KY: Charles T. Dearing, 1900).

11

RECEIVING WATER BAPTISM 'IN JESUS' NAME': ACTS 2.38 AND JOHN 3.5 IN EARLY ONENESS PENTECOSTALISM

ANDREW RAY WILLIAMS[*]

Introduction

David Reed's landmark monograph on the doctrinal development of the Oneness movement, *'In Jesus' Name'*, traces the movement through the early years to a period of organizational permanency in mid-century.[1] Oneness Pentecostalism received its spark in April 1913 at an international Pentecostal camp meeting at Arroyo Seco outside Los Angeles, where Canadian evangelist R.E. McAlister preached a baptismal sermon.[2] In his sermon, McAlister made the observation 'that the apostles baptized in the name of the Lord Jesus Christ' according to Acts 2.38, not in the triune formula of Matthew 28.19. As Reed notes, these events 'precipitated a second schism' within Pentecostalism and 'launched the third stream of the modern

---

[*] Andrew Ray Williams (PhD Candidate, Bangor University, UK) is pastor of Family Worship Center, York, PA, USA and a St. Basil Fellow at the Center for Pastor Theologians.

[1] David A. Reed, *'In Jesus' Name': The History and Beliefs of Oneness Pentecostals* (JPTSup 31; Blandford Forum: Deo Publishing, 2008).

[2] David A. Reed, 'Oneness Pentecostalism', in Stanley B. Burgess, Gary B. McGee, and Patrick H. Alexander (eds.), *Dictionary of Pentecostal and Charismatic Movements* (Grand Rapids: Regency Reference Library, 1988), pp. 644-51 (644).

Pentecostal movement'.[3] Therefore, Oneness Pentecostalism was birthed within the context of theologizing around baptism.

Yet, as Reed notes, his study lacks an analysis of the 'African-American presence in the movement, a constituency that comprises nearly half of all Oneness Pentecostals in the United States'.[4] In an attempt to address this lacuna, this study will focus on the first years of *The Christian Outlook* edited by G.T. Haywood.[5] While there have been noteworthy articles, chapters, and monographs emerging from Pentecostal scholars employing *Wirkungsgeschichte*, little attention has been devoted to early Oneness Pentecostalism. In response, this study will survey the major and consistent themes that emerge from the Oneness Pentecostal reception of baptismal verses, particularly in Acts, as expressed in the periodical literature. While this engagement is not exhaustive, it is 'representative of the constituency' of an early Oneness Pentecostal group that includes both white and African American Pentecostals.[6] This survey will reveal – among other things – that early Oneness Pentecostal baptismal theology is deeply sacramental at the explicit and implicit levels of theological discourse. Finally, this study seeks not only to examine Oneness Pentecostal reception concerning baptism, but also to further the research on early Oneness baptismal theology and practice.

---

[3] Reed, *'In Jesus' Name'*, p. 1.

[4] Douglas Jacobsen's important work on the theologies of early Pentecostal leaders, such as G.T. Haywood helps fill this gap. However, Jacobsen's treatment focuses on Haywood and Andrew Urshan specifically, without giving space for other early writers found in the periodical literature. See Douglas Jacobsen, *Thinking in the Spirit: Theologies of the Early Pentecostal Movement* (Bloomington: Indiana University Press, 2003).

[5] *The Christian Outlook* is the official publication of the Pentecostal Assemblies of the World which is still in publication today. The periodical began in 1923 with Elder G.T. Haywood as its inaugural editor until his death in 1931. Following Haywood, Elder S.K. Grimes took the role of editor in 1931. In the years engaged (1923–33), the subject of water baptism was quite prominent. The earliest available issue is *TCO* 1.4 (April 1923). In some cases, issue numbers and months are not indicated.

[6] Mark J. Cartledge, 'Text–Community–Spirit: The Challenges Posed by Pentecostal Theological Method to Evangelical Theology' in Kevin L. Spawn and Archie T. Wright (eds.), *Spirit and Scripture: Exploring a Pneumatic Hermeneutic* (New York: T&T Clark, 2012), p. 131.

Receiving Acts 2.38

The central debate that led to the establishment of the Oneness stream of Pentecostalism in 1914 was over the baptism formula established by Scripture. Trinitarians used the traditional formula from Mt. 28.19-20. While Oneness Pentecostals appealed to many Scriptures, Acts 2.38 was arguably *the* most significant and informative verse for forming and authenticating the Oneness theological convictions on water baptism. The Acts 2.38 formula provided Oneness adherents (1) the biblical precedent of baptizing in Jesus' name, (2) the biblical foundation of affirming that baptism is for the 'remission of sins', and (3) the connection between water baptism and Spirit baptism. For some, these theological articulations were undeniably found in the reading of this Scripture, causing one writer to simply declare, 'Acts 2:38 is right'.[7] As G.T. Haywood saw it, 'Any person reading … the words recorded in Acts 2.38 … cannot help but see that baptism in the name of Jesus Christ was preached and confirmed in the early days of the gospel'.[8] For Haywood, this message was a central part of the gospel: 'In reading the Book of Acts you will find what was preached as the "gospel of the kingdom." Repentance and baptism for the remission of sins was to be preached in all the world in His (Jesus') name, beginning at Jerusalem.'[9]

At times, writers interpreted other Scriptures in view of Acts 2.38. For instance, T.C. Davis argues that 'Acts 2:38 is … the fulfillment of Matthew 28:19', consequently making the apostles' baptizing in Jesus' name more authoritative than Jesus' command to baptize in the name of the Father, Son, and Holy Spirit.[10] This prioritizing of Acts 2.38 is seen consistently in the treatment of Jesus' command in Mt. 28.19, that is 'if Acts 2:38 isn't the fulfilling of Matt. 28:19, then the Word of God contradicts itself. Hence there would be two ways of baptizing.'[11] To further the point, another writer states that 'when it says to

---

[7] J.R. Ledbetter, 'Our Missionary Trip Out West', *TCO* 3.1 (January 1925), p. 13.

[8] G.T. Haywood, 'Dodging the Word of God', *TCO* (August 1926), p. 115.

[9] G.T. Haywood, 'The Gospel of the Kingdom', *TCO* 4.2 (February 1926), p. 19.

[10] T.C. Davis, 'Baptism: What is it? What is it for? And in what name should it be administered?' *TCO* 3.1 (January 1925), p. 18.

[11] Leona Burnison, 'Water Baptism in Jesus' Name', *TCO* 6.1 (January 1928), p. 13.

baptize in the Name of the Father, and of the Son, and of the Holy
Ghost. It doesn't say names, But Name in the singular. And Jesus is
the Name of the Father, Son and Holy Ghost.'[12] The Oneness doctrine of God also serves as a hermeneutical stimulus, since 'Father',
'Son', and 'Holy Ghost' are interpreted to be titles for the 'NAME'
of Jesus. Since this is the case, in Haywood's words, 'why should there
be any objections to one saying, "I baptized you in the Name of Jesus
Christ"? Why should that be termed such a terrible error when it is
mentioned in Matt. 28.19?'[13]

Oneness Pentecostals also used Acts 2.38 in connection with
other verses. For example, Acts 2.38 and Acts 2.4 were referenced
together at times to argue for the 'New Birth' doctrine. As one said,
'Baptism in water in the name of Jesus, according to Acts 2.38, and
the reception of the Holy Ghost according to Acts 2.4 starts the new
life'.[14] Similarly, Acts 2.38 was coupled with Rom. 6.3 to argue for
baptism in Christ's name.

> As in Acts 2.38, 'Repent, and be baptized every one of you in
> (into) the name of JESUS CHRIST for the remission of sins and
> ye shall receive the gift of the Holy Ghost.' And in Romans 6.3,
> we read, 'Know ye not, that many of us as were baptized into
> JESUS CHRIST were baptized into his death?'[15]

Thus, Acts 2.38 was the primary scriptural source and was placed
into dialogue with other scriptures to generate a consistent thread of
scriptural witness. However, other scriptures in Acts were referenced
as well. For example, in referring to Acts 19, Haywood comments:

> They 'baptized in water in Jesus' name' and afterwards Paul laid
> his hands on them, and they were filled with the Holy Ghost.
> HAVE YOU EVER HAD AN EXPERIENCE LIKE THIS? If
> not, then you are not sealed … Go somewhere and ask the

---

12 Burnison, 'Water Baptism in Jesus' Name', p. 14.

13 G.T. Haywood, 'The Name and the Cross', *TCO* (May 1928), p. 63.

14 J.D. Goodson, 'Ye Have Not Passed This Way Heretofore', *TCO* 6.7 (July
1928), p. 101.

15 W.B.M., 'Apostolic Mode of Baptism', *TCO* 6.10 (October 1928), p. 150.

preacher to 'baptize you in Jesus Name' and you SHALL receive the Holy Ghost. See Acts 2:38.[16]

Haywood argues that water baptism in Jesus' name should be accompanied by Spirit baptism soon afterwards. Another author uses this Acts 19 account to argue that since 'the disciples of John were rebaptized in the Name of the Lord Jesus' then baptism should be followed by Spirit baptism with accompanying 'tongues … in the Name of Jesus for the Holy Ghost'.[17] And in Acts 8.6, 'Only they were baptized in the name of the Lord Jesus' and in Acts 10:48 and Acts 19:5 'all were baptized in Jesus' name'.[18] Stated simply, the overall witness of Acts served as the major scriptural apologetic for a Oneness theology of baptism, built on the foundation given in Acts 2.38. The key defense for many writers was that using the name Jesus Christ when baptizing was the only prescribed formula in Acts.[19]

Receiving John 3.5

In addition to Acts 2.38, Oneness Pentecostals employed other prominent Scriptures to reinforce their theology of Oneness baptism, such as Jn 3.5. This verse was a significant Scriptural resource to argue for water baptism's salvific affect. Haywood states, 'If one has not been baptized in water and the Holy Spirit he cannot claim to be "born again". Conversion is one thing, but to be "born of the Spirit" is another.'[20] Evidently, conversion was understood to be something separate from being 'born of the Spirit' (referencing Jn 3.5) and becoming 'born again'. Affirming this position further by offering a commentary on the verse, Haywood states that in Jn 3.5, 'Jesus declares that even a righteous Pharisee must be born of the baptismal water and of the Holy Ghost in order to be saved'.[21]

Overall, early Oneness Pentecostals were convinced that 'too many' Christians as a whole 'jump over the 5th verse of the third

---

[16] G.T. Haywood, 'The Seal of God', *TCO* (March 1924), p. 319, emphasis original.

[17] Sel., 'The Four Fold Gospel to Enter into the Four Square City', *TCO* 6.7 (July 1928), p. 99.

[18] W.B.M., 'Apostolic Mode of Baptism', *TCO* 6.10 (October 1928), p. 149.

[19] W.B.M., 'Apostolic Mode of Baptism', p. 149.

[20] G.T. Haywood, 'The Term "Born Again"', *TCO* 7.8 (August 1929), p. 112.

[21] G.T. Haywood, 'Heresy in Song', *TCO* (September 1923), p. 179.

chapter of John's Gospel',[22] and hence fail to see the salvific element embedded within water baptism. They criticized Christians for attempting to 'hide behind the thief on the cross in order to evade the subject of baptism'.[23] The unnamed writer explains,

> There is no refuge there. The thief on the cross believed in the death, burial and resurrection of our Lord Jesus Christ even before he had 'given up the Ghost' ... There is no doubt but what that thief would have been 'buried with him by baptism' had he lived to see the day of Pentecost fulfilled. There is no refuge in the thief on the cross. Our refuge is in Jesus Christ alone. We must be baptized into Him.[24]

The thief on the cross, then, does not compromise the truths found in Jn 3.5. In this Scripture, it is undisputable that 'only one "family" will be saved – those who are born of water and Spirit ... See John 3:3-5'.[25] There is no exception in salvation, Urshan comments, one must be 'born of water (Come forth up and out of the water) and of the Spirit (Come forth up and out of the Spirit, being soaked with same and clothed upon with)' or he cannot enter into the Kingdom of God.[26] John 3.5, then, helped confirm baptism's vital importance to Christian salvation.

Receiving Pauline Baptismal Scriptures

While Acts 2.38 and Jn 3.5 were significant throughout early Oneness literature, other Scriptures were important in supporting and strengthening Oneness baptismal theology. John 3.5 was tied with Paul's statement in Eph. 4.5 to argue for 'one baptism', containing two 'vital elements':

> Paul tells us that there is one Lord, one faith, one baptism. Jesus tells Nicodemus, this Baptism is a birth. Which makes only one

---

[22] Gath, 'Gospel Message of Hope', *TCO* 1.4 (April 1923), p. 13.

[23] 'The Thief on the Cross', *TCO* (February 1923), p. 4.

[24] 'The Thief on the Cross', p. 4.

[25] W.T. Witherspoon, 'Millions Now Dead Will Never Live!' *TCO* 2.9 (October 1924), p. 475. In another issue, 1 Pet. 3.20-21 is also referenced and used to argue that 'Baptism saves'. See G.T. Haywood, 'Truth vs. Error', *TCO* (June 1925), p. 104.

[26] A.D. Urshan, 'The New Birth, or the New Creation', *TCO* 7.7 (July 1929), p. 98.

Baptism, composed of two vital elements, water and Spirit (blood). For the life is in the blood and the Spirit is life.[27]

This emphasis upon 'one baptism' can be seen throughout the literature. One writer, Leona Burnison, argues that since 'Paul ... declares that there (is) One Lord, One Faith. One Baptism (Eph. 4:5) ... then there is just one.'[28] Further, Oneness proponents reasoned Pauline Scriptures argued for only 'one' baptism. For example, in one case Eph. 4.5 and 1 Cor. 12.13 are brought together to argue this point: 'In 1 Cor. 12:13 we read that "by one Spirit we are all baptized into one body, whether we be Jews or Gentiles" and in Ephesians 4:5 we see that there is "one baptism" and "one body" also (verse 4)'.[29] Because of this, the church is composed of a 'people ... who have truly repented of their sins, and have been baptized into the Name of JESUS CHRIST for the remission of their sins ... and have been baptized into the one body by the Holy Ghost (1 Cor. 12:13)'.[30] Affirming this position, Haywood states that 'all who are baptized by that "one Spirit" ... are members of that one body'.[31]

Further, baptismal verses in Romans were employed by Oneness Pentecostals as supportive of their view. Wm. Boaz MacGregor, references Rom. 6.3-4 indirectly when he states, 'our sins are not remitted until we are *buried* with Christ in baptism'.[32] Another author, engaging Rom. 6.4 directly, argues for a Oneness doctrine of God and baptism in Jesus' name by stating, 'we are buried with HIM by baptism into death, not THEM, HIM!'.[33] This Scripture is also significant for Haywood because it 'typifies death to the allurements of the world. (Rom. 6:3–13)'.[34]

---

[27] Davis, 'Baptism: What is it? What is it for? And in what name should it be administered?', p. 18.

[28] Burnison, 'Water Baptism in Jesus' Name', p. 13.

[29] G.T. Haywood, '"The Bride of Christ"', *TCO* (September 1926), p. 133.

[30] Wm. Boaz MacGregor, 'Signs of the Appearing of Christ', *TCO* 4.2 (February 1926), p. 27.

[31] G.T. Haywood, 'Mystries [*sic*] of the Son of Man', *TCO* (November 1924), p. 489.

[32] Wm. Boaz Macgregor, 'Why Such an Uproar Against the Name of Jesus Christ', *TCO* 4.7 (July 1926), p. 101. Emphasis mine.

[33] Davis, 'Baptism: What is it? What is it for? And in what name should it be administered?', p. 18.

[34] G.T. Haywood, 'In the Last Days', *TCO* (June 1925), p. 106.

dNot surprisingly, references to the baptism of Jesus were sparse. In a possible allusion to Jesus' baptism, Haywood declares that 'when you are immersed in the Name of Jesus Christ for the remission of sins, heaven will open up unto you immediately'.[35] However, this reference notwithstanding, the lack of references to Jesus' baptism is noteworthy since Haywood notes Jesus' filling 'with the Holy Spirit at the River of Jordan'.[36] Considering the consistent Oneness Pentecostal emphasis upon the relationship between water baptism and Spirit baptism, one might consider this an opportune resource. Having said this, little attention was given to those texts, perhaps because of the way in which Trinitarians used Jesus' baptism to refute the Oneness position.

The New Birth

As we have already seen, one of the most important theological aspects of Oneness Pentecostal views of water baptism is its connection with 'New Birth' doctrine. Once again, Haywood summarizes this doctrine well: 'to be baptized in Jesus' Name, to receive the Holy Ghost and to speak in other tongues is to be born of the water and spirit into that very Kingdom that began on the day of Pentecost'.[37] Urshan expresses this doctrine when he states that salvation is found in being 'baptized in water and Spirit in His name'.[38] Every Christian, then, must obey this 'command of God'.[39] If one is not baptized in the name of Jesus and Spirit baptized, the person is not born again.

Thus, it is of vital importance for believers to 'follow in His footsteps … and be baptized in His name', expecting salvation.[40] Haywood states, 'he that believeth, and is BAPTIZED, shall be saved',[41] for 'the sins of our flesh are put off by baptism in the name of Jesus

---

[35] G.T. Haywood, 'The Hiding Place from the Wind', *TCO* (November 1923), p. 213.

[36] G.T. Haywood, 'Power to Save', *TCO* (November 1923), p. 231.

[37] G.T. Haywood, 'The Two New Things', *TCO* 6.12 (December 1928), p. 173.

[38] A.D. Urshan, 'Foreign Missions: Extracts of Interests From Letters of Missionaries', *TCO* (March 1924), p. 307.

[39] B.M. David, 'Baptism from the Bible Viewpoint', *TCO* 9.2 (February 1931), p. 30.

[40] W.T. Witherspoon, 'Millions Now Dead Will Never Live!' *TCO* 2.9 (October 1924), p. 475.

[41] G.T. Haywood, 'No Compromise', *TCO* 7.8 (August 1929), p. 111.

Christ'.[42] The salvific nature of baptism, according to Urshan, is 'the back-bone of our faith, which we cannot compromise upon for the sake of membership'.[43] Baptism is essential for 'New Birth'.

Mode, Formula, and the Nature of God

Another important theme that emerges from the literature is the emphasis of Scripture over-and-against tradition. Oneness proponents believed that Trinitarians undermined the plain reading of Scripture by appealing to the long held tradition of the Trinitarian formula. For Haywood, it is critical to 'stand for the Apostles' Doctrine' concerning 'Baptism in Jesus name for the remission of sins' rather than succumb to tradition.[44] Readers are often warned to 'not allow [themselves] to be deceived by man-made theological theories and religious speculations' but instead to simply 'obey Acts 2:38 and be born of water and the Spirit, in the Name of Jesus Christ'.[45] This emphasis upon Scripture over-and-against 'tradition' and 'theological theories' is a reoccurring theme. For instance, one writer states that while many claim that water baptism is simply an 'ordinance ... an outward sign of inward purity ... such an expression cannot be found in the Word of God'.[46] And though it is 'commonly stated that baptism does not save us ... the Word of God says' it does.[47] In so doing, Oneness Pentecostals were arguing for a more sacramental emphasis to baptism than their Trinitarian counterparts.

This emphasis is also expressed in the confessions surrounding *mode* (how they were baptized) and *formula* (what name they were baptized in). Candidates were required to be baptized by immersion in the name of Jesus, for 'to be born of water means to be dipped in

---

[42] G.T. Haywood, 'Saints Marrying Sinners?', *TCO* 6.1 (January 1928), p. 3.

[43] A.D. Urshan, 'Missionary Paragraphs and News of Interest', *TCO* (March 1924), p. 311.

[44] G.T. Haywood, 'The Apostolic Doctrine', *TCO* (November 1924), p. 481.

[45] A.D. Urshan, 'The Doctrine of New Birth', *TCO* 8.9 (1930), p. 133. In this statement Jn 3.5 and Acts 2.38 are operating together to form this New Birth doctrine. This is also seen in the following statement: 'Jesus' Name,' is inseparably connected with being born of water and ALL HAVE TO take on His Name'. See also G.T. Haywood, 'The Two New Things', *TCO* 6.12 (December 1928), p. 172.

[46] B.M. David, 'Baptism from the Bible Viewpoint', *TCO* 9.2 (February 1931), p. 30.

[47] 1 Peter 3.20-21 is probably in view here.

water and come forth out of water ... done in the Name of the Lord Jesus Christ'.[48] This too was a rejection of tradition, especially for those who 'would advise sprinkling'.[49] By contrast, one writer notes, 'there are many ministers who ... ridicule water baptism as though it was a man's doctrine', but Oneness Pentecostals consistently understood Scripture 'to prove it to be of divine origin'.[50] One writer, in my estimation, speaks on behalf of the whole in his or her comments on mode:

> Sprinkling is not baptism at all. That is only man's tradition. It is not to be found in the Word of God that children or men are to be sprinkled with water. But the Bible does read that man must be born of water ... You will see that sprinkling has never been used in the Bible at all. Therefore, if you have not been buried *under* the water, you have never been baptized at all. We will give $50 to any man who can show us in the New Testament where man or child was sprinkled.[51]

Instead, Oneness Pentecostals insisted that anything short of immersion in Jesus' name was unscriptural.[52] In Haywood's words, 'there are many who are opposed to baptism by immersion because of their traditional teachings upon the subject', but Scripture is clear: 'the only way to be baptized in the NAME of the Father, and of the Son, and of the Holy Ghost is in Jesus' Name' by immersion.[53]

For early Oneness Pentecostals, Scripture is clear on both *mode* and *formula*, and its witness must be trusted over mere human tradition and reason. To get this right is of vast importance because much *is* at stake. Without true baptism there is no salvation and remission of sins. Baptism, then, must not be deferred. As one writer states, 'delay not ... to be baptized' because nothing should be allowed to 'stand between you and your God'. If it is necessary, the believer

---

[48] A.D. Urshan, 'The Doctrine of New Birth', *TCO* 8.8 (August 1930), p. 119.

[49] W.E. Booth-Clibborn, *TCO* (September 1923), p. 199.

[50] G.T. Haywood, 'Bishop Haywood's Western Trip', *TCO* 8.5 (May 1930), p. 69.

[51] B.M. David, 'Baptism from the Bible Viewpoint', *TCO* 9.2 (1931), p. 30. My emphasis.

[52] Sel., 'The Four Fold Gospel to Enter into the Four Square City', p. 99.

[53] G.T. Haywood, 'The Whole Family in Heaven and in Earth', *TCO* (February 1924), p. 283.

should be ready to say, '"Hinder me not!"' to whomever shall stand in the way.[54]

It is important to note, though, that when individuals are baptized in Jesus' name, they are affirming a scriptural position over the 'traditional' position. By submitting to baptism in Jesus' name, they are affirming that the 'the Father, Son and Holy Ghost "are one" ... and that in Christ Jesus dwelleth all the fulness of the Godhead in bodily form'.[55] In other words, 'there is positively no just reason for baptizing in Jesus's name as a matter of fact. The only solution – the only reason – the only just reason to offer for baptism in Jesus name is, in the fact, that, the Fulness of God indwells Christ.'[56] Affirming baptism in Jesus' name, then, is affirming the Oneness doctrine of God as well.

Expounding on this doctrine of God in connection with water baptism, E.N. Bell states,

> When Jesus commanded to 'baptize in the name of the Father and of the Son' they understood what the Father's name was for. Isaiah had told them it was the Lord (42.8) and Jesus had opened their understanding that they might understand the Scriptures (Luke 24.25). Knowing also that God was a Spirit (John 4.24) and that the Lord was the Spirit (2 Cor. 3.17) they could completely obey the command of Jesus by commanding baptism merely 'IN THE NAME OF THE LORD' as Peter did in Acts 10.48 or in the name of the Lord Jesus as under Paul in Acts 19.5 ... I can say in all sincerity that I do not now believe Christ ever meant to baptize with the phrase 'Father and Son' at all ... I prefer to use the real name common to both Father and Son as the Lord commanded me to baptize in 'The Name', not in a relationship phrase which is no proper name at all. Lord, help the dear brethren to see that father and son are by no means a proper name. Recognizing

---

[54] W.E. Booth-Clibborn, *TCO* (September 1923), p. 199.

[55] G.T. Haywood, 'The Fatherhood of God in Christ', *TCO* (June 1924), p. 385.

[56] Frank Small, 'Theological World Faces Reconstruction', *TCO* 8.6 (June 1930), p. 86

the whole Godhead always present in Jesus, the apostles baptized either in a part or all of His name.[57]

Accordingly, by being baptized in Christ's name, the Oneness of God is affirmed, and the candidate receives the power that is contained in His 'Name'.

Finally, and perhaps most interestingly, the overall rhetoric for privileging Scripture over 'man's tradition' is occasionally nuanced. First, in an appeal to 'tradition', Haywood argues for water baptism to be accompanied with glossolalia:

> We here quote the words of St. Chrysostom, who lived 400 years after the death of Christ: Whoever was baptized in apostolic times (days) he straightway spake with tongues ... one in the Persian language, another in the Roman, another in the Indian, and another in some other tongue. And this made manifest to them that were without that it was the Spirit in the very person speaking. Wherefore the Apostle calls it 'the manifestation of the Spirit, which is given to every man to profit withal'. That the members of the body of Christ were baptized therein and spake with tongues is further shown by the words of Augustine, who lived several hundred years after the apostles: 'We still do what the apostles did when they laid hands on the Samaritans and called down the Holy Spirit on them in laying on of hands. It is expected that the converts should speak in new tongues'.[58]

---

[57] E.N. Bell, 'A Glorious Tribute to Jesus Christ', *TCO* 4.3 (March 1926), p. 46. This testimony by Bell is significant because he was part of the original controversy that eventually split the Trinitarians from the Oneness in 1916. Bell remained a Trinitarian, but Oneness advocates continued to use his arguments. For example, in an earlier issue, they share Bell's brief testimony on how this 'new vision of Jesus' has personally impacted him: 'If people knew what God is putting in my soul by a brand new vision of Jesus and the wonders hid in His mighty and glorious name, they would cease pitying me for being baptized in the Name of the Lord Jesus Christ and begin to shout and help me praise the Lamb that was slain who is now beginning to receive some honor and praise, but who will eventually make the whole universe – sea, earth and sky, reverberate with universal praise and honor to His great Name'. See E.N. Bell, 'A Glorious Tribute to Jesus Christ', *TCO* 4.2 (February 1926), p. 21.

[58] G.T. Haywood, 'The Bride of Christ', *TCO* (September 1926), p. 138. Significantly, Haywood possibly 'borrowed' this information from earlier Pentecostal periodicals. See A.B. Cox, 'The Baptism of the Holy Spirit,' *BC* 3.10 (March 1920), pp. 17-18.

Second, Haywood also sought to provide an apologetic using church history for using the name of Jesus in water baptism:

> The trinitarian formula and triune immersion were not uniformly used from the beginning, nor did they always go together. The 'Teaching of the Apostles' indeed prescribed baptism in the name of the Father, Son and Holy Ghost, but on the next page speaks of those who have been baptized in the name of the Lord – the formula of the New Testament. In the third century baptism in the name of Jesus Christ was still so widespread that Pope Stephen, in opposition to Cyprian of Carthage, declared it to be valid. –Ency. Brit. Vol. 3, page 365. We only have to get a full proof of the fact that baptism in the name of Jesus Christ was the earliest formula of baptism.[59]

Finally, an unidentified author argued that 'since ... the close of the apostolic age the Christian Church has used' the triune formula in baptism while 'the Church of the apostolic age used the name of the Lord Jesus Christ in the same rite, according to the Acts and the apostolic Epistles'.[60]

These two writers utilize early church theologians to provide an apologetic against the triune formula and 'second blessing' theology. In so doing, Oneness writers demonstrate that in some instances the tradition of the church provided an important resource to affirm their theological confession.

Connecting Water Baptism and Spirit Baptism

There were many testimonies and reflections surrounding water baptism and Spirit baptism among early Oneness Pentecostals. In fact, water baptism along with Spirit baptism were the two most consistently reported events in their early literature. Contributors typically stated the number of water baptisms and Spirit baptisms. Testimonies reveal that more people were water baptized than Spirit baptized,

---

[59] G.T. Haywood, 'Early Baptismal Formula', *TCO* (June 1928), p. 79.
[60] 'The Problem of the Baptismal Name and Its Biblical Solution', *TCO* 7.10 (October 1929), p. 150.

because water baptism preceded Spirit baptism.[61] For example, one report states, 'Eleven were baptized in Jesus' name, nine received the Holy Ghost and others were seeking'.[62] On occasion, those being water baptized experienced Spirit baptism immediately.[63] Others, however, experienced a gap in time between these two events. For instance, Elder C.B. Gordon shares that one person 'was baptized in the name of Jesus' and then one hour later 'was filled with the Holy Ghost'.[64] This instance suggests that although they believed that speaking in tongues was part of the conversion experience, Spirit baptism generally remained subsequent to water baptism. One could be saved, baptized in water, and continue pursuit of Spirit-baptism.

Typically, after being baptized in Jesus' name, the newly baptized were still seeking Spirit baptism.[65] However, the newly baptized were always encouraged to never 'give up' on receiving Spirit baptism after they were baptized 'in Jesus' name'.[66] The testimonies, though, reveal a flexibility in the timing of these two events. One writer – J.K. Solomon – reporting on his own experience of being baptized in the Jordan River states: 'I received my baptism of the Holy Spirit, that was before I went to the Jordan. The next day we went down to the Jordan.'[67] Therefore, some did receive 'the Holy Ghost before water baptism'.[68]

Testimonies also reveal Spirit baptism during water baptism. Summarizing the experience of a congregant, Haywood reports, 'having

---

[61] In Haywood's words, 'many are receiving the Holy Ghost *after* being baptized in Jesus' name'. My Emphasis. See G.T. Haywood, 'Column of Information', *TCO* (April 1924), p. 325.

[62] J.B. Thomas, 'Foreign Missions: Bagdad, Irak', *TCO* 8.5 (May 1930), p. 73.

[63] For example, one writer reports that 'twenty-five have been baptized in the Name of Jesus and *all* have received the Holy Ghost with the evidence of speaking in tongues as the Spirit gives utterance'. Louis Pinder, 'Field Reports: Miami, Florida', *TCO* 4.3 (March 1926), p. 44.

[64] C.B. Gordon, 'Field Reports: Terre Haute, Indiana', *TCO* 4.2 (February 1926), p. 29.

[65] For example, one, pastor reports: 'there are nine here yet to have been buried with him in baptism, who have not yet received the Holy Ghost'. See T.M. Frazier, 'Field Reports: Muskegon, Michigan', *TCO* 8.6 (June 1930), p. 92.

[66] L.B. Sly., 'Field Reports: Tampa, Florida', *TCO* 4.7 (July 1926), p. 109.

[67] J.K. Solomon, 'Foreign Missions: Jerusalem, Palestine', *TCO* 8.6 (June 1930), p. 89.

[68] Glen Bordwell, 'Field Reports: East Comstock, Michigan', *TCO* 7.4 (April 1929), p. 61.

believed on the Lord and been baptized in water' this believer 'realized she had something that she did not possess before conversion … it was the Spirit of Jesus'.[69] Other testimonies reveal that some received 'the baptism with the Holy Ghost as [they] "came up out of the water"'.[70] Sister Margret Reed testified that as a man 'was baptized in Jesus' name and upon coming up out of the water, the power of God fell and he was filled with the Holy Ghost, speaking in tongues'.[71] Another report reveals a Baptist preacher being rebaptized in Jesus' name whom after coming 'up out of the water', jumped out, and began running 'around the church, hollowing, "Power! Power!!"'.[72] Some who were 'baptized in water … came out of the water speaking in tongues'.[73] Evidently, there was a widespread expectation to meet the Spirit in the waters of baptism, manifesting itself through the *charismata* and other dramatic experiences.[74] One pastor recounts another one of these sensational experiences:

> We have seen more than 200 coming up out of the water speaking in tongues. We have seen hundreds slain under the power of God in the waters and floating as long as half an hour at the time, many speaking in tongues.[75]

Oneness Pentecostals also reported occasional deliverance from demonic oppression at the moment of or shortly after water baptism. As one person put it, 'since the day that I was baptized in the name of Jesus Christ, the Lord cast all the evil spirits out'.[76] Testimonies of physical healings were also present, such as one man who was baptized 'who had been on crutches for about 35 years' and afterwards

---

[69] G.T. Haywood, 'In the Last Days', *TCO* (June 1925), p. 114.

[70] Gath, 'Gospel Message of Hope', *TCO* 1.4 (1923), p. 13.

[71] Margret Reed, 'Field Reports: Buffalo, New York', *TCO* 5.2 (February 1927), p. 28.

[72] J.M. Turpin, 'The Power Falls in Baltimore', *TCO* 2.9 (October 1924), p. 470.

[73] J.D. Bunyan, 'Voice From India', *TCO* 2.9 (October 1924), p. 470.

[74] In one instance, this 'power' evidenced itself in a 'native' from West Africa, 'Brother Peter Chea', testifying that when he was 'baptized in Jesus' Name' he gave 'up four wives and kept one'. See Peter Chea, 'The God that Cut the Cotton Tree Down: A Native Testimony', *TCO* 1.4 (1923), p. 9

[75] Chas. Lochbaum, 'A Wonderful Service', *TCO* 6.7 (July 1928), p. 105.

[76] J.K. Moses, 'Evil Spirits Cast Out', *TCO* 6.7 (July 1928), p. 106.

was able to 'walk out and leave his crutches in the church'.[77] Another elderly 'woman … who had dropsy was baptized and is now getting better'.[78] Lastly, in another case, 'a Baptist preacher was baptized in Jesus' name and was healed in the water'.[79] Whether through the receiving of 'power … [while] in the water',[80] receiving the 'Holy Ghost … before getting out of the tank',[81] or receiving 'heal[ing] in the water',[82] these accounts provide yet another variant to baptismal experiences.[83]

The only break in the narrative of water baptism being an opportunity to meet God comes from Elder J.R. Ledbetter, a missionary to Liberia, Africa. He reports that 'nearly every Wednesday, our fast day, *we* baptize from three to four in Jesus' name and *the Lord* baptizes nearly all of them with the Holy Ghost'.[84] Significantly, Ledbetter seems to posit water baptism as man's work, while Spirit baptism is God's work. However, despite this comment, Oneness testimonies seem to suggest that many understood water baptisms to be a place to encounter the Spirit.

Believer's Baptism, Infant Baptism, and Rebaptism

Testimonies also reveal that rebaptism was prominent, due to Oneness belief in the efficacy of the formula. In one case, Timothy D. Urshan, a missionary to Jerusalem, shared his personal testimony of being rebaptized in Jesus' name:

> Before this time I was immersed according to the usual form 'in the name of the Father, and of the Son, and of the Holy Ghost,'

---

[77] S.N. Hancock, 'Field Reports: Detroit, Michigan', *TCO* 7.4 (April 1929), p. 60.

[78] J.A. Jones, 'Field Reports: Newark, New Jersey', *TCO* 6.11 (November 1928), p. 163.

[79] H.S. Covington, 'Field Reports: Oakland, California', *TCO* 8.11 (December 1930), p. 172.

[80] Bro. and Sister Chas. Lochbaum, 'Foreign Missions: Honolulu, T.H.', *TCO* 6.11 (November 1928), p. 161.

[81] *TCO* 9.1 (1931), p. 75.

[82] H.S. Covington, 'Field Reports: Oakland, California', *TCO* 8.11 (December 1930), p. 172.

[83] W.E. Kelly, 'New Mission for His Name', *TCO* 4.7 (July 1926), p. 103.

[84] J.R. Ledbetter, 'Foreign Missions: Monrovia, Liberia, Africa', *TCO* 7.7 (July 1929), p. 101. Emphasis mine.

... but when I learned that Jesus Christ was 'the name' of the Father, Son and Holy Ghost I was ready to be baptized in Jesus' name ... so Brothers and Sisters, if you have not been baptized in Jesus' name, obey God at once.[85]

For Urshan, rebaptism was an issue of obedience tied to the promise in Act 2.38, even though he had already been baptized according to Mt. 28.19-20. Testimonies consistently affirm this position. Many were rebaptized when they learned that Jesus' name is the only valid formula to be used in baptism. Following this revelation, many submitted to the 'Lord and obeyed' by being 'baptized in Jesus' name'.[86] In one instance, E.J. Douglas reports a person being 'obedient to the word' by being baptized in 'fourteen below zero' weather.[87] This is the price some Oneness Pentecostals paid for 'following Jesus in baptism'.[88]

The command to be baptized in Jesus' name also extended to children. Haywood notes, all 'little folks' (children) were 'baptized in Jesus name' by immersion.[89] Timothy Urshan shares that his 'two ... own children, Lydia and Josiah' were 'baptized at the Jordan' through immersion.[90] In one case a 'five-year-old girl that made quite an impression on the people' was immersed.[91] A missionary to China reports baptizing 'six women, two girls of fifteen years of age and thirteen boys, ranging from ten to sixteen years of age'.[92] In another account, children as young as 'six years old were baptized' and even sought 'the Holy Ghost as honestly as an older person'.[93]

[85] Timothy D. Urshan, 'My Personal Testimony: "Baptized in the Jordan"', *TCO* 5.8 (August 1927), p. 117.

[86] Bessie Blessing, 'Field Reports: Otsego, Michigan', *TCO* 9.12 (December 1931), p. 152.

[87] E.J. Douglas, 'Column of Information: Beacon, Tennessee', *TCO* (March 1924), p. 313.

[88] W.E. Kelly, 'New Mission for His Name', *TCO* 4.7 (July 1926), p. 103.

[89] G.T. Haywood, 'At Christ Temple, Indianapolis', *TCO* 8.5 (May 1930), p. 67.

[90] Timothy Urshan, 'Field Reports: Jerusalem, Palestine', *TCO* 8.8 (August 1930), p. 121.

[91] W.D. Jackson, 'Field Reports: Warsaw, Kentucky', *TCO* 8.5 (May 1930), p. 77.

[92] Mae Iry, 'Foreign Missions: Taijoh, Shansi, China', *TCO* 7.10 (October 1929), p. 144.

[93] Karl F. Smith, 'Field Reports: Columbus, Ohio', *TCO* 8.5 (May 1930), p. 76.

Given Oneness rejection of efficacious infant baptism, occasional references declare the validity of childhood baptism against infant baptism. Such a case is made by a missionary to Switzerland,

> the class of people here is hard to reach, as they have their own church and ... their babies are baptized, and because of this some little children have told our children they are going to hell since they had not been baptized when infants. Then these same children swear and take the name of the Lord in vain. The young people in this place are all seeking pleasure.[94]

The writer, then, understands the 'swearing' and 'seeking pleasure' to demonstrate the expected ills of infant baptism. Other missionaries had to deal with the issue of pedobaptism when they began evangelizing people in other nations. Some missionaries ministered in places where there were 'no churches who immerse ... except theirs'.[95] However, despite the difficulty for some pastors and missionaries, Oneness Pentecostals resolutely and passionately advocated for immersion in Jesus' name for the remission of sins.

Conclusions

In conclusion, this study demonstrates how Oneness Pentecostals taught about water baptism through sermons and expositional material on scriptural texts. These reports occasionally recorded the number of people being baptized, and baptismal accounts accompanied by ecstatic experiences. Teaching on water baptism centered on the themes of New Birth doctrine, the efficacious nature of being baptized in the Name of Jesus, the illegitimacy of any baptismal modes apart from full immersion, and baptismal connection to Spirit baptism. Baptismal theology was derived from a plain reading of Acts. Critical verses include Acts 2.38 and Jn 3.5. Water baptism and Spirit baptism were deemed as separate but closely related events that make up the New Birth. Reports and testimonies overall – with only one exception – reveal an understood expectation to encounter the Spirit of God within the rite of baptism. This study has also uncovered variation in the timing between water baptism and Spirit baptism in

---

[94] Missionary Roth and Family, 'Switzerland', *TCO* 1.4 (April 1923), p. 12.
[95] M.E. Cheatham, 'From Sister Cheatham in Africa', *TCO* (June 1925), p. 112.

early Oneness Pentecostalism. Though some received Spirit baptism concurrently with water baptism, others received one before the other. Therefore, while the New Birth followed an expected pattern, testimonies reveal that in practice, there was flexibility in the *ordo salutis*.

Perhaps most significantly, this study adds a largely African American perspective to the current conversation on Oneness baptismal theology and soteriology, which as David Reed has noted, is underresearched. The 'sacramental' perspective represented in this study is one of two main schools of thought within Oneness Pentecostalism according to Reed:

> Oneness soteriology from the earliest years has been divided into two main schools of thought. One follows the baptistic tradition of the AG in which the new birth is experienced in conversion. Baptism in the name of Jesus conforms the believer to the NT pattern of Christian initiation. Spirit baptism is a second work of grace that gives the Christian power for ministry ... the other position, expressed in sacramental terms, identifies all three elements in Acts 2:38 as constituent of the new birth. To be born of water and Spirit (John 3:5) means to be baptized in the name of Jesus and to receive the Pentecostal experience of Spirit baptism ... The insistence that baptism is for the remission of sins (Acts 2:38) draws the charge of baptismal regeneration.[96]

The 'sacramental' group that Reed references is well-represented in this study. As seen in the early literature, 'by incorporating the third stage of Spirit baptism into the new birth' this sacramental group 'transfers the initial entry of the Spirit from the traditional conversion experience to the Pentecostal one', which creates a 'highly exclusive theology of salvation ... in which one is neither truly born again nor indwelled by the Spirit until the three stages of Acts 2:38 are completed'.[97] Reed rightly notes that Haywood and Urshan are two of the major proponents of this school of thought.

This study not only confirms Reed's assessment, but contributes to the body of research. The early Oneness baptismal theology surveyed almost universally expresses a sacramental view not only at the

---

[96] Reed, 'Oneness Pentecostalism', p. 651.
[97] Reed, 'Oneness Pentecostalism', p. 650.

explicit level through teachings, confessions, and theological articulations, but also at an implicit level of theological discourse found in testimonies and personal reflections. As seen throughout, there is a deeply sacramental character to the testimonies in which those being baptized experience the presence of the Spirit. Baptism proves to be an opportunity for a dynamic encounter with the living God. This study has shown that the New Birth doctrine and the ways Acts 2.38 and Jn 3.5 were received shaped a sacramental expectation among some early Oneness Pentecostals.

Furthermore, this study should give rise to discussion on Pentecostal sacramentality.[98] As I have argued elsewhere, some contemporary Trinitarian Pentecostal theologians are beginning to apply the sacramental quality of Pentecostal spirituality to their reflections on the Lord's Supper and water baptism.[99] While Chris Green has effectively shown that many early Trinitarian Pentecostals 'held a rather "high" view of the Lord's Supper, at the same time they held a relatively "low" view of water baptism'.[100] In contrast, this study demonstrates that early Oneness Pentecostals espoused a somewhat sacramental emphasis of baptism. As Oneness theologian David Norris has noted, Oneness Pentecostals have consistently understood water baptism to be a 'real action of the holy God'.[101]

In response to this study and others developing, one might consider the current 'revisioning' within contemporary Trinitarian Pentecostal scholarship to provide fresh opportunities for discussion between Oneness and Trinitarian Pentecostals on their theologies of baptism.[102] In particular, I suggest the emphasis upon the Holy Spirit's action in baptism warrants further reflection. In sum, it is my hope that this study may re-source the current conversation, and perhaps even provide further opportunities for dialogue between Oneness and Trinitarian Pentecostals. I trust that this study will inspire

---

[98] See especially, Chris E.W. Green, *Toward a Pentecostal Theology of the Lord's Supper: Foretasting the Kingdom* (Cleveland, TN: CPT Press, 2012).

[99] See Andrew Ray Williams, 'Water Baptism in Pentecostal Perspective: A Bibliographic Evaluation', *Spiritus* 4.1 (2019), pp. 69-97 (90).

[100] Green, *Toward a Pentecostal Theology of the Lord's Supper*, p. 328.

[101] David Norris, *I Am: A Oneness Pentecostal Theology* (Hazelwood, MO: WAP Academic, 2009), p. 191.

[102] Steven J. Land, *Pentecostal Spirituality: A Passion for the Kingdom* (JPTSup 1; Sheffield: Sheffield Academic Press, 1993), p. 7. For a report on a past dialogue, see 'Oneness-Trinitarian Pentecostal Final Report', *Pneuma* 30.2 (2008), pp. 203-24.

future Pentecostal scholars – Oneness and Trinitarian – to mine our rich histories.

Bibliography

Cartledge, Mark, 'Text–Community–Spirit: The Challenges Posed by Pentecostal Theological Method to Evangelical Theology', in Kevin L. Spawn and Archie T. Wright (eds.), *Spirit and Scripture: Exploring a Pneumatic Hermeneutic* (New York: T&T Clark, 2012).

Green, Chris E.W., *Toward a Pentecostal Theology of the Lord's Supper: Foretasting the Kingdom* (Cleveland, TN: CPT Press, 2012).

Jacobsen, Douglas, *Thinking in the Spirit: Theologies of the Early Pentecostal Movement* (Bloomington: Indiana University Press, 2003).

Land, Steven J., *Pentecostal Spirituality: A Passion for the Kingdom* (JPTSup 1; Sheffield: Sheffield Academic Press, 1993; Cleveland, TN: CPT Press, 2010).

Norris, David, *I Am: A Oneness Pentecostal Theology* (Hazelwood, MO: WAP Academic, 2009).

'Oneness-Trinitarian Pentecostal Final Report', *Pneuma* 30.2 (2008), pp. 203-24.

Reed, David A., *'In Jesus' Name': The History and Beliefs of Oneness Pentecostals* (JPTSup 31; Blandford Forum: Deo Publishing, 2008).

—'Oneness Pentecostalism', in Stanley B. Burgess, Gary B. McGee, and Patrick H. Alexanders (eds.), *Dictionary of Pentecostal and Charismatic Movements* (Grand Rapids: Regency Reference Library, 1988), pp. 644-51.

Williams, Andrew Ray, 'Water Baptism in Pentecostal Perspective: A Bibliographic Evaluation', *Spiritus* 4.1 (2019), pp. 69-97.

12

IDENTITY FORMATION IN AUSTRALIAN PENTECOSTALISM: A RECEPTION HISTORY OF ROMANS 8.37

STEVEN MAWSTON[*]

DENISE A. AUSTIN[**]

The Apostle Paul has been called an 'entrepreneur of identity' for his declaration, ὑπερνικῶμεν, which has been translated 'we are more than conquerors' (Rom. 8.37).[1] It is a recognition of the transformative power of Christ's love on the identity of early believers who were enduring external oppression and internal division. Pentecostal leaders of the Assemblies of God in Australia (AGA – later called Australian Christian Churches, or ACC) likewise used this term to shape corporate and personal identity. Although other studies have examined the growth and development of the Pentecostal movement in Australia,[2] there has been little attention given to how the movement received various biblical truths as statements of identity formation.

---

[*] Steven Mawston (MTh, Alphacrucis College, Australia) is a church leadership coach in Norwich, United Kingdom.

[**] Denise A. Austin (PhD, University of Queensland, Australia) is Deputy Vice President of Research and Standards and Professor of History, Alphacrucis College, Sydney, Australia.

[1] Philip Esler, *Conflict and Identity in Romans* (Minneapolis: Augsburg, 2003), p. 38.

[2] Shane Clifton, *Pentecostal Churches in Transition: Analysing the Developing Ecclesiology of the Assemblies of God in Australia* (Leiden: Brill, 2009); Barry Chant, *The*

This study focuses on three defining periods that reveal varying aspects of both corporate and individual identity formation.[3] First generation (1937–76) AGA pioneers sought courageously to forge a new identity outside traditional church denominations. By contrast, the second generation (1977–97) secured a foothold in the Australian religious landscape through expansionist church planting and rapid growth via a groundswell of charismatic renewal. The third generation (1997–2019) cemented the movement's reputation as one of the most influential Christian denominations in Australia and beyond through contemporary worship and megachurch leadership. After providing a biblical context, this research argues that, over time, AGA/ACC leaders have received Rom. 8.37 in an increasingly individualized manner from eschatological injunction, as a mandate for church growth, and finally, as a catch cry for personal empowerment.

Paul as an 'Entrepreneur of Identity'

The book of Romans was written by the Apostle Paul at a time when the church was in the early stages of forming its identity, in the face of internal pressures and external opposition. The Roman Empire was under the rule of Nero (54–68 CE) following the rule of Claudius (41–54 CE). Roman historian Suetonius recorded that Claudius issued an edict in 49 CE. He states, 'since the Jews constantly made disturbances at the instigation of Chrestus, he [Claudius] expelled them from Rome'.[4] Scholars believe this to be a reference to the same event mentioned in Acts 18.2. The edict lapsed when Claudius died in 54 CE, and many Jews returned to Rome by 58 CE. Although Nero's early reign was relatively peaceful, he later became a murderous tyrant. Paul wrote the book of Romans between these two periods of persecution perpetrated against the early Christians who were living in Rome, the capital of the all-conquering Roman Empire.[5]

Spirit of Pentecost: The Origins and Development of the Pentecostal Movement in Australia 1870–1939 (Lexington, KY: Emeth Press, 2011); Sam Hey, *Megachurches: Origins, Ministry, and Prospects* (Eugene, OR: Wipf & Stock, 2013).

[3] 'About Us', *Australian Christian Churches*, <http://www.acc.org.au/about-us/>.

[4] Suetonius, *De Vita Claudii* 25.4, Cited in Colin G. Kruse, *Paul's Letter to the Romans* (Grand Rapids: Eerdmans, 2012), p. 1.

[5] Kruse, *Paul's Letter to the Romans*, p. 1.

Modern scholarly literature is sensitive to the historical situatedness of the letter as well as its theological intent to establish corporate
and personal identity. Philip Esler uses the lens of Social Identity
Theory to examine the nature of Christian identity, namely, what it
means to be a Christian in a world where social conflict and suffering
is rife. He argues that Paul functions within a period of hardship, so
he exercises his leadership to persuade his audience to understand
their new and true identity in Christ. Esler defines leadership as 'the
process of influencing others in a manner that enhances their contribution to the realization of group goals'.[6] Therefore, Paul serves as
an 'entrepreneur of identity', a person who is capable of unifying
groups of people around a shared social identity, purpose, and goal.[7]

Craig Keener notes that Paul's use of ὑπερνικῶμεν ('we are more
than conquerors') is set against the twin polarities of two hardship
lists at the centre of a chiasmus in which the author repeats words in
reverse order. This rhetorical tool echoes the external realities of two
historical waves of persecution. The first hardship outlined in Rom.
8.35 lists seven different forms of suffering that the early believers
were experiencing, followed by a quotation from Ps. 44.22, which re-
inforces the perplexity of God's people in the face of such inexpli-
cable hardships.[8] The second hardship list in Rom. 8.38-39 catalogues
ten of the cosmic dimensions of suffering, listing heavenly ranks and
spiritual authorities including astrological terms.[9] The hardship lists
form the centre of a rhetorical chiasmus, which highlights the foundations of the believer's security and identity as super-abundant conquerors, despite being surrounded by both natural and cosmic oppo-
sitions.

Not only does Rom. 8.37 establish a secure foundation of faith
for believers, it also describes the transformative power of Christ's
love on the identity of those believers who are facing challenges. Sui
Fung Wu comments that the persecuted Christians 'displayed God's
glory by faithfully persevering in suffering'.[10] Rather than offering a
trite triumphalism, which negates the reality of the multi-faceted

---

[6] Esler, *Conflict and Identity in Romans*, p. 43.
[7] Esler, *Conflict and Identity in Romans*, p. 38.
[8] Leon Morris, *The Epistle to the Romans* (Grand Rapids: Eerdmans, 1988), p. 339.
[9] Craig S. Keener, *Romans: A New Covenant Commentary* (Philadelphia: Casemate
Publishers, 2011), p. 112.
[10] Su Fung Wu, *Suffering in Romans* (Cambridge: James Clarke & Co., 2016), p.
194.

challenges facing the first-century Roman church, Wu acknowledges that the victory can only be accomplished 'through him who loved us' (Rom. 8.37). ὑπερνικῶμεν ('We are more than conquerors') is a victory that is the antithesis of Rome's imperial conquering through military might and forced oppression. It is a super-victory that connects with the socio-political conditions of the first audience and is firmly rooted in Christ.[11] We are more than conquerors through a new nature of conquering. ὑπερνικῶμεν ('We are more than conquerors') is a word conceived by the Apostle Paul to establish the new and true identity of believers as super-conquerors, a term which reflects the intensity and totality of the victory which is corporately theirs through their relationship to the loving Christ, over all of the natural and supernatural powers that seek to oppose and oppress believers. ὑπερνικῶμεν ('We are more than conquerors') defines the victorious corporate and personal identity of those grounded in Christ's love, even in the face of extreme hardship.

ὑπερνικῶμεν ('We are more than conquerors') as First-Generation Identity Formation (1937–76)

The years 1937–76 designate the pioneering period for the AGA movement, when the first generation of its leaders interpreted and applied Rom. 8.37 as a key verse in its identity formation. ὑπερνικῶμεν ('We are more than conquerors') was interpreted by the AGA movement almost exclusively through the lens of the King James Version: 'Nay in all these things we are more than conquerors through Him that loved us' (KJV). While there has been a recent proliferation of different translations, the phrase 'we are more than conquerors' remains the one most commonly used within Australian Pentecostalism.

The first-generation period (1937–76) was marked by a series of devastating world events, including: the Great Depression of the 1930s, World War II (1939–45), the Malayan Emergency (1948–60), the Cold War, the Korean War (1950–53), and the Vietnam War (1962–72). In light of these events, church leaders interpreted Rom.

---

[11] Wu, *Suffering in Romans*, p. 195.

8.37 through the lens of eschatological injunction, social exclusion, spiritual oppression and hope for the future.[12]

Eschatological Injunction

When the AGA was formed in 1937, pioneer leaders sought to establish a new identity in response to an eschatological injunction. The first AGA general superintendent, Charles Greenwood, wrote,

> How we shall need to take unto ourselves the whole armor of God in the days that are now almost upon us. By what other means can the Church hope to conquer, only as she is clothed upon and standing in the power and demonstration of the Holy Spirit.[13]

Just two years later, Australians were plunged into World War II with all its accompanying trauma and shaken identity.[14]

The 1940 edition of *Australian Evangel and Glad Tidings Messenger* is full of conquering imagery: 'His eyes upon the year', 'forward march', 'this is no time to sleep', 'the attitude of the Christian towards war', 'the four great powers of the end time', 'Rome's empire revived', 'a great power in the north', and 'great military forces in the Orient'.[15] The cruelty and uncertainty of war caused AGA leaders to interpret ὑπερνικῶμεν ('we are more than conquerors') in terms of eschatological urgency. Barry Chant reveals that, between 1910 and 1945, in the AGA's denominational magazine, *Australian Evangel and Glad Tidings Messenger,* over 17% of articles mention the second coming of Christ and pre-tribulation premillennialism.[16]

The perceived imminence of Christ's return caused leaders to issue a trumpet call for believers to rise up as ὑπερνικῶμεν ('we are more than conquerors') against the spiritual powers which opposed them. One example of this call to arms is the 1944 article in another

---

[12] For further examples, see W.H. Akehurst, 'Spiritual Fitness', *AEGTM* 12.10 (September, 1946), p. 12; A.G. Bennett, 'The Rocky Road to Victory', *AEGTM* 17.2 (February 1951), pp. 17-19.

[13] Charles Greenwood, 'The Church and the World When Jesus Comes', *AEGTM* 4.10 (September 1938), p. 2.

[14] Joan Beaumont, *Australia's War, 1939–45* (Sydney: Allen & Unwin, 1996), p. 1.

[15] *AEGTM* 6 (1940), pp. 3-9.

[16] Barry Chant, 'Preaching in the Spirit: The Content and Focus of Pentecostal Preaching in Australia 1910–1939', *Pentecostal and Charismatic Bible Colleges* (Sydney: January 2002).

AGA magazine entitled 'The Conquest of Joy', which encouraged readers to stand against end time adversaries. It utilizes words and phrases such as: 'victory', 'spiritual warfare', 'advancing people', 'occupying new territory', 'common raid', 'setting up banners', 'counterattacks', 'advancement', 'dispossessing', 'an army terrible with banners', 'battle cry', 'shock troops', and 'carrying the flag to new fields'.[17] Early Pentecostals saw beyond the natural realm of the physical war the Australian nation was fighting, and saw themselves participating as ὑπερνικῶμεν ('we are more than conquerors') in a spiritual war that was a signpost for the return of Christ.

Following the lead of the British Assemblies of God, many AGA members stood as conscientious objectors.[18] The Australian church planter Lloyd Averill successfully argued his pacifist stance in a magistrate's court. Although a pacifist in the natural war, Averill saw himself as a victor in gathering in the end-times harvest. He ignored 'The Brisbane Line' from Brisbane to Adelaide,[19] which represented the territory that the Australian government thought could realistically be defended in the event of an enemy invasion.[20] Lloyd and his wife Edith crossed 'The Brisbane Line' in 1944, moving from Melbourne to Gordonvale in northeast Queensland to pioneer an AGA church.[21] The Averills epitomized the pioneering spirit of the AGA first generation, seeking to forge a new identity and possess new territory as ὑπερνικῶμεν ('we are more than conquerors').[22]

Reaction against Social Exclusion
The AGA interpretation of Rom. 8.37 as a corporate victory over external oppression also reveals the social exclusion faced by pioneer Australian Pentecostals. By the end of 1945, 60 million people had died across the world because of the war, including 40 thousand

---

[17] H. Luke, 'The Conquest of Joy', *Harvest Grain* 2 (October 1944), pp. 14-16.

[18] Luke, 'The Conquest of Joy', p. 27.

[19] Sean Maher, *The Brisbane Line*, Documentary, Short, Crime, 2010, accessed August 31, 2019, http://www.imdb.com/title/tt1705053/.

[20] Drew Cottle, 'The Brisbane Line: An Episode in Capital History', *Journal of Australian Studies* 25.69 (January 1, 2001), pp. 113-21.

[21] Murray Averill, interview by Stephen Mawston, Brisbane, May 2018.

[22] Denise A. Austin and Jacqueline Grey, 'The "Outback Spirit" of Pentecostal Women Pioneers in Australia', in Margaret English de Alminana and Lois E. Olena (eds.), *Women in Pentecostal and Charismatic Ministry: Informing a Dialogue on Gender, Church, and Ministry* (Leiden: Brill, 2017), p. 204.

Australians.[23] As Australia gradually began to rebuild its social, political, and religious framework, the wider community continued to marginalize AGA constituents.

One interviewee explained, 'The non-acceptance of Pentecostals in community involvement and clergy gatherings meant we … often got the cold shoulder. We had to gain confidence.'[24] Another added, 'They called us "holy rollers" and "of the devil". Tomatoes were thrown at us and drunks made fun of us in the streets.'[25] A woman said, 'I remember at the age of ten neighbors throwing stones at people because they were Pentecostals, in Chinchilla church with the Averills as pioneer pastors'.[26] Social exclusion heightened and affirmed the need for AGA first generation pioneers to redefine victory in the context of their oppression.

This social exclusion also affected young students who sought to be trained in Christian ministry. In 1947, a group of AGA youth all wanted to go to Bible college together. They applied to every college in Australia, but their applications were rejected because they spoke in tongues.[27] One interviewee states, 'we had to try to prove we were normal people and not nutty Pentecostals who climbed walls'.[28] Her husband adds, 'we experienced persecution from mainline church groups that we were of the devil and a cult. We claimed the verses in Rom. 8.36–39.'[29] Eventually, the interdenominational Sydney Bible Training Institute accepted the eight Pentecostal students. However, they all soon withdrew their enrolments when severely reprimanded for holding a Pentecostal prayer meeting. After pleading their case directly to the AGA national leaders, Commonwealth Bible College (CBC) was opened in 1948.

Response to Spiritual Oppression

The first-generation pioneers also saw the need to establish a new identity as ὑπερνικῶμεν ('we are more than conquerors') in response to perceived 'spiritual warfare'. The war years had taught people the

---

[23] Denise A. Austin, *Our College: A History of the National College of Australian Christian Churches (Assemblies of God in Australia)* (Sydney: Australasian Pentecostal Studies, 2013), pp. 29-30.

[24] Laine Willis, interview by Steven Mawston, Brisbane, March 2017.

[25] Audrey Jones, interview by Steven Mawston, Brisbane, March 2017.

[26] Janice Boddy, interview by Steven Mawston, Brisbane, March 2017.

[27] Austin, *Our College*, p. 32.

[28] Margaret Goode, interview Steven Mawston, Brisbane, March 2017.

[29] Ron Goode, interview Steven Mawston, Brisbane, March 2017.

very real destruction that an enemy could cause, and post-war AGA was very aware of the reality of a spiritual enemy at large 'seeking whom he may devour'.

In the aftermath of the war years, in which the Allies emerged physically victorious, the name 'Conquerors' was chosen by the second cohort of CBC students in 1949. A poem written by a CBC student entitled, 'We are Conquerors', reflects the call to triumph with Christ against the invisible enemy,

> CONQUERORS, Awake! For the trumpet is sounding!
> Awake to its call and obey;
> The voice of our leader cries, 'Onward!'
> So let us no longer delay.
> Conquerors, gird on the Sword of the Spirit,
> With helmet and breastplate and shield,
> And willingly follow your Captain,
> Determined you never will yield.
> March forward, Conquerors for Jesus,
> With hearts that are loyal and brave,
> Stand firm by the Cross and its banner,
> And trust in the 'Mighty to Save'.[30]

The totality of victory was assured because of their belief in the completeness of the victory that was theirs in Christ. AGA general superintendent Ralph Read wrote,

> We are CONQUERORS because of our attachment to a mighty, conquering savior. We are CONQUERORS because Christ is above all, and is our pre-eminent leader ... His conquests are forever sure ... As CONQUERORS we will be in earnest conquest, sincere in our devotion to a living Christ.[31]

Alongside the completed victory of Christ was the tension of an ongoing spiritual war. The spiritual enemies manifested through ecclesiastical suspicion and social marginalization. Perceptions of smallness and segregation were compounded by the AGA worldview of 'separation' as a form of protection against the vices of

---

[30] Mary Edwards, 'We Are Conquerors', *C.B.C. Yukana* (Brisbane: R.G. Gillies & Co., 1949), p. 20, emphasis original.

[31] Ralph Read, 'Conquerors', *AE, Special Bible College Issue* 16 (November 1950), p. 11, emphasis original.

worldliness. Speaking about AGA interpretations of Rom. 8.37 in this period, Andrew Evans (later AGA general superintendent) comments,

> If you wanted the full blessing of God and total anointing, you had to come out and be separate. Then they decided what's holy and what isn't. They felt small, and that feeling kept them small… It was the condemnation you got if you didn't keep all of the laws.[32]

The pervasive influence of legalistic teaching and internal condemnation amplified the experiences of marginalization and suspicion.

Hope for the Future
Wolfgang Vondey argues that after World War II the eschatological injunction saw an increased missionary focus to ensure the survival of Pentecostalism.[33] In Australia, CBC became a hub of missionary training and mobilization with a strong focus on Papua New Guinea.

Simultaneously, the worldwide 'charismatic renewal' was having a significant influence on emerging AGA leaders, such as Andrew Evans (Paradise Christian Church in Adelaide), David Cartledge (Calvary Temple in Townsville), and Reg Klimionok (Garden City Christian Church in Brisbane).[34] The 'charismatic renewal' meant that believers in other denominations were experiencing gifts like 'speaking in tongues' and adopting a more sympathetic approach to Pentecostals. Some of the ecclesiological suspicion was softened. AGA churches began to grow in numbers and influence, becoming less parochial in their approach gradually began morphing them from a persecuted minority to a more positive spirit as ὑπερνικῶμεν ('we are more than conquerors').

In the Silver Jubilee edition of *Yukana* 1971–72, as Australian soldiers joined the Americans in the Vietnam War, the graduating class again chose Rom. 8.37 as their key text, but rather than calling themselves 'Conquerors' they chose 'Victors'. This seems to suggest that

---

[32] Andrew Evans, personal interview by Steven Mawston, Gold Coast, March 21, 2018.

[33] Wolfgang Vondey, *Beyond Pentecostalism: The Crisis of Global Christianity and the Renewal of the Theological Agenda* (Grand Rapids: Eerdmans, 2010), p. 158.

[34] Denise A. Austin and Shane Clifton, 'Australian Pentecostalism: From Marginalised to Megachurches', in Denise A. Austin, Jacqueline Grey, and Paul W. Lewis (eds.), *Asia Pacific Pentecostalism* (Leiden: Brill, 2019), p. 372.

the ecclesiological suspicion was gradually dissipating as believers in other denominations began to experience the charismatic gifts. The tone of 'Victors' is significantly more optimistic than 'Conquerors'. One article in the college magazine states,

> Our class selected the name of 'Victors' with the accompanying text of Romans 8:37. It is our desire to do great things for God that He may be pleased with us in all things for we know that in His strength we are more than conquerors. CBC has developed, molded, guided and changed our lives for this purpose, and so as we enter the ministry, this is our desire – to be used by God.[35]

First generation AGA leaders were a minority who encountered social exclusion and were familiar with the imagery of conquest and war. While the intensity of persecution cannot be compared to early Christians in Rome, AGA pioneers were still aware of the reality of suffering and grew in their revelation that they were ὑπερνικῶμεν ('we are more than conquerors').

ὑπερνικῶμεν ('We are more than conquerors') as a Mandate for Second-Generation Growth (1977–97)

The year 1977 was a watershed for the AGA movement, as second-generation leaders interpreted and applied Rom. 8.37 as a mandate for growth. Australian society was also in a period of transition. The war in Vietnam had ended and the resignation of Prime Minister Don Chipp signaled the demise of the two-party political system in Australia. Historian Hugh Mackay describes this period as the Age of Redefinition, as every Australian institution was subject to radical change or challenge.[36]

In April 1977, Andrew Evans became AGA general superintendent at the Commonwealth conference in Melbourne. He served for an unprecedented 20 years and made significant changes to AGA that resulted in a period of sustained growth. Through the leadership of Evans, the second-generation period is marked by an emerging social identity, an increasing commitment to church growth, and a growing faith for personal overcoming.

---

[35] 'History', *C.B.C. Yukana* (Brisbane: 1972), p. 15
[36] 'History', p. 15.

Emerging Social Identity

Phillip Esler's application of Social Identity Theory in his reading of the book of Romans, defines a leader as

> someone who is highly adept through argument, negotiation, and persuasion at managing the debate, by neutralizing views antagonistic to his or her own and by stimulating a process of consensualization around a particular vision of group identity.[37]

It is reasonable to apply this definition to the leadership of Evans, and suggest that he, also, functioned as an 'entrepreneur of identity' within the AGA. His rhetoric was highly influential in challenging existing AGA perceptions to align with a new and enlarged personal and social identity.

Evans intentionally gleaned teachings from global ministries that created a desire to challenge and break free of limiting social identities. While first generation pioneers avoided secular entertainment, such as television and cinemas, Evans actively encouraged the use of the media to spread the gospel. He preached to over 10 thousand people each week via his Paradise Christian Family television broadcast. Evans writes, 'So often we have had inferiority about the media. We have been thinking we aren't good enough. But God can use you!'[38] This is a good example of 'overcoming' as Evans intentionally sought to dismantle the internal smallness and separatism of the AGA, and to foster a more expansionist approach.

Increasing Commitment to Church Growth

The subsequent shift in worldview of the AGA gave rise to the term 'Apostolic Revolution' and a consequent commitment to growth.[39] The 1977 AGA Commonwealth Conference featured David (Paul) Yonggi Cho as guest speaker.[40] At that time, his church in Seoul,

---

[37] Esler, *Conflict and Identity in Romans*, pp. 37-39.

[38] Cited in Denise A. Austin, '"Flowing Together": The Origins and Early Development of Hillsong Church within Assemblies of God in Australia', in Tanya Riches and Tom Wager (eds.), *The Hillsong Movement Examined: You Call Me Out Upon The Waters* (Melbourne: Palgrave McMillan, 2017), p. 3.

[39] David Cartledge, *The Apostolic Revolution: The Restoration of Apostles and Prophets in the Assemblies of God in Australia* (Sydney: Paraclete Institute, 2000), p. 95. Key agents of change were Donald McGavran and Peter Wagner of the Institute of Church Growth, Fuller Theological Seminary, as well as David (Paul) Yonggi Cho of Yoido Full Gospel Assembly in South Korea.

[40] Clifton, *Pentecostal Churches in Transition*, p. 157.

South Korea was the largest in the world. Cho's faith message greatly impacted the AGA movement. Cho hosted 240 AGA leaders and members at his church in Korea to expand their vision for church growth.[41] Evans describes Cho as his mentor stating, 'A lot of Dr Cho's principles and insights rubbed off onto me'.[42] By the next biennial conference, the AGA had grown by 68%, and then by another 128 percent during the following period. Cho's teachings centered on the importance of having faith, vision, and recognizing one's authority as a believer.[43]

These principles that reshaped the sense of identity as 'more than conquerors' extended from Evans right through the AGA movement. Pastors returned from visiting Korea to set significant growth goals, as a tangible response to their new sense of faith, to become true 'conquerors'. Between 1976 and 1981 the AGA grew by 87 percent.[44]

Growing Faith for Personal Overcoming
The successful growth of the AGA led to rhetoric of overcoming in practical areas of life. Evans challenged AGA constituents to become 'overcomers' in a range of practical areas of life.[45] AGA literature in this second-generation period evidences this. One poem published in the movement's magazine, entitled 'The Victor', declares:

I see the darts still burning with the flames of hell
I hear the Accuser's voice still ringing in my ears
I rise determined, once again to win this war
And overcome the mighty foe
I'll need to put my armour on
And exercise my faith
To stand in truth and righteousness
My feet announcing peace
I'll put my hand in His right hand

---

[41] Cartledge, *The Apostolic Revolution*, p. 95.
[42] Denise A. Austin, *Jesus First: The Life and Leadership of Andrew Evans* (Sydney: Australasian Pentecostal Studies, 2017), pp. 133-35.
[43] David Yonggi Cho, *The Fourth Dimension* (Monroe, LA: Logos International, 1979).
[44] Denise A. Austin, '"A Contagious Church": Theological Influences of Pentecostalism in Sydney 1916–2016', *St Mark's Review* 242 (December 4, 2017), p. 20.
[45] Andrew Evans, 'The Importance of Self Esteem', *AE* 41.6 (June 1984), p. 3.

To gain that extra strength
And I'll return a conqueror
Much strengthened in this test.[46]

The positive thinking interpretation of 'we are more than conquerors' is evidenced in a sermon by Cartledge,

> Success comes in cans! You can succeed. You can overcome, you can. You can, you can through Jesus Christ. There is no situation which God will allow us to face which we need to fail in. In ALL things we are able to be more than conquerors through Him that loved us … Dr Yonggi Cho pastor of the world's largest church, has coined a fabulous phrase. Somehow this has gotten into my spirit. It is 'I AM A CAN DO PERSON'. We are not called to mediocrity but success.[47]

The more personal focus of interpretations in this period is frequently accompanied by encouragements or instructions to believers to take specific personal faith actions. Klimionok writes,

> If you have never experienced or tasted the Victory, I urge you, plead with you to live by the power that God has given you, indeed step out and possess your possessions. Use the scriptures, the infallible Word in confession daily. When you greet the Lord each morning take and confess before Him His word as 'I am more than a conqueror' … CONFESS the scripture daily. USE your authority in Christ. OVERCOME Satan by the word of your testimony.[48]

The emphasis on personal faith is reflected in an AGA correspondence course entitled, 'Abundantly Victorious',

> Mark these tremendous statements 'If God is for us, who can be against us … we are more than conquerors … give thanks to God who always leads us in triumph …' All of these biblical statements are true of every believer in Christ. But they will not automatically

---

[46] Yvonne Johnson, 'The Victor', *AE* 41 (September 1984), p. 13.
[47] David Cartledge, 'Success Comes in Cans', Sermon, Calvary Temple, Townsville, n.d., emphasis original.
[48] Reg Klimionok, 'The Believer's Authority in Christ', *AE* 36.4 (April 1979), p. 3.

work in your life. You must call them into reality. You must transform the promise into performance.[49]

The increasingly personalized ὑπερνικῶμεν ('we are more than conquerors') was interpreted as turning a 'promise into performance' with the onus on the believer. As well as being definitive, this personal performative faith is also distinctive, as it refers to practical areas of life such as self-esteem and self-image. Rather than being victorious against eternal hardships, ὑπερνικῶμεν ('we are more than conquerors') symbolizes the battle for a pure mind.

The corporate strengthening and personalized statements represent actions that are required by the body of believers for expansionist church growth. They also guide how believers fortify themselves in order to live in the authority of their true identity.

ὑπερνικῶμεν ('We are more than conquerors') as Third-Generation Personal Empowerment (1997–2019)

The year 1997 proved to be a key turning point for the movement with the selection of Brian Houston of Hillsong Church to the position of AGA national president. During his tenure (1997–2009), third-generation leaders increasingly interpreted Rom. 8.37 as a mandate for personal empowerment. This period coincided closely with the long term of John Howard as Prime Minister (1996–2007). The nation saw strong social and economic resilience thanks to its vast natural resources. Australia survived the crashes of the digital age, the tech wreck, the Asian depression, and the 'global financial crisis'.[50] As social commentator George Megalogenis comments, 'The rest of the world wants to know if Australia has cracked globalisation's secret code of prosperity'.[51]

Adding to the general perception of stability, the increasing personalization of ὑπερνικῶμεν ('we are more than conquerors') in this period reflects the rise of the 'megachurch' or 'empowered church' movement. This post-charismatic era led to a preference of the term 'empowered' rather than Pentecostal, charismatic, full

---

[49] Ken Chant, *Faith Dynamics* (Unit 7; Diploma Correspondence Course, 1980), p. 4.

[50] George Megalogenis, *The Australian Moment* (Melbourne: Penguin Group Australia, 2012), p. 1.

[51] Megalogenis, *The Australian Moment*.

gospel or other nomenclatures.[52] The goal is personal empowerment of individual believers through building a culture of flourishing in all areas of life. Believers are called to encounter God personally through corporate dynamic praise and worship music. In this way, believers can be fortified to face the challenges of life. Remarkably, 67 percent of references to Rom. 8.37 in the *Australian Evangel* during this period refer to personal identity that demonstrates the shifting focus.

Personal Empowerment
As national president of the rebranded Australian Christian Churches (ACC), Houston initiated cultural and theological changes that increasingly focused the constituency on personal empowerment. The Hillsong mission statement was 'To reach and influence the world by building a large Christ-centred, Bible-based church, changing mindsets and empowering people to lead and impact in every sphere of life'.[53] Other multi-site megachurches within the ACC were also impacting Australian Christianity, including Planetshakers Church and Influencers Church, both led by sons of Andrew Evans.

Houston fostered a close association with North American megachurch leaders, such as Bill Hybels and Rick Warren, who effectively served as models of personal empowerment in order to flourish in life. Houston's leadership aimed intentionally to change mindsets and empower individual believers to lead and influence in every sphere of life.

Houston's sermon on Rom. 8.37 at the 2016 Hillsong Men's Conference was entitled 'Conquest'. He states,

> The phrase 'more than conquerors' occurs only once in the Bible. In Greek, it's the word *hypernikomen*. *Hyper* comes from hyperactive. It's an intensifier, it's excessive, and it's over the top. The

---

[52] Vinson Synan and Amos Yong, 'Series Preface', in Vinson Synan and Amos Yong (eds.), *Global Renewal Christianity: Spirit-Empowered Movements Past, Present, and Future – Volume One Asia and Oceania*, (Lake Mary, FL: Charisma House, 2016), p. xv.
[53] Hillsong Church, 'Vision', accessed August 27, 2019, <https://hillsong.com/vision/>. Power Ministry School (later renamed Hillsong International Leadership College) attracted students from across the globe and millions of viewers tune in to Hillsong TV. Hillsong Channel, accessed August 27, 2019, <https://hillsongchannel.com/>.

second part is *nikomen* from the word *nike*. *Nike* means victory ... Let's understand that we are called through Jesus Christ, in Him, to be excessively victorious. We are *hyper nike men*.[54]

Central to this core belief is the concept of being 'an overcomer' and a 'conqueror', taking personal responsibility to walk in the calling to be excessively victorious in Christ. Like Andrew Evans in the previous generation, Houston has served as an 'entrepreneur of identity' across ACC, skillfully persuading and inspiring people towards the realization of a shared identity and corporate purpose of pursuing their victorious life in Christ.[55]

Culture of Flourishing

A recent use of overcoming language focuses upon financial flourishing.[56] Shane Clifton traces this 'philosophy of prosperity' back to Yonggi Cho's 'theology of blessing'.[57] Houston argues that Christians are 'blessed to be a blessing', and that prosperity comes with the purpose of blessing others and causing their lives to flourish.[58] He writes,

God is committed to seeing you succeed and He desires to complete what He has started in your life. Your faith will be tested, and there will be times when you face the temptation to abandon the principles of God, but the key is to take on the spirit of an overcomer.[59]

The concept of flourishing encompasses well-being, a meaningful life, and deep relationships.[60] This idea is encapsulated in the purpose statement of The Hillsong Foundation, namely, 'Empowering people with opportunities through a large variety of programs which impact

---

[54] Brian Houston, *Hillsong Men's Conference 2016: Conquest* (Sydney, 2016).

[55] Linda Morris, 'Pentecostal Revolution in the Suburbs', *Sydney Morning Herald* (June 28, 2007), accessed May 27, 2019. Pentecostalism thrived in Australia, growing 26% between 1997 and 2007, with a notable growth of 48% in Hillsong's home state of New South Wales.

[56] Greg Bearup, 'The Lord's Profits', *Sydney Morning Herald* (January 2003), pp. 14-21.

[57] Clifton, *Pentecostal Churches in Transition*, p. 163.

[58] Brian Houston, *How To Maximise Your Life* (Sydney: Hillsong Music Australia, 2013), p. 20.

[59] Houston, *How To Maximise Your Life*, p. 42.

[60] Shane Clifton, Gwynnyth Llewellyn, and Tom Shakespeare, 'Quadriplegia, Virtue Theory, and Flourishing: A Qualitative Study Drawing on Self-Narratives', *Disability and Society* 33.1 (2018), p. 21.

and help prisoners, the sick, single parents and others needing support'.[61]

Elizabeth Miller argues that a major key to the success of ACC churches is the ability to meet individual needs in sync with a growing emphasis on individualism in secular Australia.[62] Individual aspiration is encouraged as an expression of individual purpose within the corporate mission, positively influencing both individuals in need and society. As Shane Clifton succinctly says, 'The consequence for the individual and the church is increasing affluence for the sake of increasing influence for the kingdom of God'.[63]

Encountering God through Praise and Worship

Third-generation interpretations of Rom. 8.37 are also seen through the medium of music. Donald E. Miller and Tetsunao Yamamori note that the rapid growth of Pentecostalism globally has been partly attributed to expressive praise and worship.[64] This has certainly been true of Hillsong Church. The 2008 album *You are Here* emphasizes particularly the theme of conquering. Drawing on both Rom. 8.11 and Rom. 8.37, the cover song states,

> The same power that conquered the grave
> Lives in me, Lives in me
> Your love that rescued the earth
> Lives in me, lives in me.[65]

The iconic *Desert Song* lyrics announce:

> I will rejoice
> I will declare
> God is my victory and He is here
> And this is my prayer in my battle
> When triumph is still on its way
> I am a conqueror and co-heir with Christ

[61] Clifton, *Pentecostal Churches in Transition*, p. 165.
[62] Elizabeth Miller, *A Planting of the Lord: Contemporary Pentecostal and Charismatic Christianity in Australia* (PhD dissertation, University of Sydney, 2015), p. 116.
[63] Clifton, *Pentecostal Churches in Transition*, p. 197.
[64] Donald E. Miller and Tetsunao Yamamori, *Global Pentecostalism: The New Face of Christian Social Engagement* (Berkeley: University of California Press, 2007), p. 23.
[65] 'Hillsong – You are Here', *YouTube*, accessed August 27, 2019, <https://www.youtube.com/watch?v=-2J9Ia0X6WE>.

So firm on His promise I'll stand.[66]

This deeply personal interpretation of ὑπερνικῶμεν ('we are more than conquerors') has become the inspirational norm for third-generation worshippers, not only in Australia but around the world.[67]

It may not be the music alone which forms the conquering identity. Tom Wagner views the sound of Hillsong through the lens of media ecology to explain how Hillsong's music, or 'brand', empowers believers to experience God.[68] This expression of praise and worship contains the successful formula of brand awareness and personal encounter with the presence of God. Mark Evans argues that Hillsong's signature sound serves as a 'marker of identity' for contemporary worshippers.[69] One secular journalist concludes that the Hillsong sound symbolizes 'bright, contemporary, victorious Christianity'.[70] Therefore, if a specific sound is a marker of 'identity', then the 'victorious sound' expressed through praise and worship is indeed one of a victorious identity, which empowers believers personally to encounter God.

Intentional Fortification

A focus on personal fortification, through the reception of Rom. 8.37, can be seen, not only in Hillsong, but across all ACC churches. While Australian Pentecostal praise and worship compositions have become a rich resource for churches from the smallest congregations to the nation's megachurches, music has been one of the most obvious vehicles for sharing their victorious identity.

This shared identity is attested through data collected from Christian Copyright Licensing International (CCLI),[71] a company that enables and simplifies access to licensing and copyright services for

---

[66] 'Desert Song – Hillsong Worship', *YouTube*, <https://www.youtube.com/watch?v=HUISd7LSxAQ>.

[67] This redefinition of individualization of the spiritual conqueror clearly resonated with Christians worldwide. In 2016, Hillsong United won a Billboard Award and, in 2018, a Grammy for the song 'What a Beautiful Name'. Recording Academy, Grammy Awards, <https://www.grammy.com/grammys/videos/hillsong-worship-win-best-contemporary-christian-songperformance-2018-grammys>.

[68] Tom Wagner, 'The "Powerful" Hillsong Brand', in Tanya Riches and Tom Wager (eds.), *The Hillsong Movement Examined: You Call Me Out Upon The Waters* (Melbourne: Palgrave McMillan, 2017), p. 253.

[69] Evans, 'Creating the Hillsong Sound', p. 73.

[70] Peter Munro, 'Raising Hell For Jesus', *Sydney Morning Herald* (May 19, 2013).

[71] Nate Scott (Intellectual Property Manager of Christian Copyright Licensing International), email correspondence with Steven Mawston (November 14, 2017).

Christian music.[72] For the purposes of this research, an analysis of a CCLI data report from 2,115 Pentecostal churches currently registered in Australia,[73] included 860 Australian Pentecostal churches in 2017.[74] CCLI's 'Church Count' report showed actual songs used in Australian Pentecostal worship services, identifying all variations of the word 'conquer', 'victory', and 'overcome'. The reported songs contained 1,313 references to the word groups in total, which can be broken down as follows: 'conquerors' (304), 'victory' (679), and 'overcome' (330). The data demonstrates that Pentecostal churches in Australia utilize songs which express the concept of personal fortification, associated with ὑπερνικῶμεν ('we are more than conquerors').

Further analysis of this data reveals that 20 songs sung in Australian Pentecostal churches in 2017 featured the actual words 'more than conquerors'. Six were called 'we are more than conquerors' (or a close variation of these words), three featured the phrase in the bridge, and other songs quote Rom. 8.37 in a verse. For example, one song from Wade Iedema, a Brisbane-based songwriter who wrote 'More Than a Conqueror'.[75]

This is the reason why, Jesus came and died.
And Jesus is the biggest winner ever, so If I believe in Him,
Trust Him to get me through,
I am more, more, more than a conqueror.
I am more, more, more than a conqueror.
No I won't be giving up in this race,
I am more, more than a conqueror.

---

[72] CCLI 'About CCLI', <https://au.ccli.com/about-ccli/>.

[73] The search terms for the report were: (1) Only Churches in Australia. (2) Songs reported in 2017. (3) Only Pentecostal Churches. (4) Variations of the word 'conquer' in titles or lyrics and the words 'victory' and 'overcome'. (5) Songs reported by at least one of these Churches. The report covered all Australian Pentecostal Churches.

[74] Australian Pentecostal denominations who reported were Southern Cross Association of Churches, Assoc. Mission Churches of Australasia, ACC Australian Christian Churches (AOG/CLC), Assemblies of God (ACC), C3 Church (Christian City Church International), Christian Outreach Centers, CRC International, Full Gospel Church, Foursquare Gospel Church, Rhema (Family Church), New Life Churches, Independent Charismatic, Association of Vineyard Churches, Christian Life Churches International (CLCI), Apostolic Church of Australia, Pentecostal – Other.

[75] 'Lifetone: Songs For a Broken Life', <http://www.lifetone.com/>.

Now there is no trial that I can't face,
I am more, more than a conqueror.[76]

Significantly, the song lyrics refer to 'I' as the first person singular 17 times. The song is intensely personal and empowering, repeating eight times that the individual believer is 'more than a conqueror'.

Interestingly, the lyrics of the songs sung in Pentecostal churches emphasize the corporate emphasis of 'we' in the phrase 'we are more than Conquerors', based on the traditional translation of Rom. 8.37. However, the majority of the lyrics explored the personal struggles a believer faces in their individual journey. The following lyrics were written by Nolene Prince, one of the founders of Resource Christian Music based in Melbourne.[77]

Jesus closer than a friend
Jesus with me to the end
Jesus taking all my pain
Wiping all my tears away
Turning them to healing rain
Jesus dearer than all life
Jesus Lamb of sacrifice
Jesus watching over me
Every day in every way
You make us more than conquerors[78]

The lyrics express an intimate portrayal of a personal encounter of Jesus 'wiping all my tears away'. ACC applications of what it means to be ὑπερνικῶμεν ('we are more than conquerors') are expressed through a series of declarative statements that worshippers experience through the lyrics of their Pentecostal worship praxis.

Third-generation ACC leaders have almost exclusively interpreted ὑπερνικῶμεν ('we are more than conquerors') as intentional fortification, with little ecclesiological, eschatological, or missiological corporate reference in the literature. The rise of 'empowered churches' in this period of ACC history serves as the foundation for the empowerment of individual believers. Houston served as an

---

[76] CCLI Song Search, 'More Than a Conqueror', CCLI song number 2976873, <https://au.search.ccli.com/>.
[77] RCM Publications, 'About the Founders', <http://www.re-source.com.au/about-us>.
[78] CCLI Song Search, 'More Than a Conqueror'.

'entrepreneur of identity', empowering leaders to lead and influence in every sphere of life, as excessively victorious 'hyper nike' people.[79] The experiential application of ὑπερνικῶμεν ('we are more than conquerors') is evident in the personal empowerment of believers through an infusion of the Holy Spirit's presence and encounters with God through praise and worship.

The year 2018 marked the end of the third generation with Hillsong Church announcing that it was registering with the Australian government as a separate denomination. While Hillsong retains an associated relationship with the ACC, Hillsong also needed the space to grow independently. Houston writes,

> As Hillsong Church has continued to grow, we no longer see ourselves as an Australian Church with a global footprint, but rather a Global church with an Australian base … Two thirds of the people attending Hillsong Church each weekend live in countries beyond Australia … It is my great hope that the church in Australia will continue to be healthy and unified … And it is my belief and my prayer that, by the grace of God, all our churches will continue to flourish and grow.[80]

Although Houston had resigned as ACC national president a decade before, Hillsong has continued to have a strong impact on the ACC movement. With this newly reframed 'partnership', it remains to be seen how the next generation of ACC leaders will receive Rom. 8.37 and what this will mean for the future shaping of the movement and Australian Pentecostalism overall. Most likely, the evocative power of this verse will continue to motivate both corporate and individual empowerment.

Conclusion

Paul's expression ὑπερνικῶμεν, commonly translated 'we are more than conquerors' in Rom. 8.37, has been used as a source of inspiration for Pentecostal faith. As an 'entrepreneur of identity', the Apostle Paul uses ὑπερνικῶμεν ('we are more than conquerors') as a fortification against hardship. However, reception history of

---

[79] Houston, *Hillsong Men's Conference 2016*.
[80] Brian Houston, 'Letter to ACC Pastors' (September 19, 2018).

ὑπερνικῶμεν ('we are more than conquerors') within the AGA/ACC reveals an evolving complex interplay and influence of a number of external and internal factors. The factors are relative to and regulated by the internal growth and strength of ACC, as well as the skilled leadership of 'entrepreneurs of identity'.

First-generation AGA pioneers used Rom 8.37 to combat the marginalization, suspicion, opposition, and hardship they faced within Australian society. These external factors produced an enhanced sensitivity within AGA interpretations to eschatological, spiritual, social, and ecclesiological realities. Second-generation leaders saw ὑπερνικῶμεν ('we are more than conquerors') as an unmasking of their true identity through an emerging social identity, an increasing commitment to church growth, and a growing faith for personal overcoming. Andrew Evans served as an 'entrepreneur of identity', by challenging and enlarging the social identity of the movement and by inspiring believers to understand their personal identity/authority, as overcomers in the daily life. Finally, Brian Houston stands as an archetypal 'entrepreneur of identity' for third-generation ACC leaders. He views ὑπερνικῶμεν ('we are more than conquerors') as a mandate for personal empowerment through the Holy Spirit and encounters with God through praise and worship.

As ACC leaders consider their future, it remains to be seen if the days of marginalization and hardship are a thing of the past, if a healthy focus on growth will continue, and if praise and worship, coupled with positive Biblical preaching, will continue to reflect the ever-evolving social identity of Australian Pentecostals. One thing is sure: they believe fervently in Paul's exhortation to live as 'more than conquerors'.

Bibliography

Austin, Denise A., '"A Contagious Church": Theological Influences of Pentecostalism in Sydney 1916–2016', *St Mark's Review* 242 (December 4, 2017), p. 20.

—*Our College: A History of the National College of Australian Christian Churches (Assemblies of God in Australia)* (Sydney: Australasian Pentecostal Studies, 2013).

—'"Flowing Together": The Origins and Early Development of Hillsong Church within Assemblies of God in Australia', in Tanya Riches and

Tom Wager (eds.), *The Hillsong Movement Examined: You Call Me Out Upon The Waters* (Melbourne: Palgrave McMillan, 2017).

—*Jesus First: The Life and Leadership of Andrew Evans* (Sydney: Australasian Pentecostal Studies, 2017).

Austin, Denise A. and Shane Clifton, 'Australian Pentecostalism: From Marginalised to Megachurches', in Denise A. Austin, Jacqueline Grey, and Paul W. Lewis (eds.), *Asia Pacific Pentecostalism* (Leiden: Brill, 2019).

Austin, Denise A. and Jacqueline Grey, 'The "Outback Spirit" of Pentecostal Women Pioneers in Australia', in Margaret English de Alminana and Lois E. Olena (eds.), *Women in Pentecostal and Charismatic Ministry: Informing a Dialogue on Gender, Church, and Ministry* (Leiden: Brill, 2017).

Bearup, Greg, 'The Lord's Profits', *Sydney Morning Herald* (January 2003), pp. 14-21.

Beaumont, Joan, *Australia's War, 1939–45* (Sydney: Allen & Unwin, 1996).

Cartledge, David, *The Apostolic Revolution: The Restoration of Apostles and Prophets in the Assemblies of God in Australia* (Sydney: Paraclete Institute, 2000).

Chant, Barry, *The Spirit of Pentecost: The Origins and Development of the Pentecostal Movement in Australia 1870-1939* (Lexington KY: Emeth Press, 2011).

Chant, Ken, *Faith Dynamics* (Unit 7; Diploma Correspondence Course, 1980).

Cho, David Yonggi, *The Fourth Dimension* (Monroe, LA: Logos International, 1979).

Clifton, Shane, Gwynnyth Llewellyn, and Tom Shakespeare, 'Quadriplegia, Virtue Theory, and Flourishing: A Qualitative Study Drawing on Self-Narratives', *Disability and Society* 33.1 (2018), pp. 20-38.

Clifton, Shane, *Pentecostal Churches in Transition: Analysing the Developing Ecclesiology of the Assemblies of God in Australia* (Leiden: Brill, 2009).

Edwards, Mary, 'We Are Conquerors', *C.B.C. Yukana* (Brisbane: R.G. Gillies & Co., 1949).

Esler, Philip, *Conflict and Identity in Romans* (Minneapolis: Augsburg, 2003).

Hey, Sam, *Megachurches: Origins, Ministry, and Prospects* (Eugene, OR: Wipf & Stock, 2013).

Houston, Brian, *How To Maximise Your Life* (Sydney: Hillsong Music Australia, 2013).

Keener, Craig S., *Romans: A New Covenant Commentary* (Philadelphia: Casemate Publishers, 2011).

Kruse, Colin G., *Paul's Letter to the Romans* (Grand Rapids: Eerdmans, 2012).

Maher, Sean, *The Brisbane Line*, Documentary, Short, Crime, 2010, accessed August 31, 2019, http://www.imdb.com/title/tt1705053/.

Megalogenis, George, *The Australian Moment* (Melbourne: Penguin Group Australia, 2012).

Miller, Donald E. and Tetsunao Yamamori, *Global Pentecostalism: The New Face of Christian Social Engagement* (Berkeley: University of California Press, 2007).

Miller, Elizabeth, 'A Planting of the Lord: Contemporary Pentecostal and Charismatic Christianity in Australia' (PhD diss., University of Sydney, 2015).

Morris, Leon, *The Epistle to the Romans* (Grand Rapids: Eerdmans, 1988).

Morris, Linda, 'Pentecostal Revolution in the Suburbs', *Sydney Morning Herald* (June 28, 2007, accessed May 27, 2019).

Munro, Peter, 'Raising Hell For Jesus', *Sydney Morning Herald* (May 19, 2013).

Vinson, Synan and Amos Yong (eds.), *Global Renewal Christianity: Spirit-Empowered Movements Past, Present, and Future – Volume One Asia and Oceania* (Lake Mary, FL: Charisma House, 2016).

Vondey, Wolfgang, *Beyond Pentecostalism: The Crisis of Global Christianity and the Renewal of the Theological Agenda* (Grand Rapids: Eerdmans, 2010).

Wagner, Tom, 'The "Powerful" Hillsong Brand', in Tanya Riches and Tom Wager (eds.), *The Hillsong Movement Examined: You Call Me Out Upon The Waters* (Melbourne: Palgrave McMillan, 2017).

Wu, Su Fung, *Suffering in Romans* (Cambridge: James Clarke & Co., 2016).

INDEX OF BIBLICAL REFERENCES

INDEX OF AUTHORS

www.ingramcontent.com/pod-product-compliance
Lightning Source LLC
Chambersburg PA
CBHW060254100426
42742CB00011B/1750